The Story of Architecture

second edition   **The Story of Architecture**   Patrick Nuttgens

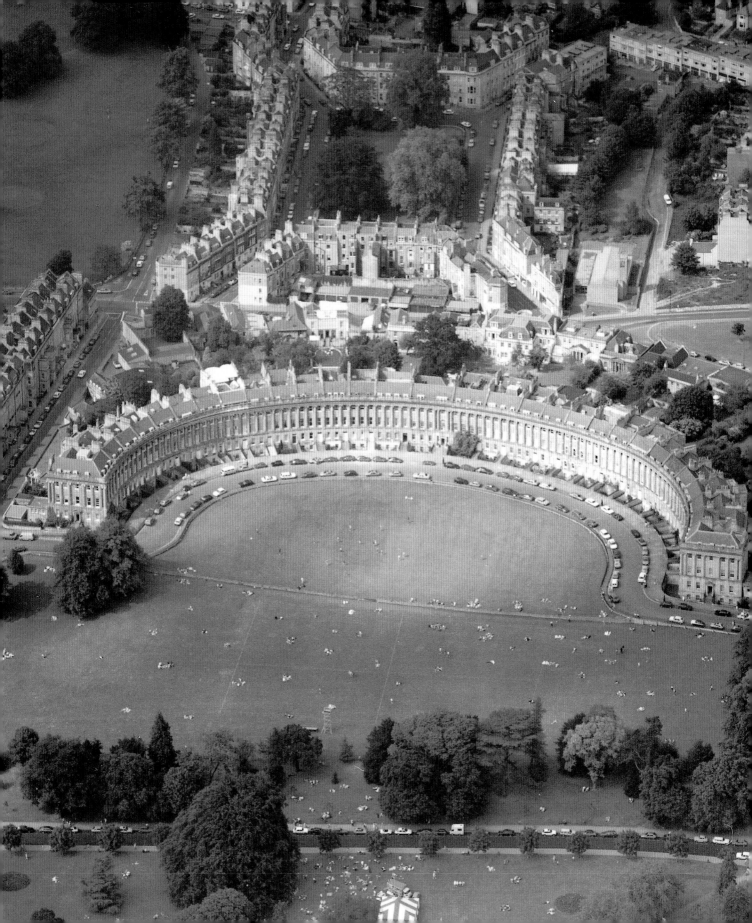

Contents

8 **Preface**

1   10   **Some Basic Facts about Architecture:** Vernacular Architecture

2   16   **Barbaric Splendour:** The First Civilizations

3   28   **The Geometry of Immortality:** Ancient Egypt

4   42   **Holy Mountain and Sacred Womb:** The Asian Sub-Continent

5   56   **Puzzles and Modules:** China and Japan

6   76   **Ritual of Blood:** Meso-America

7   86   **The Landscape of the Gods:** Ancient Greece

8   102   **The Authority of Competence:** Ancient Rome

9   116   **The Worshipping Community:** Early Christian and Byzantine

10   130   **The Order and the Sanctuary:** Romanesque

11   144   **The Flowering of the Desert:** Islam

12   158   **The Metaphysics of Light:** Medieval and Gothic

13   176   **The Scale of Human Perfection:** The Renaissance in Italy

14   190   **Crossing the Alps:** The Spread of the Renaissance

15   202   **The Drama of Shapes and Space:** Baroque and Rococo

16   218   **The Prophets of Elegance:** Romantic Classicism

17   230   **From Pioneers to Establishment:** The Americas and Beyond

18   240   **The Triumph of the Iron Masters:** The Search for a Style

19   252   **A New Vision:** The Turn of the Century

20   266   **Designing for a New Society:** The International Style

21   284   **The Architecture of Pluralism:** The End of Certainty

298   **Epilogue**

304   Maps

308   Chronological Charts

317   Glossary

321   Bibliography

325   Biographies of Architects

335   Index

351   Acknowledgements

Preface

Whether we are aware of it or not, architecture is part of everybody's personal history. The chances are that it is in a building that we are born, make love, and die; that we work and play and learn and teach and worship; that we think and make things; that we sell and buy, organize, negotiate affairs of state, try criminals, invent things, care for others. Most of us wake up in a building in the morning, go to another building or series of buildings to pass our day, and return to a building to sleep at night.

Simply from living in buildings, we all possess sufficient expertise to embark on the study of the story of architecture. But before we can do so there is one fundamental point that we have to note, which makes architecture both different from the many other arts and more difficult to judge. It has to be practical as well as attractive, useful on the one hand and beautiful on the other.

In the early seventeenth century Sir Henry Wotton, adapting the maxim of an earlier theorist, the first-century Roman architect Vitruvius, wrote that 'Well-building has three conditions: firmness, commodity and delight.' His first two conditions are concerned with the down-to-earth side of architecture; his third, with its aesthetic aspect. Commodity covers what the building is for: are the spaces formed by the building suitable for the purpose for which it is being built? Firmness concerns whether it is structurally sound: are the materials and the construction right for that particular building in that particular place, in that climate? Delight includes the aesthetic pleasure and satisfaction that both viewer and user derive from a building: and that involves a multiplicity of personal judgements.

The story that I am telling in this book covers the whole of the world. The knowledge we now have, increasing every year, of the architecture of Eastern and Middle Eastern countries and of prehistory, affects the way we look at our own immediate environment, changing its shape, its position in history and its relative importance. But I must immediately explain that my view of architecture is coloured by the fact that I was trained as an architect, to design buildings. That may be a different view from that taken by an art historian, because I have to try to understand the problem in my own way, which means to imagine what the designer was thinking as he approached the problem.

So the question I am constantly going to ask about a building is: why is it like that? There are many and various reasons. If we can discover some of them, such as the influence of history and politics and religion and social aspirations, we may be able to see more clearly why a certain designer thought the way he did and why he chose a particular way to build. For not only is there no single reason for a building, there is also no single solution to its needs. Ultimately the designer has a choice. What we have to ask is why he made that particular one.

Ludwig Mies van der Rohe, *Seagram Building,* New York, 1954–8

8

Before we can usefully start on the story of architecture, it is necessary to establish some basic facts about buildings of any kind, most easily seen and understood in the simple everyday buildings that are common in every part of the world.

Throughout the whole of history until our own century (in which we have revolutionized many techniques of building) there have been only two basic ways of building: you could either put one block upon another or you could make a frame or skeleton and cover it with a skin.

Almost everywhere in the world people have built by assembling blocks – of dried mud or clay bricks or stones. They piled one upon another, inventing ways of turning corners, leaving holes so as to get in and out, and let light in and smoke out. Finally they covered the whole structure for shelter. That was the simplest and most obvious dwelling. In some parts of the world the availability of materials led people to follow a different system. They

built by making a skeleton of wood or rushes in bundles (and later iron and steel) and covering it with skins of many kinds – animal hides, cloth and canvas, mud and straw (and later many kinds of slab).

Blocks can be made from almost anything: from alluvial mud *(fig. 1)*, sometimes bound with straw to make it more cohesive and lasting, as in ancient Mesopotamia or Egypt; from kiln-dried bricks, as in most of Europe and the Middle East; from stone, dressed or undressed; even ice, as in the Eskimo igloos of Arctic regions. Of all the materials used, the most adaptable, permanent and expressive is stone. Of the skeleton and skin type of structure, the North American Indian tepee *(fig. 2)* is the classic example, with poles overlapping, and wrapped round with animal skins. And there are many variations – the skin tents of Lapland, structures made of brushwood, of clay and reed, and the wood and paper houses of the Japanese *(fig. 4)*. They are the precursors of the nineteenth-century frame structures of iron and glass and the steel and glass of our own time.

Against that background and recognizing the basic types of structure, we must now look further and discuss some of the immediate practical problems. To the person originally thinking it out and facing the architectural challenge, the great

1 | A *pueblo* in New Mexico, forming a group of basic single-roomed dwellings built of mud

2 | North American Indian tepee

3 | Village houses built round courtyards, Mali

4 | Samurai residence, Japan

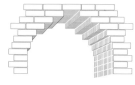

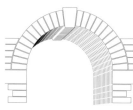

5 | Corbelled arch and true arch

occurred to them that materials could be used in only a few ways. They could be pressed together, stretched or bent. In modern structural engineering terms, strength depended upon compression or tension or bending. The block structures depend on pressing one stone or brick down on another – on compression. Skeleton structures depend on the great quality timber has – of bending, as one sees in a tree-top bending in the wind. More sophisticated structures, as well as some primitive ones, using man-made ropes, depend upon their resistance to stretching – on tension.

Because some materials are better at compression and others at tension or at bending, it follows that the kind of structure adopted in any part of the world depended upon what materials were available. Almost anything can be used for building and in practice almost everything has been used. Naturally it was the readily available materials that had the most profound effect upon architecture all over the world: stone, clay, wood, skins, grass, leaves, sand and water. But much depends on the distribution of such materials, where they are found in nature or what man has done to make them more accessible.

Of all the structural means that have been used to put those materials together, two are so fundamental and so lasting in their influence that it is worth at this point showing how they arose from the solution of basic building problems.

As any child playing with building blocks discovers sooner or later the next stage once he has made a wall is to balance a block horizontally so as to span two upright blocks and make a lintel. Primitive man discovered the same trick, sometimes investing it with magical and ceremonial significance, and siting it so that it formed a gateway for the beams of the rising or setting sun, like the stone circle at Stonehenge (*fig. 7*). Whatever its

problem from the start was not so much how to leave holes in the sides (central as those are to the character of a style of architecture, as we shall see later) as how to finish the building at the top. Again, there are two ways of doing that. The commonest is one of those described above – making a frame of wood, either flat or sloping, and covering it with some material which will keep out the sun and rain and wind, and maybe fastening it down so that it does not blow away. But the most primitive (and in the end the architecturally most exciting) is to lay the stones of the walls on one another so that the upper ones project enough gradually to curve the walls inwards and ultimately meet at the top. Such *corbelling,* as it is called (*fig. 5*), can lead to a tunnel, or, if it runs all round a building, to a dome.

The most attractive examples that still remain are in Apulia in southern Italy – the *trulli* at Alberobello (*fig. 6*). Although most of the stone-domed houses are probably no older than the sixteenth century, it is known that they are replacements in a tradition that goes back to primitive times, merely becoming more decorative with the centuries.

Now let us take the problem a stage further. When the earliest house-makers were devising ways of building their homes, it must sooner or later have elaboration, the post and lintel is the fundamental form used in buildings all over the world. The Egyptians translated it into columns supporting entablatures, leading to its metamorphosis into the classical colonnade of Greek architecture, which was used to confer power and dignity upon important buildings such as the Parthenon in Athens. The Chinese, with ready supplies of light wood, adapted it to that material, evolving a roof-structure composed of a pyramid of decreasing post-and-lintel gateways, piled one on top of the other to carry the wide eaves of the roofs. The Japanese used the form in the gateways to temples.

The second fundamental structural form is the arch. We have already seen a primitive form of it in the arrangement of stones in a wall, where each course of stones on either side of an opening juts out beyond the course below until, without the need of a capstone or lintel, they meet to form a bridge. That corbelled arch was developed in many parts of the world – in the brickwork cisterns of Mohenjo-Daro in India's earliest civilization, in the Chinese vaulted tombs of the third century BC, in the arches supporting the waterways that fed the hanging gardens of Babylon. The true arch, built of radiating wedge-shaped stones or *voussoirs*, arranged to form a semicircle, was an act of the imagination that released all sorts of architectural possibilities.

Having looked at the basic materials and the basic structural forms, we shall now look at the basic kind of building – that is, the house.

Man's earliest dwellings were single rooms, sometimes caves or semi-caves hollowed out of the ground and covered with a tent structure or with mud bricks and entered from the roof. Such early dwellings are found all over the world. There are very early examples in Jordan and Anatolia (now Turkey), some of which date back to around 8000 BC.

Another example (200 BC–200 AD) is the Yayoi tent-house of the Japanese, which is sunk into the ground and has a roof of sticks and turf. However many variations his successors later made, the early house-maker seems to have used only two basic shapes for a house and two basic ways of grouping its components.

In shape a house could be either round or rectangular. Round buildings probably came first, if only because they did not pose the problems of making a corner, which requires the cutting of stone or the making of bricks. Even when the shape was rectangular, as in the early bothans of Scotland and the clachans of Ireland, the corners were rounded. Rectangular houses are usually found in regions where there was timber available for spanning roofs or making frames. For example, the long houses of the Scandinavian countries and the cruck-framed houses of England – made with timber-framed arches with their feet stuck in the ground and the walls and roof built around them.

As soon as people began to go beyond the single unit for dwelling, they

6 | *Trulli*, Alberobello, Apulia, Italy, with roofs formed by corbelled domes

7 | *Stonehenge*, Wiltshire, England, *c.*2000 BC

had two ways of grouping the component rooms. They could make a multiple dwelling—that is, one made up of a number of separate units, each with its own roof system, grouped together closely or more freely. The *trullo* at Alberobello, referred to earlier, is the best surviving example of that type; the vaulted stone rooms could be grouped together in twos, threes or fours, and ultimately made into an elaborate and fascinating complex. Tents, as in Arab desert settlements, could be similarly grouped together. Especially fascinating is Skara Brae, Orkney. In 1850 a great storm undid the work of another storm possibly 3,000 years earlier and uncovered a Stone Age village of single-roomed stone houses which probably had turf roofs resting on rafters of wood or whale-bone. The houses were connected by covered walkways, and had stone hearths, stone beds, and even stone dressers and cupboards.

Alternatively, people could make a single compact dwelling with all the rooms under the one roof. Originally that entailed the housing of animals and humans under the same roof. The earliest houses of the Scottish Highlands and islands were like that. They housed people on one side of the fireplace, which later became a wall, and cattle on the other. Once the animals had been put out and given a separate shelter, that type developed into the cottage of two

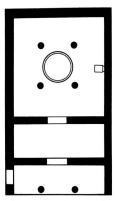

8 | *Megaron*, Mycenae, Greece, *c.*1250 BC, plan

rooms (the but-and-ben), one for living and one for sleeping.

This pattern became more sophisticated when one room was assigned more importance than the other. The classic pattern was the Greek *megaron* (*fig. 8*), which is first found on the mainland at Mycenae – a hall with an entrance room off it. That simple pattern was in due course to become the basic component of any great house or castle. Then houses moved upwards. The addition of an upper floor or a balcony required the construction of a stair, either internal or external.

Further refinements came with the development of ways of regulating the temperature. For the sake of coolness it became common in the East to group houses or rooms around a courtyard (*fig. 3*); it was a pattern adopted by the earliest monks, the desert hermits, and was found so convenient that it spread by way of European monastic establishments to academic institutions like the universities. In harsher climates like that of most of Europe, especially the northern parts, the most important development was the making of a fireplace. In the earliest houses the fire was in the centre of the floor, the smoke escaping through a hole in the roof, with or without an angled shutter to keep the rain out. It was the moving of the fireplace to the wall, usually the outer wall in a rectangular house, and the gradual development of a chimney, at first of timber and then of stone, which created the house form. The increase in convenience and fresh air more than compensated for the heat that may have been lost by having the fireplace on the outside wall. It was probably the first architectural exercise in putting comfort before technical efficiency – a process which has continued ever since.

But at this point we must make an important distinction. Everything said so far concerning the basic facts about architecture refers to the most basic of all types of building – that is, the dwelling, the house. If the house was the start of the most elementary, most ordinary and common kind of architecture – what has come to be known as *vernacular* architecture – the start of what has come to be known as *great* architecture is not the house but, as we shall see, the tomb and the temple.

The story of great architecture is the astonishing story of how individuals and groups have taken the structures, groupings, plans, access and service arrangements originally evolved to satisfy basic human needs and transformed them into some of the greatest manifestations of the human spirit. It is that story that we shall now tell.

The story of architecture begins with the story of civilization, when primitive men and women gave up their nomadic ways and established settlements. Until then our ancestors had moved around, living off seeds and berries and following animals they could hunt down for food. Of course even in warm climates they still needed shelter, not only against the weather but against wild animals or enemies who might attack them as they slept. But they made use of natural shelter in caves and trees as they moved around. Only when they started to sow their own crops did the need for permanent shelters arise. Inevitably, they found it advantageous to work together to harness water sources and till the land – and so we have the start of society and the start of a city.

So intimate is the connection between man's building of the first cities and his development of a civilized way of life that the very word 'civilization' comes from the Latin word *civis*, which means citizen, or dweller in a city. Kenneth Clark points out that a sense of permanence is the prerequisite of civilization, and what could more explicitly indicate that a man meant to give up his wandering ways and settle down than his building a city? Men, said Aristotle, come together in cities in order to live; they remain there to live the good life.

Where and when did it all start? We have to remember that much of what we know of early cities comes from the findings of archaeologists. From the Renaissance onwards, antiquarians set about examining the ruins of classical civilizations, and this led to the exploration of even earlier societies. Napoleon gave an enormous boost to the study when, during his Egyptian campaign in 1798, he shipped across with him to Egypt not only his armies but 151 doctors, scientists and scholars. It so happened that, for political reasons, he had to rush home in a hurry, leaving many of his entourage behind in Egypt, and it was these men who produced the first detailed reports on the pyramids and other ancient Egyptian antiquities. However, for much of the nineteenth century, archaeology was conducted in a very amateur way by bored diplomats and businessmen posted to stations in the back of beyond, who were looking for an interest to absorb their time. Important finds in our own time are constantly extending our knowledge of early settlements, and, by the same token, changing our ideas about them; and in the same way the development of new scientific methods of dating means that we must constantly revise our ideas of who and when and where. What seems to be clear is that remains are regularly being found to be much older than we thought they were. It looks as if man has been civilized for much longer than the older books say.

9 | Aerial view of Kalaa Sghrira, Tunisia, showing the typical dense pattern of narrow streets and courtyard houses; cf. fig. 11

Nevertheless, the earliest indications of this settling-down process can still be fixed with the agricultural villages of between 9000 and 5000 BC discovered in the hill fringes of Anatolia (modern Turkey) and the Zagros Mountains (such as the shrine houses of Çatal Hüyük) and south and west in Syria, Jordan and through to the Mediterranean in, for instance, the thousand whitewashed beehive houses of Khirokitia in Cyprus. Jericho, today a palm-tufted oasis town dotted with lemon orchards in the Jordanian desert, shares with Çatal Hüyük the distinction of being referred to by prehistorians as a 'town' – Jericho on account of its fortified walls and towers which date back to the seventh millennium BC

10 | Remains of tower and defensive wall, Jericho, Jordan, c.7000 BC

(fig. 10), and Çatal Hüyük from evidence of an established trade in flint and obsidian. But it is to the large cities and complex organizations further east that we look to find the earliest known urban architecture proper.

The land now generally accepted as the cradle of civilization was known to the Greeks as Mesopotamia, 'the land between the rivers'; in the Bible it is the Land of Shinar. This land occupies an area which is today partly in Iran and partly in Iraq, along the 700-mile course of the rivers Tigris and Euphrates from their sources near Lake Van in Anatolia southeastwards down to the Persian Gulf, and is said by tradition to have been the site of the Garden of Eden, the place where, according to Genesis, human life began.

Today it looks unprepossessing. But archaeologists have established that, during the 5000-year gestation period of civilization, this desolate area was a rich alluvial plain, teeming with fish and wild-fowl. It was, as Leonard Cottrell described it in *Lost Cities*, 'the most fertile land on earth, mile after mile of flat green fields, palm-groves and vineyards, criss-crossed by a network of canals…which at dawn and sunset still show as dark lines across the alluvial plain.' The Gulf War and the draining of the southern marshes may now have dealt a final death blow to such a vision; but it should be noted that even in these early millennia, when the area really was the 'fertile crescent' that historians speak of, it was only fertile because of human effort. With little rainfall, the tribes who wandered into the area as hunters and gatherers found they could only survive by harnessing the two rivers in massive irrigation works. Of course, such co-operation provides the classic condition for developing the kind of complex organization that characterizes civilization and promotes the founding of cities. Today, as each generation discovers more remains of early man, the shape resembles less a crescent than an ink blot seeping out between a scattered circle of seas – the Black and Caspian Seas, the Persian Gulf, the Red Sea and the Mediterranean.

From at least 5500 to the first millennium BC, Mesopotamia was the hub of the world and a melting pot of vast tribal immigrations. These tribal settlements grouped themselves into city states, small by our standards (it is estimated that Uruk, the largest of the Sumerian city states, had a population of about 50,000). Across the millennia, they grouped and regrouped, rose to power, were conquered and disappeared beneath the advance of a new invader – then sometimes reappeared and resumed dominance for a further period.

Since our concern is with architecture, we can concentrate on the three greatest civilizations of Mesopotamia. The earliest, Sumer – Akkad (c.5000 to 2000 BC) occupied the southern area south of present-day Baghdad, and included the marshy area known as the Chaldees which stretched down to the Persian Gulf. As well as Uruk their cities included those with the gritty names of Eridu, Lagash and Ur of the Chaldees. Agade, the capital city of Akkad, has not yet been found.

Somewhere about 2000 BC, an Amorite tribe whose kingdom held the same name as its capital, Babylon, assumed dominance. Its ruins lie about 56 miles (90 km) from Baghdad, and it became mighty in two phases, the second when it was rebuilt in the sixth century by Nebuchadnezzar II *(fig. 11)*. Babylon eventually gave way under repeated assaults from the third great Mesopotamian power, the Assyrians, a people of Semitic stock in the northern parts of the country. Their capitals, Ashur first of all, later Nimrud in the ninth century BC, Khorsabad between 722 and 705, and Nineveh in the seventh century BC, were among the earliest excavated and have yielded some of the best and most telling remains.

Why the Assyrian capitals have survived better than their southern counterparts is quite simple: in the north there is stone to use for building. So the architecture of this area resembles less that of Sumer and Babylon, which lacked wood and stone and all minerals, and is closer to that of countries with a similar topography such as Anatolia, where the Hittites (c.2000 – 629 BC) were the dominant power. Little is left of their large Bronze Age

capital, Hattusash, but clearly it was not just fortified but a complete fortress in itself – which speaks of wars and threats of war. It is perched on a ridge above the modern Turkish city of Bogazköy and surrounded by sheer cliffs down which cataracts plunge. The fortified cities of Assyria and Anatolia have so much in common that we will look at them together. For the moment we must close this brief chronological account with the demise of Assyria – a long-drawn-out decline at the hands of many enemies, culminating in the overthrow of their

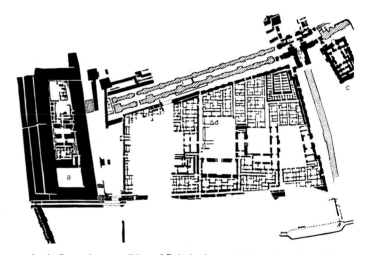

11 | Babylon, plan of part of the northern sector of the city under Nebuchadnezzar II (605–562 BC), showing the citadel (A), the Ishtar Gate (B) and the Temple of Ninmah (C)

empire in 614 BC by a coalition of Babylonians and Medes. The new Babylonian empire itself became part of the Persian empire in 539 BC.

If stone is the building material of the north but not the south, what on earth did the Sumerians build with? When in the nineteenth century early archaeologists like the traveller Sir Austen Henry Layard or the French diplomat Émile Botta started to excavate, the fertile crescent was fertile no longer. Instead, 'lone and level sands' stretched far away, punctuated by the strange mounds that had aroused the curiosity of previous travellers. They totally failed to appreciate that, in a country where the common building material was sun-baked mud, the mounds were in fact buildings or even cities which had crumbled back into the landscape from which they had come. In their efforts they may well have demolished what they had come to find. We know that J.E. Taylor, sent out by the British Museum and the Foreign Office, hacked off at least the top two terraces from the ziggurat at Ur before he was (mercifully) recalled.

Any description of these ancient cities must allow for a modicum of conjecture. What we do know is that Sumer was not so much a country as a collection of city states, each with its own organization and proprietary rights to one particular god. It had a continuing Mesopotamian culture in the thousand years of its dominance before one state, Akkad, under Sargon the Great (c.2370–2316 BC), conquered all the others and welded them together into the world's first empire, which lasted a brief but brilliant 150 years. Akkad under Sargon also made history by establishing Akkadian as the writing for all Mesopotamia – cuneiform writing, that is wedge-shaped marks made with a reed on a clay tablet. We also know that Sumer used bronze for artefacts (there is an impressive head, thought to be of Sargon, and a bronze lady with her legs tucked under her looking somewhat like a mermaid) a good 1,500 years before the Chinese, whom we always think of as masters in bronze working.

We can talk of Sumerian and Babylonian architecture together since much of the tradition of Sumer–Akkad continued in the Babylonian culture, crucially because these woodless and stoneless areas used the same building material – mud brick. It is now clear that the planning and architecture of Mesopotamian cities were closely related to their civic and religious organization. From the plan of Babylon we can see how all the main buildings and chief temples were gathered together in one sector of the city. This area was raised above the rest of the city and was allocated to the city's special god. Here the god lived, and the priests and princes, as the god's agents, ruled. In the north-west corner of Ur, for instance, Nanna the Moon God had his raised walled enclosure in which was included his house (the ziggurat, *fig. 12*) surrounded by a semicircle of five temples with thick, fortress-like walls.

12 | *Ziggurat of Ur-Nammu*, Ur, Iraq, c.2100 BC

The largest was dedicated to himself, and one of the smaller ones to his wife, Ningal. The temple area also contained the administrative buildings from which officials dispensed justice and collected taxes on the god's behalf. These activities called for a treasury, a tax office, and storehouses, since each citizen belonged to a temple and paid his taxes in kind. If we add to this that the temples owned craft shops and factories, worked in by women, we will get some idea of how the temple area hummed with life.

Inside the excavated temples have been found tablets with temple hymns, myths and histories of the temples, as well as mathematical tables which give square and cube roots, and which may point to advanced astronomical calculations. There were also fountains and water troughs lined with bitumen, and tables built of brick and grooved with knife-scores from cutting up sacrificial victims. These animal sacrifices were cooked on the hearth in the temple kitchens, the same kitchens used by the priests for daily use. The discovery of bread ovens particularly delighted Professor Woolley who wrote in his excavation diary: 'After 3000 years, we were able to light the fire again and put into commission once more the oldest kitchens in the world.'

Life at the top appears to have been quite luxurious, to judge from the artefacts of gold, silver, lapis lazuli and shell found in the royal graves of about 2500 BC at Ur, and the marvellous collection of clay tablets discovered in the library of Ashurbanipal (669–627 BC) at Nineveh, many of which form parts of the world's oldest story–the Epic of Gilgamesh. In Nineveh itself, an estimated 350,000 people were packed into five square miles of alleys and bazaars and courtyards, the mud-brick houses close-built up against each other for structural support, and to keep the blazing sun out of the living quarters. This is a pattern we can recognize in the vernacular houses in the same areas of the world today (*fig. 9*); and that goes also for the use of wood, for those who could afford it, in an outside stair, normally leading up from the courtyard to a simple wooden balcony off which the upstairs rooms open.

Babylon was even more impressive. It was situated on the east bank of the Euphrates at the closest point to its fellow river, the Tigris, about 25 miles (40 km) south of present-day Baghdad. Hammurabi's city of about 1750 BC, contemporary with the northern capital of Assyria, Ashur, was a planned and grand affair. When it was rebuilt under Nebuchadnezzar II (605–562 BC) a smaller city was added on the west bank, connected by canals and bridges. A great processional way swept along parallel to the river, and six bridges crossed the moats to six gates. The Greek traveller Herodotus left us this description of what was to be seen in the fifth century BC:

> *The city stands on a broad plain and is an exact square. It is surrounded by a broad and steep moat behind which rises a wall … As fast as they dug the moat, the soil from the cutting was made into bricks which were baked in a kiln and used to brick the borders of the moat. For the wall they used hot bitumen as cement, and interposed a layer of wattled reeds at every course of bricks.* [Bitumen is a by-product of oil, a substance with which, we now know, that area of the world is saturated. Used as cement it formed a bond so strong that, 3000 years on, it is difficult to break apart even with a pick.] *Along the top of the wall are single-chambered buildings, leaving between them room for a four-horse chariot to turn. In the circuit of the wall are a hundred gates, all of brass, with brazen side posts and lintels. The houses are three to four storeys high, and all streets run in straight lines, both parallel to the river and with*

13 | *Lion Gateway*, Mycenae, Greece, *c.*1300 BC

cross-streets leading down to the waterside. There is an inner wall almost as thick as the outer. In the centre of each division of the city is a fortress–on one side the palace of the kings, and in the other the temple of Jupiter Belus [probably Marduk, the city god of Babylon] *with gates of solid brass.*

Excavations have now revealed that Babylon was both a commercial and religious capital with 108 temples (55 of them to Marduk) and over a thousand chapels and altars. Among other things Herodotus may have seen was, standing just off the processional way and rising to the exact height of the Statue of Liberty, the Temple of Etemanenki, a ziggurat which was probably the original of the Tower of Babel; and the Hanging Gardens of Babylon, listed by the Greeks as one of the Seven Wonders of the World. These were in fact stepped terraces, built over a corbel-vaulted building which contained not only the wells whose pumped waters

made the trees and flowers flourish at the different levels, but also an ice-house or refrigerator to store, it has been suggested, sherbet for the delectation of the Medean princess for whose relaxation the gardens had been created.

In Babylon we see how much the decorative arts had improved from the simple method adopted by the early Sumerians, who ornamented their fortress-like walls with characteristic protruding and recessed panels and clay cones. Remains in the very early Temple of Warka in Iraq show that these cones were sometimes coloured cream, black or red, and pressed into the mud-skimmed walls to make patterns of circles. By contrast, one of the glories of Babylon was the use of glazed bricks, predominantly blue, tinted with lapis lazuli, with gold for contrast–the very colours we will find later in the sumptuous decorations of the palaces and mosques of Islamic architecture, in much the same area of the world. Nebuchadnezzar's Ishtar Gate (*fig. 16*)

14 | *Lion Gate* guarding the south-west approach, Hattusash, near Bogasköy, Turkey, *c.*1300 BC

Barbaric Splendour: *The First Civilizations*

is resplendent with blue tiles patterned with 152 golden beasts, almost life-size. These are variously identified as bulls and lions, alternating with the mythological 'sirrush', which had the front legs of a lynx, the back legs of an eagle, and the head and tail of a snake. Recent studies have suggested that Babylon was such an attractive place that the leaders of the Israelites had considerable difficulty in persuading their countrymen to go back to Israel when Nebuchadnezzar ended their captivity and set them free.

Not all the states of Mesopotamia appear to have been so humane. Although the standard of sophistication in Nineveh was so high that King Sennacherib (705–681 BC) brought drinking water into the city by canals and stone aqueducts, the Assyrian cities generally presented a harsher aspect, as did those of the Hittites in Anatolia.

Massive fortifications were essential for states that were constantly threatened by rival states and tribal war. Materials for fortification varied with local supply—mud brick in south Mesopotamia,

stone in Anatolia, usually with a superstructure of mud brick. They were often built in concentric rings, a practical defensive pattern which persisted into the Middle Ages, indeed until the invention of gunpowder made the fortified city obsolete. The outer wall was studded with look-out turrets and punctured with gateways, some built with posts and lintels, some with elliptical arches, like those at Hattusash, the Hittite capital (*fig. 14*). The main gateway was guarded by sentinel towers, and would have animal or warrior guardians sculpted on the gateposts. Similar massive stone defences can also be seen further west, in the contemporary citadels of Mycenae and its port Tiryns on mainland Greece. At Mycenae, the city of King Agamemnon, leader of the Greeks in the Trojan War, two huge stone lions guard the main gate (*fig. 13*).

Both the Assyrians and later the Persians decorated exterior and interior walls and bronze doors with reliefs depicting their history (*fig. 15*), sometimes with cuneiform inscriptions to explain the

16 | *Ishtar Gate*, Babylon, *c*.580 BC, re-erected in the Vorderasiatisches Museum, Berlin; cf. fig. 11

15 | *Babylonian and Bactrian tribute-bearers*. Detail of processional frieze on the east façade of the *Apadana (Audience Chamber) of Darius*, Persepolis, Iran, 5th century BC

17 | *Ziggurat of Choga Zambil, near Susa, Iran, 14th century* BC

scenes. Those on the walls of the palaces of Ashurbanipal and Ezarhaddon in Nimrud bear out the reputation for bloodthirst ascribed to the Assyrians in the Bible: 'I built a wall before the great gate of the city; I flayed the chief men of the rebels, and I covered the wall with their skins. Some of them I enclosed alive within the bricks of the wall; some of them were crucified with stakes along the wall; I caused a great multitude of them to be flayed in my presence and I covered the wall with their skins.'

The architectural achievement of these early nations remained simple in both structure and plan. In only one building type did Mesopotamia achieve distinctive form: the ziggurat. This is a stepped pyramid made of rubble and mud brick, with great ceremonial staircases rising to a temple room at the top. In the plain of Sumer these temple-mounts were landmarks, and people working in the fields or date orchards far from the city could assure themselves that their gods were keeping a protective eye on

them. But they were also unquestionably a manifestation of the power of the ruler who was identified with the city's god. Each individual brick in the ziggurat at Ur is stamped with the name of UR-NAMMU, KING OF UR, WHO BUILT THE TEMPLE OF NANNA.

The origin of the ziggurat may have been accidental. The short life of mud brick meant that constant rebuilding was required, but since the god owned the temple area in perpetuity, each successive rebuilding took place on an accumulative platform made from the debris of previous temples; possibly, too, the high priest's grave was embedded in the platform and built over. Herodotus adds a little more to our knowledge:

In the middle of the temple precinct is a tower on which is raised a second, on that a third up to eight. The ascent to the top is on the outside by a path that winds round the towers. Halfway up are seats and resting places. On the topmost tower is a temple where there is a large couch, richly decorat-

Barbaric Splendour: *The First Civilizations*

18 | Throne Room, *Palace of Minos*, Knossos, Crete, c.1600 BC

ed, and beside it a golden table. But there is no statue, and only one person may sleep there: a native woman whom the god has chosen above all others, say the Chaldeans who are the priests of this dynasty.

Unquestionably, too, it had a symbolic significance as the world mountain on top of which the heavens rotated – a recurrent theme connected with worship of the sky gods that takes material form in circular temples and stone circles like Stonehenge.

Although there is some superb masonry, as in the most beautiful ziggurat, that of Choga Zambil in the little kingdom of Elam, now in Iran (*fig. 17*), where three of the original five staircases are still basically intact, there is nothing very sophisticated about the structure of even the most important of these early buildings: stone was piled on stone or brick on brick and the roof finished off with plaited reeds or corbelling. Sometimes the scale of the stonework is so enormous it looks as if it had been built by a race of giants and is therefore sometimes referred to as 'cyclopean'. What leaves us open-mouthed with wonder is the megalomania of these expressions of power, fierce and elaborate, rich with carvings and figures – aspiring gloriously to the mountain tops in an architecture of ramps and stairs which arrogantly disregards the ordinary man in his reed hut below. It is an architecture of barbaric splendour.

With all these fiercely aggressive and defensive civilizations struggling for survival and dominance in a hard world, it is a surprise to come across a society, existing in the third millennium BC, which appears to have been much gentler. This was the Greek civilization called Minoan on the island of Crete. Even here, we have to swallow the myth of the minotaur monster raging in his labyrinth in King Minos's palace, demanding his diet of young men and women, but the impression given by the tapering, seeming upside-down, red columns and the frescoes of princes and maidens idling in flowery meadows as reconstructed by Sir Arthur Evans in the throne-room of the palace at Knossos (*fig. 18*) are much more suggestive of ease and comfort. It is possible that this carefree attitude spelled the downfall of their civilization – that they were attacked by the warlike Greeks from the Mycenaean mainland, the palaces at Knossos and Phaistos burnt and obliterated. However, another possible explanation for the abrupt end of this

19 | West stairway of the *Apadana (Audience Chamber) of Darius*, Persepolis, Iran, 5th century BC

20 | Vault (*iwan*) of the *Banqueting Hall*, Ctesiphon, Iraq, *c.*550 AD

civilization about 1500 BC was that there was a volcanic explosion and that the sea between Crete and the mainland is in fact a crater. Ancient murals, similar to those of Crete, excavated on other islands which could lie round the rim of the crater such as Santorini (Thera) would support this explanation.

But the architecture of Crete is no more structurally complex than what we saw in Mesopotamia or Anatolia. True structural sophistication does not appear in the fertile crescent until the sixth century AD, over 2,500 years later, by which time not only Knossos, but Sumer and

Babylon and Assyria were no more. Here, the builders of a revived Persian empire, the Sasanians, set their kiln-baked bricks obliquely to raise parabolic vaults over the great hall or *iwan* of the palace at Ctesiphon on the Tigris (*fig. 20*). One arch end remains for us to see today. A previous Persian dynasty, the Achaemenid, had brought us on to more familiar architectural ground in Persepolis, the capital built between 518 and 460 BC by Darius I, Xerxes I and Artaxerxes, for here we find echoes of Egypt and anticipation of Ancient Greece in the use of columns – of which, much more shortly. In Persepolis, great flights of steps lead to the podium on which the palaces were built, with a carved frieze of 23 vassal states bringing tribute to the Persian Emperor (*fig. 15*). A gateway and passage along the north side of the platform give access to the Apadana or Audience Chamber (*fig. 19*) on the western side and the throne room on the eastern side. Behind these ceremonial rooms on the south lay the living quarters. Only the stumps of the 100 columns of Xerxes's throne room survive; the pillars of Darius's Apadana are topped with unique capitals shaped like the forefront of an animal. These drastic and awe-inspiring ruins remind us that the Achaemenid Persians created the largest empire the world had known up to that time, absorbing all the civilizations we have talked of so far, as well as Egypt and the people of the Indus Valley. No wonder Christopher Marlowe makes Tamburlaine (Tamerlane), the Mongol conqueror of Persia, thus give utterance to his dreams of greatness; 'Is it not passing brave to be a king, and ride in triumph through Persepolis?' All these civilizations were eventually destroyed and dispersed in the fourth century BC by Alexander the Great, the legendary young King of Macedonia who is reputed to have once wept because he had no more worlds to conquer. But by Alexander's very conquests the influence of previous civilizations spread to India and thence to China and Japan, and ultimately round the world.

But long before that, in those countries far from the fertile crescent, metamorphosis into civilization had taken place, commencing, as in the Middle East, along fertile river valleys. In India a series of settlements have been discovered along the valley of the Indus and its tributaries (now in Pakistan) dating back to between 2500 and 1500 BC. Somewhere about the mid-eighteenth century BC, when Hammurabi was in power in Babylon and Crete was still in its Golden Age, China's cultural chrysalis broke into

early civilization probably first along the Yellow River. Across the barriers of the great seas, the New World cultures developed in Central America.

We shall follow the story to those countries in chapters 4, 5 and 6. But first we shall stay in the Middle East and explore the most inscrutable of all the early civilizations – that of ancient Egypt.

The key to Egypt's story is the Nile, that river with the singular characteristic that it never dries up: although virtually no rain falls along its course, it is constantly filled by the White and Blue Nile from the great lakes of Central Africa and the mountains of Ethiopia. The two distinct topographical areas into which the river divides provided the basis for the division of Ancient Egypt into a Lower and Upper Kingdom. Even after the two kingdoms were joined together by Menes when he built his capital at Memphis somewhere about 2400 BC, an obsession with duality seems to have hung on in the Egyptian consciousness—dark and light, night and day, flood and drought—and we will see it exerting its effect on the architecture.

Dotted along the west bank of the Nile for some 50 miles (80 km) south-west of Cairo, about 80 pyramids raise their inscrutable and monumental bulk to the sun's disc. Our immediate reaction might be that here was a civilization very similar to those of Mesopotamia. After all, they all started along river valleys and in the Middle East, and at roughly the same era in evolutionary terms, and they are all characterized by mammoth buildings, whether ziggurats or temples or pyramids. But in fact their architecture is very different. Where Mesopotamia exhibits the aggrandisement of defence and aggression, Egypt reflects 3,000 years of splendour, security and mystery. Its

culture and its architecture have a conservative, unchanging, almost unyielding character which is quite amazing over such a long period.

The plains of Mesopotamia were so located as to make them a seething cauldron of races seeking lands through settlement or war. In contrast, Egypt, isolated in the fastness of the Nile Valley, had, one might say, peace thrust upon her. Her people had no need to pack together into fortified cities for defence. In fact, she was slow to develop cities at all; the earliest approximation to cities were cities of the dead, with streets of tombs, sometimes modelled like little houses, laid out in a grid pattern. Living cities only figure in the Old Kingdom (2686–2181 BC) where the Pharaoh commanded the building of a town to house men working on his pyramid or on other public works, as in the narrow grid of little box-dwellings for Necropolis workers at Deir el-Medina, on the Theban west bank. Egypt was vulnerable to penetration only up or down the Nile Valley, from the Mediterranean (as was ultimately to happen in the Greek and Roman conquests) or down the Nile from Nubia in the south. Even here, nature afforded some protection, for in Old Kingdom days the boundary was marked by two islands which could be defended, Elephantine and Philae, and by a series of cataracts. Man added to nature with a string of forts and

21 | *Great Temple of Rameses II*, Abu Simbel, *c.*1250 BC

22 | *Kiosk of Trajan* or *Trajan's Bedstead*, Philae, 1st–2nd centuries AD

accompanying temples on the Upper Nile. One of these, the dramatic fort at Buhen, had castle-like buttressed walls with a perimeter of a mile. It is now under Lake Nasser, at the time of its creation the world's largest man-made lake, which backs up the Aswan Dam. When the dam was built, some of the most beautiful temples were moved from the encroaching waters. The Temple of Isis with its

pylon gateways was moved from the island of Philae to Agilkia; and a little gem from the period of Roman occupation known as the Kiosk of Trajan, or by the more disrespectful as Trajan's Bedstead, (*fig. 22*) was also saved. The little Dendun temple has gone abroad; it was taken apart and reconstructed in New York's Central Park. The most exciting rescue in engineering terms was raising the

The Geometry of Immortality: *Ancient Egypt*

temples of Abu Simbel up 200 feet (70 metres) on to higher ground. The architects of the New Kingdom had carved the temples into the sandstone mountain, so they had to be cut away, and a steel dome, camouflaged to look like stone, was erected to re-create the original atmosphere. Today, the four enormous effigies of Rameses II (1279–1212 BC), one headless, continue to sit, immense and implacable, intimidating invaders from the south with their basilisk stare as they have done for 3,000 years, and waiting for the sun to penetrate the temple at the equinox (*fig. 21*). The main hall of the Great Temple (*c.*1250 BC) is 30 feet (9 metres) high, with 8 pillars carved with the head of the god Osiris; behind is a smaller hall, and randomly placed chambers open off either side.

For both kingdoms, the Nile below the cataracts provided a perfect waterway. Prevailing winds conveniently blew north to south and carried boats up river. During the Middle Kingdom (2040–1782 BC) mud-slips were built so the boats could be pulled upstream to bypass the cataracts and establish access to trading forts and ports in Nubia. On the return journey, the big brown sails were furled and the current swept the boats swiftly home.

Enormous blocks of granite from the quarries at Aswan were brought down on barges or rafts in this way to build temples or tombs, and by this route too came the traffic in spices, ivory and skins as well as gold and jewels from the mines in the interior of black Africa over which the pharaoh exercised a monopoly.

The river also dictated much about the architecture. Both ordinary dwellings and buildings intended to last – tombs, pyramids and temples – were sited on the edge of the desert, beyond the high flood mark which was, of course, also the edge of the fertile strip, which in the growing season started so abruptly that one could stand with one foot on crops and the other in the desert. Within this area on the western bank, the land of the dead, were the causeways leading to the funerary temples and complexes and the villages for the workers in the Necropolis, the city of tombs with which, in the New Kingdom period (1570–1070 BC), the cliffs of the Theban hills were honeycombed.

On the eastern bank, the bank of the living, were the wharves and boat-building areas, quayside beer and eating shops, and beyond, the great temples, often with an avenue of sphinxes leading up to them from the quay, along with the ordinary dwelling houses, shops and workshops that made up the town. Most dwellings were of mud brick and there are no remains today. But little flat, almost two-dimensional models called 'soul houses' found in the tombs suggest they were not so very different from those lived in today (*fig. 23*). The houses of the noblemen were luxurious with loggias and gardens, fountains, ornamental tanks for fish, used to keep down mosquitoes, and suites of many rooms, enclosed behind high mud walls. Entry was through a single door, and, inside a rich man's house, corridors led to the several living quarters. Details of a vizier's house painted on the wall of his tomb show three corridors. One leads to the servants' quarters, one to the women's quarters and the third to the living areas, which included lofty reception rooms, the roof supported on columns painted dark red and bearing lotus capitals, while the walls were covered in paintings of flowers and birds.

On both sides of the river, mud-brick walls protected buildings from unusually high floods, just in case the pharaoh and his priest-astrologers, who measured the rise of the Nile at nilometer stations along the bank, failed to predict the correct flood level.

By September to October the river had returned to its natural level, leaving lush farmland behind, until as the year moved round it became cracked baked mud, turning from dark brown to grey under the fierce sun. These mud blocks probably formed the building material for the primitive houses, until it was discovered that a stronger block could be made by moulding the brick and incorporating straw and cattle dung. But the flooding of the Nile had a more profound effect on Egyptian architecture. For at least three months of inundation, between May and September, farming was not feasible. The pharaohs had therefore at their disposal an enormous labour force of peasants, augmented by races enslaved in time of conquest. The pharaoh set them to work on the pyramids or tomb-complexes, which were their lifetime's preoccupation.

The availability of such an enormous

23 | 'Soul house' found in an Egyptian tomb, c.1900 BC

force has been advanced as an explanation of how the massive pyramids were built. But it leaves so many questions unanswered that it is safe to say the whole thing is still a mystery. We have only to remember that stone was floated down the Nile on barges from as far away as Aswan, and that, for the pyramid of Cheops, two million stone blocks were used, some of them weighing fifteen tons. Or we can ponder how some of the columns in the hypostyle hall of the Temple of Amun-Ra at Karnak are so enormous that, even today, it has been estimated that there are only two cranes in the world that could lift them. But the Egyptians did not have cranes – possibly they did not even know the principle of the pulley, although they certainly used the lever.

The techniques available to them were really very simple. They never learned to harden copper, so, although they had both saws and drills of copper, the tough granite of Aswan had to be split from the rock face, first by hammering vertical trenches into the rock with balls or hammers of a hard rock called dolorite and then by driving in wedges either of metal

or of wood that was soaked in water until it expanded. The stones, some of which still show quarrymen's marks, were brought on the Nile to the pyramid site and dragged on sleds to the work site.

We assume, from the remains of a builders' ramp found at Karnak, that after the first course of stones was laid on the level bed, they worked from earth or mud-brick ramps which they built up as the work proceeded. But here we hit another problem. Anybody who has ever pushed a disabled person in a wheelchair knows how impossible it is to push or pull the weight of even a person up a ramp if the gradient is too steep, and building a mud-brick ramp to work on a pyramid rising to 480 feet (146 metres) would itself be an incredible feat. And how did they organize the logistics of getting the stone quarried and down to the building site with the right timing to employ these hundreds – thousands? – of workmen? The truth is, we are still very far from knowing how the Egyptians did it.

The first major monuments were mud-brick tombs, known as *mastabas*, for nobles and royalty. They began simply enough, with mounds of earth raised over

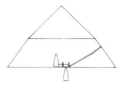

24 | Sections through the *Stepped Pyramid of King Zoser*, Saqqara c.2630–2610 BC, and the *Bent Pyramid of Snefaru*, c.2570–2250 BC. The Bent Pyramid represents the last stage leading to the development of the true pyramid

25 | *Stepped Pyramid of King Zoser*, Saqqara, c.2630– 2610 BC

26 | *House of the North*, Saqqara, c.2630–2610 BC, showing papyrus-umbel columns

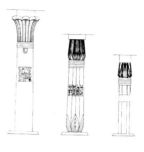

27 | Egyptian capitals: palm leaf, papyrus bud, lotus, 'tent-pole', papyrus umbel

store-room opening off. Beside the tomb a little offering temple was built so that offerings of bread and wine and other food could be left there for the departed spirit. These ancillary rooms eventually became incorporated into extensive walled complexes. When later in the Old Kingdom royal tombs became enclosed in pyramids, nobles continued to build mastaba tombs, first in brick, later in stone.

From about 2630 BC, during the Old Kingdom period, the stone mastaba which was being built west of Memphis for King Zoser (Djoser) of Dynasty III developed through several changes into a stepped pyramid (*figs. 24, 25*), and at this point Egypt's unique contribution to architecture manifests itself. Thanks to the Egyptian cult of the individual, the name of the architect has been preserved for us—Imhotep, counsellor and vizier to the king and a man of inventive and original mind. He was priest, scholar, astrologer and magician, and so skilled in the arts of healing that 200 years later he was deified as the god of medicine. The funerary complex he built for King Zoser at Saqqara covered a vast area enclosed in a white wall 32 feet (9.7 metres) high, and incorporated, as well as the six-stepped pyramid towering 200 feet (61 metres) over the shaft that tunnelled deeply down to the burial chamber, eleven separate burial pits for other members of the royal family. In his funerary complex we find features which were to become some of the mainstays of architecture.

First of all Imhotep used stone, translating into this strong medium techniques previously used for building in wood and mud brick. His is the first use of *ashlar*, or dressed stone, that is to say, stone slabs laid smoothly together so as to present a continuous surface, as distinct from *rubble* stonework, in which the stones are separately identified and picked out by the pointing which surrounds them.

pit graves in which the dead were laid, preserved in natron, a form of salt (there are salt deposits close by the pyramids at Giza). The earliest remains of a royal mastaba of the Archaic period (3150–2686 BC) are at Saqqara, on a bluff of the desert overlooking Memphis. These tombs are rectangular, the sides sloping inwards with an angle (known as a 'batter') of 75 degrees to a flat top. It is reasonable to suppose that, like the pyramids later, they were built up by a step technique. They might rise to a height of 25 feet (7.5 metres), containing an outer chamber, whose walls were often decorated, and an inner secret chamber holding statues of the family. The burial chamber itself was cut deep into the rock below— normally a single room, perhaps with a

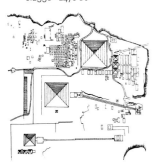

28 | *Pyramids*, Giza,
c.2550–2470 BC

29 | *Pyramids*, Giza, plan

But of even greater importance was Imhotep's translation of the bundles of reeds, used in vernacular buildings to hold up mud-packed walls, into stone architecture's basic component: the column. Left on one remaining side of the House of the North, an administrative building in the Saqqara complex, are three crisp, beautiful *engaged* (i.e. partially attached) columns, based on the papyrus reeds which grew in the marshes of Lower Egypt (*fig. 26*). The shaft imitates the triangular stem of the plant, and the *capital*, or block at the top of the shaft on which rests one of the cross-beams that support the roof, is here shaped like the open umbel of the papyrus. In the companion House of the South, the capitals were shaped like a lotus flower, the emblem of Upper Egypt. Egyptian architects repeated this conceit in the furled papyrus-bud capitals on the Temple of Amun-Ra in Luxor and in further lotus and palm-leaf capitals (*fig. 27*), while Greek classical architecture later adopted it, as we shall see, in the fluted columns based on bundles of reeds, and in the capitals derived from native Greek plants such as the acanthus leaf.

The great era of pyramid building in the Fourth Dynasty (2613–2498 BC) was probably ushered in by Huni, last pharaoh of the Third. He continued Imhotep's work by converting what appears to have been originally conceived as a seven-step pyramid at Meydum into the strange and fascinating geometrical form we associate with Ancient Egypt: four triangular walls rising from a rectangular base and sloping upwards and inwards to meet at a point. The three best-known are the pyramids of Cheops or Khufu (to give the pharaohs both their Greek and Egyptian names), Cephren or Khaefre, and Mycerinus or Menkaure. They stand in a group at Giza, now on the edge of Cairo, Cheops's pyramid with the three little pyramids of his queens at his feet (*figs. 28, 29*).

The pyramid was the pharaoh's bid for immortality. He did not build a great city to demonstrate his power, as Nebuchadnezzar did at Babylon, Darius and Xerxes did at Persepolis, as Alexander did at Alexandria, or Constantine did at Constantinople. His intent was more practical and more pressing. He believed that to gain immortality he must ensure the physical survival of his body, his earthly appearance, and the appearance of what life was like for him during his lifetime, at least in the form of models. Then, when his spirit had finished roaming the earth in animal form, his corpse and home would be there, ready for him to inhabit as his eternal home. For this doors and cavity windows were left open to allow the spirit to move freely and also to look through to keep a protective eye on his own corpse.

First the body must be embalmed – a long and complicated process, taking 70 days if properly done, and requiring the building of embalming chapels round the tomb. To perpetuate the dead man's appearance, death masks were made, like the famous gold mask of Tutankhamun, and portrait busts were ranked all round an entire funerary chapel. Round the walls were painted the story of the man's life with charms and identifying hieroglyphs, and other rooms contained models of his house, garden, boat and other possessions he wished to continue to enjoy in the afterlife. Frequently provision was made for the burial of wives, concubines and other members of the family.

Once the architects had provided for all this activity, the pyramid and its contents had to be safeguarded both from the severities of the weather and from robbers in quest of the riches buried with the dead. Hence the entrances were concealed, usually at an unspecified distance up the north side of the pyramid. A shaft, whose degree of slope was arbitrary, led to the tomb chamber, and might have a bend in it. In Cheop's pyramid there appears to have been a change of plan, for the shaft that burrows downwards from the entrance to what one would expect to be the tomb chamber appears to have been abandoned, and another cut, this time ascending through the Great Gallery to the King's Chamber which is in the heart of the pyramid and positioned exactly over the centre of the pyramid base (*fig. 30*). But maybe it was all to foil a potential thief, as were the labyrinths of corridors regularly found, sometimes leading to galleries, used both for ventilation and access to other tombs if it were a family complex, or to store-rooms. Sometimes the thief would be deceived by fake entrances as in a maze, or by blocked-off access corridors, or come to an abrupt end in one of the pits in the floor which also served to collect any rainwater that had penetrated the tomb surface. The pyramid was built in advance to the level of the burial chamber, and only after the pharaoh's body had been put in position were the shafts for building access filled in and sealed off.

Or so we think. For the three great pyramids at Giza again present us with both structural and factual puzzles.

We know that they spread a thin layer of mortar between the stones that face the pyramids, more, it is believed, to float one stone up against its neighbour on the

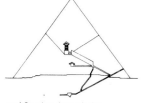

30 | Section through the *Pyramid of Cheops*, showing the King and Queen's chambers, the Grand Gallery, entries and shafts

incline than to hold them in place. But how on earth did they calculate and put in place the enormous facing slabs, never mind the corbelled slabs that roof the Great Gallery leading to the King's Chamber in Cheops's pyramid? This gallery ascends at an angle of 26 degrees along a 153 foot (46.5 metre) length. Another strange thing is the empty sarcophagus in the burial chamber and the lack of any grave goods. Most amazing of all, there are no paintings and inscriptions of the titles and mighty deeds of these pharaohs on the walls of these pyramids. This has given rise to a conjecture that the Giza pyramids were symbolic rather than actual tombs, and that they had a more important religious significance in reference to the myth that the dead pharaoh climbed to the skies to become a star-god.

A text from the pyramid of Onnos (2375–2345 BC), last king of the Fifth Dynasty, says: 'A stairway to heaven is prepared for him, and on it he ascends to heaven. He rises in a great cloud of incense. Onnus flies like a bird.' A connection is now being made between the myth that on death the pharaoh became the god Osiris and the layout of the three Giza pyramids (the two largest in line and that of Mycerinus off to the left), which exactly mirrors the relative positions of the three stars in Orion's belt. This may explain shafts in the king's tomb which

31 | Pylon gateway of the *Temple of Horus*, Edfu, 237–57 BC

The Geometry of Immortality: *Ancient Egypt*

would have been trained on the Orion constellation in Cheops's day. For the moment it simply adds another strand to the Egyptian skein of mystery.

However, whether or not the three Giza pyramids escaped burglary as this thesis presumes, most other pyramids and tombs undoubtedly did not, and the threat of robbery was one factor in the change from pyramids to rock-cut tombs in about 2000 BC. The pharaohs of the New Kingdom, beginning with Thutmose I (1524–1518 BC), cut into the 1,000-foot (300-metre) orange-yellow cliffs of the isolated Valley of the Kings in the Theban hills – still in the Land of the Dead, the west bank of the Nile, but far enough from the funerary temples to preserve the secret location of the tombs. The entrance followed the pattern of the pyramids in that it was placed at a random height on the rock-face; from the door a funnel-shaped passage down which the funeral sled could be pulled was bored

32 | *Temple of Amun-Ra, Karnak, Thebes, c.1500– c.320 BC, showing the obelisks of King Thutmose I and of Queen Hatshepsut*

into the cliff to a T-junction; here, at the point where passageways led off on either side to other rooms, was placed a statue of the dead man so that the morning sun could shine down the entry on to his face. A system of tilted bronze mirrors reflected light down to the inner passageways and chambers for tomb-artists to work by. The change from pyramids to rock-tombs seems to have been little more successful in foiling tomb-robbers, however, except in the case of Tutankhamun, who died young and was buried in his vizier's tomb.

The enigma of the pyramids is intensified by the contrast between the crafty irregularity of the internal arrangements, and the extraordinarily simple external appearance, rising sheer out of the desert – like sculptures in an exhibition. The pyramid of Cheops is orientated precisely to the four points of the compass, and the four sides are almost exact equilateral triangles, built at an angle of 51–2 degrees to the ground. The geometry is amazingly exact. The base of Cephren's, although big enough to swallow up six football pitches, is a perfect square to within 15 millimetres. How, we wonder, did they arrive at this shape? The question is sharpened by the presence of two other geometrical forms the Egyptians appear to have invented in the New Kingdom and the Late and Ptolemaic periods (1070–30 BC), the obelisk and the pylon. One of the finest pylon gateways (enormous sloping or battered buttresses on either side of the opening) is of the third century BC at Edfu (*fig. 31*). One hundred feet (30 metres) high, it forms the entrance elevation to the Temple of Horus, son of Osiris and falcon-god, of whom the pharaoh was said to be a reincarnation. In the temples of Amun-Ra and the moon-god Khons at Karnak (*c*.1500–320 BC), they erected both obelisks and pylons (*fig. 32*).

The battered walls of the temples may have had a constructional purpose. The

33 | *Temple complex of Amun-Ra*, Karnak, Thebes, *c.*1500–*c.*320 BC

temples were built just beyond the flood-line in order not to encroach on the valuable farming land left by the annual inundation, but a certain amount of subsidence was only to be expected. Clearly a broad base to the walls offered a more secure foundation. Then, because the walls inside were flat, the outside batter meant that the walls got thinner as they rose and exerted less pressure on the mud brick.

As for the obelisk, the pylon and the pyramid, the likely answer to the puzzle is that these were not so much geometrical forms as abstractions from nature – perhaps shafts of sunlight. They all derive from the worship of the sun, whose dominant presence in Egyptian life made him the greatest god of all, in the form of

Amun-Ra or the less austere Aten. That the pyramids were stairways to the sky is again suggested by the habit of gilding the tips of both pyramids and obelisks with electron, and of inscribing winged solar disks on each face of the pyramids and over temple gateways. Here again we encounter the Egyptian dualism of light and dark. Outside was the relentlessly powerful blaze of desert sun taking concrete shape on the outside of the pyramid; inside, the sooty darkness which H.V. Morton described so vividly when he visited the tomb of Cheops in 1937.

It was one of the most sinister apartments I have ever entered, a really horrible place, and I could well believe it might be haunted. The air was stale

The Geometry of Immortality: *Ancient Egypt*

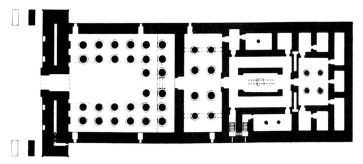

34 | *Temple of Khons,*
Karnak, Thebes, plan

and hot, and the foul reek of bats so
strong that I kept glancing up, expect-
ing to see them hanging on the corners of the walls. Although this room
(the burial chamber) is 140 feet [43
metres] above the level of the sunlit
sandhills outside, it gives the impression of being in the depths of the
earth … It was indeed the darkness of
the grave, and joined to the darkness
the silence of death.

In the New Kingdom period, Thebes
became the capital and religious centre
for the cult of Amun-Ra, and was then the
greatest city on earth, incorporating both

Karnak and Luxor, with their massive
temples and colossi connected by an
avenue of ram-headed sphinxes. The
building of the temple and palaces
reached their peak during the three
dynasties of the New Kingdom, particularly in the reign of Rameses II. This was
Egypt's imperial phase: the boundaries
were pushed north and east as far as the
Euphrates and southwards into the gold-
rich lands of Nubia or Kush. Some temples were built over a long period, with
successive pharaohs adding further
courts and halls, as happened in the temple of Amun-Ra at Karnak (*fig. 33*). The
extraordinary thing about this temple is
the unity of the whole concept when one
considers that the building started about
1500 BC, and the famous hypostyle
(roofed and columned) hall was added
400 years later, while the entrance pylon
was the last of six and not built until the
fourth century BC.

We can note here a pattern that we
will see in holy places all over the world:

35 | *Temple of Amun-Ra,* Luxor,
Thebes, *c.*1460–*c.*320 BC, showing papyrus-bud columns

36 | *Funerary Temple of Queen Hatshepsut*, Deir el-Bahri, Thebes, *c.*1458 BC

that of axis. The rooms or spaces of the temple are set one behind the other, moving back from larger public spaces, through smaller and élitist areas for special people (here, the priests and the pharaoh) through to the image room, the god's house, the inner sanctum, the holy of holies. Usually as you go further back, the rooms become smaller, darker and more secret. We will find this very strongly in the next chapter when we look at the Hindu architecture of the Indian subcontinent. In the Egyptian temples there is some degree of the tunnel effect, for there is a rise in floor level, usually via some shallow steps, from the more public hypostyle halls into the more private areas, and at the same time the roof of each surrounding room becomes lower,

until the back sanctum, the room containing the image and the sacred barque on which it was carried in procession, is only dimly lit by roof-grills.

For all its elaboration through the centuries, in the Temple of Amun-Ra we can still distinguish this axial core, although it is much easier to see it in the simpler Temple of Khons, the moon god, at Karnak (*fig. 34*). In the Temple of Amun-Ra we can recognize the typical monumental massing of the temples: the great open outer court contrasting with the covered hypostyle hall, crammed with 134 columns with capitals carved like the open and closed umbels of the papyrus reed; the pylon gateway outside, guarded by colossal priest figures (a life-sized figure between their feet reaches up only

The Geometry of Immortality: *Ancient Egypt*

to their knees); the typical processional approach, the *dromos* here sweeping between rows of ram-headed sphinxes, the ram being the symbol of Amun-Ra. We have some impression of just how breath-taking the temple must have been if we picture it on a ceremonial occasion: the courtyard and the hypostyle hall crowded with priestesses brought to dance before the pharaoh, musicians with trumpets and cymbals, and ranks of shaven-headed white-robed priests ready to conduct the pharaoh into the inner sanctum.

Before Imhotep turned their attention to stone, Egyptians were highly proficient in working in wood, a skill probably developed for shipbuilding. We know they could make plywood of up to six layers, had mastered wood inlay, and had developed most of the joints we use today, including mortice and tenon, for native woods like willow and sycamore yielded only narrow planks, which had often to be joined together. Building traditions more appropriate to timber than to stone continued in the temples; they used no arches or vaults (except in tombs), so in the hypostyle halls the great spaces spanned by stone lintels became forests of columns, lit either by clerestory grills or by light reflected back from the white alabaster floor paving which increased their mystery as well as their grandeur.

The great temple of Amun-Ra at Luxor (*fig. 35*) was the most stylish and elaborate; that at Karnak, in whose erection the Queen Pharaoh Hatshepsut (*c.*1479–1458 BC) played an important part, the biggest and most awe-inspiring. The temples of the Ptolemaic period and the period of Roman occupation, like the temple of the hawk-god Horus at Edfu or the similar temple at Dendera dedicated to Hathor, the cow-goddess whom the Greeks were to identify with Aphrodite, were smaller. Many of the best temples were funerary temples, associated with the tombs, notably that of Queen Hatshepsut at Deir el-Bahri on the west bank (*fig. 36*). It

maintained religious commerce with Thebes on the opposite bank in the Beautiful Feast of the Valley, when cult statues of Amun-Ra were ferried across from Karnak for ceremonies. The cool, well-bred horizontal lines of the complex, which included valley temple, mortuary chapel and causeway, contrast impressively with the vertically scored precipice under which it is set; the terraces of smooth post-and-lintel arcading, linked from level to level by massive ramps, are serene, elegant and commanding without pomposity or aggression. This is surprising, for the woman for whom they were built, the only female pharaoh, had her share of both pomposity and aggression. She usurped her young stepson Thutmose III, and took over herself. Thutmose, assuming his rights after her death, informed posterity of his feelings by knocking the head off all the statues of the Queen in the valley temple.

Hatshepsut's temple is a satisfactory place to leave the Egyptian phase of our story, for we have only to set its picture alongside that of the colonnade in the Temple of Poseidon at Cape Sounion, Attica, to see that the Greek temples are of the same lineage as the Egyptian. Indeed, though some of the Queen's columns are square, some are as much as sixteen-sided like an embryonic Doric column, a prefiguring of classic Greek architecture that has been noted in some other Egyptian buildings, such as the fluted and tapered columns at the entrance to rock-cut tombs of the Middle Kingdom at Beni-Hassan.

However, before we move on to Greece and Rome and through them follow the main current of Western architecture, we must step aside to look in the next few chapters at other areas of the world, whose civilizations, though often not much younger than those of the Middle East we have traced so far, have made their own very individual contributions to our story.

It is difficult to decide at what point we should look at the architectures of India, South East Asia, China, Japan and pre-Columbian America because chronologically their story does not parallel Western developments. While the Western world romped its way through all sorts of styles and modes of building, those civilizations which did not pass away altogether – as did Mesopotamia, Egypt and ancient Persia – often remained at the same level for many centuries.

In this part of the story we find ourselves in a vast area of peninsular sub-continents hanging like a frontal into the eastern seas from a wire of mountain ranges that continue from the Hindu Kush in the west to the mountains of Sechwan, China, in the east. Obviously there was a wide variety of available building materials and climatic conditions in such a vast area.

In this chapter we are not so much concerned with the earliest Indian cities so far found – the civilization of the Indus Valley and its tributaries, which we mentioned fleetingly in the chapter on the early cities. We think that these sites may have been occupied as far back as 6000 BC by a people called the Dasus people, and that the civilization may have lasted for a thousand years at its peak – between about 2500 and 1500 BC. Over 100 sites have been found since the first archaeological discoveries in the 1920s; and two

centres, now separated by desert (probably due to over-grazing) are of special interest: a northern (Punjab) group on the Indus tributaries whose main city was Harappa, and a southern group in Sind on the Indus itself, whose chief city was Mohenjo-Daro. Both cities appear to have been large, possibly 3 miles (5 kilometres) across, with grids of criss-crossing streets overlooked by a citadel, walled and towered, on a platform of mud brick. Harappa was unfortunately devastated in the nineteenth century to obtain brick for ballast for railway and house building, so Mohenjo-Daro has more to tell us. It had a complex of important buildings including that known by the archaeologists as the 'assembly hall', wonderful granaries with a maze of passages, and 'Great Baths' (*fig. 37*) which are so grand, with a series of dressing rooms or small baths around, that they must have had some ceremonial significance, possibly religious. We do rather expect religious beliefs to figure in the lives of early peoples, but, if the Baths were *not* religious, our conviction that early architecture is that of the temple and the tomb breaks down here: no temples or tombs have been found, although a statue of a priest-king, with what look like phylacteries bound round his upper arm and temples, has been found to tantalize us. Perhaps we must wait till their script has been deciphered before we learn any more.

37 | *'Great Baths'*, Mohenjo-Daro, Sind, Pakistan, *c.*2500 – 1700 BC

38 | *Borobudur Temple*, Java, *c.*800, Buddha and bell-stupas

39 | Carvings on the south entrance of *Hoysalesvara Temple*, Halebid, Mysore, India, 14th century AD

Probably the Indus civilization was gradually destroyed by the Aryan or Indo-European people who started making incursions into India via the Khyber Pass about 1750 BC, a destruction aided by repeated flooding of the Indus which occurred at this time. The invaders appear to have gone through the usual progression from hunters to settled farmers, and to have gradually taken over the land, by 900 BC reaching the Ganges, a century later moving into the Deccan plateau and pushing the aboriginal people of that area, the Dravidians, further south. This is known as the Vedic period, because most of our picture of India in

the last two millennia BC is gleaned from the *Vedas* of the Aryans – a Sanskrit cycle of hymns which includes two long exciting epic poems of the origins and legends of their race. The *Vedas* were not written down until the eighteenth century but clearly enshrine an oral tradition of great antiquity. The Vedic religion appears to have given way to Hinduism from about the fifth century BC; eventually, about the start of the Christian era, substituting the *trimurti*, the Hindu trinity of the three greatest gods, for the many blurred and confusing deities of Vedism.

We are still searching out clues to the architecture of this period. The vernacular buildings in bamboo and thatch have of course vanished without trace, and the paucity of other remains suggest that wood was the main building material – softwoods, top-grade teak from Burma and *sisham*, poor man's teak, growing in the valleys of India or floated down from forested mountain regions. Occasionally, in the river plains of Bengal, and in the Punjab and in Sri Lanka and Burma, remains of brickwork which recall the superb tradition of brick-building of Mohenjo-Daro have been discovered. But for the great cities mentioned in Sanskrit writings we have nothing to go by for 1,500 years, until we pick up mention in the Muslim conquest of 1565 of the destruction of a great palace complex in the Vijayanagara kingdom of the south. This has now been identified as the seat of the Hindu Vijayanagara kings, founded in 1336 AD, and splendid buildings such as the Ladies' Baths, the Elephant Stables, and a temple to the god Shiva have now been discovered. But a thousand years before the Christian era, kingdoms and republics had developed all over India, setting the scene for a move to the first all-Indian Empire by Chandragupta Maurya (316–292 BC). It was under his grandson, the Mauryan dynasty emperor Asoka (273–232 BC), an important figure, that the first dressed stone was used. Stone then became accepted as a 'sacred' material for building the temples which comprise the surviving contribution to the story of architecture. In areas where stone was scarce, it was used as a facing material over rubble walls. Sri Lanka had no problem of supply and distinguished herself in temple building. India had sandstone and marble south of the Indus, and sandstone in the more southern mountain plateau, the Deccan. But woodwork techniques were constantly employed in stonework, telling us much of those lost wooden buildings – even to the point of using carpentry joints; and even today we can spot a similarity of artistic expression between

the rustic hand-carving and peasant poker-work on boxes and trays carved by Indian craftsmen, and the superlative all-over carving that covers many of the temple fronts.

The architecture of this area was spread and animated by two enduring world religions: Hinduism and Buddhism. Perhaps no architecture reflects more vividly the underlying philosophies of its builders than that of this wide area, especially when one looks at its decorative sculpture. If we take the fourteenth-century AD Hoysalesvara Temple at Halebid (*fig. 39*) with its tiers of

40 | Buddha figures, *Gal Vihara*, Polonnaruwa, Sri Lanka, 12th century AD

elephants, lions and horsemen rising to a many-armed god as typical of Hindu architecture, and lay it side by side with a twelfth-century Buddha in enlightenment after death from the Gal Vihara at Polonnaruwa, Sri Lanka (*fig. 40*) – his countenance bland and beatific as the lotus flowers on the soles of his feet – we become aware of the contrasting atmosphere of the two religions. The more mundane architectural provision of the two religions shows a less emotional and more practical contrast: while Hinduism is a religion of individual daily devotion with public ritual performed by the priests, Buddhism is strongly community-oriented, leading to the establishment of monasteries (*viharas*) with cells grouped round courtyards, *chaitya* or assembly halls, and stupas – temple-mounds round which gather pilgrims and large congregations. But of course it is simplistic to labour the differences between the two. These religions have lived not merely side by side but intertwined for so many centuries that beliefs and forms of worship or devotion become confused – often bewilderingly so, to the outsider. Hinduism, originally called Brahminism after its priestly caste, itself arose from a strange fusion. On one side was the dark, earthy Dravidian religion, writhing with cult images and fertility symbols; on the other, the idol-less worship of the pale-skinned Aryans.

A key to understanding Hindu architecture is to be found in reconciling elements which at times seem contradictory. We have to reconcile the erotic pages of the *Kama Sutra* and the pornographic fantasies we see translated into stone in the tortuous forms on many temple walls with the near-impossible asceticism of yoga – at its most intense in the holy *saddhu*, sitting motionless in the fierce heat, heedless of time or of the clamours of the flesh. But to the Hindu there is no paradox: all are aspects of the same god. This Janus-face is constantly mirrored in the architecture of Asia – in abstract plans and symbolic outlines combined with a profusion of bulbous towers clotted with carvings, luxuriant as jungle growth, frenzied with many-armed gods and gibbering monkeys.

Buddhism was one of two movements that broke away from the stranglehold of the Brahmin priests, the other being Jainism which is less important architecturally. Buddhism was based on the teaching of the 'enlightened one', Siddhartha Gautama, who, born in the sixth century BC into the knightly caste in a state on the northern Ganges plain, preached an Eightfold Noble Path, whereby any man irrespective of caste might free himself from constant rebirths and achieve nirvana (ultimate liberation).

In 255 BC, Asoka, the third Mauryan Emperor of North India, became a convert to Buddhism and established it as the state religion. Asoka was an active ruler who consolidated the first unified Indian empire by modelling his administration and military exploits on those of Alexander the Great, whom his grandfather, Chandragupta, had met when part of India was encompassed by Alexander's empire. Asoka also built the Royal Road – today's Great Trunk Road – from Patna to the north-west. In repentance for a particularly bloody campaign against Kalinga in east India, when 250,000 of the enemy were slaughtered, he turned to religion, ordering the first cave shrines (probably based on Achaemenid tombs in Persia of the sixth and fifth centuries BC) to be cut for Jain ascetics in the Barabar Hills; thereafter he extended his empire spiritually, sending missionaries as far as the Hellenic world, Nepal and Sri Lanka. The overlapping control of the entire known world by these enormous empires – the Persian, Alexander's, and now the spiritual empire of Buddhism – explains the two-way traffic of cultural influences which we can so often observe in the story of architecture.

Testimony to Asoka's influence, for instance, can be found all over India in the carvings of ethical teachings on pillars and rock faces, in rock-cut shrines and monolithic accessories to shrines, in thousands of tumuli or stupas (he is said to have erected 84,000 in three years) and in the ruins of a palace with an immense hypostyle hall at Pataliputra (now Patna).

Underlying Buddhism, Jainism and Hinduism is the concept of the universe as a vast ocean in the middle of which floats the world. The centre of the world is a great mountain made of five or six ascending terraces of which mankind occupies the bottom one, guardian deities the middle tiers, rising to the 27 heavens of the gods. It is amazing how often we can trace architectural forms and details back to this basic concept, which has already been alluded to in relation to the ziggurat form.

In the first place, the concept of the holy mountain dovetails exactly with the Hindu belief that the gods live in mountains or caves, a belief which prompted, when they came to build a temporary

dwelling-place for the god on earth, what we may call mound and womb architecture. All Hindu temples are temple-mountains, and the classic Buddhist structure, the stupa, is less in origin a building than

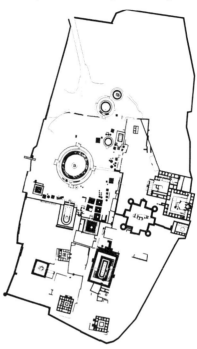

42 | *Great Stupa*, Sanchi, plan of complex

41 | *Great Stupa*, Sanchi, India, 1st century AD

43 | *Swayambhunath Stupa*, Kathmandu Valley, Nepal, founded *c*.400 AD, rebuilt many times

a shrine—an enormous mound of earth, solid and impenetrable, which gradually became encased in brick or stone for increasing permanence.

Few of the earliest stupas remain. The Great Stupa at Sanchi, central India, in spite of much reconstruction and restoration in the nineteenth century, retains the basic form given it by Asoka between 273 and 236 BC. The present mound (*figs. 41, 42*), which probably dates from the first century AD, presents the typically wide, shallow shape, 105 feet (32 metres) in diameter and 50 feet (15 metres) high. All the classic stupa features are here: the railings or carved stone balustrades to separate the sacred area from its secular surroundings, broken at the four points of the compass with high carved ornate gateways called *toranas* (which were to influence the Chinese *p'ailou* and the

Japanese *torii*); the ambulatories running round the mound linked by stairways to the flattened stupa top, where a shrine or altar is situated. All stupas are holy monuments and reliquaries, since, even if they do not house an actual relic from the Buddha's life, they mark a spot which he or his followers once hallowed with their presence.

The symbolism is laid out in copybook fashion. The great dome of heaven revolves round the cosmic axis, which is visually indicated by a pinnacle formed of umbrellas, symbolizing the soul's passage through layers of consciousness. The four gates ornamented with the Buddha's signs—the wheel, the tree, the trident and the lotus—face the four points of the compass. Railings demarcate the walkway—an important element—designed so that the worshipper

Holy Mountain and Sacred Womb: *The Asian Sub-Continent*

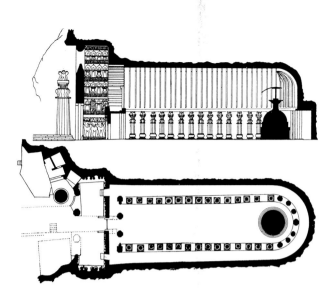

44 | Rock-cut *chaitya hall*, Karli, Deccan, India, 78 BC, section and plan

45 | *Chaitya hall*, Karli, interior

may carry out the devotional exercise of passing clockwise round the shrine, studying carvings of the Buddha's life on the walls.

The stupa evolved many fascinating forms. The original shape was retained in Sri Lanka, as we see in the third-century AD Ruvanveli *dagoba* (for so stupas are called in Sri Lanka) in the ancient capital of Anuradhapura, where we can also see pillars from the ruins of the monks' cell complexes. This city is distinguished by ruins as extensive as those of Babylon or Nineveh, and columns can still be seen from two of the palaces, the Peacock Palace and the Brazen Palace, of which the latter is reputed to have once boasted many storeys roofed in brazen tiles and, within, halls of pearl and gold and an ivory throne decorated with the sun, moon and stars.

In Pagan, once the capital of Burma, there are still 5,000 of the 13,000 bell-shaped temples that once ran for 20 miles (32 km) along the Irawaddy river before the destruction by Kublai Khan, the thirteen-century Mongol emperor of China who attempted to conquer South East Asia. Some, like the Schwe Dagon Pagoda in Rangoon, are still plated with gold leaf over the coating of hard polished plaster that encases the stupa. In the Swayambhunath Stupa in Kathmandu

Valley (*fig. 43*) we find the Nepalese style: on the square sides of the temple the slanting, hooded, all-seeing eyes of the Buddha gaze from beneath a helmeted roof of the thirteen umbrella rings of the Buddhist heaven. Since the stupa form is interpreted in so many ways in different areas – from mounds to bells to stepped tombs to pagodas – it is difficult to make a distinction between temples and stupas. Basically, temples are sanctuaries and involve congregational worship, but this will always revolve (literally, since circumambulation is so important in worship) round a stupa-model or a Buddha image.

So much for the mound. The opposite of temple-mountain architecture, womb architecture, is a form of religious expression that is used by all three religions.

46 | Entrance of *Cave Temple 19*, Ajanta, India, *c.*250 AD

Hindus, Jains and Buddhists all preserved the tradition of very early Indian architecture in cave-shrines and assembly halls, hewn with staggering skill and hard labour from the living rock from as early as 200 BC until the ninth century AD.

Chaitya was originally a general term for a shrine, but is today most often applied to the Buddhist assembly halls often accompanying a *vihara* or monastic dwelling. The rock-cut chaityas were sometimes stupas in reverse: instead of a mound of earth rising up, a mound of earth was excavated from the hill. The walkway here forms a processional ambulatory similar to what one might find in a Christian church. It is separated from the hall by a row of columns of naked rock and forms an apse at the end. At Karli in the Deccan (78 BC; *figs. 44, 45*) the pillars are squat with capitals like ribbed fruit – a detail that persisted in Indian architecture for a thousand years. The first-century AD chaitya at Bhaja, which was used by Buddhist monks, had a high barrel-vault as at Karli. In the apse there characteristically stood a small stupa, surmounted by a telescoped umbrella finial, often carved from a column of rock arising directly out of the floor, and reproducing the crowning umbrella on a stupa. Chaityas were often lit by horseshoe windows, such as the one of about 250

AD at Ajanta (*fig. 46*), where there was a monastic university with schools and chapels cut into the rock. Ajanta, an overgrown ravine in central India, where jackals whine at dusk, boasts 29 caves, hollowed out across a long period from the second century BC to about 640 AD, when the Chinese traveller Hiuen Tsang described them. The window traceries – the window bars, surrounds and grilles – of these cave shrines resemble carved timber whether they are in fact made from wood or cut from rock.

The Hindu version of the temple is different. It moves from architecture hollowed downwards into the rock to buildings which are almost sculpture, carved from the face of the living rock inwards and upwards. For the Kailasa Temple, Ellora (750–950), designed as a replica of Mount Kailasa in the Himalayas, which was sacred to Shiva, 2,000,000 tons of black volcanic rock are estimated to have been cut away to create the form of the temple carved from the solid rock (*fig. 47*). In the courtyard rises a *stambha*, a free-standing pillar carved with inscriptions, sometimes used as a pedestal for a human figure or a light source. The lower storey of this temple was added later by burrowing still further into the rock and carving it out in the form of elephants, symbolizing strength and monsoons, which appear to be carrying the temple on their backs. In the monoliths of Mahabalipuram near Madras, south India, single blocks of granite were cut *in situ* into chariots (*raths*) and life-size elephants, by the kings of the Pallava dynasty in the seventh and eighth centuries (*fig. 48*). Only the entrance hall of the Temple of the Sun at Konarak, Orissa (thirteenth century), was built, but its power consists in the fact that the whole pavilion is sculpted as the sun god's chariot (*fig. 49*), rather than in its bands of famous erotic sculptures round the outside. Surya, an Indo-Aryan deity, daily circles the globe in his chariot, drawn by

Holy Mountain and Sacred Womb: *The Asian Sub-Continent*

47 | *Kailasa Temple*, Ellora, India, 750–950 AD; engraving

sometimes four and sometimes seven horses; and the red sandstone temple is given twelve wheels to match the signs of the zodiac and to give the impression of motion. The interior of the ninth-century Elephanta Temple on Elephanta Island in Bombay Harbour has a carved cornice and square pillars, with capitals resembling ribbed fruit, much like those at Karli.

The earliest ruins of a free-standing temple are in Afghanistan and date from the Gupta rule of the second century AD. The Hacchappayya Temple at Aihole in the Deccan (320–650) is one of the earliest examples extant to emerge from its cave-womb and sit above ground. But the symbolism has not faded away–far from it. The womb is still there, the little dark unlit shrine called the *garbha griha*, at the heart of the Hindu temple on the ground floor, in which the god sits. This is the holy of holies, where only priests may enter to dress, tend and feed the god. In Orissa and other parts of southern India, a common pattern is to have a series of vestibules to the shrine, and these are laid out one behind the other on the same axis as the shrine chamber, just as we observed in the Egyptian temple (*fig. 50*). Often forming a plinth base to the temple, there is the *mandapa* or dancing hall. Directly over the shrine and indicating its presence from the outside is the *sikhara*, meaning a mountain peak–a spire-like roof. The sikhara is formed by receding courses of stone and is quite hollow: its sole purpose is to simulate a mountain and to indicate to the outer world the position of the sacred cosmic access–an invisible rod of power–which connects cave and mountain. There is great variety in the size and shape of the sikharas in different areas, but it is always in the sikhara, with its commanding

48 | *Raths*, Mahabalipuram, Madras, India, 7th–8th centuries

49 | *Temple of the Sun (Surya)*, Konarak, Orissa, India, 13th century

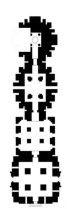

50 | *Lingaraja Temple*, Bhubaneswar, Orissa, India, 9–10th century, plan

height and impressive carving, that the god's dignity is demonstrated, rather than in the chamber for the cult image underneath, which tends to be poky, dark and airless. This is very apparent in the two remaining shore temples of the eighth century that stand on the beach at Mahabalipuram (*fig. 51*), the larger facing east and the smaller towards the setting sun. Age has somewhat blurred the features of Shiva's Nanda bulls who guard the approach, but the pyramidal sikhara, ringed by three walkways, the floor of each providing a roof for the one below, is still very impressive.

The south Dravidian temple (from about 600 to 1750), found in the states of Madras, Mysore, Kerala and Andhra, is the only kind of Hindu temple that is not confined to accommodating the god's shrine and the priests who attend the god. It provides for community worship and daily life by a more complex grouping of courts, towers and mandapas covered by repetitive roofs under a series of sikharas or a series of stepped roofs rising around the ascending sikhara. Seventy examples remain with, typically, several courtyards set along the axis one behind the other, some of the inner ones with flat roofs, and each one entered by a towered gateway called a *gopuram*–stepped pyramids, oblong in plan, that grow smaller as they approach the central shrine. But the gopurams are certainly not self-effacing pieces of architecture: their receding stepped sides, writhing with figures, clustered with domed model houses, represent the holy temple mountain and are often patterned frenetically in an ascending order of creation from man on the bottom step to gods at the top.

The Great Temple at Madura (1623), which has long corridors supported by 2,000 columns shaped like lions and galloping horses, is a good example of the South Dravidian type (*fig. 52*). It is virtually a small town, the original little shrines to Shiva and his consort Menakshi almost lost amid the later bustle of courts, halls and gateways, vividly proclaiming the union of sacred and secular in Indian life, with busy bazaars, trumpeting temple elephants and worshippers washing

51 | *Shore temples*, Mahabalipuram, Madras, India, 8th century

52 | Three main gopurams of the *Great Temple*, Madura, India, 1623

themselves and their clothes in the lake-size Tank of the Golden Lilies.

What all the temples have in common is a walkway lined with sacred carvings, either immediately round the shrine within the mandapa or outside the temple. A Hindu temple is an object of veneration in itself, and it is an act of worship to move round it – clockwise from an eastern entry for a living temple, and anti-clockwise from a western entry for a funerary monument like the great Khmer temple, Angkor Wat, in Cambodia. Another feature they have in common is that, however much they appear to go up in the air or burrow into the ground, all the usable space is in fact at ground level, either inside the building or in the area around it. This is not surprising in hot lands, where much of the daily life is lived in the open air. In silhouette and plan, temples varied from place to place according to local stylistic predilections, available materials and factors such as rainfall, which affected

roof and sikhara shape and pitch. Whether the temple is of a simple northern type, composed of tower and vestibule surrounded by an ambulatory and then a wall of about 6 feet (1.8 metres) to separate holy from secular ground, or the more complex South Dravidian type with courts on an axis, the separate elements can be clearly distinguished from the outside. They may be linked together by passages, but they are planned as separate entities. Inside the

53 | *Brahmesvara Temple*, Bhubaneswar, Orissa, India, 9th century

temple the two main structures are a broad-based assembly hall for worship, frequently low and squat in silhouette, and a small shrine room over which rises the sikhara. The ninth century was a great period for temple building in Orissa, and the Brahmesvara Temple at Bhubaneswar (*fig. 53*), a growing capital there, shows very clearly on its exterior the three elements I am speaking of: a plinth base, a band of ornate carving and the dominating sikhara. Brahmesvara is the greatest surviving Orissa-style monument from the 7,000 which once encircled the sacred lake; its sikhara rises like a corn cob, topped with a ribbed disc resembling a flat, plush-velvet cushion, but executed in stone.

Whatever the type of silhouette, the temple is always an image of the cosmos, informed by the life-giving spirit of God. Astrological advice was sought in order to decide when a temple should be erected, and the plans of some of the more complex have the satisfying symmetry and mystical perfection of a mandala—in other words, they are geometric diagrams of the cosmos and the process of creation. The stupa at Sanchi with its railings and gateways on the compass points states it with absolute simplicity.

Of the many beautiful expressions of Asian art, we must pick out two spectacular buildings which make an unforgettable impact—Angkor Wat in Cambodia and the Buddhist temple-mountain

Borobudur in Java. Both have the advantage of impressive natural settings. Borobudur stands against a background of volcanoes, whose shape it mirrors; it was originally carved out of a mountain. Angkor Wat (*fig. 54*) rises out of jungle, islanded from the trees by a moat 2½ miles (4 km) long. Suryavarman III (1113–50), King of the Khmer empire and Deva-Raja (god-king), built here as a dynastic monument the world's largest religious complex, so enormous that pilgrims attempting the full ritual circumambulation find that they have let themselves in for a 12-mile (19 km) walk. The centre of the temple rises in five terraces to a height of 215 feet (65.5 metres), and is crowned with five fir-coned towers, symbolizing Mount Meru; it is reached by a raised road and a cruciform entry platform.

'To enter by causeway and lilied moat', says Rose Macaulay, in *Pleasure of Ruins*, 'was to be caught into some delirious dream.' She goes on to describe how visitors move from one terrace to another, up twisting or straight steep flights of stairs from which grasses grow, finding a route through the maze of courts and long corridors, whose walls 'sway gently' with Apsaras, the dancing nymphs, 'and always the musing god', until eventually they look down on 'a forest that surrounds the nearby city of Angkor Thom'. For after the fall of the Khmer empire, the forest rushed back, engulfing the cities of the kingdom. The god's snake symbol, transformed into a balustrade that wraps itself round the temple enclosure, was through the centuries rivalled by more constricting snake forms—the creeping roots and branches of fig and banyan trees. This tremendous piece of architecture remained stifled in their vicious embrace not for a mere one hundred years like the palace of the Sleeping Beauty, but for five hundred. However, sooner or later, Prince Charming must come; and in 1861 he appeared

54 | *Angkor Wat*, Cambodia, 12th century

55 | *Borobudur Temple*, Java, c.800, aerial view

in the guise of a French naturalist and writer, Pierre Loti, who, while hunting for a rare tropical plant, stumbled on and gave the kiss of life to the prize of Khmer art. Painstaking work had by 1973 restored much of the temple to its former glory. Alas, since 1975, under the military supremacy of the Khmer Rouge, its lovely terraces have become once more prey to neglect and rain, fungi and vines; and few gods can still muse, for vandalism and pilfering have robbed most of them of their heads.

The temple of Borobudur, the Buddhist *pièce de résistance* of about 800 AD (*fig. 55*), has the fascination of the elemental. This is partly due to its origin as an outcrop of rock, partly to its enormous size; seen from below, the massed masonry of its terraces, dotted with niches containing Buddhas, seems not man-made, but rather a natural cliff of crumbling rock, pocked with hermits'

caves. The whole is an image of the soul's journey to nirvana, for pilgrims must, as at Angkor Wat, pass along long corridors, ever upwards and inwards, through the nine stages of self-abnegation in the approach to enlightenment. From the plinth pilgrims pass through four square enclosed terraces to three open concentric terraces, where sit, inside 72 bell-stupas of chequered stone lattice, 72 buddhas – some, who have lost their bell-lids, visible from the waist as if sitting snug in their bath-tubs (*fig. 38*) – until they achieve the apex, the little enclosed and pinnacled stupa in which, no pilgrim could doubt, must surely lie, eternally waiting, the mystery at the very heart of existence.

The architecture of the Far East shows extreme individuality, compelling and memorable, stemming from a culture that is cool, aloof and self-sufficient. Aloof, of course, as seen from the West. Geographically, China turns her back on the West and looks East, to Korea, Japan and the rising sun. Behind her, on the west, massive mountain barriers separate the Far East from the rest of the world.

Our knowledge of China's early architecture is patchy, partly because of her tradition of building in wood – a highly perishable material – and partly because for a long time neither the Chinese nor the Japanese showed much inclination to enshrine pomp and circumstance, whether worldly or heavenly, in monumental or permanent architecture. But in the 1970s hundreds of imperial tombs of the Ch'in dynasty (221–206 BC) were uncovered from the orange earth of the Yellow River valley. Among them was the tomb of the conquering Ch'in king who united China and took the name of Ch'in Shih Huang Ti, which means First Emperor of China. In 1996 his tomb was found intact, although at the time of writing it has not been opened. Shih Huang Ti not only built a new capital, Hsienyang, and the Great Wall of China (by filling in gaps between piecemeal previous defences) to repel Mongol incursions, but also in the course of 36 years dragooned some 7,000 conscripts to create an underground 'spirit city' containing dummies

of those who at an earlier period would have attended the king to his tomb in person – 600 terracotta figures, 6 feet (1.8 metres) high (were the Chinese a tall race in 200 BC?), each with a different face as if modelled on individual soldiers. There was also a model of the Ch'in idea of the heavens with sun, moon and stars moved by machinery, and, most informatively for us, a layout model of the Ch'in kingdom. Here are the Yellow and the Yangtse rivers reproduced in mercury and made to flow by some mechanical contrivance into an ocean; and here are the buildings of the old capital reproduced in pottery – farms, palaces and pavilions.

These and later tomb models (*fig. 56*) have substantiated the picture of early Chinese wooden architecture which historians had previously deduced from wooden buildings in Japan traditionally reputed to be rebuilds at many removes of Chinese buildings, due to an obliging Japanese habit of building replicas on adjacent sites every 20 or 30 years. Shrines of the sun-goddess of the ancient pantheistic Shinto religion of Japan, such as the Ise Shrine (*fig. 57*) and the Izumo Shrine, are cases in point, lovely examples of vernacular architecture.

It is relatively easy to put clues together and come up with something that approximates Chinese society of 3,500 years ago because China appears to have evolved her sophisticated culture early and in isolation,

56 | Pottery model of a house from an Eastern Han Dynasty tomb, China, 1st century AD

57 | *Ise shrine*, Mie Prefecture, Japan, believed to have been rebuilt on the same site at 20–30 year intervals since the 7th century

58 | *Himei-ji Castle*, the 'White Heron', Hyogo Prefecture, Japan, *c.*1570

and then chosen to pursue only those technological developments which suited the national temperament, remaining relatively static in many fields of activity until the present century.

The persistent use of wood had, by the nineteenth century, threatened to replace a land of jungle with a landscape bald and denuded. It was not that the Chinese did not know how to use brick and stone. From the third century BC they used brick arches in tombs and vaults. Buddhism brought with it in the second and third centuries AD the Indian and Burmese traditions of brick and stone building, exemplified in pagodas such as the Liao dynasty (907–1125) brick pagoda in Manchuria, in the *p'ailou*, the striking triumphal arches used as city gates (*fig. 59*), and in the bridges which, in this well-watered country, have always been features of great beauty. There was superb brickwork too,

in the palace of Kublai Khan (1214–94), the founder of the Mongol Yuan dynasty (1260–1368), in its successors built in the Ming dynasty (1368–1644), and in many fortresses.

But undoubtedly it was wood that the Chinese found most pleasing. The wooden trabeate or beam structure, which developed first in China and was then passed on to Japan, is one of two distinctive features of Chinese architecture. The second was a body of rules – a sort of kit of unwritten planning by-laws, strictly adhered to – which governed the planning of any town or building, controlling siting, orientation, plan and even colour. These laws stemmed not only from physical, social or political requirements, but from a philosophy of design which embraced harmony in nature and what the oracles had determined was 'propitious', called *Feng-shui*. They were about the use of space, the

Puzzles and Modules: *China and Japan*

61 | *Foguang Temple*, Mt Wutai, Shanxi province, China, *c.*857

eternal theme of architecture, and about creating spaces; and space was all-important in Chinese philosophy – more, some commentators insist, than time, and certainly more than structure. But we must look at structure first if we are to have an image of the buildings.

No doubt it was the abundance of wood that first prompted its use in the early building types. In the northern areas along the river Amur, the earliest dwellings were not so much caves as holes in the ground over which a roof was set, supported by tree-trunk pillars driven into the ground. Early Japanese buildings were similarly created with a thatched roof resting on the ground (Jomon culture), and in the later Yayoi culture with a tent-shaped roof held up by a ridge-pole between two forked sticks, perched above a wattle-and-thatch wall that looked like a natural grass mound. This has remained the vernacular farm-

house pattern in Japan. In southern China, South East Asia and Indonesia, the likelihood of flooding prompted the raising of wooden buildings on piles; this has remained the vernacular type in these areas.

What was to become the classic Chinese structure was developed in the middle Yellow River valley – a wood-frame building on a platform. Earthquakes, fairly frequent in China and endemic in Japan, may well have influenced the evolution of this structure. The need was not for solid walls, which could be cracked and rent apart by any upheaval of the earth's crust, but a structure which at best might be able to ride the heaving earth like a boat, shifting and settling back into position, and at worst, would be disposable, easily rebuilt after devastation. Possibly the base platform could act like a raft.

A famous example of early Chinese

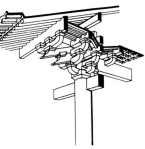

60 | *Kou-tung* bracket cluster

62 | Red-painted columns in the interior of the *Kasuga Shrine*, Nara, Japan, founded 768

architecture is the Foguang Temple in the Wutai Mountains of Shanxi province, built in the ninth century (*fig. 61*). Here are the three basic elements of Chinese and Japanese buildings: a raised platform, a frame wall and a roof. Typically, the podium was solid – there were never any cellars – and could be made of stamped earth, sometimes faced with brick or stone, or of pounded clay, rubble or uneven stones, or even of laid brick or ashlar. On this the wooden frame of the house was erected. This is the first time in our story that we have found a national building pattern for their 'great' architecture which is on the frame principle – that is, the roof is supported on a frame with corner pillars;

the walls are later in-fill. In the wooden houses of the Far East we can see the structural principle exemplified in naked simplicity, with the minimum of obscuring cladding.

Another early Chinese building is in Korea, the Chil-Song-Gak (Hall of the Pleiades) in Bo-Hyan-Su Temple in the Myohyang Mountains (Diamond Mountains), dating from the seventh and eighth centuries. The Hall of the Pleiades has solid stumpy tree-trunks as corner pillars, typical of the early type of architecture, and a single lintel beam (architrave), which usually became double in later classic versions. Columns of pine or cedar were generally set on protective bases of stone or bronze

Puzzles and Modules: *China and Japan*

that, through time, became increasingly elaborated with carvings or engravings. Also for protection from weather or termites, the pillars were painted with lacquer or an oil and hemp mixture which had brick dust mixed into it; from this may have come the custom of painting columns and brackets all in one colour, frequently a vivid red (*fig. 62*). (Lacquer, also frequently bright red, from the sap of the lacquer tree, which hardens when exposed to oxygen, was used in a similar way to coat load-bearing structures like columns or bell-frames from early times, but particularly from the third century BC.) On the columns was set the distinctive lintel structure which supports the roof. There were no chimneys: heating was by portable stoves, and the smoke escaped from the side or under the ridge of the roof. This was no problem in the humid heat of the south, where the walls were filled in by mere decorated screens, often only half-height; even in the bitter north, where timber walls might be 40 inches (100 centimetres) thick, it was customary to leave a gap below the roofline. Window glass was often of paper, which could be rolled up like a blind to let in the breezes on a hot day. Le Corbusier once pointed out that windows have three functions: to let in light, to see out of, and to let in air. In countries that are exposed to the sun for much of the year, the first of these three functions does not apply; windows primarily exist as air-vents. In Japan, both outer and inner screen walls might be of paper.

The roofs were remarkable. They did not use the triangular tied construction of the half-timbered houses of medieval Europe. The Far East never used the diagonal reinforcing strut; diagonal wood strips on the surface such as appear on some Han tomb farmhouse models are purely decorative. The wide eaves of Chinese and Japanese houses are supported on a trabeate pyramid (*trabis* is Latin for a beam). As well as the purlins on which the rafters rest, the lintel beam between the two

corner columns supports short vertical members which carry a beam of shorter size. This pattern may be repeated with lintels of decreasing length up to the roof, the weight being forced back down on to the two original kingposts. To help carry the weight, or to allow for sideways expansion and to achieve greater eaves overhang (the classic method of providing a shaded balcony or courtyard area where the family might sit out of the sun or rain), extra pillars would be added at the sides, each carrying its own post-and-lintel construction.

The additional columns provided galleries and aisle-like spaces inside. To meet the need of architects who wished to extend the eaves overhang without cluttering the interior with columns, they evolved a clever system: they cantilevered the overhang outwards on clusters of brackets known as *kou-tung* (*fig. 60*). These were works of art in themselves, locking together like Chinese puzzles. Attention was further drawn to the brackets by the tradition of painting the beams and the rafters they supported in gay colours. The inspiration for these kou-tung may have come from Persian sources by way of India. Their importance was emphasized in the Song era (960–1279), the Silver Age of Chinese culture, when, following the publication of a master-builder's manual in 1103 – *The Methods and Design of Architecture (Ying*

61

Zao Fa Shi) by Li Chieh – a module for the
spacing of pillars and beams (previously
often charmingly irregular), based on bracket size, was established for use throughout
the empire. When a new module was put
forward in the seventeenth century by
the Ching dynasty (1644–1912) Palace
Office of Works, it was again based on
the bracket arm.

Altering the angle of the brackets made
possible the marvellous undulating swags
of Chinese roofs (*fig. 63*), and combined
with a chosen roof-shape – gabled, hipped,
half-hipped or pyramidal – created fascinating outlines. From the Han dynasty (206
BC – 220 AD) onwards, eaves hang in catenary curves and have curved ridge lines
and hip seams; sometimes they sport
serrated edges like dragons' teeth and
exuberantly winged corners hung with
little bronze bells. The ridge pole was considered so important that a special ceremony took place when it was set in position.
For good measure, tiles might be grey in
the north, and elsewhere either blue or
green or purple or yellow. Yellow was the
imperial colour, and a bird's-eye view of
Beijing in Ming times might have established the social status of different areas
according to roof colour.

65 | *Enemy Observation
Pagoda* (*Liao Di Ta*), *Kaiyuan
Temple*, Dingxian, Hebei
province, China, 1001–50

The pagoda is sometimes considered
the characteristic form of the Far East.
Certainly, practically every town in China
boasts at least one pagoda, often sited to
block the entry of evil spirits into the town
from the north-east – the 'direction of the
devil'. But in fact the typical Chinese building pattern was one-storey, or at the most
two-storey, rectangular buildings grouped
round courtyards. It is interesting to note
that, in contrast to most countries where
sacred structures set the standard 'quality'
pattern for the national style, temples in
China and Japan were built in the style of
ordinary domestic housing. This reversal
of sacred and secular may be typical of the
mentality of the Far East, perhaps account-
ing for the sacred nature of Japan's domestic tea ceremony.

It has been suggested that the pagoda,
which was generally attached to a temple,
may have developed from a typical house
of which we show a model from a Han
tomb – a rectangular hall with above, in the
centre, a single first-floor study room, to
which the master might escape for serious
thought, topped by an attic granary. Another plausible explanation is that it developed
under Buddhist influence – a type of sikhara
or pyramid of Buddhist umbrellas. However, the tiered *lou* was already an ancient
form in China, and can be traced back to
models of watch or water towers in the
Han tombs. Very likely it evolved from a
combination of the three.

We can trace the evolution through
three pagodas. First, through the twelve-
sided Songyue Pagoda on Mount Song,
Henan province, the oldest surviving brick
building in China, dated 520 AD, and highly
reminiscent of an Indian temple (*fig. 64*).
Second, through the lighthouse-like Song
dynasty Enemy Observation Pagoda (Liao
Di Ta) of 1001–50, a watchtower for the
frontier between the Liao and Song territories at the Kaiyuan Temple, Dingxian,
Hebei (*fig. 65*). Not until the Sakyamuni
Pagoda, Yingxian, of 1056 (*fig. 66*) do we
find the form has developed into what

66 | *Sakyamuni Pagoda*,
Yingxian, Shanxi province,
China, 1056, section

67 | *Great Wall of China*,
completed 210 BC

we think of as typically Chinese. An all-wooden pagoda on an octagonal plan, it has the uneven number of floors which was to become *de rigeur* (usually seven or thirteen). The Chou belief that heaven had nine layers caused nine to be favoured in the early Buddhist period. In the Foguang temple we have five floors, indicated on the exterior by jutting roofs, with the intermediate gallery floors unexpressed. Originally the pagodas were shrines or reliquaries attached to Buddhist monasteries. They housed an image on the ground floor and were hollow above, like the Indian sikhara, or sometimes contained a giant image that went up through several floors, or carried a series of images on galleried floors.

For all the similarity in form, the Chinese pagoda never had the mystical significance of the sikhara as a vertical axis round which the cosmos turned. The Chinese were concerned with the cosmic axis, but for them it was horizontal, on the ground. The points of the compass were crucial, their separate identities linked with colours, animal symbols and seasons. Black stood for the north, winter and night – death of the day and the year – and from this direction evil came, not surprisingly when one thinks of the cold winds from Mongolia. And so from the earliest examples discovered, it appears that Chinese towns and houses were laid out on a north – south axis, the towns on a grid with

68 | *Hall of Prayer for Good Harvests, Temple of Heaven, Beijing*, 1420

the main street running north to south, the houses with doors facing south, the good direction of the Red Phoenix and the summer sun. The west was seen as white autumn, the white tiger at the evening of the day and the year, white peace and white mourning robes at the end of life. The importance of ancestor worship therefore makes the south-west corner of the house the sacred area: no utilitarian offices were placed here.

But there were 24 cardinal points to contend with, in addition to the main compass points, when siting a house, grave or town. Diviners interpreted the local forces of good or ill luck (harmony with the 'cosmic breath') by means of the ancient 'science' of Feng-shui (literally, 'wind and water') which we mentioned earlier. Such diviners are still consulted today, even for a project as up-to-date as the revolutionary Hong Kong Shanghai Bank in Hong Kong of 1982–3. Feng-shui not only dictates the site in relation to hills, roads and streams, and the building's orientation, but also the position of the doors (one Singapore bank constantly lost on business deals until it changed its entrance), the relationship of house-blocks within a compound, and even the number of rooms in a house (three, four and eight bedrooms are unlucky and must be avoided).

After the site was chosen a wall was built, again often in association with Feng-shui, to block any evil influences from an unpropitious direction. Walls and the privacy

Puzzles and Modules: *China and Japan*

69 | Coffered ceiling of the *Hall of Prayer for Good Harvests, Temple of Heaven,* Beijing, 1420

70 | View from the Meridian Gate (Wu Men) across the horseshoe canal and the great expanse of ceremonial space to the *Gate of Great Peace* (Tai He Men), *Forbidden City*, Beijing

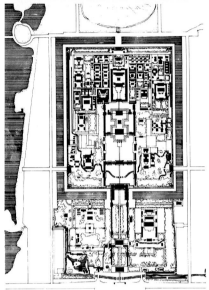

71 | *Forbidden City*, Beijing, 1406–20, plan

they give are important to the Chinese. Fittingly, the first emperor, Ch'in Shih Huang Ti, joined into the Great Wall of China (*fig. 67*) all the stretches of the wall along the northern frontier that feuding neighbouring clans had built against each other. The only man-made feature that can be seen from outer space, it is a superb example of interaction between man and his environment as it loops its way, following the natural contours of the hills, 2,383 miles (3,813 km) from the Gulf of Bohai to Jia Yuguan in Kansu Province. Completed in 210 BC, the Wall was maintained by successive emperors and finally given the refacing we see today by the Ming dynasty from the fifteenth to the sixteenth century.

We talked earlier of the wooden trabeate structure and the kit of building regulations as two vital characteristics of Chinese architecture; we can add the obsession with the defensive wall as a

third. In the first place, the defensive wall explains the puzzling lack of defensive castles in a country whose long history was patterned with fighting between clans and feudal overlords. The nobleman's town was his castle. The Ch'in capital of Xianyang was planned to hold 10,000 people, and the Imperial City at Beijing was built big enough to harbour within its walls the entire population of the city if need be. Ch'in unification in the third century BC had brought about a hierarchical feudal system, and towns became the bureaucratic and administrative centres. The system of walls for bureaucratic identity, privacy and defence was repeated from macrocosm to microcosm: the country was walled, each city was walled and had its own god of wall and moat, each dwelling within the city would normally consist of several buildings within a walled courtyard to house the customary extended family, which might comprise a hundred relatives. Indeed the word for 'wall' and the word for 'city' were the same.

Beijing, the northern capital, epitomizes the system. Its fortunes as a capital oscillated until in 1552 the Ming emperors built a new wall, 9 miles (14.5 km) round with seven gates, to take in the southern suburbs, which had developed under the pressure of a population explosion. This gave the city its four famous walled enclosures, and also put within the outer enclosure the Temple of Heaven (Chi Nian Dian) of 1420 (*figs. 68, 69*), built, as was the custom, in the open air on a mound to the south of the capital city. Moats and bastioned walls encircled the Outer City to the south and the Inner City to the north; inside the Inner City were the walls through which one had

72 | Chinese courtyard houses, Beijing

Puzzles and Modules: *China and Japan*

煙霞天成

73 | The Long Walk in the gardens of the *Summer Palace*, near Beijing, originally laid out in the 18th century

to pass by the Gate of Heavenly Peace (Tian An Men) into the great public square (Tiananmen Square) which formed the entrance courtyard to the Imperial City. To penetrate to the heart of the complex, the Forbidden City (*fig. 71*) one had to breach another wall by the Meridian Gate (Wu Men), cross the horseshoe canal by one of the five bridges, and pass through first the gate-house buildings, guarded by the Emperor Qian Long's great bronze dog-lions, and then the Gate of Great Peace (Tai He Men), before reaching the podium on which the Palace of Great Peace itself stood (*fig. 70*). One is reminded of those ingenious boxes within boxes which the Chinese excel in carving out of ivory, and which hold a sort of mystical anticipation that within and within one may penetrate to the seat of power and majesty. Thus enclosed, each part of Chinese society could keep itself to itself, forging relations with the outer world on its own terms.

The same aloofness informs the planning of both city and house. The latter is conceived from the inside looking out, the opposite attitude to the one we find in our Western streets where each house proudly shows off its position, station and beauty to the passer-by. Clues to the

74 | *Phoenix Hall, Byodoin Temple*, Uji, near Kyoto, Japan, 11th century

status of the house-owner can in fact be picked up from its compass position in the city or in the street-block (or *fang*) within the city grid; and once inside the gate there are factors like the height of the platform on which the house stands and the number of inner courtyards which indicate status. Under the Ming dynasty imperial legislation fixed the number of bays of a single-halled dwelling–nine for an emperor, seven for a prince, five for a mandarin and three for a citizen. But what can be seen from the street are blank walls. Houses look inwards to their inner courtyards (*fig. 72*), so there are no windows to be seen in the walls rising round the entrance courtyard, and even the view through gateways is blocked by 'spirit walls'–screens set just inside the entrance to obstruct the passage of evil spirits, who can only move in straight lines. However, the top of a flowering tree may be glimpsed in the entrance courtyard, and the spirit walls themselves are often very beautiful–carved in geometric or naturalistic patterns of crazy-paving or 'cracked ice', with lotus flowers or bamboo wands, or perhaps painted white with a single good-omen character in black.

Frequently the entrance court is approached through a side gate, but no impressive façade greets the visitor–simply one long wall of the house with the doorway placed at the centre (never in the gable wall). All houses must for good luck have a back door as well as a front door, and the two must not be in line, again to foil evil spirits. Rules of etiquette decide from this point whether the visitor will be invited further in to discover for himself the symmetrical division of the house into the bright (*ming*) public rooms to the front and the cool dark shady (*an*) apartments at the back, which are the private family rooms. This layout, no doubt in part caused by the need to create cross-draughts within the interior, reflects a certain element of Chinese formality and privacy: steps to left and right, which lead, respectively, the host on the east and the guest on the west separately towards these back rooms, give the guest a clear understanding that he penetrates to the family areas on the host's terms and may not make himself free of the house.

Gardens have been a feature of Chinese architecture from long before the building guidelines were set down in the *Ying Zao Fa Shi* in 1103. The T'ang Empress Wu (690–705) even turned the imperial gardens at Chang'an into something of a wild-life park, enclosing it in 100 miles of wall and importing rhinoceros from India to roam among hills, lakes and woodland. The watered and wooded landscape surrounding the Summer Palace 6 miles (10 km) north-west of Beijing is dotted with charming and idiosyncratic architectural features – pavilions with circular octagonal and fretwork doors, pagodas, covered walkways round the lake promontory, bridges, gateways, steps (*fig. 73*). Here waters spout, purr and tinkle, leaves rustle, paths meander, waterlilies sway gently on the surface of the lakes like full moons – 'Now sleeps the crimson petal, now the white, Nor wakes the cypress in the palace walk; Nor winks the gold fin in the porphyry font ...' All is a dreamy fantasy misted in almond blossom.

In palace as in humble dwelling, the building is geometrical and formal, the garden free. The macrocosm/microcosm duality persists. The house is a small version of the Chinese view of the world: a five-sided open box with the sky for a lid. The garden is a miniature version of nature, of mountains reduced to rocks, forests to plants and mosses, rivers and oceans to brooks and pools. There are no straight lines: all is sloping and sinuous to foil those lurking evil spirits. In the same way, the structures that connect house to garden – gates, balconies, screens, railings, steps – abandon the angular geometry of the house for rounded and flowing lines and the irregular patterns of natural forms – cracked ice, jointed stems, tasselled fronds, ferns uncurling, bamboo quivering.

Commentators have associated the contrasting styles of house and garden with the two great indigenous Chinese philosophies, Confucianism and Taoism. The founders of both were seeking for a principle of unity in life during a turbulent period of Chinese history. In the sixth century BC Lao Zi set out his philosophy in the *Dao De Jing* (*The Book of the Virtuous Way*). Confucius, on the other hand, was a government official (Kong Fuzi) in the fifth century BC, and preached a civil servant's solution to the problems of life. Conservative and authoritarian, he respected the traditions of the ancestors (*li*) and advocated a Way (*tao*) of social order and peace, brought about by rational and competent administration. We can trace the effect of his philosophy in the united empire of the Ch'in, which succeeded the years of the Warring States (475–221 BC), in the establishment of a bureaucratic feudalism so strong it lasted till 1911, and in the order, hierarchy and exact geometry that characterizes houses. In contrast, the garden reflects the Taoist concern for the life of feeling, intuition and mysticism. It is a movement away from rationalism, order and symmetry, to freedom, experiment and contemplation.

China has an ancient legend that in the beginning the Supreme Lord sent out two opposite forces, the *yin* and the *yang*, to share control of the universe. In the Chinese house and garden we see the two polarities reconciled and shown to be complementary.

When we turn to Japan we find that so great was the effect of Chinese culture that much of her architectural story has already been told. Japan, a string of rocky volcanic islands lying out in the Pacific, 125 miles (200 km) from the Asian mainland, was, until recently, very isolated. Her history has alternated between periods of native rule and culture and occupation from abroad. The original Neolithic Jomon culture and the indigenous Shinto religion were first disturbed by Yayoi immigrants from China, who came by way of Korea from the first to the fifth century AD; and hard on their heels came Buddhism. The highest architectural expression of this import of Chinese religion is probably the Amida Hall of the Byodoin Temple above the river at Uji, south of Kyoto (then known as Heien), usually called the Phoenix Hall, because its plan is shaped like a bird. Dating from the eleventh century, its frontage was copied from a T'ang palace, and its rich embellishments of gold, silver, lacquer and mother-of-pearl show the sumptuous Chinese/Japanese/Buddhist style at its height (*fig. 74*).

After the fall of the T'ang dynasty in China, Japanese vigour reasserted itself;

75 | *East Pagoda of the Yakushi-ji Temple*, Nara, Japan, 680

the Emperor moved his capital to Heien, and from the eighth to the twelfth century, the first indigenous domestic architecture appeared in the form of rambling country houses for the lords who headed the clans. The usual pattern was a series of rectangular buildings connected by corridors, set down irregularly in a landscaped garden with pools and islands.

Continuous clan skirmishing, culminating in a century of civil wars, resulted in the transference of power from the Emperor to a military commander who bore the name of *Shogun*, or Commander-in-Chief. From the twelfth to the nineteenth century the

chief power resided in the shoguns with their private armies, the *samurai*. The architectural consequences of the power of the Shogunate and of the introduction of gunpowder were the marvellous garrison castles, which in Japan replaced the Chinese walled city system of defence. Often moated and set on high platforms of dressed granite or other stone to resist fire (a major threat to their log superstructure), and with a curved batter to resist earth movement, these impressive buildings have towns huddled at their base, and are clearly in command of the surrounding countryside.

In the 1630s, Ieyasu of the Tokogawa

Puzzles and Modules: *China and Japan*

Shogunate expelled all foreigners, closing the borders to traffic upon pain of execution. Christianity, which had come in with the Dutch, Spanish and Portuguese explorers in the sixteenth century, was crushed. Japan entered the so-called Floating World period, a time of middle-class affluence and a golden era for the arts: music, puppetry, *No* theatre, *haiku* poetry, painting and woodcuts, especially of blossom or Japan's volcano, Fujiyama. In the next 200 years of prosperity, the population soared to 30 million and the standard of literacy was high. By 1854, Japan was ready to resume relations with the outside world and eventually take her place as one of the world's leading technological nations.

What are the distinctive features of Japanese architecture? The Chinese type originally adopted was the rectangular building set on an open platform of wooden stilts; to this the Japanese added an extra verandah, often called a fishing gallery because, wherever possible, dwellings were sited on the edge of a pond or lake, so that fish, a staple part of the Japanese diet, could be obtained fresh. The original tent roof persisted for at least 2,000 years, with its characteristic V-shaped fork at either end of the ridge pole. But the most general roof shape is a combination of gable and half-hip in which the

77 | Japanese roof bracket system in the *Main Hall*, *Toshodai-ji Temple*, Nara, 8th century

gable eaves curve backwards slightly to disappear behind the wrapped-around hip, achieving from the front a strange silhouette like a farmer's broad-brimmed hat.

The Japanese pagoda with its five linear roofs is more refined than Chinese versions. The roof-shape here, tauter, slimmer, hovers with wide wing-span over the building. In some cases, the eaves overhang is as much as 8 feet (2.4 metres). Roofs, sometimes of unequal size, are stacked on a shady square-core tower like discs on a spindle, and topped by a high, thin finial called a *hosho*—the sacred crowning gem—so spindly that it appears to trail away in the sky like the cry of a wild bird. The silhouette of the pagoda often resembles a calligraphic character or the pine trees that typify Japanese scenery. On the East Pagoda of the Yakushi-ji Temple at Nara of 680 (*fig. 75*) the roofs are alternately narrow and wide, with an entry door on the lower of each pair. But only the

78 | *Golden Pavilion,
Kinkaku-ji*, in the grounds of
the Kitayama Palace, Kyoto,
Japan, 1397

They had much practice, both because of
the need for rebuilding after earthquake or
hurricane, and because for many centuries
before the permanent capital was fixed at
Nara in 710 AD, the imperial court was peri-
patetic, and craftsmen had to evolve buildings finely jointed and carefully slotted
together to allow rapid dismantling and re-
erection (*fig. 77*). Even early gateways to
Shinto shrines, the equivalent of Chinese
p'ailou known as *torii* in Japan, exhibit masterly workmanship in their twin-beamed
simplicity; as does the earliest extant
wooden building in Asia, the *Kondo* main
hall of the Horyu-ji Temple at Nara, which
was originally founded for Buddhist monks
by Japan's early hero, Prince Shotoku
(574–622). The brackets carrying these
enormous eaves are robust and beautiful.

The Chinese preoccupation with symmetry was early shaken off. Precincts
started off adhering to a north–south axis,
but when the Horyu-ji precinct had to be
rebuilt after a fire in 670, the architects
incorporated an existing mortuary chapel
in the Golden Hall (the Kondo) and set
the pagoda, which holds a clay sculpture
tableau of the nirvana of the Buddha, next
to it. In 733 the Hokkedo was added on
rising ground within the temple precinct.
Like the Kondo, it was a basic single-unit
building, with the typical early unevenly
spaced pillars, but it was gentler and
prettier, with the old pattern of shallow
roof in silvery-grey tiles and gently
curving eaves.

Where the tradition of orientation was
maintained it was for practical purposes.
To cope with the overpoweringly strong
afternoon sun on the west, the long side
of the house would be on the east–west
axis, with the living rooms facing south or
south-east; in addition, it was common to
have a seasonal change of living quarters
and move into the darker parts of the
house in high summer. Eventually, the
movement away from Chinese models
passed beyond finding their own axiality to
a distinctive preference for asymmetry. A

door on the ground floor provides access;
those above to the galleries surrounding
the floors are sham. The five roofs of the
pagoda of the Horyu-ji Temple at Ikaruga
near Nara, originally dating from *c.*670–714,
(*fig. 76*) subtly decrease in size as they
go upwards, in a proportion of 10:9:8:7:6.
Castles have the most exciting roofs of all,
because the Japanese managed to solve
the intricate structural problems involved in
piling up storeys with gables facing watch-
fully in different directions. Perched above
the water and with their white-plastered
rendering, the castles suggest the movement of a cluster of great white seabirds
about to lift off from a rocky perch – so that
it is no surprise to discover that Himei-ji
Castle of about 1570 in the Hyogo Prefecture is known as the White Heron
(*fig. 58*).

The Japanese skill in woodwork
surpassed even that of the Chinese.

taste for variety of façades developed and led to an interest in the natural qualities of materials and the lovely contrasting use of surface texture which, as we will see when we look at the modern movement of the 1960s and the conservation of old buildings which became such an important movement then, was to form part of the Japanese legacy to modern architecture. Typical is the 1397 Golden Pavilion, Kinkaku-ji, in the Kitayama Palace grounds at Kyoto (*fig. 78*). Permutations of the pleasure given by different detailing and surfaces on each storey are multiplied by the reflection in the lake.

Interest in texture was promoted by the Zen Buddhists, a sect whose rise to importance coincides with the rise of the Shoguns. Their insistence on simplicity influenced the economy in line, colour and detailing in modern Western architecture. It also complied with one ancient principle of Japanese architecture: the use of a module. The house itself, the size of internal areas, and the screens which created the bays along the elevations of the house, were established by a module of 6 x 3 feet (1.8 x 0.9 metres), the size of the rice-straw floor mat, the *tatami*. Originally laid side by side loose, mats were later set into the floor, and eventually, after 1615, standardization of the module was formalized when the capital moved to Edo, today called Tokyo. By that time the early pattern of corridors joining separate buildings had long since given way to corridors within the house formed by paper screens. After the twelfth century, runners were fixed to the floor to allow the screens to be pushed aside so that new areas could be opened up, or in summer, to open the entire side of the house to the garden. The Japanese traditionally do not have furniture: they sit back on their heels and eat from trays and sleep on mats. This has two effects. Life is lived at a very low level: ceilings can be low, and the beauties of the garden are admired from a couple of feet above the ground. But the second effect is more

important: it gives the house space enormous flexibility. Traditional houses had two raised areas – the chief one, for living and sleeping, was furnished with floor mats, and slippers were removed before it was entered; the other, floored in wood, was used for corridors and verandahs. A lower, unfloored area usually supplied hall, bathroom and kitchen areas. The Japanese thus possessed a traditional domestic architecture which became the envy of the West; a system so flexible that it could retain individuality while lending itself to the mass-production of building components.

The tea-houses built for *cho-no-ya*, the tea ceremony, epitomize the cool economy of Japanese module architecture, as do their flower arrangements of a single spray of blossom set against a white wall. Tea-drinking was originally associated with Zen Buddhist monks, who drank green tea to keep themselves awake during contemplation. A Zen priest called Shuko prevailed upon his friend the Shogun Yoshimasa to build him a special little tea-house in the grounds of the Silver Pavilion in Kyoto. Tea-houses were thus based on a monk's simple study, contemplative, pure, beautiful (*fig. 79*). Walls and door panels were white or else translucent to let in the light reflected from the ground outside – the chief source of illumination under those deep eaves. Mats covered the floor and furniture was confined to shelves to hold the tea-making equipment and possibly an alcove displaying a single work of art – perhaps a painting or a bowl or a slim flower arrangement.

That spirit of Japan we find distilled in the tea-house is also apparent in the gardens. Zen Buddhism in particular affirms the need to be at one with nature, and gardens, whatever their size, were important. Like Chinese gardens, they represent the world in miniature, but here art more particularly contrives nature. You may walk in a Japanese woodland and moss garden, but a sand-garden you can only view from

79 | *Tea-Room of the Shokintei House, Katsura Imperial Villa*, Kyoto, c.1590

a terrace or verandah. As with flower arrangements, great painters were employed to design gardens, such as So-ami's sand garden adjoining the tea-house of a Kyoto temple. Like the black-ink paintings of which the Japanese were so fond, sand gardens should be a study in dark and light – rock formations created from carefully searched-out *objets trouvés* (to split a rock would be to violate nature), white sand raked into hillocks and wave or whirl-pool patterns, miniature trees, water in lakes, ponds or tiny waterfalls according to the space available (*fig. 80*).

From the sixteenth century onwards,

the Chinese influence is apparent in the art and architecture of Europe. But in the long run it has been Japanese architecture that has proved more influential. Among the features the world has drawn from Japan are the standardized building components based on a module; the rethinking of internal space with fitted carpets and floor-cushions, as well as bean bags and bedding rolls (futons) to replace furniture, all of which can be safely stowed away in fitted cupboards when not in use; space made flexible with screen-dividers; the use of untreated natural materials producing contrasting textures (linen, wool, rafia, hemp,

Puzzles and Modules: *China and Japan*

80 | Japanese moss/sand
garden, Ryoan-ji Temple, Kyoto

wood) within a narrow range of colours
(white, black and natural) which accentuate
the structure, and finally the interchange
between house and garden, which
assumed a full role in twentieth-century
architecture.

In the sixteenth century Charles I of Spain sent his conquistadors to the New World, where they found strange civilizations dating from the first millennium BC. When, after landing on the Mexican Gulf, they pushed their way through rain-forests, thick-set with thorns and infested with mosquitoes, to the Aztec city of Tenochtitlan, the site of Mexico City today, there was plenty of reason for native Indians and Spaniards to stare at each other with wild surmise. The apparition of the Spaniards fulfilled a prophesy among the Indians: the Aztec emperor Montezuma II and his men believed they were witnessing the second coming of Quetzalcoatl, the plumed serpent god, who, it had been predicted, would come again, white and bearded and majestic from the East. They were riveted by the strangeness of the armed warriors with flashing steel, popping firearms and thunderball cannons, mounted (most fearsome of all) on monsters with thudding hooves, tossing manes and lashing tails. For these people possessed neither iron nor steel, and did their fighting with poison-tipped arrows and weapons of bronze and obsidian. Moreover, the Pre-Columbians never discovered the wheel and had never seen a horse. Indeed, in this country, except in the high Andes of Peru where llamas were sometimes used as pack animals, man was the beast of burden – a tradition so deep-seated that even today building workers often prefer to shift massive stones on their backs in great woven baskets supported by headbands, rather than use wheelbarrows or trolleys. As for the horse, it was of course a historic meeting, indeed the start of a centuries-long love affair.

And what was there to stop the Spaniards in their tracks? The area which they invaded, south of where Christopher Columbus had landed some 27 years earlier in 1492, was the isthmus that connects North America with the west coast of South America; and in this region (which today comprises Mexico, Yucatan, Honduras and Guatemala) and in an area on the Pacific coast of South America (comprising modern Peru and the fringes of Bolivia and Chile), the ancient civilizations in the Americas were in their final phase. The Spaniards, pushing their way inland through Yucatan, may have first stumbled on some of the enormous stone heads, eight or nine feet (2.5 metres) high, which the ancient Olmec race had left behind, along with remains of the two classic Meso-American architectural forms, the pyramid and the ball court; and may have caught glimpses of the crested temples of the Maya, marooned among the tufted trees. For it is possible that these ancient tribes, the Olmec and the Maya, had inhabited that area for 2,000 years.

At last, under the terrible blue-ribbed

81 | *Temple-Pyramid I*, Tikal, Guatemala, *c.*687–730

volcanoes of Mexico, they were stopped in their advance by a people far outnumbering their own handful of troops and quite unlike any they had come across before: dark, pulsing, powerful and warlike. These were the Aztecs, migrant tribes who had come into the area, slaughtering as they went, searching for an eagle that would be sitting on a cactus and eating a snake–the sign, according to their vicious humming-bird war-god Huitzilopochtli, which would identify the place where they had to settle. The symbol, which now graces the Mexican flag, was spotted on an island on saline Lake Texcoco. And so in 1325, they founded on two neighbouring islands, their cities of Tlatelolco and Tenochtitlan, where Mexico City spreads itself today, using a light, local volcanic material called *tezontle*–a sort of dull red pumice stone–so that the city foundations should not sink into the marshes of the lake.

The Spaniards were very impressed by Tenochtitlan, laid out, as was characteristic of the Meso-American cities, on spacious town-planning principles which would be acceptable today, with vast plazas surrounded by temples and palaces raised on great pyramidal mounds, the different areas linked by traffic on the canals and by bridges connecting great sweeping causeways, wide enough to take eight conquistadores riding abreast; with fresh water brought in by special canals, and gardens lush with flowers. But there was a stench in the air, and even the bloodthirsty Spanish soldiers recoiled from a rose-red city dyed with human blood. Blood often figured in the ancient worship of the jaguar (*fig. 82*), of Huitzilopochtli and of Quetzalcoatl, the feathered serpent, which was common to most Meso-American tribes. Nightly, the priests indulged in ritual blood-letting, and public worship involved the sacrifice of animals and humans. It was for such ceremonies that the standard city centre had developed: vast squares for public assemblies,

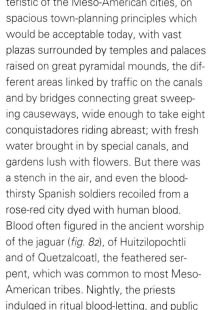

82 | Stone lintel from Yaxchilan, Mexico, *c.*600–900, showing the Maya King named Shield Jaguar being armed for battle

religious dancing and games, laid out before pyramid temples, up which great flights of steps soared to the god's little house at the zenith. There would be a statue of the god at the top of the steps, and here priests performed the public rites of sacrifice, tiny figures impressively close to heaven on a plinth that towered over the packed piazza of frenzied worshippers. One of these pyramid temples, the Santa Cecilia Temple outside Mexico City (*fig. 83*), was unearthed by archaeologists in good condition under a crumbling superstructure, so we now know what they looked like.

The Aztec ritual was particularly bloodthirsty, for Huitzilopochtli had to be supplied with a diet of human hearts, cut still beating from the victims' breasts, if he was to permit the sun to continue to make its daily pilgrimage across the sky. And so the processing priests descended, pulled their victim up the great flight of steps, and bent him backwards, priests on either side pulling arms and legs taut, over the sacrificial stone which stood before Huitzilopochtli's image. 'Thereupon,' says a Spanish chronicler, 'they gashed his breast open … seized his heart … then rolled … his body over, cast it hence, bounced it down.' From the top of the 91 steps of the pyramid at Chichen Itza

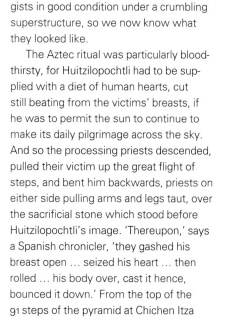

83 | *Pyramid Temple of Santa Cecilia*, near Mexico City, *c.*500–900

they threw the hearts down into the lap of Chac, the cruel rain god.

Until recently it was thought that all that had remained of the cities were descriptions in letters and reports back to Spain that had been preserved in the royal and monastic archives. But in recent years, excavation of tunnels for a transport system and for sewers and electric cables in Mexico City has yielded exciting finds which tie in with the Spanish accounts. On the site of the final Aztec defeat in the Plaza of the Three Cultures remains of the Temple of Tlatelolco in red igneous rock stand beside a Spanish church and monastery. Close behind the great Baroque Cathedral of Mexico City, with the vast square of the Zocala outside, the foundations of the Great Temple of Tenochtitlan itself have been unearthed, the temple whose consecration in 1487 involved the sacrifice of a great many victims, variously estimated between 10,000 and 80,000, ritually slaughtered four at a time, from sunrise to sundown, for four days.

Whether the ancient Meso-American cultures developed autonomously has long been a matter of dispute. There may have been tribal movements from east to west, from North Africa across the Atlantic, from Peru to the Polynesian Islands, which would explain puzzling similarities in such wide-flung cultures, including their architecture. It could explain why a mere handful of tribes – Maya, Olmec, Aztec, Zapotec, Totonac, Toltec and Mixtec – all from this middle belt, developed such advanced civilizations while to north and south the Indian tribes remained at a primitive stage. It could explain why, when the tribes to north and south made huts of branches and leaves, these people, like the Mesopotamians, used adobe bricks of mud and straw to build square houses, which sometimes showed sophisticated features such as several floors, gutters, streets, sewers and aqueducts. It would explain why in jungle or desert coasts they brought stone long distances to build stepped pyramids.

Their land-surveying, calculation of time and astronomy probably excelled those of Babylon and Egypt. Tunnels and

84 | *Caracol Observatory*, Chichen Itza, Mexico, *c.*900

85 | *Ball Court*, Chichen Itza, Mexico, c.900–1200

strong resemblance to the mandala plan of Borobudur. But there is no suggestion of cross-influences here; the mandala does appear to be a universal symbol, full of subconscious meaning and satisfaction to human beings. The Caracol (Snail) Observatory at Chichen Itza (*fig. 84*) dates from the time of or before the resuscitation of that late Maya city by the Toltecs in the ninth and tenth centuries. The snail is a tower 10 feet (3 metres) high, with two circular viewing tiers around the core spiral staircase which gives it its name; set on a series of stepped terraces, it is the only circular building so far found to have a classic Maya corbelled vault.

Amerindian complexes distinguish themselves by the grandeur and spaciousness of their public areas, which are set apart from the domestic quarters of the city. Even the Puuc-style buildings of the northern Maya in lowland Yucatan, characteristically long and low here where they are sited on open ground and do not have to rise above the jungle, are still set on high platforms. The 330-foot (100-metre) long Palace of the Governor at Uxmal, for instance, stands on a man-made esplanade 43 feet (13 metres) high. It is estimated that 2,000 men, working three years, each consisting of 200 working days, would have had to shift between them some 1,000 tons of building materials a day in order to create the esplanade. The pattern for the central ceremonial area was established in Teotihuacan, north-east of present-day Mexico City, a city which was the cultural capital of Meso-America for several hundreds of years (*fig. 86*). Although its origins are disputed, it was probably founded in the fifth century BC by the Toltecs, and by the first century AD, under Aztec control, it was bigger than Imperial Rome. Here, temples piled one against the other are set around an area reserved for dancing and cannibalistic feasting.

One of the first Meso-American colonnades is to be found in the later Toltec

angled holes in their observatories for siting the rise and fall of celestial bodies give some clue as to how astronomical calculations were made. At Monte Alban, the Zapotec 'city of the Gods', there is a boat-shaped observatory with a central siting tunnel that dates from between 500 and 700 AD. At about the same time, before 600 AD at El Tajin, their Gulf Coast capital, the Totonacs built the Pyramid of the Niches (*fig. 94*). Archaeologists gave it this name when they excavated it in the 1950s because they thought its many recessed window embrasures, one for each day of the year, had lost their statues. But we now understand that the niches had astrological significance for the Indians. Seen in plan the pyramid bears a

86 | Side view of the stairs and façade of the *Temple of Quetzalcoatl*, Teotihuacan, Mexico, with the heads of Quetzalcoatl (centre bottom) and Chac, the Rain-God (right bottom), c.400–600

87 | Warrior columns with butterfly breastplates, originally supporting the roof of the *Temple of Quetzalcoatl*, Tula, Mexico, c.700

capital, Tula. Here the pillars tell the story of Toltec conquest: those at the temple doorway are the standard Quetzalcoatl pillars with the snake's head, spikily fanged and feathered, at the base, and the tail holding up the door lintel (a motif common to several tribes), while at the front are enormous pillars in the shape of inexorable Toltec warriors, wearing feathered headdresses and breast-plates shaped like butterflies (*fig. 87*). At Chichen Itza, the Toltec influence is seen in the colonnades and porticoes that connect ceremonial areas.

Also in Chichen Itza is the largest and grandest example of another Meso-American ceremonial space: the ball court (*fig. 85*). The object of the game was to knock a solid rubber ball (there was plenty of rubber about; the Spaniards referred to the Olmecs as the 'rubber people') of about 10 inches (25 centimetres) in diameter through stone rings set high on the walls of the court, using the hips, elbows and thighs. Murals on the walls of the courts showing that the vanquished team was sometimes ritually sacrificed bear out the religious importance of the game, also suggested by the siting of courts near temples, often with a connecting way to a viewing platform for the priests and dignitaries.

In contrast to the grand exteriors, the interiors of buildings were cramped, windowless and dark. The little temples set atop the soaring pyramids were exact copies of the adobe huts in which peasant Maya may still live today. Even the palaces, for example the Palace of the Governor at Maya City of Uxmal (*fig. 91*), lack windows. They were lit by natural light through the doorways and had dark narrow rooms assembled, it appears, on a unit basis, sometimes in double rank, as at Uxmal, more for the occasional show than for everyday living, which was conducted out of doors.

There are particular details that can be used as clues to distinguish between the ruins of one Meso-American tribe and those of another. Characteristic of the early Mayan cities, which have in the last century been disentangled from the stifling embrace of the jungle, are the steep pyramids crowned by little square temples with corbel-vaulted roofs surmounted by a plumed ruff of stone standing up behind their roofs, known in Spanish as *cresteria* (*fig. 89*). Often this protrudes above the vegetation and gives the whole pyramid the appearance of a raised ornamental throne – a seat of authority. The god presumably looked out from his little house over his jungle kingdom. It was made possible by the abundance of tropical hardwood which, used for the lintels, was tough enough to support such a superstructure. Perhaps the

89 | *Temple of the Sun*, Palenque, Mexico, *c.*700, with its roof-comb, the *cresteria*

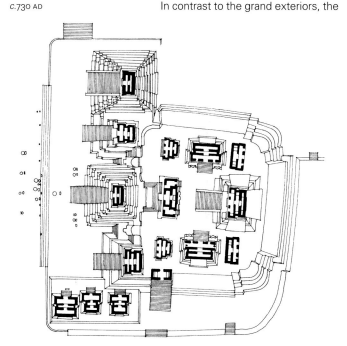

88 | *Tikal*, Guatemala, plan of the North Acropolis, *c.*100 BC– *c.*730 AD

90 | *Turtle House*, Uxmal,
Yucatan, Mexico, *c.*600–900

best examples are the five main temple-pyramids of the religious centre of Tikal (*figs. 81*, *88*), which rises above the Petén jungle in southern Guatemala. These belong to the high Maya period, which appears to have started about 1000 BC and reached its peak between 200 and 900 AD. The temples are among some 3,000 structures so far dug out of the jungle since Tikal was first explored in 1877.

Nine was the sacred number for the Amerindians, and many pyramids have nine basic stages. The arrangement of steps varies. Some climb in sheer flights to the top – as in the Castillo at Chichen Itza (*figs. 92*, *93*), where four flights of stairs, in perfect symmetry, sweep up the four sides of the pyramid; on other temples the steps are arranged in a series of shallow swooping flights which often fail to correspond to the stages of banked earth and rubble that form the actual temple mound – as in the Maya Pyramid of the Magician at Uxmal. This pyramid shows the Maya feature of corbelled vaulting, in which only the last two jutting stone-

91 | *Palace of the Governor*,
Uxmal, Yucatan, Mexico,
*c.*600–900

92 | *El Castillo*, Chichen Itza, Mexico, *c.*1000

courses meet under a great cross beam whose weight stabilizes the structure. This sort of vaulting is also found at another Maya city, Palenque, along the fa ade of the Multiple Court and in the crypt chamber of the priest-king in the Temple of the Inscriptions, a rare Meso-American example of a burial pyramid, which is entered by a triangular door from a staircase built within the walls. Arrow-headed corbelled openings occur also in the later Puuc-style buildings of the northern Maya, for instance in the arcades connecting the two wings to the central block of the Palace of the Governor at Uxmal.

The well-preserved friezes around the buildings of the dry lowland Puuc area of Yucatan are remarkable not only because we know they were executed with only

bronze and obsidian tools, but also because they are so varied. The smooth warm dignity of the Turtle House at Uxmal (*fig. 90*), almost classical Greek or Egyptian in its simplicity, contrasts with the band of decoration on the Governor s Palace, in depth almost half the Palace s total height and giving it a curiously arresting, boxy, beetling appearance. Different again are the complicated repetition masks of Chac, the rain god, that decorate the Codz-poop or Palace of the Masks at Mayan Kabah, near Uxmal, where the assembly of thousands of identical segments would have been impossible had they been so much as half an inch out.

In the Mexican isthmus, in the ancient Toltec capital of Teotihuacan and later cities, buildings are distinguished, in

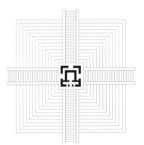

93 | *El Castillo*, plan

94 | *Pyramid of the Niches*, El Tajin, Mexico, *c.*500–600

addition to the use of standard proportion and silhouette, by rectangular panels called *tableros*, which emphasize the stages of the stepped pyramid: the *tablero* is normally cantilevered forward over the sloping wallface known as the *talud*. The silhouettes suggest that the Meso-Americans had a good eye for incisive outlines and contrasts of light and shade created by the brilliant sunlight. The same features are displayed in Oaxaca, the area stretching northwards from the southern Mexican coastline, in the very beautiful south façade of the Palace of the Columns at Mitla, a Mixtec city of about 1,200 inhabitants, its long, low lines and crisp geometrical friezes reminiscent of Puuc-style Maya, and in the Pyramid of Quetzalcoatl at Xochicalco near Cuernavaca, with the feathered serpent squirming all over it. Xochicalco, a city fortress, displays Maya, Toltec, Zapotec and Mixtec influences from successive occupations by different tribes.

In the Pyramid of the Niches at El Tajin (*fig. 94*) flying cornices jut over hollow recesses to produce a marvellous chiaroscuro effect. The builders' intention may have been less to fulfil an aesthetic demand than to use the niche frames to reinforce the structure and keep the central core of packed earth in place. Traces of red, blue and black paint remaining on the pyramid suggest that most Pre-Columbian temples had a layer of brightly coloured plaster, made from burned limestone laid over the facing stonework or adobe mud brick, and in some cases murals were painted on to this background.

Finally, we must look at the contribution made by the architecture of the Incas in Peru, which is different from that of the isthmus cultures. Does this mean that the Incas were an Indian tribe who, presumably like the others, had crossed the Bering Straits from Asia in the last Ice Age, but had through the millennia wandered even further south than the Isthmus tribes? We can only conjecture, but what is clear is that, having settled about 1000 AD in the Cuzco Valley, the Incas had created a great empire by the time of the arrival of the conquistadores under Francisco Pizarro in 1531. The chief distinguishing feature of Inca architecture is its large-scale masonry, built in courses and tightly jointed without any mortar. Some of the most skilful masonry in the world can still be seen in the lower walls of some streets in Cuzco, one-time Inca capital; and the scale of the pieces in this cyclopean jigsaw can be judged from seeing a herd of llamas feeding or a man standing below the three-tier ramparts of Sacsahuaman, the fortress which stands guard above the capital. This masonry was probably achieved by hoisting the great blocks up on rollers with liana ropes, and swinging them backwards and forwards until they ground into place between their fellow mammoth stones.

But masonry is not the only Inca achievement. Today, as you climb higher and higher into the Andes at altitudes so great that guards on the train offer the passengers oxygen, you can see evidence of Inca fortresses and their network of communications – roads and bridges over chasms and ravines – as well as waterworks and agricultural terraces, superbly carved in serried ranks from precipitous canyon sides. They were made possible by the existence of a highly regulated and no doubt tyrannical feudal society, in which the young and fit were annually conscripted to contribute to public works. In return for this service, a virtual welfare state operated, providing insurance against famine, sickness and old age.

One hill fortress, Machu Picchu, which may have been the sanctuary sought by the Inca King, Manco II, from the invading Spaniards, is one of architecture's most breathtaking achievements (*fig. 95*).

The excavations are not complete, but houses, stairs, courts, temples, granaries and graveyards have been identified as well as a novitiate convent for the maidens known as Virgins of the Sun, who served in the Inca temples. As if aware that they could not improve on nature's grand conception, the builders tucked the city into an inaccessible saddle between two majestic cloud-wreathed sugar-loaf peaks. Far below this garrison of sheer living rock, the river Urubamba snakes its way. Solid and void defy definition or delineation. Ghost houses enveloped in mist and snow materialize out of the very mountain, for man has incorporated the rocky outcrops into the house walls in a grey-green osmosis of man-vegetation-mineral, of past and present, of living and dead, of earth and heaven. Machu Picchu not only epitomizes the piercing excitement of architectural experience, but also in the interaction of man and his environment provides a fleeting glimpse of some elemental reality.

95 | *Machu Picchu*, Peru, *c.*1500

With the architecture of ancient Greece we return to the mainstream European tradition. One of the most aesthetically perfect bodies of work in the Western European tradition, it was also the foundation of many subsequent styles in different parts of the world. It therefore occupies a unique place in our story, and we must look at it carefully and ask how it took shape. Its growth and development forms one of the most entrancing episodes in architectural history. It has a logic and inevitability about it, like the drama that the same civilization was able to invent and perform.

To the traveller approaching Attica by boat and seeing the white columns of the Temple of Poseidon at Cape Sounion (*fig. 96*) for the first time (not one of the earliest buildings; it dates from about 440 BC) the immediate impact, with the ruins gleaming above the blinding blue sea, is of the landscape and the light. The land, with its unexpected humps and hills, its moments of drama, its untidy olive groves and bleached grass, is evocative, moody and memorable. The light, praised by everyone from Plutarch to John Henry Newman, who speaks of its 'special purity, elasticity, clearness and salubrity', must have played a crucial part in the evolution of the classical orders of architecture. The clear, dazzling sunshine makes for strong shadows and encourages clean, powerful forms in the landscape.

And the materials were there to make that possible – the local limestone, at first often covered with a marble stucco, and then marble itself.

Against this background there emerged the most impeccable architecture, the expression of an exquisite, mature national consciousness. Like that consciousness, it took its shape gradually. For Greece was not, for most of its history, one country. With its mountainous mainland and scattered islands it began as a group of city-states, usually in rivalry with one another. What brought the culture – and the architecture – to a climax was the supremacy of Athens. In the golden age known as the Hellenic period (800–323 BC), the city-state was established as the basis of society, new cities were founded and Athens emerged as the supreme power after decisive victories over the invading Persians. The zenith was reached in the fifth century BC, known as the high classical age because of its astonishing flowering of philosophy, architecture, art, literature and drama. The Parthenon, which we shall discuss in some detail, was one of the supreme achievements of that period. The independence of the Greek city-states was destroyed by Alexander the Great, whose conquests extended as far as India. During the period after his death in 323 BC, which is known as the Hellenistic period, his empire was divided among Greek

96 | *Temple of Poseidon*, Cape Sounion, Greece, *c.*440 BC

successor kingdoms, including Ptolemaic Egypt. These were finally swallowed up in the Roman Empire by 30 BC.

As we have already seen, the region that later became Greece saw its first civilization in the island of Crete, which reached its peak at the palace of Knossos (*fig. 18*). That was the Minoan civilization (3000–1400 BC), and the plans of its great buildings (if not the structures) were every bit as complex (literally labyrinthine in the haunts of the Minotaur) as those of any other state at the time. It was succeeded by a culture at Mycenae and Tiryns on the mainland (*c.*1600–1050 BC), possibly less elegant architecturally but, especially in the Fortress of Mycenae, lowering over the Argive plain from its menacing heights, more warlike and formidable (*fig. 13*). The military aspirations of most of the Greek states continued right through to Alexander the Great, who although he was tutored by the philosopher Aristotle, made his mark as a ferocious warrior of incomparable vigour and genius, and did much to destroy the inheritance of the great early civilizations; certainly the Persians saw his bloody victories as the destruction of art and ordered life. That makes it all the more remarkable that Athens was able to witness such a flowering of culture in the fifth century BC. Architecturally, the story moves from the fortress to the market-place, from the citadel to the agora. A Greek philosopher remarked that high ground was the place for aristocracy and low ground the place for democracy. What took the place of the fortress was the temple, which in Athens reached the pinnacle of perfection; what completed the market-place were social and communal buildings that brought people together to talk, argue and trade. What brought unity to Greek architecture was the column and the lintel.

Discarding the arch, even though they knew about it and could have used it had they wished to do so, the Greeks concentrated on perfecting the constructional element that most perfectly suited the climate, materials and society that used the buildings. For it was a society that used – and therefore saw – architecture not as interior rooms, but from the outside. Both the temples and the other buildings of the agora or market-place were exterior architecture. They put all the fun and the refinement on the outside. For it was not in the dark and inaccessible interior that things happened; the interaction between men and gods happened in the open air, where the welcome fingers of the breeze played through the slim colonnade as if on a lyre, where a shaft of light emphasized the clarity of an Ionic column, and the hide-and-seek of sun and shadow was petrified into a moulding.

Before we can go any further we must therefore look at the temple, starting with one built in a manner that was to become the first of the three major styles that have been used ever since throughout the world – the Doric style.

If we look at a Doric temple and mentally pull it apart, we can immediately identify the primitive structural elements we saw being put together by the Egyptians or the Persians. We see how the bundles of reeds tied together to form door-posts or roof-supports have been discarded and replaced by fluted columns, first in wood, then after about 600 BC in stone. We see that these columns go down into the earth – a base was a refinement which was only to make its appearance with the Ionic style. The flat block of wood placed on top of the reed bundle to carry the roof structure is there still as the *capital*. This is the feature of a column that we look to first, to check which order of Greek architecture – Doric, Ionic or Corinthian – the architect is using in the building. During three centuries (seventh to fourth century BC), the wooden beams that span the space from column to column (the joints

occurring over the middle of the capital) changed to blocks of stone which form the *architrave*. Sometimes a wide capital will carry two parallel blocks of stone, as we can see if we walk between the columns and look upwards in the so-called Theseion (the Temple of Hephaestus) in the Agora at Athens (445 BC). About 20 feet (6 metres) was the maximum span possible, so anything wider meant that additional columns had to be inserted. Above the architrave is the decorative frieze, composed of *triglyphs* and *metopes*. We can easily appreciate that the triglyphs (meaning three slits) –

protruding blocks scored with three grooves – originated as the ends of the cross-beams of a wooden roof, and clearly we are looking here at the translation of a timber structure into stone. In between these beams-ends the Greeks hung decorated terracotta plaques, and in stone temples the surface of these spaces (the *metopes*) were carved with figurative scenes. A narrow projecting course of stones called the *cornice* ran along the edge of the roof and along the base of the triangular pediment which filled in the gable end under the wide, sloping eaves. Both cornice and eaves performed the

97 | **Mnesicles**, *Propylaea*, Acropolis, Athens, *c.*437 BC

89

98 | The Greek orders: Doric, Ionic, Corinthian, Composite

Julius Caesar attributes to this the fact that his troops did relatively little damage taking the city.

The Greeks did not use mortar, but made the bed for the stones slightly concave, and ground each stone into position with sand to produce hairline joints in a manner similar to that later adopted by the Incas in Peru. The short drums, of which a column was made up, were fitted together with a central wooden (and later iron) dowel wrapped in lead: iron clamps fixed with molten lead linked blocks of stone together, and iron bars were used for strengthening as, for instance, in the architrave of the Propylaea on the Acropolis (*fig. 97*). The carving of friezes and columns was enormously extended once marble had come into general use for temples from about 525 BC. The glowing Pentelic marble from quarries near Athens was used for the temples on the Acropolis. Yet the Greeks were not content with that material. They painted their buildings, statues and details in what we would consider garish colours – red, blue and gold – just as the eyes, lips and nipples of their bronze statues were inlaid with coloured stones.

The odd thing is that even after the second half of the eighteenth century, when Greece was included in the fashionable itinerary for the gentleman's Grand Tour, it was still thought that there was no colour in the temples. The Greeks, it was said, were not interested in colour – only in form. Even today, the image with which we opened this chapter of the white colonnade outlined against the blue sky and the blue sea, is amazingly enduring. The architectural critic, Vincent Scully, actually opens his book on the social architecture of ancient Greece by alluding to 'white forms, touched with bright colours', whose geometric forms contrast with the mountains and valleys in which they are set. 'These', he says, 'were the temples of the gods.'

Let us return to those very temples.

practical task of throwing off rainwater. All these features from the top of the column to below the triangular pediment (that is the cross-beams forming the architrave, the frieze with its triglyphs and metopes, and the cornice) are collectively known as the *entablature*.

Wood persisted as a roofing material, even in the stone temples, and its susceptibility to fire offers a convincing explanation of why so many temples, such as those on the Acropolis, have been left to us as roofless ruins. However, stone roofs do occur, becoming more common in the Hellenistic era (323–30 BC). The Temple of Hephaestus has a stone ceiling coffered (that is, cut away between the stone beams so that it looks as if made from upturned empty boxes) to lighten the great weight of the stone. The Hellenistic city of Alexandria in Egypt must have been largely stone-roofed, for

The classic temple plan of the fifth century BC did not become much more complex in structure than the megaron, the hall of a Mycenaean chief (*fig. 8*). The statue of the god replaced the hearth, and the row of pillars down the centre, necessary to carry the roof, was reorganized to form a colonnade right around the outside of the rectangular building. The entry was usually between the customary six columns on the short side, and through the open door the statue would face the rising sun. Often, an entrance porch was screened off by a second rank of six pillars, and, to balance the porch, there might be a treasury, entered from the back, at the other end of the temple.

We begin to find what distinguishes these temples from those of other great civilizations – the throne-room at Knossos, Darius the Great's palace at Persepolis (*fig. 19*), or the Temple of Amun-Ra at Karnak (*fig. 33*) – when we come to examine the three types of *orders* under which, as we have already noted, Greek temples can be grouped. The term 'order' is really quite a good one, because it not only implies the organization of the components of the temple, but it also suggests the satisfying relationship and proportion that these components bear to each other and to the whole. In fact, the Roman writer on architecture Vitruvius introduced it, and it comes from the Latin *ordo*, a rank; the Greek word for 'order' in the sense of tidy organization was 'cosmos'. The first two orders, the Doric and Ionic, evolved from the seventh to the fifth century BC, the Ionic slightly after the Doric. The third, the Corinthian, came later in the fifth century in Greece and continued to overlap with the Romans, who created a combination of Ionic and Corinthian known as the Composite (*fig. 98*).

Earliest and simplest, the Doric temple, with no base, plain capitals and undecorated grooving along the shaft of the pillar, appeared between 700 and 500 BC in mainland Greece, the lands settled

99 | *Temple of Hera*, Paestum, Italy, *c.*530 BC

100 | *Choragic Monument of Lysicrates*, Athens, 335–334 BC

flutings along the column are scalloped at top and bottom, and are separated from each other by a narrow flat fillet; metopes and triglyphs have disappeared, but the frieze and pediment are likely to be fully carved. The steps to the *stylobate* (the plinth on which the temple stands) in the classic Ionic are often less massive than the Doric – and therefore easier for the worshipper to climb. The Ionians had a treaty port on the Nile Delta, and this contact with the enormous Egyptian temples influenced the magnitude of the later Hellenistic Ionic temples by comparison with the Attic Doric. The Temple of Artemis (Diana) at Ephesus, for instance, was so large that Antipater in the first century BC included it in his list of the Seven Wonders of the World.

The Corinthian capital, shaped like an upturned bell surrounded by serrated leaves, on the one hand evaded what had always been a problem with the corner pillars of the Ionic, namely that the capital is made to be seen from the front; and on the other, offered possibilities for elaborately carved symmetry, which was to find great popularity in the lavishness of the Roman Empire. But undoubtedly it has a charm of its own when used delicately as in the Choragic Monument of Lysicrates in Athens (335–334 BC; *fig. 100*), which was its earliest external use. Its use was more dramatic in the Temple of Olympian Zeus in Athens, begun in the days of the tyrants in the sixth century BC, but not completed until the first century AD by the Roman emperor, Hadrian.

But for classic examples of the first two orders, we need go no further than the Acropolis (*figs. 102, 103*). Today the rock is approached by an impressive flight of steps, broken in the middle by a path for animals on their way to the sanctuary to be sacrificed, but these date only from Roman times. The ancient Athenian crossed the agora diagonally by the processional way and then zigzagged up a path to the great entrance gateway, the

by Dorian invaders from the Balkans. The stocky, silent grandeur of the Doric pillars in the early Temple of Hera at Paestum, a Greek colony in southern Italy (*c.*530 BC; *fig. 99*), can be contrasted with the precision of detail and the serene simplicity that give ineffable dignity to the later Doric (490 BC) Temple of Aphaia at Aegina.

The Ionic temple is usually found in the islands and on the coasts of Asia Minor, the areas settled by Greeks who had fled from the Dorians. Its columns are slimmer, lighter and more delicately sculpted and can be readily identified by volutes on the capitals that look like rams' horns or a scroll lightly rolled up at either end. A glance at the total profile of this order reveals how much more complex it is than the Doric. The slender column is set on a tiered and decorated base; the

The Landscape of the Gods: *Ancient Greece*

101 | **Callicrates**, *Temple of Nike Apteros*, Acropolis, Athens, c.450–424 BC

everything is in perspective, at an angle. Greek architects put symmetrical buildings into unsymmetrical and irregular places and manipulated the levels of the ground so that the sense of unity was experienced by moving around the site, like the procession on the main day of the Panathenaic festival, rather than by viewing buildings separately from a stationary position.

The earlier temples of the Acropolis, dedicated to the guardian deities of the city, were totally destroyed by the Persians. But Pericles, after the victories of Salamis and Plataea (480–479 BC), was inspired to devote some of the war-fund collected from the Greek city-states to rebuilding the temples, a move which –initiated the first recorded controversy over the mismanagement of a disaster fund, and eventually led to the Peloponnesian Wars between the Greek states (431–404 BC), after which Athens lost her supremacy.

The rebuilding was conducted under the supervision not of the architects but of the sculptor Phidias. A sculptor as overseer made sense at the time, because the temples were in some ways exhibition halls for sculptures of deities or even of victorious athletes, and sculpture was considered the superior art. And so the pilgrim's first encounter would have been with Phidias's bronze statue of Athena, by all accounts so big that the sun flashing off her helmet was used by sailors at sea as a beacon by which to set course for Piraeus, the port of Athens.

Propylaea. With wings jutting forward on either side, the Propylaea opens its arms to pilgrims from the west. Isolated on a bastion to the right of the entrance is the tiny Ionic temple of Nike Apteros (the Wingless Victory), designed by Callicrates c.450 BC but not built until 424 BC (*fig. 101*), and the sole survivor of the small temples which originally ringed the rock. The Propylaea was built by Mnesicles in about 437 BC and used Doric on its outer columns, Ionic on the inner, in a fittingly restrained manner so as not to pre-empt the glory that burst upon the worshipper as he passed through the gate into the sanctuary. Here an important aspect of the layout can be seen. Nothing is direct,

overleaf

103 | Acropolis, Athens

102 | Acropolis, Athens, plan, showing the Parthenon (A), Erechtheum (B), Propylaea (C), Temple of Nike Apteros (D), Theatre of Dionysus (E)

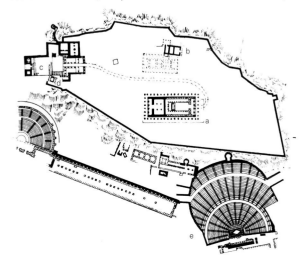

104 | *Caryatid Porch, Erechtheum,*
Acropolis, Athens, 421–406 BC

Phidias's statue retained the site of its predecessor outside the wall of the earlier temple.

The statue no longer stands on the Acropolis, and today on entering the *temenos*, or sacred enclosure, the eye is drawn to the right of centre, to the highest point on the rock, where stands the Parthenon. In ancient times a second statue of the goddess Athena by Phidias, this time of gold and precious stones, stood within the temple itself. Today, it is possible to clamber into the ruins over the stylobate, without troubling about doors, but in the fifth century BC the temple turned its back on the Propylaea, and pilgrims had to walk round the outside to the entrance oriented towards the rising sun on the eastern side. To the north, beyond the site of the Parthenon's predecessor, is the little temple of the Erechtheum (421–406 BC), which in its day played a bigger part in the rituals of the goddess Athene than the Parthenon itself. Because the temple steps down the hillside on two levels, a continuous colonnade was impossible; but it makes an ingenious use of the Ionic by rising through two levels on the side where the hill falls away, and being half-height on the adjacent façade. Most unusual of all is the porch, where a row of powerfully

built maidens, known as Caryatids, replace the columns (*fig. 104*). These Amazonian ladies have been so eroded by pollution that in recent years they have been replaced by fibre-glass casts – a move that has raised much academic controversy.

But we must pause at the Parthenon (*figs. 105, 106*), not simply because it is the best-known of all Greek buildings, but because it has been the subject of meticulous study which has revealed some of the mathematical secrets of its perfection of form and proportion. Built between 447 and 432 BC by Ictinus and Callicrates under Phidias's direction, it obeys the canons for classic Doric proportions generally adopted after the sixth century BC, except that the customary six columns on the east and west ends have been increased to eight. But its power to enchant and satisfy lies in the subtleties of line and proportion. Even in its own time these refinements were legendary.

When, in the nineteenth century, it was measured in detail, it was discovered that there is scarcely a straight line in the whole structure: every surface is hollowed or swollen or tapered in such a way that the eye can slide along its contours unobstructed by optical distortion, so that nothing jars, all is harmony. Most Greek buildings of this golden period use *entasis*, the device whereby tapering columns are given a slight swelling about a third of the way up to counteract a tendency of the eye to see them as curving inwards from either side, the most extreme and bulgy example being the Temple of Hera at Paestum. But on the Parthenon this exercise in optical illusion is not limited to the columns. All the horizontal lines (such as the architrave and the stylobate), which, left to themselves, would appear to sag slightly in the middle, are similarly corrected; the corner columns are thicker and stand closer to their neighbours, so that they will not appear spindly against the sky,

105 | **Ictinus** and **Callicrates**, *Parthenon*, Acropolis, Athens, 447–432 BC

and, furthermore, they tilt inward slightly at the top to avoid an illusion of falling outwards; the triglyphs are spaced progressively further apart as they reach the centre front and back, so that they will not create hard lines by being directly over a column. The design of the Parthenon called for meticulous measurement; precision in calculation; mastery in masonry; and a unique fineness of perception and response. The result is breathtaking.

Still in Athens, let us look down from the Acropolis at the city as a whole. The ordinary dwelling-houses at this time were an undistinguished huddle of windowless single rooms giving on to court-

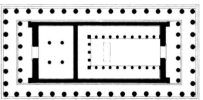

106 | *Parthenon*, plan

yards linked by narrow twisting alleys, under the hill. It was where people congregated that interesting architectural events happened. Especially impressive was the open space, the agora, which, officially the market-place, gathered around itself the meeting-halls used for government and law. Here, democracy was born. It was a limited democracy (indeed, the Roman system made for

108 | *Stoa of Attalus*, Agora, Athens, *c.*150 BC, restored

greater equality), since the right to vote, to be elected to the assembly and to hold public office was denied to women, to slaves, on whom the Athenian economy depended, and to foreigners, irrespective of how long they had lived or worked in Athens. But here was established the principle of representative democracy and with it free speech, a principle which was to affect education and the advance of thought in the West. Here Pericles made his famous funeral oration, celebrating the distinctive character of Greek civilization. Here, under the colonnades of the *stoas* (sheltered promenades lined with shops and offices which became the characteristic feature of the agora) loitered the philosophers and their disciples who were to lay down the foundation of philosophical enquiry for the Western world—Socrates, Plato, Aristotle, and of course the Stoics (who actually took their name from the structure).

The *stoa* was a simple but enormously influential invention of the Greeks, which took the principle of the column and lintel, but linked them together to form a long colonnade which had many uses. It was a method of grouping together a lot of shops and workshops, which would otherwise have looked like a random collection of sheds and huts, and of giving them a dignified unity. It provided a space for people to sit in or walk under in the shade, where they could talk and barter their goods. And if it had an upper story it

107 | **Polykleitos**, *Theatre*, Epidauros, Greece, *c.*350 BC

could provide offices and other rooms. It was the major unifying feature of the agora. The two-storeyed Stoa of Attalus, under the Acropolis, was built in about 150 BC (*fig. 108*). It has been restored by the American School of Archaeology as a museum and gives a very accurate impression of how a stoa must have looked. Other stoas were scattered around irregularly to north and south of the Athenian agora; in later Hellenic-planned towns both agora and stoa are geometrically defined and orderly in layout.

Other important buildings were the assembly hall, the town hall, the gymnasium, the stadium and the theatre, which played a significant part in the life of the Greeks. In Athens the theatre of Dionysus, dating from the early sixth century BC, lies to the south of the Acropolis on the site of successive wooden theatres. Primitive banks of seats, taking advantage of the lower contours of the rock, were not replaced by stone seating until after the earth and timber seats collapsed in 499 BC. While temples were not required to cater for public worship, theatres were. They were associated with the frenzied rituals in honour of Dionysus and had to be large enough to include a circular or semicircular stage, or *orchestra*, for the chorus and the dancing involved in the rituals, an altar for the libations with which performances commenced, and space for a vast seated audience. It was here that Aeschylus, Sophocles, Euripides and Aristophanes presented their plays, laying down the pattern for Western drama and theatre. The theatre at Epidauros, built by the architect Polykleitos in about 350 BC (*fig. 107*), could hold 13,000 people and the acoustics are so perfect that any whisper from the circular orchestra can be heard in any of the seats; an effect partly due to intensifying the bowl shape by making the rake on the upper set of seats steeper than on the lower, partly to the

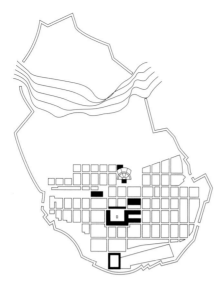

109 | Priene, Asia Minor, plan, dating mainly from *c.*350 BC

ingenious use of resonators in the form of large pottery urns beneath the stone rows of seats. In the Hellenistic-planned towns, the theatre tended to be outside the town proper. The bowl-shape which had been found to be acoustically effective did not fit into the grid plan; and it was moreover the Greek habit to hunt out a site where the natural contours of the ground could be readily converted into an amphitheatre. And they had to be very big.

The other major building type was the stadium for games. Stadia, which had to be at least a *stade* long (200 yards, 183 metres) for the races, were also placed outside the town walls. The Athenian stadium of 331 BC could accommodate 60,000 spectators. The embankment of earth around the narrow stadium at Olympia, the little town in the Peloponnese which established from the eighth century BC onward the competitive games every fourth year, provided standing room for 40,000 people. In addition to the stadium, all Greek cities had gymnasia where the local young men trained as an essential part of their education – a principle which we see firmly entrenched in the European and American educational systems. Salamis in Cyprus has good examples of both

theatre and gymnasium, the latter remodelled by the Romans.

All these types of building were represented and grouped into a synthesis in the new planned cities of the Hellenistic period. Some were rebuilt on the higher ground above cities of the Ionian Greeks, originally sited on estuaries of rivers which had since silted up; others, in Asia Minor, were founded after Alexander's conquests. The common pattern, adopting principles attributed to Hippodamus of Miletus (fifth century BC), was for the city to be laid out on a grid plan below an acropolis, with a central agora, thoroughfares crossing the town, and separate zones scheduled for commercial, religious and political life. Hippodamus himself had been brought to Athens by Pericles to lay out the port of Piraeus, which is five miles from the Acropolis and connected to the city by a walled road known as the 'long walls'. Miletus was similarly planned in 466 BC after the Persian Wars. Priene (*fig. 109*) and Pergamum are later classical and Hellenistic examples in Asia Minor. Gracious living made its appearance in these cities; streets were wide and paved, temples large, theatres, gymnasia and council chamber spacious enough to accommodate all adult males with the right to vote; sanitation was improved and some private houses became more imposing.

The Greek genius for bringing man, nature and the gods together in an awe-inspiring unity is to be found at its most dramatic at Delphi (*fig. 110*). Delphi was the most sacred of the sacred sites of ancient Greece, the sanctuary of Apollo and the place of the oracle. Like many a successful sacred site, it was a magnet for pilgrims; and as in many others the behaviour of the locals in making as much money from the faithful as possible was often disgraceful. But as a total experience of landscape and buildings cunningly, never obviously, sited (for as we have seen in Athens, the Greeks never

The Landscape of the Gods: *Ancient Greece*

110 | Delphi, Greece, looking down from the *Theatre* (*c*.150 BC) to the *Temple of Apollo* (*c*.510 BC) and the *Athenian Treasury* (lower right, *c*.490 BC)

produced elementary axial symmetry in their landscapes, whatever they did in the buildings within them), Delphi is a masterpiece of imaginative layout, every turn and corner of the route carefully considered as to its emotional impact on the pilgrim.

The first building that a traveller would see after climbing the ragged hills from Athens was the Tholos, a circular temple whose architectural purpose was to turn the attention towards the slopes of Parnassus, where the shrine of Apollo was constructed (mostly from the sixth century onwards). The Sacred Way leads upwards from the sanctuary, never in a straight line, but turning back upon itself past the Athenian Treasury (the first Doric building constructed entirely of marble), zigzagging, so as to give a succession of carefully contrived views, to the Temple of Apollo, which stands proudly in its Doric majesty upon a huge level plinth of cyclopean stones. Then, ever upwards, to the Theatre (early second century BC), which is acoustically superb, with a dramatic view across the fierce ravine below. Still further up and to one side is the Stadium. It is a magical place – as it was intended to be. And the magic is made by the unity and coherence of the buildings with the land.

Under the Roman Empire, architecture, buoyed along by new techniques, achieved a prowess that, in some areas, European architecture was not again to reach until the seventeenth, eighteenth or even nineteenth century. But this is not apparent at first sight, particularly if we have just been looking at Greek architecture and our eye is attuned to Greek proportions and orders, because, content to leave matters of art to the Greeks, the Romans borrowed many of the external trappings of that older civilization's very external architecture. So, viewing the Forum of Rome from the west (*fig. 112*), we might at first see this as a straight translation of an agora.

It is only when we come to examine some of the buildings in detail that we realize how superficial are the similarities between the two peoples. Where the Greeks sought for man's harmony with the universe, communed with the abstract, and expressed their cosmic consciousness in art as fine as man's purest ideals, the Romans had no time for such idealism. They were a robust practical people with sharp logical minds, who excelled in the making of laws, in engineering feats and in administering territories. The harmonies they sought were not of the spirit nor among the celestial spheres, but in their immediate home circle and in the territories they had conquered. Their religion revolved around the

family, with lamps burning before household gods, the *penates*, in the *atrium*, or hall, of their villas; the virtues that they extolled the most (along with physical courage) were *pietas* (loyalty to parents and ancestors) and *gravitas* (responsibility). They considered the Greeks effete. They were convinced that the Roman way of life alone was right, as we see from the following quotation from Vitruvius, a military engineer in the service of Julius Caesar and later Augustus in the first centuries BC–AD, who wrote the only extant treatise on architecture before the fifteenth century.

But although southern nations have the keenest wit, and are infinitely clever in forming schemes, yet the moment it comes to displaying valour they succumb because all manliness of soul is sucked out of them by the sun. On the other hand, men born in cold countries are indeed readier to meet the shock of arms with great courage and without timidity, but their wits are so slow that they will rush to the charge inconsiderately and inexpertly, thus defeating their own devices. Such being nature's arrangement of the universe, and all these nations being allotted temperaments which are lacking in due moderation, the truly perfect territory, situated under the middle of heaven, and having on each side the entire extent of

111 | *Pont du Gard aqueduct,* Nîmes, France, 14 AD

112 | *Imperial Forum*, Rome, *c*.27 BC–14 AD, view from the west

the world and its countries, is that which is occupied by the Roman people.

Ten Books on Architecture, Book VI. The legendary origins of this conceited race are strangely romantic, involving the illustrious but illicit union of Mars, god of war, with a vestal virgin, and the subsequent rescue of their abandoned twin sons by a she-wolf, whose bronze statue stands today on the Capitoline Hill in Rome, the spot where one of the twins, Romulus, founded the city. That was, reputedly, in 753 BC, the year from which the Romans counted their dates (*ab urbe condita*), but in fact not much of a city is likely to have existed prior to 600 BC, and the celebrated bronze dates from the Renaissance. Indeed, by the time when elsewhere in the world great things were afoot – Buddha teaching in India, Confucius in China, Jimmu, the first emperor of Japan, ascending his throne, Judah undergoing the Babylonian captivity, and the Persians sweeping all before them and yet to encounter the Greeks – Rome was little more than one among many village-states in mid-Italy. Then in 509 BC she took her first step towards greatness by expelling the tyrannical Etruscan kings

The Authority of Competence: *Ancient Rome*

and declaring herself a republic. The national temperament now began to show itself in systematic conquest, first of her neighbours so that by the third century BC she dominated Italy; in the third and second centuries BC, the three Punic Wars secured North Africa and Spain; by the first century BC, Rome possessed the entire Hellenic world, and when Augustus established the empire (30 BC), all the known world was theirs, and the Mediterranean truly was, as its name implies, the sea at the centre of the world.

Victory achieved, the vanquished were not forced to bury their national identity and customs; these could be retained with Roman citizenship, provided they were prepared to accept Roman law, taxes, military service and an undemanding religion. In race and religion toleration was probably greater than under the vaunted democracy of the Greeks. Even in regard to class: although aristocratic patricians dominated the Senate, plebeians had an established right to constitutional office; and although the slave-labour force – swelled with each new conquest – had no political voice, there was a kind of apprenticeship system towards citizenship.

'The Roman Empire', says A.N. Whitehead (in *The Aims of Education*, chapter V), 'existed by virtue of the grandest application of technology that the world had hitherto seen: its roads, its bridges, its aqueducts, its tunnels, its sewers, its vast buildings, its organized merchant navies, its military science, its metallurgy, and its agriculture.' It meant the dissolution of political and commercial frontiers, and a supply of commodities from abroad. It meant running water in homes; public lavatories, sometimes arranged in groups (*fig. 113*), in the grandest of which people sat on marble seats between sculpted dolphins, reading and chatting for all the world like gentlemen of leisure at their clubs; it meant hot and cold public

baths to relax in, forums for law and politics, double-hairpin-shaped circuses for chariot races, and amphitheatres for gladiatorial fights or for watching Christians being eaten by lions; and theatres for drama, of which the most popular were not intense tragedies like those of classical Greece, but rather the slapstick and social comedy of Plautus and Terence.

It is therefore not surprising that the architecture built by such a people was directed to immediate practical purposes rather than to aesthetic satisfaction. The Romans were ready to leave matters of art to the Greeks, and leaned heavily on Greek forms and tastes when buildings of serenity, dignity and power, suitable to a great empire, were called for. These qualities are apparent in the series of new forums built by successive emperors to accommodate increasingly complex social, legal and commercial needs. Augustus (31 BC – 14 AD) initiated the first by building a new Forum in Rome in contrast to the accumulation of buildings that had grown piecemeal round the old one: he set a colonnaded stoa along both sides of a great rectangular space, closing the vista at the end with a Temple to Mars. Although the original inspiration was Hellenistic, the Roman imprint quickly appears. Buildings are not sited in response to the natural environment, in mystical communion with the contours of the place; instead, there emerges a new concept: planned space enclosed by architecture. The new forums are less concerned with individual temples than they are with the total design, conceived as awe-inspiring set-pieces that demonstrate imperial power. A series of geometric shapes unfold as one walks through the forum at Baalbek, Lebanon; and in Augustus's Forum at Rome, contrived views and vistas are enclosed by a temple façade.

In the amphitheatre known as the Colosseum, the architecture was distinctively Roman. While the Greeks used

113 | Public lavatories in the Roman city at Dougga, Tunisia, 3rd century AD

114 | *Theatre*, Orange, France, *c*.50 AD

115 | *Theatre*, Orange, plan

their theatres exclusively for drama, the Romans required circuses and amphitheatres for races and contests. Many Roman theatres and amphitheatres are still standing. The theatre at Orange (*c*.50 AD; *figs. 114, 115*), in the south of France, of awesome proportions, is particularly well preserved, although the wooden awning that sheltered the stage, supported at the front by two great chains fastened to high masts rising from corbelled piers at the back, no longer exists; the amphitheatres at Arles and Nîmes in Provence (both of the late first century) are still used for bull-fights. But the Orange theatre is unusual for, like the Greek theatres, it is at least partially hollowed out of the hill. And here we have the basic difference between Greek and Roman forms. The Greek concentration on the exterior is, in the theatre, turned inside out: the theatre has no outside, being sited in a natural hollow below a hill, usually outside the main city. Its sloping seats were built into the hillside, and nature provided her own backdrop of hills or sea for the players on the stage.

In contrast, the Colosseum, built by the Emperors Vespasian, Titus and Domitian between 72 and 82 AD (*fig. 116*), stands in the city centre, elliptical in shape, on level ground. For amphithe-

atres such as this both an inside and an outside architecture were required, and for drama even the backdrop must be man-made, like the *scenae frons*, now reconstructed behind the stage in the Roman theatre at Sabratha in North Africa of about 200 AD. Once inside the Colosseum, whose enormous auditorium could seat 55,000 spectators, and which continued to be used for animal games until the sixth century, we can gaze upwards at the remains of four tiers of seats, and downwards, through where the floor of the arena once stretched, to a web of circulation passageways; and we are left in no doubt that this is internal architecture of the most complex design. Vaulted passages between the wedges of seats (all worked out mathematically) at each level gave speedy access to seating and, moreover, speedy exit, so that the auditorium could be cleared quickly in case of fire. Below stage, cages and detainment areas for beasts and criminals were provided by passageways closed by portcullis gates, and mechanical lifts and ramps were used to bring performers up to the arena floor.

It was, clearly, a much more sophisticated and intricate construction than a rectangular temple dependent on columns holding up lintels. What gave us

116 | *Colosseum*, Rome, 72–82 AD

the idea that the Roman amphitheatre was a straight translation of the Greek? If we return again to the outside, we immediately see what it was that deceived us: the four floors of the Colosseum present a copy-book façade of the Greek orders: Doric on the ground floor, Ionic on the second, Corinthian on the third, and on the pilasters running along the top storey. But we now realize that the orders play no part in the structure: the supporting members are built into the bodywork of the building, and the columns are simply a decorative device applied to the front.

The Romans made much use of the orders, their favourite being the Corinthian with its florid, luxuriant possibilities. Whether there is truth in the story that its designer was inspired at a banquet by the sight of a goblet wound round with acanthus leaves, there is a certain feeling of Bacchanalian revelry about this order, which is taller than either Doric or Ionic and seems in accord with the enormous size of some of the Roman temples, such as those (now ruins) at Baalbek, Lebanon (*fig. 117*). Here the smaller of two temples, the Temple of Bacchus, is bigger than the Parthenon. The Romans adopted two more orders into their repertoire – the *Composite*, a combination of Ionic and Corinthian, and the *Etruscan*, or Tuscan, a stumpier version of Doric. But characteristic of Roman architecture is the use of non-structural columns, frequently wholly or partially embedded in the walls – a device known as *engaged* or *semi-engaged* columns; sometimes the columns are flattened and squared off and are then called *pilasters*.

107

117 | *Temple of Bacchus*,
Baalbek, Lebanon,
2nd century AD

or a Severus, and the gratitude of the Senate and the people of Rome to their mighty ruler, is so clear and impressive that it forms the basis of the typefaces of the Renaissance and our own times. Whether the form has one arch, as in the Arch of Titus on the edge of the Forum (*c.*81 AD), or is designed in triple motif (small, tall, small), as in the Arch of Constantine (315 AD), the massive architrave on which the dedication is carved is carried like a banner, as unflinching as if held aloft by a legionary marching into battle.

The device is clearly exhibited in another Roman architectural type: the triumphal arch. Often sited at an entrance to a forum, such arches were erected to commemorate victories. They had to be wide and grand enough to allow a triumphal procession to march through between cheering crowds, driving before them carts laden with booty and prisoners in chains. The lettering used for inscriptions on these arches, detailing the victories of a Titus, a Constantine (*fig. 118*)

Because the orders and classical motifs were no longer required structurally, the way was opened to playing with the forms decoratively. Interior decoration in Pompeii foreshadowed Baroque caprices in mock marbling and painted architectural vistas. One of the most attractive of these architectural whimsies, thought to date from the second century AD, is the miniature round temple set between the sides of a broken pediment on the upper floor façade of the

118 | *Triumphal Arch of Constantine*, Rome, 315 AD

rock-cut El-Deir (Monastery) Temple, in Petra, one-time caravan trading city, cut into the rose-red rocks of the Arabian desert (*fig. 119*).

The Romans did not have to rely on the post and lintel structure of the Greeks because they had developed a much more effective method of support in the true arch. They did not invent it: the true arch may go back as far as 2500 BC in Egypt, and we have an extant example in the tomb of Rameses II at Thebes of about 1200 BC. The Romans were not a particularly inventive people – probably less so than the Greeks. But perhaps the superior comments of Vitruvius have some justification: the Greeks had ideas, but often failed to carry them into practice, as if they did not choose to soil their hands with the practical. The Romans' command of abstract geometry and theoretical science might have lagged behind that of the Greeks, but they had no inhibitions about putting others' knowledge to practical ends. And so, while Greek mechanical and hydraulic devices often remained on paper as ingenious toys – steam-operated doors to temples or oracles, or penny-in-the-slot holy-water dispensers – the Romans set their knowledge to improving everyday life.

The same with structures. They speedily perfected the timber tied-truss roof construction, which the third-century Greeks had done no more than toy with. Their attention then turned to the true arch which (unlike the corbelled arch where stones jutting from either side meet in the middle) is held together by pressure on the wedge-shaped stones, called *voussoirs*, radiating around the arc. During building the arch was supported by a temporary scaffolding called *centring* – usually a wooden structure or a mound of earth. A series of arches with padding in between to form a tunnel produced a *barrel vault*, and where two barrel vaults met at right-angles they formed a *groin vault*.

119 | *El-Deir (Monastery) Temple*, Petra, Jordan, 2nd century AD

The exploitation of this structure went hand in hand with the development of concrete. The properties of volcanic soil mixed with lime to make a waterproof concrete were early recognized on the volcanic island of Thera (rechristened Santorini during the Fourth Crusade), but the best substance for concrete-making was *pozzolana*, a red volcanic soil from Puteoli (today Pozzuoli), a port near Naples. The Romans used several kinds of concrete aggregate, collectively called *caementum*, which varied from a random collection of stone and brick rubble and even potsherds to carefully organized layers of brick and pumice such as tufa, particularly suitable for the dome or the upper part of a structure where lightness of weight was called for. As a rule they poured concrete into a permanent framework or casing, preferring this to removable shuttering, which leaves an exposed concrete face, and is often used today. The framework might be in traditional squared blocks of stone (*opus quadratum*) or a rough stone frame (*opus incertum*); if the framework was of brick, the bricks were either laid diagonally to form teeth for the concrete to cling to (*opus reticulatum*) or were triangular in shape, laid point inwards (*opus testaceum*).

The combined arch/concrete structure, by rendering pillars unnecessary, opened up a new world of spatial design. Engineering invention flowered in structures which were not to be emulated

120 | *Pantheon*, Rome, 120–4 AD

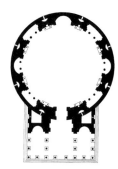

121 | *Pantheon*, plan

until the architects of the Renaissance read the manuals of Vitruvius or used classical models. For instance, the dome of the Pantheon (*figs. 120–2*), the temple of the gods built by the Emperor Hadrian between 120 and 124 AD, with a diameter of 143 feet (43.5 metres), remained the widest dome until the nineteenth century. It is built in concrete between permanent frame walls, with a total thickness of 23 feet (7 metres), brick on the outside and marble facing on the inside. Here was a temple, in direct contrast to the Greek temples, designed to be looked at from the inside as well as the outside. An

122 | *Pantheon*, interior, painting by G.P. Panini, *c.*1734

even, diffused light penetrates everywhere, and it is a moment before one realizes that, since there are no windows (from the outside the whole building appears solid), the light must be flooding in from the unglazed hole, the *oculus*, or eye, in the centre of the dome. The dimensions are exactly planned; the dome is a perfect hemisphere, its radius equal to its height, and it starts its ascent at a height equal to the radius of the drum which forms the body of the temple. The upper parts of the dome are made from volcanic tufa, for lightness, and are cut away in panelled coffering, itself cut back in frame after frame, a device which is both decorative and structural. The oculus cleverly dispenses with weight at the top of the dome. But there is another clever way in which the dome is supported. If we look at the building from the inside, we see that the dome springs from the second storey, but if we look from the outside, we see that there are three floors indicated on the outer wall; the dome is, in fact, set inside the drum, which forms the main body of the temple, and one storey of drum rises up around it on the outside, forming a buttress. The Romans made much use of buttresses, and every type of buttressing then known occurs in the Pantheon. The entrance portico, screened from the interior by Corinthian columns, was

built using the remains of a little temple, built by Agrippa, Augustus's son-in-law, in 25 BC.

The power of arch and concrete to act on the environment spread to all areas of everyday life – roads, bridges, aqueducts, harbours, theatres, housing, water-supply and drainage. Water was usually piped underground, but where pipes had to emerge to cross a valley, aqueducts carried it along arched bridges, which, like those that carried roads, are among the most beautiful functional pieces of architecture in existence. Augustus's aqueduct at Segovia, Spain, has 128 arches of white granite 90 feet (27.5 metres) high. The water supply to Nîmes, France, which was 25 miles (40 km) long, includes the famous Pont du Gard (14 AD; *fig. 111*) with its dry-stone masonry, still standing as an eloquent tribute to Roman engineering.

Civilizations before the Romans had, of course, known of sanitation. Terracotta pipes led water into terracotta baths, and running water passed below lavatories in the Palace of Knossos in 2000 BC; Sargon I of Assyria (721–705 BC) had jugs of water by his lavatories; his successor Sennacherib (704–681 BC) and Polycrates of Pergamum both constructed aqueducts. The Romans, however, planned drainage for whole cities. The main drain into the Tiber, the Cloaca Maxima, built by the

123 | *Baths of Caracalla*, Rome, 212–16 AD

Etruscans before 510 BC, was the only major sewer in Europe until the seventeenth century.

Inside the houses (*domus*) of the affluent, water ran from taps, bath-water was led along pipes from boilers on the top of furnaces, and there were individual lavatories. Heating was largely by braziers of coal carried from room to room; but in cold areas like Britain and Gaul, and

124 | *Insulae*, Ostia Antica, near Rome, 2nd century AD

for country villas and public baths, the *hypocaust* was used, that is, the floor was raised up on brick pillars, and heat from slow furnaces beneath rose into the rooms through patterned slits.

Life was less luxurious for the working people who inhabited the 46,602 *insulae*, or high tenement blocks, listed in the census for the city of Rome of 300 AD. They were lucky if there was a common lavatory on the ground floor, and they had to collect water from a tap in the street.

The lot, however, of men, in particular, was much ameliorated by the high standard of the public services. Public baths were either free or cost very little, and were often in sumptuous buildings. The public baths of the Emperor Caracalla in Rome (212–16 AD; *fig. 123*), today used an opera house, were surrounded by gardens and gymnasia, and boasted a round room with a dome which was divided into a hot room (*calidarium*), a medium-hot room (*tepidarium*), vaulted and lit from the clerestory, and an open-air swimming pool (*frigidarium*). Plans of baths, as with later forums such as that at Baalbek in Lebanon, show the Roman genius for arranging volumes of space, something that later inspired the architects of the Renaissance.

Insulae were often three or four storeys high, and may even have reached five or six at one stage. Those at Rome's port, Ostia Antica (*fig. 124*), although now in ruins, show the common arrangement of arcaded shops on the ground floor. The pattern was taken up during the Renaissance by designers of palaces for merchant princes, and it is still being followed today. As in tenements today, inhabitants of insulae were prey to exploitation, and the poet Juvenal, in his satires written at the end of the first century AD, talks of how landlords arrested the collapse of their property by shoring it up with 'gimcrack stays and props' and 'papering over great cracks in the ramshackle fabric'. They were also easy prey to fire, so that, says Juvenal, 'by the time the smoke has got to your third-floor apartment (and you still asleep), your heroic downstairs neighbour is roaring for water and shifting his bits and pieces to safety. If the alarm goes at ground level, the last to fry will be the attic tenant.' According to Tacitus, after the fire of 64 AD the height of the insulae was limited to 70 feet (21 metres) and party walls were forbidden; instead of timber, the use of fire-resistant stone from the Alban Hills was recommended,

125 | *House of the Vetii,* Pompeii, 2nd century BC

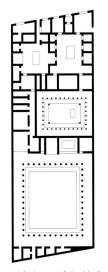

126 | *House of the Vetii,* plan

and flat roofs on the porticoes to give fire-fighters access became obligatory. When the burnt-out city was rebuilt, arterial roads like the present Via del Corso were cut through previously built-up sites to act as firebreaks in future emergencies. A fire corps, whose officers held army status, had already been created by Augustus when a fire in 6 AD had destroyed a quarter of the city.

The standard of living of the rich far exceeded the bare physical needs and safety precautions of the poor. The eruption of Vesuvius in 79 AD set a death-mask of molten lava over the commercial city of Pompeii (*figs. 125, 126*) and its seaside companion, Herculaneum. All was transfixed—paved streets, fountains on mosaic walls, where water had once spouted from lions' heads, shops and taverns, graceful houses with mural paintings, delicate mosaic floors, fan-lights, architraves over doors and colonnaded peristyles.

The rich used their country villas as a refuge from noisy Rome. Set in small self-supporting estates, they were usually run, in the master's absence, by a bailiff and a staff of freedmen and slaves, and included arable land, olive groves, vineyards, orchards, barns, granaries and workshops. Entered inconspicuously from the road, Roman villas (like Chinese dwellings) looked inwards to the *atrium*,

a mosaic-paved courtyard with a central pool, an *impluvium*, used for bathing or simply to hold goldfish. The impluvium also served to collect rainwater from the pitched red-tiled roofs which surrounded the atrium and jutted forward a little for shade. From the atrium opened the dining-room with three long couches placed along three sides of a table (for the Romans ate in the reclining position), the study, the library, the guest and owner's bedrooms, and the lavatories. Sometimes the formal rooms were grouped around the atrium, and the family lived in two-storey quarters to one side. Larger houses extended around an open courtyard with a Greek peristyle, and this, like the formal garden which most villas possessed, was laid out with grass, fountains and statues, bay hedges, rose and vine trellis-walks, and perhaps even a dovecot. Just how much thought and pride were put into the design of these country retreats can be gleaned from a letter from Pliny the Younger to a friend whom he is trying to entice to his villa at Laurentum, not far from Rome. Among its attractions were a D-shaped courtyard enclosed by colonnades, a dining-room with folding doors, windows all round and a view of the sea from three sides, a library with bookshelves, a winter bedroom with underfloor heating, a sun-parlour,

127 | *Hadrian's Villa*, Tivoli, Italy, 118–34 AD, showing the remains of the Maritime Theatre

rosemary and box hedges along the drive, a garden where mulberries and figs grew and a terrace filled with the scent of violets.

As for the palaces, inhabited by god-like emperors, it is scarcely surprising that their opulent apartments and grounds should put us in mind of Imperial China. At Spalato (Split, Croatia), Diocletian built a palace to retire to in 305 AD. Modelled on a legionary fortress, it is almost a city in itself, entered into from a street on one side, its grounds extending to an arcaded frontage and wharfs on the Adriatic. Hadrian's Villa at Tivoli (118–34 AD) was virtually a little kingdom. What remains of its seven miles of gardens, pavilions, palaces, baths, theatres and temples may still be seen (*fig. 127*).

In the public sector, a new type of lofty hall, the *basilica*, first appeared in the city in the Basilica Porcia of 184 BC and grew popular under the Empire to house the increasingly sophisticated legal and commercial activities. Made sometimes from stone, sometimes in brick and concrete, which allowed large spaces uncluttered by columns, a plan evolved for housing big assemblies. The pattern was taken up by the Christian Church and established as the norm in the early Christian and Byzantine era. Usually rectangular, the length twice the width, the basilica divides into a main hall (the nave) and single or double side-aisles screened with columns. The roof was normally timber, and, since the main nave rose above the side aisles, light entered through a

The Authority of Competence: *Ancient Rome*

128 | *Basilica of Maxentius*, Rome, *c.*306–25 AD

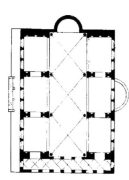

129 | *Basilica of Maxentius*, plan

row of clerestory windows on both sides of the upper walls of the nave. A semicircular apse at one end held the tribunal, sometimes raised, for the seat of the presiding magistrate. In what is left of the Basilica of the Emperor Maxentius, completed by his successor Constantine (*c.*306–25 AD), we can appreciate how impressive the simplicity and grandeur of the barn-like confines of the basilica form must have been to the Romans (*figs. 128, 129*). There were two apses in this basilica, the second added by Constantine, and the roof was deeply vaulted in concrete hexagonal coffering between brickwork ribs.

The basilica carries us architecturally across the divide between the Western Roman Empire and the Eastern Empire of Byzantium, the link being made by the new religion, Christianity, which was to become the chief architectural inspiration for the next ten centuries. Constantine and his basilica provide the bridge, for, before his death in 337 AD, he had started to build the church of St Peter in Rome, and had transferred the imperial capital to Byzantium, renaming it Constantinople (it is now Istanbul).

Early Christian architecture picks up from where the Romans left off, with the basilica. It was to become the stock Western church type for the next 700 years and led directly to the subsequent architectural phase, the Romanesque. But, as we have seen, it started as a secular hall of justice, and not as a religious building at all. In fact, during the first centuries, the Christians built no churches. Poverty and the need to hide from persecution were not the only reasons for this. The whole ethos of Christianity at this stage was in direct opposition to the combined trappings of state and religion to be found in the pagan temples, where gods and emperors were worshipped side by side. A bricks and mortar establishment held little interest for the early believers; their concern was with the promised second coming of Christ, and they lived in daily expectation of meeting him in the street or market-place.

The Acts of the Apostles gives us some idea of how they shared this period of waiting, wherever possible living together in a community. Since most of them were ordinary working people, their cells were likely to be over a workshop belonging to one of their number or in an average vernacular house – a succession of rooms opening off a courtyard. A similar attitude towards the community led to the development of the catacombs. Christians, believing in the resurrection of the body, did not adopt the Roman custom of cremation; they liked to be buried beside their brethren, if possible near the grave of an apostle, often under tombstones simply made from slates stuck into the ground. As the graveyards filled up, they hollowed out the earth to create catacombs in which passages were lined with tiers of alcoves for the bodies (*fig. 131*).

But Christian remains are not the only ones that are scarce from this period; we have very few secular post-Roman remains at all. As the Empire went into a long drawn-out decline, masonry structures of all sorts – temples, roads, bridges – became neglected, fell into disrepair and were eventually used for quarries. It was the period facilely called the Dark Ages, the period of the crumbling of the ancient Roman Empire, when Europe was subjected to incursions of Germanic tribes collectively called barbarians, a name long before coined by the Greeks for all foreigners whose uncouth speech sounded to them like 'Ba-ba-ba'. Angles, Saxons, Jutes, Franks, Huns, Goths and Vandals infiltrated the Roman provinces, bringing about a racial and cultural restructuring of the whole civilized world other than the Far East.

As with any large institution, erosion came from both outside and within. In the third century, Diocletian abandoned Rome as the capital and moved to

130 | *Santa Costanza*, Rome, *c.*350

131 | *Catacomb* off the Via Latina, Rome, 4th century

Nicodemia, about 50 miles (80 km) from Byzantium; later emperors were to establish capitals at Trier in Germany and at Milan. In 402, harried by Goths and by malaria from the surrounding marshes, Honorius moved the Western capital from Rome to Ravenna, a move of architectural consequence. Eight years later, Alaric the Goth did indeed sack Rome, but it was at Toulouse that the Goths preferred eventually to set up their capital. By 475 Rome was finally occupied – and the Western Roman Empire crumbled.

In 285 Diocletian appointed a co-emperor for the East, and although Constantine briefly reunited the empire in the fourth century (as Justinian was to do again in the sixth), the division was finalized when, on Theodosius's death in 395, the imperial possessions were shared between his two sons – Honorius, who would rule the West from Rome, and Arcadius, who would rule from Constantinople, Constantine's city on the Bosphorus. In 476 the last emperor of the West, Romulus Augustulus, abdicated, so Western Rome went as it had come – with a Romulus.

The Christians, heroically defending their new faith, might be seen as an internal cancer, eating away at the Empire. But in some ways the new Church and the old Empire appear to have nursed each other through the centuries of barbarian invasion. Once the Christians had grasped that Christ's message was not only for the Jews, but was for the whole world, they found a ready-made international vehicle in the Empire. And after Constantine declared Christianity the official imperial religion in 313, Rome found in the Church a refuge and sanctuary for her classical traditions. Not surprisingly with Europe in the melting pot, there was a long period of ambivalence between the old and the new religions, and exclusively Christian forms took some time to appear. A baptismal font in Tuscany shows pre-Christian gargoyles, and Celtic interlaced ornament continues to be largely composed of pagan forms even on Christian crosses as late as the eighth century. Constantine, who thought of himself as the thirteenth apostle and dedicated his new city of Constantinople to the Virgin Mary, nevertheless set up a statue of Delphic Apollo in the Hippodrome, and a temple to Rhea, mother of the gods, in his new market-place.

To compound the confusion, after Theodosius in 380 had declared all religions other than Christianity heretical, temples were taken over lock, stock and barrel as Christian churches, or looted to build new churches. The Corinthian columns of the nave of the basilica of Santa Sabina in Rome (422–32), for instance, are antique.

Basilicas became increasingly used to house the choirs and big assemblies that were part of the religion that was now official. But at first the simple Christians persisted in using the basilicas for communal living as if they were rooms in their house-churches. They would curtain off the side-aisles and use them for discussion and the instruction of catechumens who, until they had received baptism, were denied participation in the eucharistic rite. Since the eucharist was originally part of a communal meal, the altar-table was placed anywhere in the basilica – in

132 | *Santa Maria Maggiore,* Rome, 432–40

front of the apse, where the Romans had placed their pagan altar for the sacrifice which initiated the conduct of business, or even in the centre of the nave, but not in the apse itself. The apse from where the tribune, assessors and praetor had once presided, later came to have stone seats built around it for the clergy, with, in the case of cathedrals, a central throne for the bishop.

In the East, less harried by barbarian invasion, there was more time and leisure for theological controversy and liturgical changes, and the clergy more and more took over the nave. Sometimes, particularly in Syria, the nave had a raised semi-circular chancel, called a *bema*, with railings around it, for the clergy to sit on during the early part of the Mass. The congregation was pushed out into the aisles, which became increasingly wider to accommodate it, a tendency which eventually resulted in the cruciform church characteristic of the East, and into galleries built over the side aisles. In the West, the plan and shape of the older basilican hall was retained as the liturgy became formalized. The chief variation at this stage lay in whether the nave arcading adopted the classical trabeate style, where a series of lintels rest on the pillars, as in Santa Maria Maggiore, Rome (*fig. 132*), which dates from the classical revival of Pope Sixtus III (432–40), or was formed by arches resting on the pillars, as in Santa Sabina on the Aventine

Hill in Rome (422–30; *fig. 133*), allowing nave and aisles to interpenetrate in greater light and freedom. This second type became characteristic of the churches of Ravenna in its period as capital during the fifth and sixth centuries, and remained popular in Italy beyond the twelfth century.

The first surge of building for the new creed came after 330 when Constantine, the first Christian emperor, transferred his capital to Byzantium, an old Greek trading colony on the Bosphorus, and laid out a whole new city with roads, civic spaces and a blaze of churches. One of his first acts as emperor was to hand over the Imperial Palace of the Lateran in Rome to the Bishop of Rome, and to build alongside it the church of St John Lateran (*c.*313–20), a basilican church modelled on the basilican audience chamber he had built at Trier, Germany, when he was Western co-emperor there. In the Holy Land, he built the Church of the Nativity in Bethlehem (*c.*339; rebuilt after 529; *fig. 134*) over the reputed site of the cave in which Christ was born. Its atrium, or front courtyard, is now part of Manger Square, where today buses park. He replaced the customary apse at the end by an octagonal chapel, and pilgrims could peer down through an *oculus*, or eye let into the floor, into the sacred cave below. This octagon was replaced in the sixth century by a sanctuary with a trefoil

133 | *Santa Sabina*, Rome, 422–30

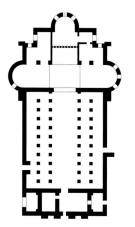

134 | *Church of the Nativity*, Bethlehem, rebuilt 6th century, plan

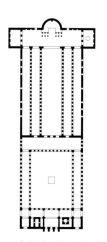

135 | *Old Basilica of St Peter*, Rome, c.330, plan

apse off it. Today, entering the church by the low door, placed either for defensive purposes or to prevent animals straying in, it is easy to be swept by, without being aware of it, through the dark cavernous stretches of Constantine's church with its dull-red Corinthian pillars on the way to the birth-cave with the star let into the floor.

In Rome, the first church of St Peter, built in about 330 over a graveyard near the site of the Circus of Gaius and Nero, had an impressive nave 400 feet (122 metres) long and double aisles, all ending in arches which led on to the first recorded transept or cross-aisle, placed across the head with one central apse off it (*fig. 135*). The transept was designed so that pilgrims could revere the tomb of the apostle – a typical *aedicula* of the period, composed of a slab on two small pillars before a wall niche. This plan was to live on, notably in Carolingian and Frankish architecture in Tours (995) and in the church of St-Rémi, Rheims (1000), but it is that first transept which is particularly important.

There are two distinctive features about these early basilican churches. First, they eschewed the complicated technology of vaults evolved by the Romans for their baths; possibly for the sake of cheapness, they reverted to the simple construction of slim walls – brick-faced concrete in Rome, stone or brick elsewhere – and columns holding up wooden roofs. Second (except in Constantinople where Constantine was building an entirely new city) they were normally placed on the outskirts of the town, either because the poor Christian community could not afford highly priced sites in the built-up areas or because of their desire to build over the burial place of a saint, and Roman graveyards were outside the boundary walls. We find churches like Sant'Agnese fuori le Mura, Rome, built in 630 to replace the one Constantine had built in 324 over the

saint's tomb, and San Paulo fuori le Mura, one of the best early examples remaining, more ornate than Santa Sabina, with a plan like old St Peter's, which we can still see, for although it was burnt down it was rebuilt in replica in 1823. Twin towers on the façade, which we tend to associate with Romanesque churches, appeared amazingly early. A carved ivory casket of about 400 symbolizing Jerusalem, the holy city, shows twin round towers, and they were quite common in Syria from the fifth century onwards. The freestanding bell-tower, or *campanile*, which features on the sixth-century churches of Ravenna, was also developed early. That of San Apollinare in Classe (c.534–49; *fig. 136*), erected by Justinian on the site of a temple to Apollo, is one of the earliest examples of a round tower.

The exterior of the basilican church tended to be simple and austere, perhaps to prepare the humble penitent for the vision of heaven awaiting him inside. Here the muted colours of Roman-style pavings built up through the marbles of the pillars and gave way to a burst of mosaic covering the walls. Galla Placidia's little Mausoleum (420; *fig. 137*), which is said to house her tomb and those of her husband and her brother the Emperor Honorius, has a deeply spiritual character that is created by the blue mosaics made by Byzantine craftsmen, whose patterns follow the lines of the

136 | *San Apollinare in Classe*, Ravenna, c.534–49

137 | *Mausoleum of Galla Placidia*, Ravenna, 420

arches and domes. At one with the structure, the patterns could now flow untrammelled from the floor up over the walls, swelling and ebbing over the arches, and gathering to a consummation in the central dome, usually in a great figure of Christ, pale-faced with sad and compelling eyes – a countenance of power, wordlessly teaching the lesson of Eastern mysticism: Be still and know that I am God.

Between the early Christian basilica and the domed church of the Byzantine period there was a third type of church linking the two forms – the centralized church. This type commenced as a mausoleum, or shrine, and was later used for baptisteries and reliquaries. A rotunda was built over the shrine of the Holy Sepulchre, Jerusalem, by the end of the fourth century. St Peter's in Rome, although a basilica, was built as a shrine, not a church, so attention was focused on the tomb, and it therefore originally had no altar; its place was taken by the first transept, which provided circulation space for pilgrims to the tomb. Inspired by Roman classical mausoleums or polygonal audience halls like the so-called Temple of Minerva Medica in Rome or the rotunda incorporated into Diocletian's palace at Split, the suitability of the circular or octagonal form for assemblies around a sacred object began to be appreciated. In square or rectangular churches as well as in circular ones, this centralized plan was often indicated on the exterior by the fact that the roof was raised over the central space, either as a timber pyramid or as a dome. We see this in the mausoleum of Constantine's daughter, Constantia, in Rome (c.350; converted into a church, Santa Costanza, in 1256), which is a rotunda with an outer encircling aisle, while the roof of domed brick is held up over the central tomb-space by an inner girdle of pillars which, in effect, forms an inner dodecagon (*figs. 130, 138*).

structural arches, and by the golden glow from the alabaster windows. In Ravenna the mosaics were at their most fabulous during the extensive building programme of Justinian's reign (527–65).

The particular intensity of light and refraction in Byzantine mosaic comes from the fact that the cubes are covered with a thin layer of gold leaf or coloured glaze, and finished off with a top film of glass. Commencing in the brick and plaster basilicas, where the design of the mosaics was necessarily repeatedly interrupted by the angularity of the structure, this wall-clothing was to become fully liberated in the Byzantine structure of

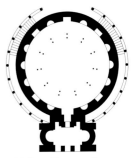

138 | *Santa Costanza*, Rome, c.350, plan

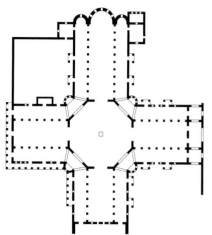

139 | *Monastery and pilgrim church of St Simeon Stylites*, Qal'at Sim'an, Syria, 480–90, plan

Constantine's Church of the Holy Apostles in Constantinople, which no longer exists, represented by all accounts the next phase in development: the amalgamation of the congregational basilica with the centralized shrine. Since Constantine considered himself the thirteenth apostle, his tomb was to stand in the central space, surrounded by twelve columns to symbolize the other twelve; and from this centre not one but four great naves were to project in the form of a cross. A similar plan was used at Qal'at Sim'an in north Syria (480–90), where an eight-arched octagon was built round the pillar-like hermit's cell in which the eccentric Saint Simeon Stylites squatted for thirty years. Four churches, each with a nave and two aisles, radiated in cross-form from the octagon (*fig. 139*); and the whole sanctuary complex, complete with porticoed monastery, was pitched between the quarries that provided the stone and the ceremonial gateway from which a sacred way ran down to a pilgrimage town of hostelries and convents.

In the Eastern Empire (which, at this stage, included Greece and the Balkans, Anatolia, Syria and Egypt), the Greek-cross plan with four arms of equal length was to become standard. It was theologically acceptable, since the Eastern Church laid great emphasis on the cross, just as it insisted on the observance of a hierarchy in its wall-paintings – the saints at the bottom, then the Virgin Mary, and the Trinity or Godhead at the top, in the dome. It was also liturgically suitable. There was no need for vast choir and congregational areas in the Eastern liturgy, which was largely carried out by the priest behind a screen, while the people worshipped individually, perhaps by candlelight before ikons, pinned on to the iconostasis or ikon screen, in the dark, mysterious spaces of the church. The shrine-like plan, where the cross arms projected from the central space – square, circular or octagonal – was not, however, the only plan; frequently the entire cross was contained within a square or rectangular plan, or else the arms were quatrefoil apses contained in a square, circle or octagon. And this form of a cross within a square was structurally useful because of the support that the *exedrae*, or areas opening off the central space, gave to

140 | *San Vitale*, Ravenna, 540–8

141 | *Santa Fosca*, Torcello, 11th century, interior of dome showing squinches

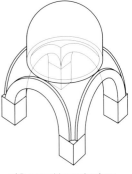

142 | Dome with pendentives

that space and the dome it was likely to support.

The revolutionary aspect of the Byzantine dome was that it was set on a building of square plan. Domes had been built before, on the Roman baths and on the massive circular walls of the Pantheon. There are even domes on square tombs of saints in Persia, but since these are tiny buildings with a small dome span it was possible to rest the dome on an octagon, simply made by throwing a stone bridge diagonally across each corner. Such a solution would not serve for a dome of heavy weight, so instead a pyramidal wooden roof was often used as, for example, on the Martyrion of St Byblas in Antioch Kaoussie (*c.*379). San Vitale in Ravenna (*c.*540–8; *fig. 140*) side-stepped the problem with an unusual structure of light pots fitted together. Then some unknown genius in Sassanian Persia was inspired to replace the corner lintel with

an arch, known as a *squinch*; the earliest known example is from the third-century palace at Firuzabad. The eleventh-century church of Santa Fosca at Torcello used two squinches, one above the other, to bring the vertical walls upwards and inwards to carry the round drum supporting the dome (*fig. 141*).

Squinches did not, however, provide the answer, especially where, as in a cruciform church, the dome would rest not on four solid walls but on the four arches which gave entry to the arms of the cross. The weight of a large and heavy dome not only bears down with crushing weight on the supporting pillars, but it also tends to push those pillars outwards. The solution, called a *pendentive* (*fig. 142*), came by resorting to the elementary technique of building out brick courses to make a beehive dome. Each beehive shape would start at the corner junction of two supporting arches, but stop when

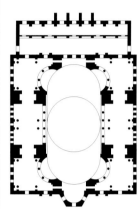

143 | *Hagia Sophia*, Istanbul, 532–62, interior

145 | *Hagia Sophia*, plan

level with the top of the arches, forming curving triangles (the pendentives) that met in a ring poised on top of a canopy formed by the pillars and the arches; on this ring the dome would rest, thrusting the weight back down on to the massive corner piers. The dome could now vary in size, sometimes, as in Hagia Sophia, pierced all around with windows.

It is difficult to exaggerate the effect of that invention. What the pendentive achieved can be appreciated if we compare the Pantheon, the Romans' greatest domed building, with the interior of Hagia Sophia, the Byzantine masterpiece, built by Justinian to replace Constantine's church, which had been destroyed by an earthquake in 532 (*figs. 143–5*). The uniform suffusion of light in the Pantheon illuminates its containing, igloo-shaped

144 | *Hagia Sophia*

walls, strong, smooth, clear-cut mouldings, exact triangular architraves over the niches – all calculated with the mathematical precision one would expect from an empire which had sorted out and organized the known world with admirable efficiency. Structurally it played safe by incorporating every form of buttressing known to Rome. In contrast, Hagia Sophia shows the ability to take a risk, essential to the pioneering of a new structure. The demand for our admiration is not dependent on a recitation of the statistics of this great building – that it has a square plan with a nave and galleried aisles; that it has a shallow central dome (almost as big as the Pantheon's and only eight feet smaller than St Paul's, London) which has 40 brick ribs and is held up by four arches on massive piers; that the dome is buttressed on either side by a semi-dome of the same diameter, each with three little satellite domes to support it; that on the exterior the building is austere but for the rocket-like minarets added at the four corners when it became a mosque after the fall of Constantinople to the Turks in 1453 – all such details seem irrelevant compared with the impression that one is a tiny creature in a living space.

Such breathtaking architecture could only be achieved by a revolutionary structure. In the course of the construction

146 | Byzantine capital from San Vitale, Ravenna

adaptations had to be made, and at one stage the architects, Anathemios of Tralles and Isidore of Miletus, told Justinian that they doubted that it would hold up. Justinian, with the courage of faith or architectural perspicacity, told them to continue to build the arches till they met, when they would support each other. Hold up it did. A historian of the time, Procopius, speaks of how the parts have been 'fitted together with incredible skill in mid-air and floating off each other and resting only on the parts next to them, producing a single and most extraordinary harmony in the work'. In his inaugurating sermon, Paul the Silentiary said the dome appeared to be 'suspended from heaven by a golden chain'. As for Justinian, when he saw the masterpiece, he declared, 'O Solomon, I have outdone thee!' While in the Pantheon light limits and defines the enclosure, here shafts from the 40 windows around the drum below the shallow, floating dome mingle and interfuse with the light pouring through the arches from apse windows or those above the galleried side-aisles in a way that makes it difficult to distinguish space from light. Where the Romans hid arches in the structure of concrete walls and vaults, the Byzantines opened up arches into apses, dome or semi-dome, giving the impression that, rather than building up walls and roofs to mark off and enclose

stretches of usable space, the architects have tunnelled into space itself.

Hagia Sophia is now a museum, and in spite of the admirable work done by the Byzantine Institute of America in replacing the veined marble that clothed the walls leading to the galleries, some of its former splendour has disappeared under the whitewash with which its Turkish owners obliterated the human figures forbidden by Islam, leaving their Kufic script still painted around the domes. Yet the glory remains. Here too, as in Ravenna, we find the cushion-shaped Byzantine capital, often carved with a filigree of leaves (*fig. 146*).

This first Byzantine masterpiece was never surpassed. But the style it established took on a new and more homespun quality—less filled with light, more dark and cavernous with candles catching the gilt of mosaic or ikon—and spread from Sicily in the south (there are famous mosaics at Cefalù, 1131, Monreale, 1190, and Palermo, 1170–85) through Italy, Turkey, Bulgaria, Armenia and north into Russia, where, cut off from Byzantium by Mongol invasions, the Russians built their own brand of the style as late as 1714, in the Church of the Transfiguration on Khizi Island.

Each area developed its own version. Typical of Greece and the Balkans were the monasteries at Daphni (*fig. 147*) and Hosios Loukas, where the cross-plan is

147 | *Monastery Church*, Daphni, Greece, *c.*1080

148 | *Monasteries*, Mount Athos, Greece

human or animal—has been permitted entry for a thousand years. Since Greece was at this period an unimportant outlying province of the Empire, its thirteenth-century cathedral at Athens, the Little Metropolitan, is the smallest in the world—35 by 25 feet (10.7 x 7.6 metres) and a midget Byzantine gem.

In the fifth century, refugees from the barbarian hordes crossed the Adriatic lagoons and created Venice as part of the eastern Byzantine Empire; so it remained for 500 years. In the ninth century some of her merchants returned from Alexandria with the body of St Mark the Evangelist and built a shrine for it, replaced in the eleventh century by the present St Mark's Cathedral (*figs. 149, 150*). The Greek architect based his Greek-cross, five-domed church on Justinian's Church of the Holy Apostles in Constantinople, which no longer exists. In spite of spangled additions to the outside, including antique bronze horses looted from

expressed on the exterior by separate pan-tiled roofs over the different sections. A late flowering of the style is seen in the fourteenth-century churches at Mistra which tumble down a hillside above the plain of Sparta. A fantastic elaboration occurs in the 20 monasteries on precipitous Mount Athos in north-east Greece (*fig. 148*), where no female—

149 | *St Mark's*, Venice, 11th century

150 | *St Mark's*, Venice,
interior

Constantinople, Gothic crockets or mini-
spires and religious mosaics in semicircular lunettes, it has retained something of
the magic of Hagia Sophia. The façade
builds up in three tiers of semicircular
shapes: on the ground floor, five magnificent doorways, deeply imbedded in the
surface between a two-tier paling of little
pillars; on the floor above, five rounded
gable ends hold the lunettes, each with a
quizzical ogee eyebrow (a moulding made
up of a convex and concave curve) that
remind us of Venice's Eastern affinities;

on the roof, the shape is echoed in the
lead-covered domes with their garlic-bulb
finials. Inside it is entirely sheathed in a
molten skin of gold mosaic.

For Armenia, on a high plateau east
of the Euphrates, the Byzantine period
was her finest hour. Today abandoned
to grassland, Ani, the capital, was once
known as the city of a thousand churches. The reputation of her architects was
such that in 989, after the dome of Hagia
Sophia had been destroyed in an earthquake, the Armenian architect Trdat, who

151 | **Trdat**, *Cathedral*, Ani, Armenia (now Kemah, eastern Turkey), 1001–15

later built Ani Cathedral (*fig. 151*), was asked to restore it. Armenia was the earliest country to adopt Christianity as the state religion in 301. There is a child-like quality in the primitive carvings of biblical scenes on the walls of their churches and in the conical caps fitted over domes that reminds us of early Christian wall-paintings.

As for Russia, her distinctive contribution to the Byzantine style is the onion dome, which swells outwards before curving inwards. This appears to have evolved in the twelfth century in Novgorod, the farthest north the style had penetrated, where shallow domes tended to give way beneath the weight of winter snow. The early wooden churches, set up by Prince Vladimir of Kiev after he

established Christianity as the state religion in 988, have perished. The first masonry church, Santa Sophia in Kiev (1018–37), built originally with one large dome to represent Christ and twelve smaller apostle domes, was during the seventeenth and eighteenth centuries so elaborated with extra aisles and domes that it is not easy today to see its original form.

It is difficult to reconcile solemn Red Square, Moscow, with the gay and skittish appearance of its cathedral, St Basil's, built by Ivan the Terrible in 1550–60 in thanksgiving for his victories. Its central tower, scalloped with upraised eyebrows, is clustered around with a collection of smaller domes, which must

The Worshipping Community: *Early Christian and Byzantine*

152 | *St Basil's Cathedral*, Red Square, Moscow, 1550–60

have been individual enough when they were first built, but which, since they adopted many-coloured tiling in he seventeenth century, present an appearance of Oriental extravagance one expects from a fairground (*fig. 152*).

It was the critics of the nineteenth century who first recognized and gave a name to an architectural style that reached its zenith in Western Europe during the eleventh and twelfth centuries. They called it Romanesque because its structural basis was derived from ancient Roman construction. This does not mean that its builders were concerned with the classical elements, such as the orders – although they might pick up and incorporate the odd classical column as the early Christian architects had done. Even in those places (usually in Italy) where quasi-classical details were specially designed, we can observe a distinctive character that belongs neither to the original classical period nor to its revival in the Renaissance. This can be seen in the Corinthian columns of the basically basilican church of San Miniato al Monte in Florence (1018–62; *fig. 154*), or in the cathedral at Pisa (1063–1272; *fig. 156*), where the tiers of delicate arcades on the west front culminate in a little temple-end. But it is its strong foundation on the Roman vault that puts the 'Roman' into Romanesque. It is generated by an obsession with security; each building, whether castle or church or abbey, is a stronghold, a fortress. Indeed, the purpose of all buildings at this time was semi-defensive.

One of the extraordinary things about the Romanesque is that both secular and religious buildings seem to have gained dignity from their ambivalent inspiration. The fortress-like quality is not surprising when we remind ourselves that this was the first settled and cohesive building programme to appear in Europe out of 700 years of turmoil. What had happened was that in the course of the several centuries that preceded the millennium, those barbarian hordes we saw in the Dark Ages devastating cities and destroying culture had undergone a transformation. They had not only settled down, but had gradually become peoples whose leaders, in partnership with the Church, were to establish a new order – medieval Christendom.

The first to become 'establishment' were the Franks, when Pope Zacharias approved the election of Pepin as King in 751. Then Charlemagne revived the lost idea of empire – a political entity embracing several peoples – by uniting the western Frankish kingdom. He was a shrewd man. Although he could hardly write his own name, he brought the learned monk Alcuin from the cathedral school at York across to Tours to set up a school where a new generation of Frankish rulers could be educated in the classical culture which had been preserved through the writings of Christians like St Augustine and Boethius. The Pope crowned him Emperor on Christmas Day 800. Wandering minstrels of the eleventh and twelfth

153 | *Aachen Cathedral, 792–805*

154 | *San Miniato al Monte*, Florence, 1018–62, interior

centuries sang of his valiant deeds in their *Chansons de geste*. Some even wanted him canonized. The best example of what is called Carolingian architecture is Charlemagne's Cathedral at Aachen (Aix-la-Chapelle) of 792–805 (*fig. 153*). Modelled on San Vitale, Ravenna, it is of the centralized tomb/shrine type, built by Charlemagne for his burial. It is a 16-sided outer polygon, with an inner octagon of light columns, which supports a dome. Other chapels, aisles and a Gothic choir were added later. But the focus of attention is on the tomb: 'Beneath this tomb lies Charles the great and orthodox Emperor, who nobly extended the kingdom of the Franks, and reigned prosperously 47 years. He died in his 70s in 814.'

Contributions to the new age by the one-time barbarians are patterned through the new culture. The workmanship of Frankish, Lombard and Visigoth ornament – wide bands of gold studded with enormous gems – found its way into the devotional furniture of the medieval Church, in the cross, chalice, reliquary and tabernacle doors. The grandeur and barbarism are exemplified in the tenth-century reliquary of Ste Foy in the pilgrim church at Conques, Auvergne. The casket enshrining the remains of the little martyr who refused to give her body to a lewd and pagan emperor was, ironically, honoured by being decorated with the gold

mask of a fifth-century emperor's face sent as a gift to the church by Pope Boniface.

One late group of barbarians, the Norsemen of Scandinavia, made a remarkable contribution to the emerging culture, not least in architecture. From Charlemagne's time their cruel-prowed Viking ships had preyed along the coastlines of Europe and, as we know now, had even crossed the Atlantic to North America. The Normans applied their skill in using naturally curved tree-trunks for the prows of their boats to the *cruck*, the combined timber-post and roof structure of England and northern Europe. In all the places where they made firm settlements – Normandy in 911, England in 1066, southern Italy and Sicily – they established a distinctive and influential form of Romanesque known as the Norman style, seen at its best in the interior of Durham Cathedral, built mainly in the twelfth century (*fig. 155*).

At the same time a strong independent tradition flourished in the Celtic fringes which had remained unaffected by the European mêlée. From Ireland, which had been converted to Christianity through the Roman occupation in the fifth century, Christianity flowed back to the Continent by way of the British mainland. From Ireland came interwoven decoration on stone crosses, churches and illuminated gospels (for example, the Book of Kells); and, of course, missionaries – Columba, Aidan, Alcuin and Boniface. The little Anglo-Saxon church of St Lawrence at Bradford-on-Avon, Wiltshire (*fig. 157*), dating from the cultural renaissance after Alfred, victor of the Danes, whose beautiful ashlar stonework may well have been reused Roman masonry, is an example of the Christian tradition that had existed in England for 600 years before William the Conqueror arrived from Normandy.

There was also the Saracenic influence. The tide of Islam's advance had swept as far as central France when

155 | *Durham Cathedral*, nave, 1110–53

Charles Martel, Charlemagne's grandfather, stemmed its flood at the Battle of Poitiers in 732. Even at the time of the First Crusade (1096), the Moors still occupied southern Spain – in fact the Kingdom of Granada remained a Muslim state until 1492. We can see this influence in the Moorish capitals in the cloisters of Segovia and, combined with Norman, in the Cathedral at Cefalù, Sicily (1131–48).

What had been the Western Roman Empire – France, Germany, Italy, England and northern Spain – was assuming a more settled identity. The inspiring principle was supplied by the Church. The system which unified and controlled society was that developed by the Normans and expressed in their dominant building types. That was feudalism, a hierarchial system of mutual obligations in which people owed service to their masters in return for security. If the abbey was the expression of the Church, the castle was the direct expression of feudalism.

The feudal system was, in many ways, a harsh one, in which life was poor and coarse for the serf at the bottom of the social ladder and not much more refined or sensitive for his lord. They were probably both illiterate, for book-learning was the prerogative of the clergy. The labourer lived in a hut of

overleaf
156 | *Cathedral, Baptistry* and *Leaning Tower*, Pisa, 1063–1272

133

157 | *Church of St Lawrence*, Bradford-upon-Avon, Wiltshire, 10th–11th century

brushwood or of wattle and daub, a construction wherein thin strips of wood, woven together like a basket, were covered by a mixture of dung and horsehair and finished with whitewash or plaster. The lord's hall, the forerunner of the manor house and the castle, was also primitive: one great room, heated from a central hearth with louvred smoke-hole above, and furnished with sleeping-benches around the walls. The servants would bed down round the fire with the dogs.

Change came as daily life became more civilized. Chimneys began to be built in the outside walls of castles. Then stairs led out of the hall to upper quarters for the family, and, later still, kitchen and servants' wings were added. Lighting was primitive, perhaps mercifully so, since, until the thirteenth century, when soap became more common, people were not very clean. Insufficient water supplies and sanitation contributed to the lack of hygiene. The towns had the worst of it. By the eleventh century all the ancient aqueducts in Rome had ceased to function. The aqueduct which the Emperor Julian had built for bringing water to Paris was destroyed by the Norsemen in the ninth century. Not until the monasteries, always carefully sited by spring or stream, started to channel fresh water in and sewage away, and Greek and Arab medical texts were brought back from

the East, was anything practical done about these vital matters.

Two other phenomena are crucial to an understanding of the Romanesque. The first was the passion for pilgrimage. Trade routes had already opened, but it was religious enthusiasm that made the heart of the community beat. It was manifest in visions, miracles, legends, saints and relics, wreathed in superstition and clothed in beaten gold encrusted with gems, each of which had a mystic significance; and it pumped the traffic of the time – monks and friars, pilgrims and crusaders – through the arteries of Christendom. With that traffic went the spread of Romanesque architecture, of wide naves and broad transepts that afforded space for the daily ritual and processions to a shrine. Local pilgrimages (like the Canterbury pilgrimage that Chaucer so vividly portrays) provided opportunity for social encounters, and, since saints were the heroes of the day, to visit the shrine of Becket at Canterbury or of Ste Foy at Conques and actually to see the relics must have provided the glamour and excitement that fans today get from hearing their pop idol live in concert. And some pilgrims went a long way, to Rome or Jerusalem. After the Arabs had been forced out of the Basque region, the popularity of the shrine of the apostle James at Santiago de Compostela in north-west

158 | *Pilgrim Church of St James*, Santiago de Compostela, Spain, 1078–1122, plan

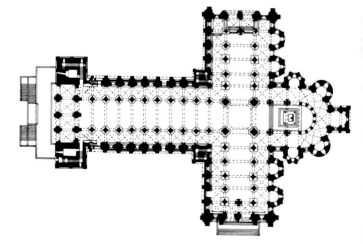

The Order and the Sanctuary: *Romanesque*

Spain (*fig. 158*) provided a new magnet, and the Cluniac Benedictines organized a fan of routes crossing France diagonally, from St-Denis and Vézelay and Le Puy and Arles.

The second phenomenon was the Crusades, the attempts by kings and barons and their retainers, urged on by popes and bishops, to recapture the Holy Land from the Turks. The Crusaders, some of whom spent ten years away, brought back from the East not only the impact of walking on the soil once trodden by Christ, but also tales of the sun glinting off scimitar and coats of mail, the sharp smell of sweetmeats and danger, Greek scientific texts preserved in Arabic, Saracenic decoration and the techniques of siege. Their tombs were given pride of

place in many a country church, where their effigies lie proudly with legs crossed to indicate that they probably participated in that great adventure to the glory of

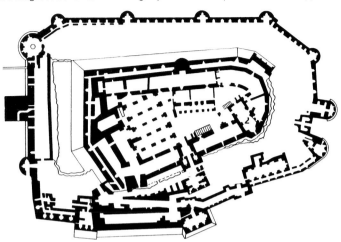

160 | *Krak des Chevaliers*, plan

159 | *Krak des Chevaliers*, Syria, *c*.1142–1220

God. The orders of the Knights Hospitallers and the Knights Templar were expressly founded to protect the Holy Land from the Saracens. They left in their wake not only handsome churches, monastic buildings and pilgrims' hostels, but also marvellous robust castles like the Krak des Chevaliers in Syria (*c.*1142–1220; *figs. 159, 160*), spoken of by a contemporary as 'the bone in the Saracen's throat'.

The key building in the spread of devotion was the abbey. And the creators of the abbey were the religious orders. Neither St Benedict, who, from his cave in Subiaco at the end of the fifth century, founded the first monastic order, nor St Bernard of Clairvaux (1090–1153), the ascetic Cistercian reformer, who was said to have averted his eyes from a sunset for fear it would distract his thoughts from God, nor St Francis, born in 1181, who wanted his wandering friars to sleep on the forest floor with their brothers the birds and the beasts, could be considered a patron of the arts. Yet, as their orders spread and became richer, abbey churches soared upwards all over Europe. The Benedictine Abbot Hugh of Cluny (1024–1109) (whose new abbey church was then the largest church in Christendom), was superior over several hundred abbeys. The Abbey of Cluny, founded by William of Aquitaine in 910 and given by him to 'St Peter and his successors the popes', that is, the Church, was responsible for building most of the churches on the pilgrim routes on plans similar to Hugh's abbey. Cluny became very powerful, particularly from 1309, when the popes moved to Avignon, and its abbey played for the Romanesque a role similar to that which Abbot Suger's church at St-Denis was to play for the Gothic.

Monasteries were often sited just outside the city gates, generating a little suburb, with shops of their own, by their social importance in providing work, medical care, education, hostels for travellers

and even sanctuary for hunted criminals. They were the power-houses of inventive talent. The Cistercians, the biggest farming order, initiated the agricultural developments of the time, especially in grain production, sheep-rearing, dry-stone walling techniques, water wheels and land drainage. Workshops were attached to all abbeys, where masons, carvers, joiners and engineers worked on the inspiration, experimentation and building techniques that were to blossom into the Romanesque style.

The earliest known drawing of a great abbey, the Benedictine abbey of St Gall in Switzerland, was made in the year 820 and illustrates the scale and complexity of the buildings inhabited by these great communities (*fig. 161*), which played a central role in the economy of the times, in agriculture and in industry. In their

161 | Plan of the *Abbey of St Gall*, Switzerland, drawn by the monk Eginhart, 820

162 | *Notre-Dame la Grande*, Poitiers, France, 1130–48, west front

churches and associated buildings, they reflected the dominance of the Church. From about 1000 the power of the Church increased, until by 1500 it informed all aspects of life. 'Shortly after the year 1000', wrote a monk of that time, Raoul Glaber, 'all Christian peoples were seized with a great desire to outdo one another in magnificence. It was as if the world shook and cast off its old age, everywhere investing itself with a white mantle of churches.' Like daisies in May, white-stone or lime-washed, they spread over the green fields of Christendom in a surge of relief that the millennium celebrating Christ's birth or death had not, after all, brought the predicted end of the world.

The typical abbey church was cruciform in plan, liturgically oriented with the altar at the east, the direction of the rising sun, and the main door at the west, in keeping with the contemporary obsession with symbolism. The east end was sometimes built up with the altar over a crypt and, in a pilgrim church, had a *chevet*–an ambulatory with chapels opening off it–behind the altar, whose pile-up of roofs with semi-conical caps would fittingly emphasize the position of the altar on the exterior. The same pattern was apparent in monastic churches, where crypt or chevet chapels provided space for a large congregation of priests to celebrate Mass daily, as gradually became the custom. Some churches had a tower over the crossing, but the German pattern developed a second transept, as, for example, St Michael's, Hildesheim (1001–33), and would often have two towers dominating a massive west façade, known as the *Westwerk* (fig. 164).

Characteristically, the west front of the churches of Burgundy is decorated by massive sunken portals and is richly sculpted with figures spilling out from a Christ-figure on the tympanum over the main doorway to cover the entire front, in a manner now recognized as typical of the Romanesque. Such a church is Notre-Dame la Grande at Poitiers (1130–48; *fig. 162*). We know who carved the tympanum of Autun Cathedral (*fig. 163*) by the signature 'Gislebertus hoc fecit' ('Gislebertus made this'). It portrays Christ in Judgement, with the damned writhing in a frieze below his feet; while on a nearby

164 | *Worms Cathedral*, Germany, c.1016, showing the twin towers of the western apse

163 | **Gislebertus**, *sculpture of the Three Magi Sleeping*, Autun Cathedral, France, c.1120–40

165 | *St-Sernin*, Toulouse,
France, 1080–1100

column, the Magi are being roused by an
angel from their sleep under a semicircular crochet blanket.

Stone is the usual material, but many
Italian churches adhere to the local custom of using brick with marble facings, as
in San Miniato al Monte in Florence. We
can recognize a Romanesque building
(whether it be a cathedral or a castle)
by its massive and sheer stretches of
stonework – ashlar on churches, rough-
stone on castles – covered with masons'
marks telling the 'lodge' or workshop
where the mason was trained. This suggests that skill in stonework was prized.
Stonework, whether plain or carved, was
slit by relatively few window openings,
a feature that creates the fortress-like
appearance of the style. It is in direct
contrast to the Gothic architecture of the

second half of the Middle Ages, from the
twelfth century onwards, where a new
structure brought in walls almost entirely
of glass.

Perhaps the classic feature of the
Romanesque church is its semicircular
shape, the shape of the round-headed
arch and its extension, the barrel vault,
which was adopted from the ancient
Romans as the mainstay structure of
the period. It runs through plan, three-
dimensional structure and even decoration – in the section of a round, smooth
pillar, in the chevet with its semicircular
chapels bulging off it, in the semi-conical
caps to roofs.

In Aquitaine this geometrical shape
appears in domed churches, the domes
set over square bays, which may indicate
cross-fertilization from the East. On the

exteriors, it is to be traced in an ornament of pilaster strips and blind arcades, often interlaced, which first appeared in Lombardy. They are therefore sometimes called Lombard bands, and act as decoration and as a form of buttressing. Even in the castles, round towers appear bulging from the corners, just as the side-chapels bulge from the chevets, and again the motif is structurally valid since the round towers make crossfire possible and the rounded corners make it more difficult to undermine the wall.

The semicircular motif is petrified in the arc of the barrel vault, which is the structural basis of Romanesque architecture. It is at its most beautiful in the tunnel-vaulted nave of St-Sernin, Toulouse, the surviving pilgrim church on the route to Santiago de Compostela, built between 1080 and 1100 (*fig. 165*). However, barrel vaults are heavy, requiring massive walls and buttressing; two vaults intersecting at right angles to form a groin vault can be particularly clumsy. Experiments in Lombardy towards the end of the eleventh century led to a general adoption of ribbed vaults. The ribs were first calculated and built like the spokes of an umbrella, defining and emphasizing the groins, with infilling in between. The vault probably came to Burgundy from the East. We have already noted its use in Persian palaces. Autun Cathedral (1120–32), for instance, was probably based on the Benedictine monastery at Monte Cassino of 1066–71, on which workmen from Amalfi, a city which traded with Baghdad, were employed. Because this structure sits best over a

166 | *Rochester Castle*, Kent, *c.*1130

square plan, the nave or aisle was divided into square compartments by *diaphragm* arches. The roof of each compartment consisted of a groin vault. Where the arch of the nave was particularly high, two bays of the aisle were allowed for each groin vault. This structure may be recognized as one walks down the nave, even before one looks up at the roof, because the aisle arcades have alternatively a pillar and a heavy stone pier to carry the weight.

By the end of the period the evolving structure was explicitly stated in the fabric of the building–in contrast to those early Roman models, where brick arches and vaults are hidden, embedded in the concrete walls. Possibly the enfolding arc of the vault, embracing like a mother's arm, appealed to an age sufficiently troubled to look for security. Spiritually, as well as physically, man was safe within the church.

In the castle, the same feature is also apparent. Here the watchful towers protruding from the sheer defensive sweep of the round keep, or *donjon*, make an aggressive and defensive gesture that reflects the reasons why they were built. However, in feudal society their function was not only military, it was also administrative. The castle became the seat of local government.

Between 1066 and 1189, the Normans built some 1,200 castles. The original castle form was the motte and bailey, the motte being a mound, sometimes a natural hill, often an artificial one, encircled with a ditch or moat, on top of which stood a timber structure which could be anything from a lookout post to a wooden dwelling, according to the space available. Looping from the motte's foot and connected to it by a wooden bridge was the bailey, a wide area protected by ramparts and earthworks. The bailey acted as a parade ground and storage area, and would include retainers' houses, stables, and even armouries, depending on its size. The Norman development was to transmute the flimsy wooden dwelling on the motte top into a strong stone keep. The earliest examples are rectangular, holding a common hall and private chamber side by side on the first floor over the ground-floor storage area. After 1125, it became a round tower, with the private chamber above a great hall. Later examples had circular or octagonal keeps with more complex plans. In some remains, such as the keep at Rochester Castle, Kent, of about 1130 (*fig. 166*), the crucial well-shaft which supplied the water from top to bottom of the keep can still be seen.

Feuding families in Italian city-states would build their houses in the form of towers, solid at the base with single apartments on the upper floors, and sometimes a warning bell added on top. San Gimignano in Tuscany bristles splendidly with examples of such defiance (*fig. 167*). At Bologna, where once 41 towers stood, two remaining towers, the Gli Asinelli at 322 feet (98 metres) and La Garisenda, draw attention to themselves by leaning together at a dangerous inclination only a little less than the famous bell-tower at Pisa. The slants of these towers are almost certainly due to inadequate foundations, a common fault at this period, and the probable reason why, of the English Romanesque cathedrals, only Norwich has retained her tower intact over the crossing. However, they provided the security required of them at the time, and given that the Bologna towers have been leaning since 1119, they have not done so badly after all.

But ultimately a castle indicated the beginning of a town, often, like the castle, a walled one. Most existing city walls date from between 1000 and 1300. The castle and the church towers would rear up above a wonderfully varied roofscape that resulted from the fact that the house fronts (the better ones arcaded) were not aligned but scattered along twisting

167 | *Tower houses*, San
Gimignano, Italy

streets that looped up and down over
untamed contours. There seems to have
been little sensitivity to spatial planning,
and anyway civic pride expressed itself in
processions in honour of a patron saint
rather than in town-planning. But the
castle, like the abbey, was at the centre
of an emerging society which we will see
in some of its more glorious moments in
the Gothic period. We must at this point,
however, examine the Islamic architecture that developed in the East at the
same time as Romanesque in Europe.

For two hundred years after 1096 the Christian knights of Europe fought the Muslims in more or less continuous Crusades to retain the holy places – Palestine, where Christ had lived, and Constantinople, where Constantine had established the seat of the first Christian empire. Yet when you go there today it is the architecture left by Islam that is the more impressive. And that is all the stranger because the Muslim religion originated from a nomadic Arab people who lived under black tents in the desert and had, before religious fervour drove them to seek to conquer the world, few architectural pretensions. To trace that story and try to explain what happened there is no better place to start than Jerusalem.

Ever since it was built, between 688 and 692, the golden cupola of the Dome of the Rock (*fig. 169*), rising above the western wall and the creamy-brown rolling panorama of the city of Jerusalem, has commanded the attention of pilgrims, whether they were Jews, Muslims or Christians, and from whichever direction they approached over the hills. Close by, down some steps but on the same axis, Caliph al Walid, son of Ibn el Malik, who built the Dome of the Rock, started in 710 to build the El Aksa mosque (*fig. 170*), rebuilt many times since, and at present having a dome of silver. These are two of the oldest Islamic buildings still in existence. They stand upon a naked white

podium, with dark, tufted trees at its perimeter, that lies between the congested houses and tunnelled bazaars of the Old City on one side and the rising terraces of the Mount of Olives on the other. The podium is in fact the levelled-off top of Mount Moriah up which Abraham brought his son Isaac for sacrifice. It is also known as the Temple Mount, because Solomon's temple was built against one side of it.

Neither their exposed position nor their architecture is entirely typical of Islamic buildings, which tend to be hidden behind high walls and to concentrate on their interior arrangements. But they represent a tradition in its early evolutionary stages. The Dome of the Rock is used as a mosque today, but it is primarily a shrine, holy both to Jews and to Muslims. It is built around the hollow rock from which Muhammad is said to have made his leap to heaven in about 639. Structurally it is Byzantine. Its octagonal plan was suggested by the shrine of the Holy Sepulchre, which already stood in the Old City, not far away. A double ring of columns provides an outer ambulatory resembling those of the Roman-based Byzantine tombs and shrines, such as, for example, Santa Costanza in Rome. It is roofed with a shallow pitch, made imperceptible from the outside by the device – later carried to extremes on Persian gateways – of carrying the wall

168 | Spiral minaret of the *al-Malwiya Mosque*, Samarra, Iran, begun *c.*848

169 | *Dome of the Rock*, Jerusalem, 688–92

up sheerly into a parapet to provide an uninterrupted surface for decoration. Originally glass mosaic, the decoration, dating from the sixteenth century, is now a sheath of blue and gold ceramic tiles. The drum, also faced in tiles, is supported by an arcade of antique pillars and carries the double-skinned wooden dome, clothed on the outside in gilded lead originally, today in anodized aluminium. The columns, gleaned from ancient sites, do not quite match and have been wedged between makeshift block-like bases and capitals. Islamic whims or a healthy attitude to recycling is a probable explanation for this, since in the Great Mosque at Cordoba, Spain (about 785; *fig. 172*), there are classical columns sawn off and jammed in in the same way. Early examples of the pointed arch, a recurring motif in Islamic architecture, are to be found in the screen wall.

The style of the El Aksa Mosque, despite much rebuilding, reveals its Christian origins; nevertheless, its atmosphere is that of a mosque. This is Islam's holiest shrine after Mecca and Medina, and more accessible than those two, for the Prophet's Mosque in Medina and Islam's central shrine, the Ka'aba in Mecca (a strange cube-shaped building housing the sacred black stone – a relic of pre-Muslim worship; *fig. 171*) are forbidden to non-Muslims. The El Aksa consists of one long carpeted prayer-hall, and has typical

timber bracing-beams cutting at capital level across from arch to arch of the arcade. It also has crosswise arcading so that worshippers may kneel on the floor facing the *qibla*, or wall oriented towards Mecca.

In Damascus, another city to take its turn as Muslim capital, the Great Mosque (*fig. 173*), the earliest mosque to survive intact, preserves other features typical of the mosque in its development phase. In 706, Caliph al Walid took over a *temenos*, originally a Hellenistic sacred precinct containing a temple and later harbouring a Christian church, and turned it into a congregational mosque. The caliph made use of the existing square towers and turned them into the first minarets. The pierced stone patterns on the window grilles, on the other hand, show the kind of geometrical detail that was to become standard Islamic, after figurative decorations were forbidden to Muslims in the eighth century (as they already were to Jews under the prohibition against the making of graven images).

All three of these mosques are impressive buildings by any standards. But what was it that inspired men in the East to build this kind of building, a full century and a half before Charlemagne was crowned Emperor in Rome, at a time when in the West the basilican form of Early Christian architecture was still unchallenged? It was the prophet Muhammad, born in about 570 in Mecca,

170 | *El Aksa Mosque*, Jerusalem, 710

171 | The *Ka'aba*, Mecca, *c.*608

a city on the camel-routes, who was the inspiration. His revelations, couched in rhyming prose, were arranged according to length to form the *Qur'an* (*Koran*), which Muslims learn by heart and recite daily. This, with the late addition of two other holy books (the *Hadith*, comprising Muhammad's sayings, and the *Law*, drawn from the first two), formed the basis on which scattered Bedouin tribes united to surge forth from the Arabian desert and along the Mediterranean as far as France in a tide of holy war.

It was not until 732, at Moussais-le-Bataille, near Poitiers, that Charles Martel managed to stop the invasion of Arab tribes into Europe. A measure of their achievement is that they had started to build the Great Mosque at Kairouan, Tunisia, some two thousand miles (3,200 km) from Mecca, around 670 (*figs. 174, 175*), before Muhammad had been dead forty years. It was rebuilt in 836, but the base of its minaret is the oldest extant Muslim structure.

Islam presents a life so simple, practical and complete that it has never lost its appeal across the centuries. There is only one basic dogma: that there is one God, Allah, and Muhammad is his prophet; and one basic requirement: submission to the omnipotent will of Allah. *Islam* means surrender, and a *muslim* is one who submits. This practical requirement is expressed in a daily way of life, which includes ritual prayer five times daily, fasting, paying taxes to support the poor and making a pilgrimage (*hajj*) to Mecca once in a lifetime.

The buildings of Islam enshrine this pattern of everyday life. The importance of leadership was readily accepted by the Bedouin faithful, who knew from experience that a leader was needed to protect them from the threat of one shepherd doubling his fortune by killing his neighbour and seizing his flock. Such a leader under Allah was the caliph who occupied Muhammad's place. Such are the three officials in the mosque: the *muezzin*, who

172 | *Great Mosque*, Cordoba, Spain, *c.*785, interior

173 | *Great Mosque*, Damascus, 706–15

calls the faithful to pray, the *khatib*, who preaches and leads prayers from a pulpit called the *minbar*—often the only furniture in the mosque—and the *imam*, the paid official who represents the caliph. They are not priests: there is no sacrificial ritual and therefore no sanctuary as such in a mosque. All worshippers have equal rights to prayer.

Islamic architecture inevitably developed regional differences, which were mingled with the flavour of Syria, Persia and Samarkand as well as of Mecca and Medina. But none of them explains the character of Islamic architecture. The key fact is that Islam was a highly powerful society which had absolutely no tradition of 'great' building. And so what became Islamic architecture developed, like her rituals, directly from the everyday life of the believers; it is an architecture of the oasis. This applies to the characteristic features not only of mosques—in particular the *Ulu Jami* (Friday) congregational mosques that developed from the seventh to the eleventh century—and the *madresas*, the theological colleges dating from the tenth century onwards, but also the palaces, luxury houses and the dervish hostels on trade or pilgrim routes. They all consist of a high-walled compound for protection against enemies, thieves and the sun, with shady arcades and halls around it, and a water-source, a

fountain, pool or well or, in some cases today, a large tank, often in the centre of the courtyard.

The main concern of the dwellers in these parched lands was water, and it was soon built into Muslim daily life with the ritual ablutions that preceded prayers. Under nomadic tents, no distinction is made between *inside* and *outside*, and an expression of this can be observed in how mosques and palace buildings and gardens may mirror each other—the symmetrical layout of rugs inside, or streams and flower-beds outside, repeating each other. We can see this in Middle Eastern carpets, in which 'rivers of life' flow between arbours of blossoms, flower-beds and pools (*fig. 176*). A similar arrangement can be seen in the axiality and symmetry of the Shalimar Garden, Lake Dal, Kashmir (1605–27; *fig. 177*), which is on three levels linked by elegant canals and pools with, as its focal point, a black marble pavilion surrounded by fountains.

The early palaces, whose high enclosing walls often make them appear fortresses from outside, reveal them-

174 | *Great Mosque*, Kairouan, Tunisia, *c.*670, interior showing bracing-beams

175 | *Great Mosque*, Kairouan

selves structurally from within as a series of simple pavilions set in parks or gardens. Their furnishings may be rich and sumptuous, with silk hangings and gold and silver work, but in architectural terms they are little more sophisticated than the Bedouin tents. It is easy to be so dazed by the fairy-cavern impression of the fourteenth-century Palace of Alhambra (Qalat al-Hamra) at Granada, Spain, with its tessellated filigree of fretting and stalactites, that we fail to grasp that its plan is simply made up of a series of pavilion units linked by elaborate courts (*figs. 178, 179*). Even in more complex buildings we find (as in China and Japan) that rooms and areas are rarely designated for particular functions such as eating or sleeping, but are more likely to be seasonal – winter and summer areas.

The major buildings are in cities. Mosques and palaces were isolated behind walls in the heart of the cities both for protection and to signify withdrawal from worldly concerns. Likewise, inside the mosque, the prayer-hall was placed farthest from the entrance.

Nowhere was the principle of defensive planning carried so far as in the magical city of Baghdad on the river Tigris, city of Haroun al Raschid and the Arabian Nights, not far from the ruins of Babylon and Ctesiphon, those magnificent capitals of past empires.

Caliph Mansur in the eighth century so planned the city that his palace and administrative buildings were in the middle of a great open space, encircled by three concentric rings of walls with an outer 4-mile (6.5 km) circumference. The city itself lay between the inner and the middle walls and was divided into four quarters by two intersecting roads. The four gates on the compass points were named after the provinces to which they gave access, and had bent entries – a device adopted by the Crusaders. Military barracks lined the roads by the gates, and the circle between middle and outer walls remained open so that the caliph was in

176 | *Persian garden carpet*, *c.*1700. Victoria and Albert Museum, London

177 | *Shalimar Garden*, Lake Dal, Kashmir, India, 1605–27

a position to mobilize troops in order to defend himself from external aggression, as well as from rebellion from within the ranks of his own people.

Isfahan, a royal city of Shah Abbas, a contemporary of Queen Elizabeth I of England, shows similar protective planning, culminating in a great open space, the *maidan*, which was the royal polo-ground, flanked by two mosques, the palace, and royal caravanserais. The entry to the Masjid-i-Shah from the maidan is through a great *iwan*, or vaulted gateway, backed by a half-dome that is cut into the extraordinary flat façade, with twin minarets 110 feet (33.5 metres) high on its portal. The iwan leads into an inner court, off which the corresponding iwan leading to the mosque had to be set at an angle of 45 degrees in order to orient the mosque correctly. Over the internal courts rises the mosque's great dome,

set on a pierced drum and subtly bulbous, adazzle in peacock, kingfisher and jade faience speckled in white like the glory of the southern heavens at night.

Masjid-i-Shah (*figs. 180, 182*) was a royal mosque. All mosques had certain essential features. They had either flat roofs supported on beams and wooden columns, or gently pitched roofs that rested on arcades running around three sides of the courtyard. The arcades provided stabling for camels as well as shade and sleeping-shelters, for mosques had many functions that were not strictly religious. Since community administration and community law were part of the Muslim

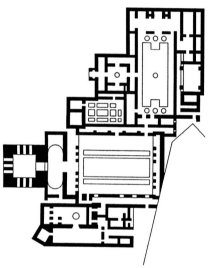

179 | *Palace of Alhambra*, plan

tradition, clerks were permanently attached to the mosque, and the law was dealt with there. Treasures, too, were stored there. Their concern for ventilation dictated the open arcades; and even after these arcades were enclosed in prayer-halls running the length of the inner *qibla* or Mecca-facing wall of the courtyard, they still kept lofty arches as a feature to encourage coolness.

The classic mosque form, which developed from the most straightforward practical considerations, is well illustrated in the plan of the Great Mosque at Samarra, Iraq, of 847, of burnt brick buttressed with round towers, the largest ever built,

178 | Court of the Lions, *Palace of Alhambra*, Granada, Spain, *c*.1370–80

having an outer enclosure (a *ziyada*) that measures more than a fifth of a mile square (10 hectares); and in that of the Ibn Tulun Mosque, Cairo, of 876–9 (*fig. 181*). The courtyard of any mosque must have a water supply, usually a fountain in the centre, for drinking and for the ablutions which became obligatory before prayers. The entrance wall of the courtyard was pierced by the great iwan portal, which could be flanked by minaret towers, or have a single central minaret, according to the regional pattern. Arcades, to provide shelter from the sun, sometimes two deep, typically ran round the inner entry wall and the two adjacent walls of the courtyard. At the Ibn Tulun Mosque, date palms make up the roof of the arcades, a technique much used in ancient Mesopotamia. But along the opposite wall of the courtyard, the qibla wall, which was the sacred prayer area, there could be four, five or even six rows of arcades. When Islam spread to colder areas, it was these arcades enshrining

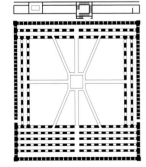

the qibla wall which were roofed over to form an enclosed mosque.

The courts, the minaret, the fountain or ablutions pool, the arcades and the qibla wall together with the *mihrab* (a recessed niche in the centre of the qibla wall) make up the essential features of the mosque. The function of the mihrab was to indicate the direction of Mecca, so that believers knew which way to face in prayer. Originally a spear stuck in the sand had been used for this purpose. However, the alcove early became a distinctive feature and one on which the most beautiful decoration was lavished. Among the Egyptian labourers used in the renovation of the Prophet's House Mosque at Medina in 707 there were Coptic Christians who, perhaps, accustomed to building apses on the side walls, decided to incorporate one here. At least, that is one commonly cited reason for the mihrab taking the form of a large niche. From here the imam could lead prayers while visible to the worshippers,

182 | *Masjid-i-Shah*, Isfahan, Iran, 1612–38, tiled interior

and could himself survey his congregation wherever they knelt on the floor. The conversion of Christian churches with their long east/west axis into early mosques in Syria, where Mecca lay to the south, established a pattern for the qibla to be one long side-wall facing which the believers prostrated themselves in prayer. This established a pattern, so that when Islam spread across the world there were many examples— in the Great Mosque at Kairouan, Tunisia, for instance–of a southwards orientation quite incorrect in that part of the world. The mihrab in the south wall signified that the mosque had to be entered from the middle of the long northern wall. This

made it necessary to emphasize the mihrab. It was commonly done by introducing another set of arcades in the prayer area opposite the mihrab, running at right-angles to the qibla, so that in an east—west oriented building they would run from side to side across the width of the mosque. The central arcade might be taller than its fellows and might stop short with a dome over the centre of the prayer space opposite the mihrab to give further emphasis—external as well as internal, for it can be identified by the raised roof on the outside. Such a dome appears in the Aghlabid Mosque of 836 at Kairouan, and in the many-domed mosques of the Turkish Seljuk dynasty.

The Flowering of the Desert: *Islam*

183 | **Koca Sinan**,
Suleymaniye Mosque,
Istanbul, 1551–8

Rugs on the floor, a pulpit called a *minbar* to the right of the mihrab, and sometimes a railed enclosure for special worshippers such as the caliph, or women, normally complete the sparse furniture of the mosque.

Presumably Muhammad, in his garden at Medina, asked one of his followers to climb on the wall and call to the others when it was time to pray. Just as the mihrab is possibly an adaptation of the side apse, so the towers of the Christian church at Damascus gave birth to another Islamic component: the minaret. The first purpose-built minaret of which there is a record dates from 670 and is to be found in the 16-aisle, open-court Great Mosque at Kairouan where, incidentally, we also find the first use of the sumptuous glazed tiles which were to become the hallmark of Islamic architecture. Mosques in Mesopotamia and North Africa usually have a single minaret, placed at the entrance to the courtyard; coupled minarets are typical of Seljuk and post-Seljuk Persia, while in Turkey a single

minaret off-centre between courtyard and prayer-hall is common. Some caliphs gave expression to their grand concepts by building four or even six minarets around the prayer-hall. The Ka'aba Mosque at Mecca is unusual in that it has seven.

Minarets may be cylindrical or tapering – looking like a factory chimney except that some are covered in incredible patterning in basket-weave and geometrical and calligraphic forms. Some minarets are fretted, some tiered and stepped like a lighthouse tower, ending perhaps, in a mode peculiar to Cairo, in an open pavilion. Some are free-standing and show the idiosyncrasies of their origin. At Samarra, one-time capital on the Tigris, the minaret at the north end of the ninth-century al-Malwiya Mosque is a spiral ramp, reminiscent of early Assyrian ziggurats not far away, so wide that the caliph could ride up it to a pavilion 150 feet (45.5 metres) above ground (*fig. 168*). Four slim needles rising at the four corners of a square complex are the hallmark

The madresa is the last of the court-yard forms we ought to look at. It is a theological or teaching college that developed in the tenth century, particularly in Seljuk Turkey in Anatolia, for the Turks were devout propagandists. Attached to mosque or palace, and part of an extended complex, it normally took the form of a series of cells round a courtyard. What is probably the world's first university was attached to the El-Ashair mosque in Cairo in 971. Some of the best examples were built under the Bahri Mamelukes in Egypt during the thirteenth and fourteenth centuries. Often, they were built from brick that had already been used, but in Anatolia they show how Turkey had learnt from the superb Syrian traditions of ashlar stonework. Sometimes they housed the tomb of their founder, as in the Madresa of Sultan Hassan (1356–62) in Cairo.

Entry to the madresa courtyard was through four vaulted chambers, the iwans, their enormous portals much-sculpted in a series of receding and diminishing arches and sometimes vaulted with a semi-dome. In the twelfth century, emphasis on the main gateway made it bigger and surrounded it with an upright rectangular panel (known as a *pishtaq*), which made a superb base for the fashionable mosaic of tiles in blues

184 | *Jami (Friday) Mosque,* Yazd, Iran, 1324–64

of Ottoman buildings in Turkey and Istanbul, especially those of the greatest (and only named) early Turkish architect, Koca Sinan (1489–1578 or 1588), such as the Suleymaniye Mosque in Istanbul (1551–8; *fig. 183*). Some of these minarets rise like horns from both sides of the iwan façade of mosque or madresa. (The Ottoman rulers had ousted the Turkish Seljuk dynasty in the thirteenth century, and established the enormous Ottoman Empire which lasted until 1918.)

185 | Tomb of the Sultan Iltumish, *Quwwat-ul-Islam,* Delhi, India, 1230, showing decorative brickwork

154

and greens and golds, which derived from Persian and Mesopotamian sources. The best example of a pishtaq is probably the Jami Mosque at Yazd, Iran (1324–64; *fig. 184*), a city set in the desert, but possessing its own water supply, making possible the creation of a city and even the cultivation of mulberry trees for the silk trade by Tamerlane (Timur the Lame), the Turkish conqueror who, with his son, resurrected this area after the devastation caused by the invasions of Mongols and Turkish tribesmen during the thirteenth and fourteenth centuries.

What is fascinating about Islamic architecture is how its extreme simplicity of arrangement and structure could give rise to so many diverse shapes and decorations, many of which carry the seeds of future structural developments. The arcades of the mosques, for instance, started as mere supports for light, awning-type roofs, and this left their creators free to invent a multiplicity of arched forms: pointed, stepped, round, horseshoe, trefoil, scalloped, ogee or shaped like inverted ships' keels, or double-tiered as in the arches with variegated voussoirs at Cordoba. Whereas a round arch is one-centred (since in a semicircle, both height and width are radii from the centre point) these arches of complex design may be two- or even three-centred.

The fact that figurative representation was forbidden perhaps gave impetus to the exploration of shapes, resulting in a rich spectrum from robust battlementing of Crusader origins to intricate but delicate interlaced arabesques developed from calligraphy. Part of the magic springs from the freedom with which shapes and patterns can be swapped from one use or medium to another: where else has ink brushwork or cursive writing been translated into brick (*fig. 185*)? When later, Islamic faith extended into colder regions like Anatolia, where the Seljuks had to abandon open-court mosques for enclosed buildings, experimentation with the arcades continued, aided by the pavilion form, in which they were not required to support an upper storey.

The countries that adopted Islam were in no way backward in structural evolution. We saw how the Persians were originally far in advance of Byzantium in working out the squinch, forerunner of the pendentive, to carry a brick-domed

186 | *Blue Mosque*, Istanbul, 1606–16, showing tiered domes

187 | *Taj Mahal*, Agra, India,
1630–53

roof. The squinch was originally used at
the corners, but after the eleventh century its use was extended so that it covered
the entire alcove, recessed portal or hall-
pavilion. No longer used as a method of
supporting a dome or vault, vast numbers
of tiny squinches were often used in
Islamic architecture as a decorative conceit; they were built up in overlapping
layers, like the scales of a pineapple or a
fir-cone, until they created a magical cave
of little stalactites (called *muqurnas*).
We can see how in the Hall of Lions and
the Hall of Judgement in the Alhambra
Palace, Granada, the muqurnas in
lath, plaster and stucco have been

transformed into filigree resembling frost-
flowers on a window pane. We see these
Islamic patterns persisting right through
the medieval period in Sicily, in Cefalù
and in the Royal Palace at Palermo.

Structures and flowing decoration
come together in the roof silhouette. The
tomb, which made an important contribution to Islamic architecture, made possible small-scale invention in dome shapes,
again often betraying local origins.
Domes were placed at important points,
such as over the entrance or over the
bays before the mihrab. Sometimes in
Persia and in Mesopotamia, each bay of
mosque, madresa or palace had its own

188 | *Gur-i-mir*, Samarkand, 1404

dome. The Ottoman struggle to make all subordinate to the central dome can be seen in the Selimiye Mosque, Edirne, Turkey (1569–74), and the Blue Mosque, Istanbul (1606–16, *fig. 186*). When Islam came to India with the Mogul conquerors in 1526, they too adopted the domes of their Persian cultural background. But they look slightly different to Persian or Ottoman domes. Domes on Indian tomb-complexes display a calm, disembodied beauty, although they tend to be more bulbous in silhouette. The best example is the Taj Mahal at Agra (1630–53), the beautiful marble palace which Shah Jehan built in memory of his wife. He set it in the midst of gardens by the river between four sentinel minarets. There is a still, breathless perfection about its massing, with four octagonal towers carrying the central pavilion (*fig. 187*). On the façade, a great open iwan rises two storeys to the drum and floating dome based on the earlier Tomb of Humayan at Delhi (1565–6).

Iran, however, sometimes built odd tall tomb-towers with conical caps resembling rather superior farm silos, like that of the Gunbad-i-Qabus dating from 1006–7. In Samarkand, now in Uzbekistan, a city on the silk route and once a capital of the Abbasid caliphate (750–1258), Tamerlane has left us an exotic legacy. This includes a tomb-city, and the lovely Gur-i-mir (The Grave of the Sovereign), his mausoleum (1404). Its turquoise dome, shaped like a fig and with distinctive gadrooned ribbing, rises amid a flight of pigeons up to a lilac evening sky (*fig. 188*). Much of the calming influence that the tyrant's tomb has on the onlooker is due to the builder's proportioning of substructure, drum and dome according to strict aesthetic rules, so that they are in a perfect relationship of 3:2:2.

There is no doubt that much Islamic architecture was inspired by the effect strong sunshine has on shapes and carvings and stucco mouldings in relief, emphasising hollows, shadows, knife edges and raised areas and making them appear even more stunningly extravagant.

Occasionally in the story of architecture there occurs a particular person, place or building that we can point to as a milestone, saying *here* started such a style. In the transition from the first to the second half of the Middle Ages, that is from Romanesque to Gothic, we have such a milestone. The man is a Benedictine abbot called Suger, the place the Abbey Church of St-Denis on the edge of Paris, the year 1144 and the occasion magnificent—the consecration of the new abbey choir (*figs. 190, 191*), rebuilt after one of those disastrous fires so common when wooden roofs were vulnerable to lightning from without and to flares and tapers from within.

Abbot Suger belonged to the religious order that had for so long controlled Romanesque church building from Cluny. He was an important man in both Church and state, an adviser to kings and popes, a well-known theologian and a superb administrator. Before embarking on the rebuilding of St-Denis, he meticulously sorted out all the Abbey lands to ensure a stable income during the building period. And he set down on paper his thinking and aims in rebuilding St-Denis.

Suger's writings—a pamphlet on the *Consecration of the Church of St-Denis* and a *Report on the Administration*—present us with a rare description of the sources of Gothic architecture. His thesis was that 'the dull mind rises to truth through that which is material'; and his genius grasped how he could appeal at several levels to the dull mind by using the rib vault. He could create soaring arches which would draw the spirit of man up to heaven; he could transform walls into screens of glass which would teach the worshipper the doctrine and origins of his faith in picture stories while submerging him in celestial light. Anybody who has walked along the triforium gallery at Chartres Cathedral, bathed in the liquid fire of ruby and sea-green that flickers from the robes of the prophets, will know how successfully Suger's followers gave flesh to his vision. In church one was to have an experience of heaven on earth.

'This is the House of God and the Gate of Heaven', says the psalmist in the liturgy for the consecration of a a church, a liturgy systematized at this period (the Gothic mind was full of systems).

Suger caught the temper of the times, which were swinging away from the obsession of the early Middle Ages with life's grimmer aspects, sin, guilt and death, to a triumphant Church which had put down the Albigensian heretics and achieved romantic success in the Crusades. The view of God's world was now one of beauty and comparative safety, in which the ordinary man could rejoice. Nature was let loose on choir stalls, portals, canopies and chapter houses, in an

189 | *Chapel of the Holy Thorn (La Sainte-Chapelle)*, Paris, 1242–8

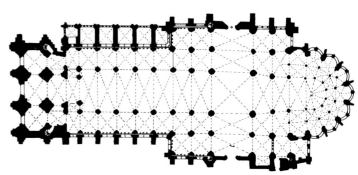

191 | *St-Denis*, plan

190 | *St-Denis*, Paris, 1144, choir

exuberance of tendrils and leaves, birds, animals and flowers. St Francis, founder of one of the new orders of friars, went around exhorting his brothers and sisters—men, women, animals, birds—to praise and exalt the Lord above all things for ever.

The French called this new translation of beauty into stone 'le style ogival', recognizing the debt its shapes owed to the East. But the name by which it has come to be known was the scornful soubriquet of 'Gothic', or barbaric, with which it was dubbed by the sixteenth-century art historian Giorgio Vasari. The prestigious congregation at the consecration of St-Denis, which included Louis VII of France and his Queen, 17 archbishops and bishops from all over France and from as far away

as Canterbury, did not see the style as barbaric. The soaring thin-ribbed vaults and walls, incandescent with the 'uncreated light of the Godhead', clearly impressed them. It appears that, on returning home, they all took the first opportunity proffered them by fire or by disrepair to build in Gothic. Within 25 years of the consecration, every diocese represented at the ceremony had raised a Gothic cathedral to the heavens.

What the new style offered in practical terms was the following. Liturgically, it preserved the basic cruciform plan with the altar at the east end, space for processions up the nave, and side chapels for celebrating private Masses. Structurally, it did away with the need for massive masonry, yet made possible higher and more varied vaults. Wall space thus freed could be used as a means of instructing the simple worshipper through sculpture, painting and glass. In this way, an architectural synthesis was created, coherent in structure and detail, and capable of inspiring a vision of ultimate truth and reality.

Yet not one of the features by which we distinguish Gothic architecture was new—not the pointed arch or window, nor cross-vaulting, flying buttresses or twin towers on the façade. What then was essentially Gothic in the way that these components were structurally combined in those cathedrals that followed St-Denis? One of the first things to be exploited was the freedom given by the pointed arch. In the semicircular Romanesque arch, height and width from

The Metaphysics of Light: *Medieval and Gothic*

a central point had, of course, to be equal, being the radii of the same circle. However, the pointed arch, having several different curvatures, could be varied in width and still retain its original height, thus making possible an arcade with some columns closer than others, yet all having the top of their arches at the same level. Furthermore, they could be varied in both height and width and joined at right angles to vaults which could also vary in height and width. Thus a low side aisle could give on to a higher transept, and the transept on to a higher and wider nave. The architects recognized a further possibility opened up by the pointed arch. They realized that by thinking of the main structural elements as cutting across the cathedral as well as running the length of it, they could send the main forces from the roof down to the aisles and then by way of flying buttresses to the ground. This made it possible to treat the outside walls no longer as structures holding things up but as panels which could be almost entirely glazed. The cathedral could now be a lantern of glass.

The pointed arch and all that it implied could coexist with the cruciform plan. In France a chevet could be punctuated by side chapels running round the east end behind the choir. The plan remained open-ended; nave and transepts could be added on to as needs dictated, and the monks' choir, behind the altar from which the daily office was sung, and chevet or side chapels, where each priest offered his private daily Mass, could be extended.

The basis of the whole design had radically changed from the Romanesque for this reason: builders no longer had to assemble the structure over a series of cube-shaped units of space. The space they were enclosing could now be widened or narrowed, and, above all, it could extend upwards. Vaulted roofs no longer planted their weight, heavy-footed, on the massive shoulders of the side walls; instead the weight swung down through simple arches built transversely and diagonally across each bay, like the ribs of an umbrella. Until recently it was thought that the ribs were carrying all the weight and transferring it through the buttresses to the ground. However, instances in the Second World War, where the ribs were destroyed and the infill sections (like the webbing between a duck's toes) remained standing, have shown that the structure depends on a delicate balance and disposition of loads and thrusts throughout the whole

192 | *Rheims Cathedral,*
1211–1481

prey to lightning, until Benjamin Franklin invented the lightning conductor in the eighteenth century. While the outer roof might be struck and would burn, the inner stone vault protected the church. In rainy weather, however, the roles were reversed; the wooden roof protected the shallower vault below. The roof also provided space for the hoisting-gear needed to heave the stones of the vault into position. That is why, as the vaulting became more complicated in the late Gothic English, German and Austrian churches, the roofs became steeper, like St Stephen's Cathedral in Vienna. There are medieval cathedrals which still shelter their hoisting gear between the two roofs.

Bit by bit, the Gothic builders learnt how much they could cut away from wall,

building. Villard de Honnecourt's 33-page parchment sketchbook (probably commissioned as a source-book for his masons' lodge), made in the thirteenth century, is a rich source of information about medieval building methods. His sectional drawing of the stately royal cathedral of Rheims (1211–1481; *fig. 192*), the site where the kings of France had been crowned since the fifth century, gives us some idea of the intricate problem of weight distribution, often adjusted as building progressed. Further clues to building methods are given by work guidelines that have been left on some sites. At York and Wells we have found the reusable plaster tracing-floor on which master masons drew out plans and diagrams for apprentices to follow. Renovation work on Westminster Abbey uncovered level boss stones at the point where the ribs of the vault meet, scored to show where the lines of the ribs were to come in.

It is surprising how often what we take to be mere ornamentation shows itself on further examination to be an integral part of this delicate balance of weights. The pinnacles on the top of the outer buttresses, for instance, are not just spiky decoration, but are built up to counter the thrust of the nave walls.

Nor did the double Gothic roof – wood outside and stone vault beneath – arise from mere whimsy. Tall buildings were a

arch or buttress without impairing the functioning of the structure. The beautiful but simple late twelfth-century spokes of the early buttresses at Chartres (*fig. 193*), had, by 1500, become a fretwork of traceried gables and buttresses such as those of La Trinité, Vendôme (1450–1500), and St-Maclou, Rouen (1436–1520). The more solid expanse of wall, exemplified in the early cathedral of Sens (1145), becomes increasingly aerated as greater confidence in the

194 | *Bourges Cathedral,*
1190–1275

195 | *Wells Cathedral*, west front, 1215–39

structure develops. In Chartres, a triforium passage is cut into the thickness of the wall; Bourges Cathedral (1190–1275), with its unique pyramid shape of nave flanked on each side by two aisles of decreasing height (*fig. 194*), is perforated right through to the outside from aisle to aisle; and in the Chapel of the Holy Thorn, built by St Louis in Paris, usually known as La Sainte-Chapelle (*fig. 189*), the translation from solid wall to glass screens is complete. Here the stone mullions that hold the glass together are so slim that one can hardly perceive them for the dazzle of the stained glass. What the architect of 1242 had in effect achieved was to take Suger's example to its logical conclusion. He extended the upper, glassed-in area of Suger's apse on the end of the choir at St-Denis and made this the whole chapel, glass right down to the ground, so that the building glows like a reliquary casket cut from a faceted jewel.

The paring down of solid walls meant that glass increasingly took over. Early Gothic windows were simple lancets, as at Coutances (1220–91), and in plate tracery, as at Chartres and the Basilica of St Francis at Assisi (1226–53), a geometric pattern was, as it were, simply punched out of the wall surface. In 1201, bar tracery

was invented: instead of the stone face of the wall being punched out into shaped holes, the glass was slotted into linear frameworks – stone mullions and window bars, carved into slim patterns as pieces of sculpture in their own right. These traceries are not fully appreciated from the inside, where the glory of the stained glass against the light claims all attention. But on the outside they take their place in an overall intricate pattern of lines and figures, which may cover the entire front of a Gothic cathedral, in the French manner at Rheims or Strasbourg (1245–75), or make a screen as if of carved wood in characteristic English fashion at Wells, Somerset (1215–39; *fig. 195*). Here the frontage 150 feet (46 metres) wide obscures all indications of the component units and is covered with 400 statues – a brave sight, no doubt, in the Middle Ages when all were painted and gilded, but today providing a major headache for the cathedral architects who are attempting to preserve the façade.

The basic early window-shape of two lancet lights, a circle poised between their tips and all enclosed in a pointed window frame, later became freed from the circumscribing shape like a plant

196 | *Milan Cathedral*, Italy, 1385–1485

growing and putting out tendrils. The circles shot out petals or rays in the energetic manner that was to give this phase of French Gothic the name of Rayonnant. In England patterns of trefoils and leaves developed along with geometric patterns to give the term Decorated to the corresponding phase there. From the end of the thirteenth century the leading ideas were to be found in England, whose Gothic period was to culminate in the staid upright dignity of the Perpendicular of the east end of Gloucester Cathedral (1337–77). But before this example of typically English aloof reticence, the Decorated phase became more extravagant in the Curvilinear style, which undoubtedly owes much to England's contacts with the East, through trade and the Crusades, giving us excitingly mobile forms that

reach their peak in the ogee traceries and carved hoods of the seats in the Lady Chapel at Ely (1321), a building set apart from the main cathedral in the manner of a chapter house. Even in the purity of the Perpendicular, where all the lines of the traceries are pulled upwards, straight and smooth within a vertical rectangular panel, there is more than an echo of the pishtaqs of Isfahan.

The fashions in Gothic were carried through Europe from Norway to Spain by the master masons, who travelled widely from job to job, so that by the fourteenth century they were referring to themselves as 'free' masons (although it should be mentioned that some historians think the term rather indicated that 'free' masons were qualified to work in freestone, that is, fine-grained limestone or sandstone that lent itself to carving). Charles VII of Bohemia snatched the opportunity of Prague's lucky escape from the plague to employ Matthew of Arras from Avignon and one of a famous family of masons, Peter Parler from Gmünd, on his new cathedral (1344–96). William of Sens built Canterbury Cathedral (1174–84); Etienne of Bonneuil went from Paris to work at Uppsala, Sweden; and a bevy of foreign experts from Paris and Germany worked on Milan Cathedral (1385–1485; *fig. 196*).

198 | *Church of the Convent of Christ*, Tomar, Portugal, 1510–14, west end

197 | *Burgos Cathedral*, Spain, 1220–60, star lantern

It was by such interchanges that the flowing English Curvilinear form of decoration came to the Continent, there to be translated into particular national versions from the fourteenth to the sixteenth century. In Spain it manifested itself in the ornate style known as Plateresque, from the much-chased silverwork of the time, for example Burgos Cathedral (1220–60; *fig. 197*). The Portuguese version, known as Manueline (*fig. 198*), often has a nautical flavour with knotted ropes and encrusted sea symbols, for, like the English, the seafaring Portuguese were embarking on world exploration. In Germany, English influence was far-reaching, as we shall see when we compare vaulting forms. And in France in her late blossoming – the Flamboyant of the churches of Rouen, for instance – it inspired traceries that whirl and lick across the windows like leaves tossed by an autumn gale or the flames of the bonfires that consume them. In the rose windows, one of the most glorious architectural forms in Gothic architecture (*fig. 199*), patterns changed across the years from wheels to roses, from roses to flames.

Clearly, trial and error played their part in the development of the vault. The early vaults were divided into four parts by the two hooped diagonal ribs that intersected at the boss stone. In the twelfth century, in Sens Cathedral, the rib number was increased to three hoops, so that the division of the vault became six. Closely

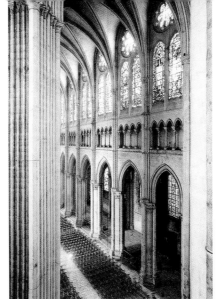

linked with the development of the vault was the question of height, an important factor in producing the verticality so characteristic of French Gothic. It is thought that individual masons' lodges each had their own rule-of-thumb as to the relation of height to width, but little more than that broad proportion was specified. If we compare the section of Rheims showing weights, buttresses and roof positions with the interior of Chartres, we have some insight into the factors controlling the building of vaults.

Chartres is the classic example of early French Gothic (*figs. 193, 199–201*). Its basic shape was built in 27 years, between 1194 and 1221; that is, all but its towers, which were built centuries apart, the simple octagonal south spire in the early thirteenth century, and the more elaborate north spire in about 1507; they were built, it should be noted, without any attempt to match the later to the earlier. However, it is not only in the matter of towers that Chartres is classic. Unlike the typical Romanesque church, built and financed by a great abbey, Gothic cathedrals belonged to the town. They were built not only in competition with neighbouring towns to the Glory of God, but also out of civic pride. As at St-Denis, much of the physical work was done by the parishioners themselves, peasants

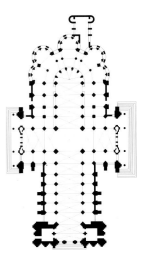

200 | *Chartres Cathedral*, interior, showing nave arcades, triforium passage and clerestory windows

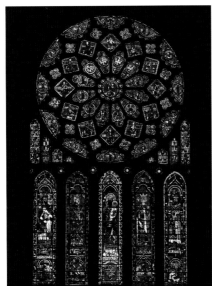

199 | *Chartres Cathedral*, 1194–1221, north rose window

201 | *Chartres Cathedral*, plan

202 | *Amiens Cathedral*, 1220–70

203 | *Bristol Cathedral*, choir, 1300–11

where even a fourth level, a gallery, was introduced, but that was a relatively short-lived fashion.

Between the windows are the flying buttresses, connecting with the piers of the vault. These piers are always slimmer than the smooth expansive boles characteristic of Romanesque columns, but in some of the earlier cathedrals like Laon (1160–1230) and Notre-Dame, Paris (1163–1250), the arcade is still made of single round columns, at least as far up as the capitals and the springing of the arches; it is only above that we find the characteristic Gothic clustered shafts resembling bundles of wands. However, from the building of Bourges onwards, in the thirteenth century, such clustered pillars became typical. In Chartres, Rouen, Soissons, Rheims, Amiens (*fig. 202*), Tours, Strasbourg, Auxerre, Cologne, Toledo and Barcelona and in many English cathedrals, the upward movement of the clustered piers, like a fountain, starts from the floor and spurts, unfettered, into the roof vaults. The style reaches its pinnacle in the choir of Bristol Cathedral of 1300–11 (*fig. 203*), where not so much as a capital causes a break in the upward surge.

Just how high they could shoot upwards without overreaching themselves had to be learnt from experience. Beauvais Cathedral, whose bishop is said to have suffered from the sin of pride, courted disaster: the double-aisled choir (begun around 1220), probably built by Eudes de Montreuil, a master mason who accompanied St Louis on his Crusade, speaks volubly of ambition, as does its soaring vault. And sure enough first the roof, and later the tower, fell. Nevertheless, rebuilt at nearly 158 feet (48 metres), it remains the highest Gothic vault.

But regal Rheims Cathedral drew herself up to 125 feet (38 metres) without incurring heavenly displeasure. Inside, the sensation of height is cleverly

dragging the carts with stone from the quarries, tradesmen and craftsmen laying down their tools and deserting other jobs to meet the wagons at the town gate and pull them to the cathedral site.

Structurally, Chartres provides the classic three-storey model: an *arcade*, or row of arches, down either side of the nave, supported on piers; a middle row of arches, often quite low and frequently with a walkway, running round the inside of the church, called the *triforium*; and an upper row, or *clerestory*, that is heavily glassed. Figure 200 shows the two great sources of light: first, from the side aisles, filtering through the nave arcades, and secondly, from the clerestory. The triforium runs inside the roof-space of the aisles and has no outlets to the exterior. There are examples where the triforium is pierced through to give light, and some

The Metaphysics of Light: *Medieval and Gothic*

204 | Henry VII's Chapel, *Westminster Abbey*, London, 1503–19

exaggerated by making the bases of the pillars shoulder-high, so that, standing in the aisle, one is dwarfed by the pillars before they even commence their upward climb. The unusual pyramid-shape of Bourges, with its double side aisles of decreasing size, masks its height; it is only when you go into the inner aisle and look upwards and note that it has its own arcade, triforium and clerestory as if it were a nave, that you realize the very aisles swoop up to a vault as high as that of many a cathedral nave.

All things, says St Thomas Aquinas, should be ordered towards God, and so the clustered shafts draw the eye in two directions. Firstly they quicken and flicker towards God-made-man in the sacrament of the altar at the east end of the church; secondly, they carry the eye upwards, to God-in-heaven, as in a copse of slim birch trees, where one naturally looks up to where the sunlight is filtering through the leaves. In contrast to the barn-like

austerity of the preaching-churches of the friars in Germany and Italy, we find the occasional late Gothic church, like Brunswick Cathedral (1469), where (to carry on the metaphor) the copse becomes tropical forest, with extravagant shafts spiralling like tendrils up to star-shaped serrated capitals which then burst into a canopy of palm-leaf vaulting – brightly painted, what's more!

Some countries emphasized verticality on the exterior. Germany and Bohemia, particularly, liked towers; the soaring spire of Ulm Minster, designed by Ulrich Ensinger at the end of the fourteenth century, but not completed until 1890, was the highest of all.

But impetus in the development of pillars and vaulting came from England. In France, the classic period ends in about 1300, and there is a gap before the flourishing of the Flamboyant. The first half of the fourteenth century (before the Black Death killed a quarter of the population in 1348–9), was a particularly rich period in England. During this time there emerged window, vaulting and roofing styles which were to be highly influential in Europe.

In England Gothic started quite humbly when the Cistercian orders

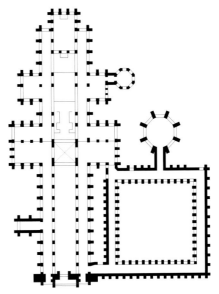

205 | *Salisbury Cathedral*, 1220–66, plan

167

settled there, establishing sheep farming and the woollen industry that were to provide the source of much of her wealth during the middle Ages, as well as international contacts through her membership of the Wool Staple. Durham (1093–1133) had early experimented with pointed arches along with the round-headed Romanesque. But the classic French cathedral pattern, apparent in Canterbury, Lincoln (rebuilt after 1185) and Henry VII's Chapel at Westminster (built later, but consciously modelled on the French; *fig. 204*), was introduced when

206 | *St Wendreda's*, March, Cambridgeshire, angel roof, 15th century

a French architect was recruited by the Chapter of Canterbury Cathedral. William, a native of Sens, a city then engaged in building a cathedral, persuaded the Chapter that the Norman remains, unsafe from a fire in 1174, should be scrapped and the project started afresh; and so, up until the time that he was injured falling off a scaffold and had to pass the work to another architect, he built at Canterbury a cathedral similar to the one at Sens.

But the native tradition, which can be traced back through the Norman Romanesque to the Anglo-Saxon church of St Lawrence, Bradford-on-Avon (*fig. 157*), doggedly persisted, however fashionable French ways were. It was this

more rugged tradition which gave English Gothic its original characteristics – square-ended choirs without chevets (a direct continuation of the Saxon plan), exaggeratedly long naves, as at Lincoln, and sometimes double transepts. Most characteristic of all, in contrast to the astringency of French plans, where everything is economically drawn together within one over-all outline, English cathedrals have no concentration of space, but scatter their component units around in irregular patterns. If you look at all those differently shaped structures on the plan of Salisbury (1220–66; *fig. 205*), for example, and remember that they all have to be roofed, it is not difficult to understand that experimentation in roofing and vaulting emanated from England.

There was another factor that encouraged English builders to experiment in roofing. Britain had always been to the fore as a seafaring nation, and was given to making full use of wood from the forests which still covered much of the land – land often owned by the Church. It takes no feat of the imagination to see the similarities between the upturned keel of a boat and the vaulting of a church. All over England at this time, village churches sprang up, many built to the highest standard. Between the Conquest and the Gothic Revival of the nineteenth century, at least 1,000 parish churches were built.

Apart from the use of a rich variety of local materials – different stones, brick, flints and tiles – their roofs and silhouettes are an interesting feature. There is an enormous variety of towers and spires, which are often bell-towers, particularly in the coastal areas, where the bells could be used to give warning of invaders; and inside there is a marvellous use of wood, both in the rood screens on which the *rood*, or cross, was carved or painted, and above all in the roofs.

The wooden structures, which bear names like trussed-rafter roofs, tie-beam

roofs, collar-braced roofs and hammer-beam roofs, were to provide important ceilings in many of the grand secular buildings of the late Gothic period, demonstrating a continuing link between structure and beauty at a time when stonework decoration had ceased to have functional significance. In villages like March in Cambridgeshire, one can chance on a hammer-beam angel-roof, in which the hammer-beam construction sends the weight of the roof-beams through the struts on to cantilevered-out hammer-beams, and marvel at the sheer beauty of the flight of angels (*fig. 206*).

When those wooden techniques were translated into stone, the ribs on the vaulting were multiplied, far beyond structural necessity, so as to create a decorative web of carving comparable to the intricate work that was being developed in the window traceries. These extra struts have lovely names: *tiercerons* are the ribs that fan out from the wall shafts to meet the ridge, forming palm-tree shapes, as at Exeter Cathedral (1235–40), while the small decorative struts between the ribs, visible in the roof of Ely Presbytery (1335) are called *liernes*. After that, ribs proliferated in English cathedrals, and were rapidly adopted and further exploited on the Continent, notably in Germany, Bohemia and Spain, and later even in the originally simple wide hall-churches (the *Hallenkirchen* of Germany) which were popular with the friars because of their potential for preaching to large congregations. There

207 | *Cloth Hall*, Ypres, Belgium, 1202–1304

208 | *Carcassone*, France, 13th century, restored 19th century

was the skeleton vault, where the ordinary structural ribs are themselves supported by a separate series of detached vaults, seen in miniature in the Easter Sepulchre Chapel, in Lincoln. Perhaps the most thrilling examples of star vaults are in Germany. German masons brought the complex vaults to Spain, where they culminated in the star lantern of Burgos Cathedral (1220–60; *fig. 197*). Net vaults, where the structural hooped ribs are interrupted to make lozenge and triangle patterns, provide another development.

In England there appeared the beautiful fan vault, the chief beauty of King's College Chapel, Cambridge (1446–1515), and of Henry VII's Chapel, Westminster (1503–19). A fashion peculiar to England, it was to retain popularity and develop well into the Jacobean period with extended pendant central bosses.

Gothic architecture was by no means without effect on secular buildings. Its influence was felt towards the end of the fourteenth century, several centuries later than with the cathedrals. In the first half of that century, life was too hard for attention to focus on aesthetic matters. Famine resulting from a series of bad harvests in the early part of the century had left a population without resistance to the regular epidemics of disease (1,400 people are said to have died in three days in Avignon at one point) that led to the Black Death of 1348–50. A papal inquiry estimated that it killed about 40 million, a quarter of the population of Europe. But from then onwards, whether because the weather improved or because there were fewer mouths to feed, standards of comfort began to pick up. An interest in intellectual matters emerged, which was later to blossom in the individuality, learning and commerce of the Renaissance.

The castle was the major example of Gothic in secular building. Its story is typical of the changes of the time. After gunpowder (invented between 1327 and 1340) became effective, the castle underwent several stages of evolution. The superb defensive fortifications based on the expertise of the Crusaders gave place to castles which still retained the trappings of a fortress, but whose defences were never put to the test; then came castles which retained their defences largely for stylistic reasons; and eventually there developed the fortified and moated manor-houses of England and ultimately the Renaissance palaces.

Towns also developed as trade increased. We have seen that the great Gothic cathedral belonged to a town or city, just as the great Romanesque abbey belonged to the country. Now there was another important development: the parish church. In the new atmosphere of prosperity, towns, rarely with more than 5,000 to 10,000 inhabitants, were granted charters to run markets, and market-spaces appeared, usually under the shadow of a cathedral or parish church. English towns had market crosses, from where the town-crier proclaimed the news. Many still survive, like the fine octagonal Poultry Cross in Salisbury, with its ogee ribs and crown on top.

With increasing trade, other buildings appeared round the market area–town halls, craft and merchant halls and trade exchanges, some of whose high towers indicated that the secular world was competing with the Church in daily life. The Silk Market at Valencia (1426–51) had a high vault and twisted pillars. The magnificent Cloth Hall at Ypres (1202–1304), with its 440 feet (134 metre) long façade, took one hundred years to complete (fig. 207). Although destroyed in 1915, it was so much loved that it was rebuilt. The half-timbered Guildhall at Lavenham, Suffolk, was built in 1529 during a boom in the wool trade. Few such structures were more elaborate than the beautiful Merchant Adventurers' Hall in York (1357–68) with its lovely timbering. Prosperous ports of the Hanseatic League of wool importers, like Hamburg, required harbours, wharves, customs houses and warehouses. Rich merchants built themselves beautiful houses; taverns appeared, so did theatres like the famous Globe Theatre in London, where some of Shakespeare's plays were enacted.

Some buildings developed from religious organizations and were associated with charity, like almshouses and hospitals, or with education, like the cathedral schools. But the new universities were symptomatic of a growing tendency towards independence from the Church. Neither the law school at Bologna, part of the ancient university founded in the eleventh century, nor the medical school at Salerno were associated with cathedrals. Oxford University is said to have originated from a Church–State quarrel, when Henry II, furious that archbishop Becket took refuge from him in France, decided that English students should be barred from attending the university in Paris. Architecturally, the university derived from monastic buildings, its quadrangle for walking and reading

209 | *Beaumaris Castle*, Wales, 1283–1323

mirroring the cloisters around which the monks walked and prayed. The chapel, the great hall which functioned as a refectory, and of course the library were also monastic in origin. Stairs leading to the fellows' study-bedrooms were built into the corners of the courtyards. Ablutions in these venerable and civilized surroundings may today still be some distance away in a back alley as they were in the fourteenth century.

Some great houses which were to become the homes of the rich started out under the aegis of the Church as the homes of bishops, the princes of the Church. They could be very grand, like the papal palace at Avignon (1316–64), where the popes lived during the Great Schism (1378–1417). With a defensive fourteenth-century city clustering around it, the papal palace shared with many other castles the feature of being not one building so much as a fortified town. This is also true of Aigues-Mortes, of 1240, a grid-plan town with about 150 towers around its massive walls, and of the Emperor Frederick II's early thirteenth-century Castel del Monte, Bari, Italy.

Carcassonne in south-west France is a walled town which shows the increasing

pride in symmetrical defences (*fig. 208*). Frederick II (ruled 1212–50), who was brought up among Roman remains in Sicily, set the fashion for symmetrically arranged fortifications which seem to have derived from ancient Roman forts. His castle at Prato (1237–48), and the original Louvre palace, built by Philip II in the thirteenth century, moated, with a round central keep with pointed turret, were designed symmetrically, as were other châteaux in France and above the Rhine in Germany. Characteristically these castles were protected by water – sea, river or moat – above which walls rose sheer and usually sloping inwards, with rounded corners so as to foil any besiegers' attempts to tunnel under and blow a breach across the corner angle with gunpowder. Probably the best-preserved remains of castles from this period are in Britain. They include the 'perfected' castles built by Edward I in the thirteenth century to subdue Celtic revolts in Wales – Conwy, Caernarfon, Pembroke, Harlech, Beaumaris. Beaumaris (*fig. 209*), with its double curtain walls and outer moat, and two massive gateways each with four towers, two large and two small, one facing inland and the other out to sea, is as symmetrical and as

210 | *Stokesay Castle*, Shropshire, 1285–1305

comprehensively organized for defence as any. It was the last castle Edward I built, and was supervised by James of St George, Master of the King's Works in Wales. The early Norman Tower of London (1076–8) has a similar unity and coherence, although it has been changed and rebuilt in parts at later periods.

Domestic arrangements were complex at this time, with provision in different wings or towers for the private life of families whose business made them live in the castle. Fireplaces still in the walls and the relationships of suites of rooms within a great castle like Castle Bolton in Wensleydale, Yorkshire (begun *c.*1378), where Mary, Queen of Scots was imprisoned, bear testimony to the tenement aspect of castles of this time.

Where a single family owned the castle, the standard arrangement was a central hall, used as living-space by both family and servants, going up through two storeys, with, grouped round it on one or two floors, bedrooms, garderobes or lavatories in the corners, kitchen quarters, a chapel, and sometimes a solar or private room. This arrangement, sufficient but simple, can be seen in the lovely moated manor house, Stokesay Castle in Shropshire (*fig. 210*). It was built in the late thirteenth century and today, drowsing among ducks, wallflowers and gillyflowers, looks far from warlike. The great hall has been preserved for

posterity by having been used as a barn.

In England, the progression from castle to manor house was through the L-shaped plan of great hall and tower, to the T-plan, where two-storey dwelling-quarters were set at right angles to the hall, and finally to the arrangement whereby a second wing was added on the other side to form an H-shape, so that the lord's family could inhabit one wing and the servants the other, with access to each other only through the hall. The staggered entry, a defensive feature, persisted for a long time.

In country and in town, the rich were buying themselves a civilized life and creating houses decorated with great beauty and refinement in a Gothic style which might betray their national origins. We see that in the very French Gothic house of a merchant, Jacques Coeur, at Bourges (1442–53)–with its decorated façade (*fig. 212*), fretwork balconies, fireplaces carved like little windows, statues of ladies and gentlemen leaning out to chat to their neighbours across the way, knobbly pinnacles and canopies of the sort that characteristically appear in the background of fifteenth- and sixteenth-century stained-glass windows. Equivalent forms of all these details could be

213 | *Doges' Palace*, Venice, 1309–1424

found on the façade or the furniture of late Gothic cathedrals. That kind of Gothic detail was to persist in France for some time, amalgamating with Renaissance detail and arrangements in rich houses and châteaux. France was the country most loath to relinquish the Gothic style, which had provided her period of greatest architectural glory.

A translation of English Gothic detail from religious to secular use can be seen on a house of social standing similar to that of Bourges – the house of the wool merchant William Grevel, who died in 1401 in Chipping Campden, Gloucestershire (*fig. 211*). On the bow window on the street façade, slim stone mullions connect ground- and first-floor ranges of windows in a distinctly Perpendicular-style panel. The country house of the abbot of Forde, Dorset, of 1521 is an elaboration of this style.

But the most splendid of the merchants' houses are those in Venice, the palazzi on the Grand Canal, and above all, that of the Doges, or heads of the Republic (*fig. 213*). Here the simple massing is complemented by the delicacy of the double row of arcades and discretely patterned rose and white marble on the upper storey, reminding one that Venice

214 | **Jan van Pede**, *Town Hall*, Oudenarde, The Netherlands, 1525–30

215 | *Palazzo Pubblico*, Siena, Italy, 1298

was a great trading centre that looked eastwards.

Distinctively national forms of Gothic manifest themselves not surprisingly in the town halls, the first secular expression of local civic pride. Germany and the Low Countries were well to the forefront and expressed their commercial dignity in characteristically steep-pitched roofs, often cut into with dormer windows, and combined with narrow decorative towers. Jan van Pede's Town Hall at Oudenarde, Brabant, of 1525–30 (*fig. 214*), displays the integrity of a great work of art. Its bottom arcade, two rows of Gothic windows, lacework parapets, steep roof and central crowning belfry have a total harmony of proportion and decoration. Less successful was the fourteenth-century top-heavy belfry that sticks up – not merely like a sore thumb but like a sore thumb swathed in successive layers of bandaging – over the town hall of Bourges, built in the fifteenth century. There is a similar contrast between the unusual curved façade in stone and brick and slim bell-tower of the Palazzo Pubblico of Siena (1298; *fig. 215*) and the Palazzo Vecchio in Florence, which was started only one year later, an ungainly prison-like block with a clumsy torch-like belfry stuck on top, perhaps in the vain hope of emulating the beautiful striped campanile of the Cathedral.

And so we find ourselves at the transition from Gothic to Renaissance appropriately in Florence, where Renaissance architecture began. It is there that we start the next chapter of our story.

Architectural periods are never neatly bounded. So much do movements overlap that a mason working on Milan Cathedral (the greatest and according to some the only true Gothic cathedral in Italy) in the 1420s could have travelled to Florence 150 miles (240 km) away and found work there on a cathedral that represented a quite different attitude towards design. The work in question was the dome of Florence Cathedral (1420–34; *fig. 216*), and its architect Filippo Brunelleschi (1377–1446), who had trained as a goldsmith, was revolutionizing design and taste.

There had, of course, been domes before, like the Pantheon in ancient Rome (*fig. 120*). This one was different. Brunelleschi fitted a dome on top of an octagonal drum, and made no attempt to use pendentives. He invented a complicated wooden form, around which his eight-panelled dome could be built in two layers, an inner and an outer masonry shell. Also different was the fact that the masonry ribs were tied together in a series of reinforcing 'chains' at strategic points in the form of bands of timber or stone clamped with iron. The cupola on the top was a temple of masonry acting as a weight holding the rather pointed dome together and preventing it from spreading apart.

That dome was by no means Brunelleschi's only or his most revolutionary contribution to the new move-ment. His Foundling Hospital of 1421 (*fig. 217*), simple and serene, with graceful arcades of round-headed arches above slim Corinthian columns, plain rectangular windows directly above the centre of each arch and simple triangular pediment, was another inaugural building of the Renaissance. As for the chapel he created for the Pazzi family in the cloisters of the Franciscan friary of Santa Croce (1429–61; *figs. 218, 219*), it was not only perfect, but it was also a copy-book for Renaissance buildings.

In the first place, the Pazzi Chapel, entered through a tall arch in the loggia, was a revolutionary shape–no longer a nave and aisles, but a square covered by a dome, this time using pendentives The centre of the chapel was the centre of the circle below the dome; the building seemed complete from every direction. Furthermore, the dimensions were all exact: the square of the chancel below the dome was half the total width. And the atmosphere was created by a very precise treatment of the wall surfaces, with decorative bands on the walls, arches and floor in a darker tone, indicating the proportions. Brunelleschi's two great churches, San Lorenzo (1421–) and Santo Spirito (1436–82; *fig. 220*), had basilican plans, but the same exactitude was there and domes were used at the crossings.

This kind of architecture came to dominate first Europe, then much of the

216 | View of Florence from the Belvedere showing the dome of the *Cathedral*, 1420–34, by **Filippo Brunelleschi**

world, for many centuries, and it is still to be found today. What had caused the transition from Gothic to Renaissance? On the one hand Gothic seemed played out. Every architectural style is bound at some time or another to reach a stage when it can no longer yield anything new. On the other hand, important changes had been taking place in society, especially in that section of society that employed architects.

Gunpowder changed the nature of warfare and therefore relations among nations. The invention of the compass and the development of new techniques in shipbuilding made it possible to expand the limits of the known world into China, the East Indies, India and America. Banking, no longer frowned upon by the Church, began to play a central role in society. Trade and banking made Florence rich. The hereditary nobles of feudal times were ousted by a new class of merchant princes – such as the Medici, the Strozzi, the Rucellai, the Pitti – whose commercial empires spread throughout Europe.

Merchant princes and the artists to whom they extended financial patronage became the new universal men of the Renaissance. Piero della Francesca's famous profile of Federigo da Montefeltro, Duke of Urbino (ruled 1444–82), with its basilisk eye and hooked nose, does no justice to this renowned art-patron. Ruler of a little mountainous northern Italian kingdom, the Duke was a man of principle, gentleness and humanity. He was a distinguished soldier, but the Palace of Urbino (c.1454–; *frontispiece*), built for him by Luciano Laurana (1420/5–79), a contemporary of Alberti, accurately represents the artistic side of his nature. The castle dominates the pantiled hilltop village. In the state-rooms and courtyards (one lined with a loggia based on the Foundling Hospital, another sheltering a secret garden with access from the Duke and Duchess's apartments) scholars, philosophers, musicians and artists gathered, discussed and created. The Duke was himself accomplished in all these areas. He collected one of the finest libraries in Italy, now part of the Vatican

217 | **Filippo Brunelleschi**, *Foundling Hospital*, Florence, 1421, courtyard

218 | **Filippo Brunelleschi**, *Pazzi Chapel*, Santa Croce, Florence, 1429–61

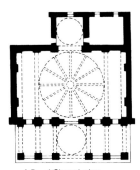

219 | *Pazzi Chapel*, plan

Library, employing, it is said, thirty or forty scribes for fourteen years to copy the great classical and modern texts.

The key to a new vision of human life and therefore of architecture came from the scholars' access to these classical texts. International trading exchanges had helped to disseminate ideas, and a group of teachers of the humanities (grammar, rhetoric, history and philosophy), who acquired the name of Humanists, played a crucial part in their propagation. These texts were spread through developments in printing. Printing was invented long before in China, but in Europe a tremendous impetus was given to the spread of ideas by Gutenberg's invention of movable type in 1450. The first printed Bible was in 1456. And architectural texts followed.

In 1415, G.F. Poggio Bracciolini, a papal secretary, had produced an improved version of the text of Vitruvius, based on a manuscript which he had discovered at St Gall in Switzerland. Now, in 1487, Vitruvius was one of the first writers to appear in print. The impact of this new means of communication was tremendous. The architectural theorists of the revived antique style – Alberti, Serlio, Francesco di Giorgio, Palladio, Vignola, Giulio Romano – all wrote treatises that

owed something to Vitruvius. These men were no longer master masons, however brilliant; they were scholars. Architecture was no longer the continuation of a practical tradition, handed on through masons' lodges; it was a literary idea. The architect was not just putting up a building; he was following a theory.

The architect had at his disposal some exciting new discoveries. A new concept of spatial relationships had been made possible by the discovery of perspective by the Florentine painters in about 1425, or possibly by Brunelleschi himself. On top of that came one of those revelations that give a sudden unity to experience and open up a whole new realm of meaning. That was the rediscovery of Pythagoras's theory that musical intervals in harmony were exactly proportional to numbers in physical dimensions. This was something that totally captured the imagination of the Renaissance. If harmonic ratios could be the same as physical ratios, not only was there a rule on which to base proportions but also music and architecture were mathematically related, and nature was displaying a wonderful unity. Thus it followed that a building could reflect in its dimensions the fundamental laws of nature and of God. A perfectly proportioned building would thus be a revelation of Godhead, a reflection of God in man.

The architect who brought such

220 | **Filippo Brunelleschi**, *Santo Spirito*, Florence, 1436–82

theories together in practice was Leon Battista Alberti (1404–72). He was himself the ideal Renaissance man. An accomplished horseman and athlete, of whom it was said he could jump a man's height with both feet together, he painted, wrote plays and music and had written a treatise on painting before he produced what was to become one of the essential books of the Renaissance. His *De re aedificatoria* (*On Architecture*), begun in the 1440s and published in 1485, was the first architectural book to be printed. He explained the theory of beauty based on the harmony of numbers and used Euclidean geometry to lend authority to the use of basic shapes – the square, the cube, the circle and the sphere – working out ideal proportions from these figures by doubling and halving. And he produced one of the crucial architectural statements of the Renaissance in defining beauty in a building as the rational integration of the proportions of all the parts, where nothing could be added or taken away without destroying the harmony of the whole.

One further aspect of Alberti was crucial to architecture and characteristic of the Renaissance – an interest in the powers and talents of the individual man. Man was, of course, as the medieval Church had stated, 'created in God's image and likeness'; but now the emphasis shifted: man assumed a new dignity in himself. Knowledge of the classics, geometry, astronomy, physics, anatomy and geography suggested that man had godlike capabilities. The humanists resurrected the adage of the ancient Greek philosopher, Protagoras, that 'man is the measure of all things.' Alberti, in laying down the conditions for the creation of a perfect church by combining ideal forms, believed that this would mean making a material image of the Godhead. And this ideal form had a human face. Vitruvius, in Book III of *De architectura*, had suggested that a building should reflect the

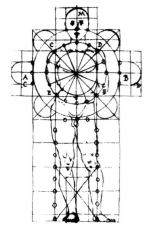

221 | **Francesco di Giorgio's** human figure superimposed on centralized cruciform church plan

proportions of the human figure, and Leonardo da Vinci developed this idea in his famous drawing relating human proportions to the ideal shapes – the square and the circle; Francesco di Giorgio's diagram related them explicitly to the architecture of the time – a centralized Greek-cross plan with extended nave superimposed on a man's body (*fig. 221*).

Alberti's buildings are some of the landmarks of the Renaissance. To the church of Santa Maria Novella in Florence he added a façade (1456–70), strictly proportioned, which is one of the

222 | **Leon Battista Alberti,** *Sant' Andrea*, Mantua, 1472–94

most memorable of all elevations. To link the nave and the lower aisles without sacrificing the horizontal layout characteristic of the new style, he designed huge scrolls which were to become part of the vocabulary of later architects. He created most of the facade of Sant' Andrea, Mantua (1472–94; *fig. 222*), out of a triumphal arch. Here emerges the ancient Roman ABA motif, which was to appear in a hundred guises on Renaissance buildings – low arch, high arch, low arch; pilaster, window, pilaster; turret, dome, turret. In the Palazzo Rucellai (1446–57; *fig. 223*), he used different orders for different floors – Doric, Ionic and Corinthian – as the Romans had done on the Colosseum. They were all very carefully proportioned. An interest was also revived at this time in Vitruvius's idea that certain orders were suited to certain types of buildings – the Doric for masculine buildings – law courts and churches dedicated to male saints; Ionic for

philosophers, scholars and churches of matronly saints; and Corinthian for churches dedicated to the Virgin Mary and young female saints.

The Palazzo Rucellai was only one of the many Florentine palaces that became a new building type. They usually presented uninviting façades to the street, using rough masonry on the lower floors, known as 'rusticated' masonry, a word meaning 'countrified', for the stones were not smoothed off, but deliberately left rough-hewn as if they had come straight from the quarry. At the top, Alberti introduced a huge, jutting cornice which virtually hides the roof. Again this tended to become typical Renaissance, giving a concentrated boxy outline to a palace. The largest of all the Florentine palaces, the Palazzo Pitti (1458–66), whose author is not known, makes a feature of the ground-floor windows by having a whole unit within an arch of rusticated masonry. If the outside of a Renaissance palace was forbidding, once inside the courtyard all was different; the prison-like exterior gave way to a scenario for gracious, hospitable and elegant living for very rich people (*fig. 224*).

Florence was the first of the three great Italian cities to foster the new style. The second was Rome and the third Venice. The phase from 1500 onwards, which reached its climax encouraged by papal patronage, is known as the High Renaissance. The architectural events in

225 | **Donato Bramante**,
Tempietto, San Pietro in
Montorio, Rome, 1502

Rome were at first not unlike what had happened in Florence. Of the Renaissance palaces, the Cancelleria, whose architect is unknown, built from 1486 to 1498 for Cardinal Riario, nephew of Pope Sixtus IV, marks the move of the hub of architectural enterprise from Florence to Rome. The elements are still apparent as the guidelines for the beautifully proportioned Palazzo Farnese commenced by Antonio da Sangallo the Younger in 1541 and finished off by Michelangelo. A tunnel-vaulted passage plunges through the central doorway into the courtyard, and on either side are similar ranks of windows with straight cornices on the ground floor, while on the first floor the pediments above the windows alternate between triangular and round-headed segments.

The architect who dominated the early years of the High Renaissance in Rome was Donato Bramante (1444–1514). He grew up near Urbino, became a painter, spent some time in Milan, where he certainly knew Leonardo da Vinci, and came to Rome after Milan fell to the French king, Louis XII, in 1499. He had already shown the influence of Alberti in his work in Milan, but it was the work of the last twelve years of his life, in which he seems to have become imbued with the spirit of the ancients, that gives him his place in history.

The building most closely following Alberti's prescription for pure classicism was the little temple Bramante built in 1502 on what was then thought to be the site of St Peter's martyrdom, the cloister of San Pietro in Montorio, on the Janiculum Hill. The Tempietto (*fig. 225*) is consciously modelled on the ancient Roman temple of Vesta. Free-standing within its courtyard, with steps rising to a circular plinth, its form is a drum encircled by a Doric colonnade, trimmed with a low balustrade, through which the drum reaches up and is crowned with a dome – possibly architecture's finest gem. Its internal arrangements obey the rules, with high-placed windows showing blue skies, but are otherwise of little account. It is designed from the outside, and has that peculiarly dense quality of High Renaissance architecture, lacking the modelling of the interior in terms of space and light which we associate with the styles which were to follow. Yet it is not heavy, nor proud and intimidating like the palazzi. The wide-spaced colonnade on its raised plinth and the cut-out

balustrade around the upper storey have all the charm, elegance and delicacy that you could ask of an ideal building.

Bramante's remarkable achievement was that, while the proportions of this building were in such harmony that it seemed that nothing could be added or subtracted without ruining the whole, its original conception has proved immensely flexible, for it has been successfully copied throughout the world. It was the inspiration for Gibbs's Radcliffe Camera in Oxford (1739–49), Hawksmoor's Mausoleum at Castle Howard, Yorkshire (1729), and the domes on St Peter's, Rome (1585–90), on Wren's St Paul's Cathedral, London (*fig. 277*), the church of St-Geneviève (the Panthéon), Paris (*fig. 289*), and even the Capitol, Washington DC (*fig. 312*).

The building which symbolizes all the spiritual pomp and worldly power of Renaissance Rome is, appropriately, St Peter's (*fig. 227*). The old basilica dated from 330 AD and was built on what had been the Circus of Nero, where St Peter's martyrdom took place, beside an obelisk from the upper Nile which had been erected on the site in 41 AD, before

227 | **Donato Bramante**, **Michelangelo** and others, *St Peter's*, Rome, consecrated 1626

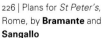

226 | Plans for *St Peter's*, Rome, by **Bramante** and **Sangallo**

228 | **Michelangelo**, staircase to the *Laurentian Library*, San Lorenzo, Florence, 1524

Nero built his circus. This obelisk, 84 feet (25.5 metres) high, had in due course to be moved–a feat of engineering which took six months and was conducted by Domenico Fontana (1543–1607).

Nor was the building of the cathedral easily accomplished. It involved many plans and major disputes on structural theory. The foundation stone was laid in 1506, but the building was not completed until over a century later, in 1626. The builders sound like a roll-call of the High Renaissance: Bramante (who was 60 when the work started), Raphael, Peruzzi, Sangallo the Younger, Michelangelo, Vignola, della Porta, Fontana and Carlo Maderna (1556–1629).

Bramante's original plan, which he and Leonardo da Vinci may well have discussed (Leonardo's sketchbook shows a design for a cathedral on a Greek cross-plan with five domes), was a Greek cross superimposed on a square with a central hemispherical dome supported on four massive piers (*fig. 226*). Each symmetrical arm of the cross protruded in an apse beyond the square, allowing for four small Greek-cross side chapels, each roofed with a little dome, to be tucked into the angle of the arms of the big cross, with a tower on each of the four corners of the square. Bramante

experimented with Roman concrete for the enormous piers and the great arches–far larger than any other used in this period. Raphael took over from him, but contributed nothing of great import. It was Giuliano da Sangallo (1445–1516) who brought the work on a step further (*fig. 226*), by strengthening the pillars and building the nave vault and pendentives to support the dome. He changed the designs for the dome from the classical hemisphere to a segmental one with ribs, some 30 feet (9 metres) higher than Bramante had intended.

But the dome, eventually completed by Giacomo della Porta (c.1537–1602) and Domenico Fontana (1543–1607), was in fact designed by the 72-year-old Michelangelo, painter, sculptor and

229 | **Michelangelo**, *Medici Chapel*, San Lorenzo, Florence, 1519

military engineer, who had turned architect in his old age. He returned to Florence for his inspiration, and to Brunelleschi's dome. The structure he designed has strong similarities to the Florence dome: it is made in two shells, it is mostly brick internally and its shape is of orange-peel segments supported by ribs held together with three iron chains.

What was Michelangelo's contribution? With a sculptor's eye for the three-dimensional, he bypassed the contemporary preoccupation with proportion to open up new concepts of scale and space–two areas in which the Baroque was later to experiment. It was, after all, through sculpture that he had come to architecture. He provided the setting for his sculptures of figures representing Night and Day, Evening and Dawn, around the chapel built on to Brunelleschi's San Lorenzo in Florence to house the tombs of the Medicis (1519–; *fig. 229*). But his stature and originality became apparent only a few years later in his designs (1524) for the Laurentian Library adjoining San Lorenzo (which was eventually to be completed with some modifications by other architects). The task here was to design a library in a long wing, where access was from a vestibule on the lower level. He made no attempt to re-create the balanced proportions of

the Renaissance. On the contrary, he exaggerated the disparity of the two elements, by running a long low room off the upper part of a high, narrow block. A popular late Renaissance Mannerist trick, as we shall see, was to emphasize perspective by lines in moulding and decoration so as to create a room, a court or a street like a tunnel. Vasari uses it cleverly in his courtyard to the Uffizi, Florence (1560–80), which sucks the visitors along and through the ABA gateway to the Arno beyond. Michelangelo managed somehow at the same time to provide a light-filled, calm atmosphere essential to the reading-room that has become the model for a host of university libraries since. The anteroom, with its triple staircase and pillars halfway up the wall supporting nothing, but indicating the upper storey, is quite original (*fig. 228*).

Another Michelangelo hallmark, to be widely adopted by Palladio and others, was the creation of giant orders, that is to say, columns running up through two or more storeys, sometimes the entire height of a façade. They are best seen on the palaces that surround the Capitol in Rome, whose reshaping Michelangelo began in 1539. It was the sorting out of a cluster of very down-at-heel palaces here that gave Rome one of her most exciting vistas. On the spot where Romulus and

231 | Baldassare Peruzzi,
Palazzo Massimo alle Colonne,
Rome, 1532–

Remus are said to have been discovered, and where Romulus founded the city, Michelangelo created a wide, shallow-stepped ramp rising to pass between antique statues of Castor and Pollux, protectors of Rome, to a trapezium-shaped piazza. A star in white stone spreads cosmic rays out across the paving in an oval pool of ripples – the first use of this shape in Renaissance architecture. On the Palazzo del Senatore (completed 1600), which closes the top of the square, and the two marching palaces to the left and right, giant orders and pilasters link several storeys together.

Michelangelo's original use of classical motifs introduces a new phase in the Renaissance, Mannerism. This late sixteenth-century style deliberately flouts classical prescriptions. Jacopo Sansovino (1486–1570), Baldassare Peruzzi (1481–1536) and Sebastiano Serlio (1475–1554) were among its exponents. The greatest Mannerist figure, Giulio

Romano (1492–1546), a pupil of Raphael and the first Renaissance artist to be born and raised in Rome, could play the classical game with as much ease as anybody. In fact, he expended as much intellectual exertion on breaking the rules as he did on keeping them, in, for example, the Cathedral at Mantua (1545–7). What the Mannerists did with classical detail was really a sort of in-joke. When Romano dropped a few wedge-shaped stones below the architrave in the courtyard of the Palazzo del Tè at Mantua (1525–34), built for Duke Federico Gonzaga II, he knew perfectly well that he was not actually making the structure unsafe, but he hoped it might make the uninitiated gasp with shock (*fig. 230*). The ruses reached fever-pitch in his Cortile della Cavallerizza of the Palazzo Ducale at Mantua (1538–9), with its pock-marked rusticated arcades and giddy columns, like mummies attempting to struggle out of their wrappings.

A more serious Mannerist building is the Palazzo Massimo alle Colonne in Rome, which Peruzzi started to build in 1532 (*fig. 231*). It has a revolutionary façade, for it is curved. It is broken in the middle by an irregular portico, formed by a pair of columns, a space and a single column, on either side of the entry to a recessed front door. The first-floor row of windows in the upper wall is unexceptional, but the two rows above are horizontally rectangular holes cut out of the façade, framed, as it were, in stone picture-frames, of which the lower row have scrolled curves like sheets of parchment. The interior of the courtyard is much more impressive, while still maintaining an oddly modern appearance. At one end, an open loggia composed of two large single Tuscan columns, well spaced, shows an open hall with the passage of the front entrance leading away behind, and stairs going up on the left. The loggia is repeated by the balcony on the floor above, through whose pillars a coffered ceiling and a

doorway beyond can be glimpsed. The total façade is much bolder and less regular than one would expect, extending beyond the private jokes of Mannerism and suggesting an impetus towards a new, broader canvas similar to that shown in Michelangelo's work.

The other great Mannerist architect was Giacomo da Vignola (1507–73), whose church for the Jesuit order, Il Gesù (1568–84; *figs. 232, 233*), became the type for many later churches. The west front was built by della Porta, but was based on Vignola's designs. But it was Vignola's pentagonal Palazzo Farnese at Caprarola (1547–9), incorporating many original features, like the circular open staircase off the circular cortile at its heart, terraces and oval paired steps, gardens and moat, that marked his work as some of the most imaginative and spectacular of the period.

The third centre of Renaissance architecture was Venice and its surrounding region. There the commanding figure is Andrea Palladio (1508–80). He was a

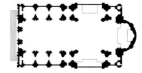

232 | *Il Gesù*, plan

233 | **Giacomo da Vignola** and **Giacomo della Porta**, *Il Gesù*, Rome, 1568–84

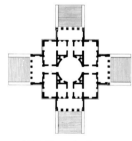

234 | **Andrea Palladio**, *Villa Capra (Rotonda)*, Vicenza, 1565–9

235 | *Villa Rotonda*, plan

precise and exact classicist. In his Villa Capra (Rotonda) near Vicenza (1565–9), a symmetrical building, he created an ideal place for a secular purpose, closely following Alberti's rules and spirit (*figs. 234, 235*). He controlled the classical rules – not they him. It was as if he distilled the essence of classicism from the Vitruvian rules and the ancient models, and held the pure and colourless liquor up to the light. His buildings have the hallmark of elegance: the same ability that a diamond has – to be cool, and, simultaneously, to sparkle. Except for two churches in Venice, his buildings are around Vicenza. They are secular, reflecting the new importance of secular rather than religious buildings that makes the architectural character of the sixteenth century onwards different from what had gone before. Undoubtedly aided by the

dissemination of his architectural treatise, *I quattro libri dell' architettura* of 1570, his work had an enormous influence in other countries, notably on the Georgian architects in eighteenth-century England, Thomas Jefferson and other architects in America, and in Russia. It is tempting to describe him as a symbol of the classical style, since he exhibits the two most prized qualities of Renaissance architecture: exactitude and centralized plans. But it is the effortless manner in which he achieves this that gives his buildings the humanity sometimes lacking in strict, formal classical buildings.

If we look at the plan of the Villa Rotonda, with its circular room covered by a dome set within a raised square, approached on all four sides by even flights of steps, we can guess that it was not particularly comfortable to live in. We

The Scale of Human Perfection: *The Renaissance in Italy*

236 | Andrea Palladio,
Il Redentore, Venice, 1577–92

shall see how Jefferson dealt with this problem in his version at Monticello (*fig. 309*). Its symmetry may undermine its comfort, but there is no questioning the beauty and dignity of its exterior and the view of the countryside it commands.

With the Basilica (Palazzo della Ragione) in Vicenza (1549), Palladio gave Europe one of its most popular architectural motifs, the Palladian motif, a central arched window or opening flanked by a flat-topped window on each side. It became one of the most widely used and effective features of great houses for several centuries. In his many other villas it was his extension of a regular plan to embrace outbuildings and the landscape that gave a lead to the landscaping movements of the eighteenth century. Rarely has an architect whose work was concentrated in such a relatively small area had such a world-wide influence upon buildings and their surroundings.

Palladio's two churches in Venice were San Giorgio Maggiore (1565–1610) and Il Redentore (1577–92; *fig. 236*). The latter, situated on the edge of the Giudecca Canal, was built by the Venetian government in thanksgiving for the end of a particularly virulent episode of the plague. It is dedicated to the Redeemer, whose annual feast in July is celebrated with fireworks over a sparkling traffic of lit-up boats. This strong and arresting building has a dome, set between little pointed turrets, that rises above an extraordinary west front made up of a series of interlocking temple fronts. This composition, which also uses both giant and minor orders, is so original it goes beyond Mannerism–it is unique.

Italian Renaissance forms were slow in crossing over the Alps. When it happened, the sixteenth-century Mannerist challenge and seventeenth-century Baroque theatricality were already opening up new fields of interest in Italy. Throughout most of this period the rest of Europe was still preoccupied in working through the national forms of Gothic they had evolved. Nationalism was emerging. In 1519, three monarchs, Henry VIII of England, the Habsburg Charles V of Spain, whose possessions included much of Italy and German principalities, and François I of France all laid claim to the title of Holy Roman Emperor. Henry VIII's daughter Elizabeth established England as a power of consequence in Europe and beyond when she sent her pirate knights across the Atlantic to explore the New World. Spain and Portugal, briefly united under Philip II, were also intent on extending their realm of gold in the Americas. As for France, successive ministers – Richelieu, Mazarin and Colbert – built up the absolutism of their monarch until Louis XIV (1643–1715) could style himself Le Roi Soleil (the Sun King) and say: 'L'état c'est moi' ('The State, I am the State').

All of this affected the changes in architecture. Before Louis XIV's time, François I had transferred his capital from the hunting lodges and the easy aristocratic life of the Loire Valley to hard-centred and politically conscious Paris.

The king's court became the administrative centre of French life – not just for law and commerce, but also for the arts and the basic services – roads and canals and even forestry. Architects were among those whose status was affected: Claude Perrault (1613–88), who was working on a new wing of the Louvre Palace in the 1660s, formally became a civil servant. England too made architectural status official; the king had long had his master mason, but in 1615 Inigo Jones received the title of Royal Surveyor.

Nationalism was not the only thing working against the import of Italian ways from the sixteenth to the eighteenth century; there was also the question of religion. To the northern countries that had embraced Protestantism, the Catholic temperament demonstrated in the later Italian Renaissance held no attractions; in some cases it actually repelled. Europe at this period was racked by religious conflict and wars.

What happened to the architecture of those countries was simply this. Mannerist Italian architects might enjoy themselves breaking the rules. Beyond the Alps this did not apply. For these people not only did not know the classical rules, but also did not know that there were any rules to break. Slowly, Renaissance details, patterns and structures filtered through, first into France and later throughout Europe. They were

237 | *Galerie François I*, Fontainebleau, France, decorated by **Francesco Primaticcio** and others in the 1530s

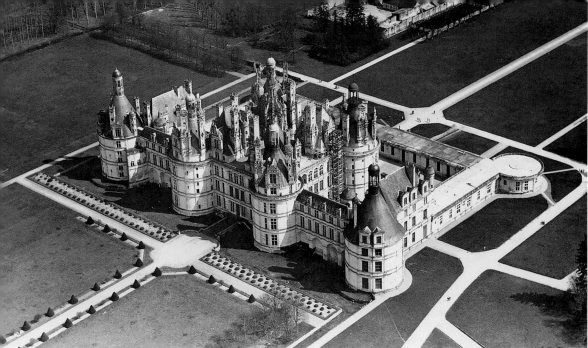

238 | *Château de Chambord*, France, 1519–47

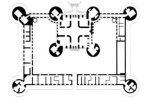

239 | *Château de Chambord*, plan

sometimes adapted, but often they were simply copied and added on quite incongruously to buildings which were still fundamentally Gothic in style.

One of François I's châteaux on the Loire, Chambord (1519–47; *figs. 238, 239*), is a case in point. At first glance, the symmetry of its plan seems perfectly respectable from a Renaissance point of view. It shows a square within a rectangle, although not concentrically placed. As with Italian palaces, the inner courtyard, surrounded on three sides by wings, is reached through a centre doorway on the front façade. But at Chambord, two-thirds of the entry façade is just a screen, and it is only the central block, the *corps de logis*, which is the actual living quarters for the family. We now see that the plan is basically that of the English Gothic castle: the *corps de logis* is the keep, the courtyard the bailey, but so well integrated is this in Renaissance symmetry that we can only fully spot it from the air or in plan when we note that there are corner towers on the corners of the courtyard and on the four corners of the *corps de logis*.

Apart from the symmetry, what other Renaissance elements can we identify? There is an arcade along the ground floor,

and horizontal rows of windows above. But while on an Italian palace each storey of windows may be different – perhaps with a different order, or one row with double or coupled columns on each side of the windows, the next with perhaps only an intermediate pilaster – here the windows are equal, and so placed that they create vertical stripes up the façade which are quite as assertive as the horizontal divisions. And what about the roof? Far from melting away behind a parapet, here are steep northern slopes, dotted with dormer windows. On the corner turrets and especially over the central *corps de logis*, there is a host of Renaissance detail in the form of gables, chimneys, lanterns and crowns. But would any Italian skyline ever permit such a mixture of shapes to jostle so violently against each other? It is like a market-day crowd; one can almost hear the hubbub. That rooftop is very medieval and very French, no matter how its architect, Domenico da Cortona (the only known of many architects involved), tried to disguise it with sophisticated Italian trappings.

And what do we make of the little miracle of engineering, the unique double spiral staircase (*fig. 240*)? It is a free-standing

240 | *Château de Chambord*, double staircase

241 | *Château de Blois*, France,
north-west wing, 1515–24

cage of stone placed at the crossing of
the Greek-cross hallways within the
square *corps de logis*. It rises through the
elliptical barrel-vaulted ceiling and up to
the central lantern on the exterior. If the
supporting piers have something in common with Gothic buttresses, its ingenious
planning (so that people entering or making a getaway might not see each other
as they pass on the same stairs) could
only have been fathered by Renaissance
intrigue. In fact, Leonardo da Vinci made
a sketch for just such a staircase.

Leonardo was only one of several
Italian artists who made their living in
France, having been recruited by François
I to his court. He died 25 miles (40 km)
away from Chambord, in 1519, the year
they started building the château. The
wars in Italy between the Emperor
Charles V and François I of France were
one reason for his move. François I's
patronage was an enormous draw, for it
ranked second only to that offered by the
papal court. Sebastiano Serlio (1475–1554),
a Mannerist whose writings were to have
an impact in Europe, came to the French
court in 1540 and stayed until his death.
He designed the château at Ancy-le-Franc
in 1546 on a somewhat similar layout
to Chambord, only really giving way to
French taste in the matter of the high,
steep roofs, and even here he dispensed
with the dormers. (Roofs were very
important to the French, one kind of roof
is even called after the architect François
Mansart who invented it – the *mansard*
roof with a steep boxy side to it that
allows the architect to stuff virtually a
full-height row of rooms into it.)

242 | **Philibert de l'Orme**,
screen (*jubé*), *St-Etienne du
Mont*, Paris, 1545

In 1532 arrived the painter Francesco Primaticcio (1504–70), a friend of Giulio Romano with whom he had worked on the Palazzo del Tè. He made the Galerie François I inside the Château of Fontainebleau sizzle with vitality (*fig. 237*). Here was the first use of strapwork – stucco shaped like curled leather – which was to prove one of the most popular and characteristic motifs of the transalpine Renaissance, particularly in the Low Countries and in Spain.

François I was an important patron of the Renaissance forms. He commissioned much of the Renaissance work on the palaces of the Loire, Chambord, Blois, Fontainebleau and, after the move to Paris, the Louvre. The Bohiers, a bourgeois family of financiers, commissioned the châteaux of Chenonceaux (1515–23; *fig. 244*) and Azay-le-Rideau (1518–27). Chenonceaux consisted of a simple *corps de logis* descended from the Gothic keep, until Philibert de l'Orme (1514–70), at the command of Henri II's mistress, Diane de Poitiers, added, in 1556–9, a ravishing five-bay bridge in white stone, along which Jean Bullant later (1576–7) added a three-storey gallery to preen and admire itself in the ripples of the blue-green water. At Blois it is undoubtedly the north-west wing (1515–24), full of Renaissance motifs, that François added to the château Louis XII had begun in 1498, and the later south-west wing (1635–9) by François Mansart (1598–1666) that excite the attention. The north-west wing is emphatically horizontal with an arcaded gallery along the garden front. Here again, built into an octagonal

243 | *Ottheinrichsbau*, Heidelberg Castle, Germany 1556–9

tower, is a sophisticated open spiral staircase (*fig. 241*).

But the coming and going of artists was not the only way in which Renaissance ideas filtered through to the rest

of Europe. Some ideas were expressed on paper, in the pattern-books that were being produced in abundance in Italy. Since most transalpine architects had never seen the ancient ruins nor their Renaissance derivatives, they were very dependent on these books, and too often, with no true understanding of the classical revival, they used them as a bran tub, dipping in and picking out ideas and employing them at random. Sometimes, where an architect had individual flair, an extraordinarily effective marriage of disparate elements took place.

Philibert de l'Orme, on the basis of pattern-books and a few brief visits to Italy, was capable of such inventiveness.

244 | *Château de Chenonceaux*, Loire, France, 1515–23, with the bridge by **Philibert de l'Orme**, 1556–9, and the gallery by **Jean Bullant**, 1576–7

245 | **Claude Perrault**, *Louvre*, Paris, 1665, east front

In the Church of St-Etienne du Mont, Paris, he built in 1545 an incredible screen called a *jubé* with a balcony across an unaltered Gothic nave (*fig. 242*). It could be reached from either side by a swelling, curving staircase. The breathtaking charm of the screen owes its sweeping concept to Renaissance freedom of approach, yet when we look at it closely we realize that the fretwork patterning is Gothic in origin.

But not all transalpine architects had de l'Orme's genius. Many misapplied the orders, transplanting them out of context,

246 | **Elias Holl**, *Arsenal*, Augsburg, Germany, 1602–7

with no reference to structure, proportion or scale. So the Renaissance effect was often only skin-deep. Matters were not helped when pattern-books of decoration only, separate from their architectural basis, started to go the rounds, mostly in the Low Countries and in Germany. Cornelius Floris (1514–75) and Vredeman de Vries (1527–1606) of Holland were two such authors; Wendel Dietterlin of Germany, who published his in 1593 and was said to be demented, was another. The writhing fantasy, verging on a Bosch-like phantasmagoria, that Dietterlin would project on to a flat wall surface gave the kind of effect to be seen on the Otthein-richsbau in Heidelberg Castle (1556–9;

fig. 243). It is as clotted with writhing figures as a Hindu gopuram.

There is another basic drawback to the learning of styles from books, namely, that prints are two-dimensional. At this time, we must remember, many architects were still coming into this field of work from outside. Francesco Primaticcio was a painter, Inigo Jones a designer of masques; Claude Perrault, who built the later wing on the Louvre (*fig. 245*), was actually a doctor. Relationship of outside to inside, which makes for truly great architecture, is not easy to achieve; not all architects are capable of thinking in three dimensions. Some façades that have evolved from copy-book plates, however originally these have been employed, retain a flat appearance which can render them very dead. The Louvre has this copy-plate flavour about it, even though Perrault made history by treating a tall ground floor as a podium on which to build a first-floor loggia of giant coupled columns.

Luckily the story at this point is brightened by the odd original. Elias Holl (1573–1646), City Architect to Augsburg, came back from a visit to Venice in about 1600 with a taste for Mannerism. A contemporary of his, Jacob van Campen (1595–1657) built a Town Hall at Amsterdam (1648–65) that was sufficiently grave and classical to be transmuted into a royal Palace. But Holl in his Town

247 | *University of Salamanca*, Spain, doorway in the main façade, 1514–29

248 | **Juan Bautista de Toledo** and **Juan de Herrera**, *Escorial Palace*, Spain, 1562–82

Hall at Augsburg (1615–20) took the bold step of adopting, as Cornelius Floris did at Antwerp, a council room that ran right through the top floor; moreover, Holl filled his with light from windows placed on both sides and by painting it white. Even more original was what he did with the Arsenal at Augsburg (1602–7; *fig. 246*). In a masterly way, he retained the tall narrow height so characteristic of a German house, traditionally set gable-end on to the road. But the Arsenal looks you proudly in the eye, in spite of the extremely mannered way in which window frames are wrenched apart on either side of the window, and its gable end culminates in a broken pediment with the oddest bulbous ornament in the middle.

The same conflict between an undiscriminating adoption of motifs and a serious attempt to build in the classical idiom can be seen in other countries. In Spain,

the Plateresque or silversmith's style of elaborate and close decoration in low relief on a flat wall surface was carried over from the Gothic of Queen Isabella with no pause—merely a further mixture of motifs. The incrustation of a seafaring scene, which we saw on the outside of the convent at Tomar, is reiterated, with the addition of strapwork and other devices, on the classical doorway of Salamanca (1514–29; *fig. 247*), the university that had nurtured so many humanists.

It was in Spain that there occurred the most bleak expression of religious feeling; it had its roots not in reformist puritanism but in Counter-Reformation Catholicism (as well, that is, as emotional desiccation on Philip II's part). Pope Pius V was deeply ascetic and zealous in his clearing up of the libertine Church of Renaissance Rome. The spirit of penitence spread to the Emperor, Charles V, who in 1555 abdicated to live out the rest of his life in a monastery. His son Philip II followed the architectural style of his father, shunning the elaborate forms being developed in Italy, and in 1562 began to build a palace that centred around a chapel and included a monastery and a college. There was no room here for private Mannerist jokes or any hint of relaxation or pleasure.

The Palace is called the Escorial (*fig. 248*) since it is built on a slag-heap on the lonely rolling plains 30 miles (48 km) from Madrid. It dominates the surrounding

249 | **Robert Smythson**, *Wollaton Hall*, Nottinghamshire, 1580–8

250 | **Diego de Siloe**, *Escalera Dorada*, Burgos Cathedral, Spain, 1524

indicates the changing social and economic climate of the time. Whereas in the Middle Ages the bulk of building was ecclesiastical, now the stock of secular building started to increase. In the Catholic countries during the Renaissance, about half the new buildings of any stature were used for religious purposes, the other half for secular. In the Protestant areas, with their emphasis on commerce, secular far outweighed religious. One reason for this was that since so many churches had been built in the Gothic period there was no need for more.

During this time in England, compact but sizeable houses mushroomed, often built to house the rich merchants. The half-timbered wooden houses of Weobley, Herefordshire, and the stone houses of the Cotswolds in Gloucestershire, a rich wool-producing area, are good examples. The E and H plans, to be found in the Tudor and Jacobean periods, now widened out. The middle section of the H was filled to create a distinctive house type that was less dependent on Gothic or Renaissance influences than on its own needs. The Elizabethan house at Longleat in Wiltshire (1572–), for which Robert Smythson (1536–1614) was mason, set the tone for that distinctive English type of building, striped vertically down its wide frontage with slightly projecting bay windows, and emphasized horizontally with slim string-courses separating the ranks of mullioned windows. In a country where it was important to let in as much light as possible, new techniques in glass-making were promptly incorporated into the new designs. Clear glass, known in the Roman Empire, was rediscovered by the Venetians in the fifteenth century, and glass-blowers brought it to England in the sixteenth. During the sixteenth and seventeenth centuries windows got larger and larger, until of another Smythson house it could be said 'Hardwick Hall, More glass than wall'. The same was true of Wollaton

village as that other palace at Urbino did, but in a very different way. The gaunt cliff of its podium base, with rows of windows higher up, suggests at first that it could be a prison. Its high severe walls enclose a symmetrical complex of courtyards and buildings, in the centre of which a classical portico with a pediment identifies the position of the domed chapel which replaces the Holy of Holies in Solomon's Temple, on which the palace was modelled. That this bleak, bloodless appearance was intended we know from recorded instructions given by Philip to his architect, Juan de Herrera (c.1530–97), who took over from the original designer, Juan Bautista de Toledo (d. 1567). He demanded 'simplicity of form, severity in the whole, nobility without arrogance, majesty without ostentation'.

In more bourgeois parts of Europe, where prosperous middle-class housing was springing up, a smaller palace design was demanded of the architects. This

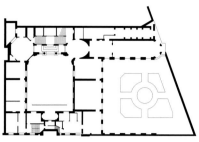

Hall, Nottinghamshire (1580–8), also built by Smythson (*fig. 249*).

Bay windows and the sharply jutting bays called oriel windows were popular. Perhaps England was more concerned with her women-folk and their comfort than were other countries; there was great play with windows and built-in window seats, where the ladies might sit and sew, and, another English peculiarity, long galleries running the length of the house on the first floor, where the ladies might promenade when the weather proved inclement. Then in the seventeenth century sash windows with chequered window-bars came to England from Holland. Their name derives from Dutch *sas*, sluice, and French *chassis*, frame. They were universally adopted and arranged in rectangles and squares one above the other, to impart the later characteristic verticality to the English Georgian terraced town-house.

Chimneys connecting with enormous hearths shaded by handsome chimney-pieces had always been important in England. Tudor houses also went in for marvellous skylines: twisted, chevroned, clustered and proudly single chimney stacks, turrets, crenellations and Dutch gables abounded, and persisted in English taste for many years. It is such details, in a period of domestic growth, that determine not only the plan but also much of the character of a house.

Stairways, for example, were highly expressive of the architectural character of the age. The medieval stair had been little more than an enclosed ladder, or, in the case of castles, a stone spiral enclosed in a turret. Now, in sixteenth-century Spain, experiments in the development of new stair types were taking place. There were three types: stairs that spiralled around a usually rectangular stair well; T-shaped stairs where the bottom flight split into two arms moving off to left and right (this form has almost unlimited variations according to stair shape, angles and balconies, for example in the Palazzo Farnese at Caprarola and the Escalera Dorada of 1524 at Burgos Cathedral, by Diego de Siloe, *fig. 250*); and stairs set around a rectangular well, with each successive flight bending sharply back to run parallel to the lower flight. This type makes its first appearance in the Escorial. To these Palladio added a fourth type: a free-standing flight fixed to the wall at one end only and supported on an arch. This last pattern was made good use of in street scenery, perhaps most excitingly in stair-bridges over canals in Venice.

The adoption of the first type of stairs, starting immediately within a hall at the front door, spiralling around an open well and lit from above by a cupola or skylight, established the pattern for English town houses built after the Great Fire of London of 1666 and up to the twentieth century. They were tall narrow houses, at first with only a few rooms on each floor, in Queen Anne's reign, sometimes with only one to the front and one to the back. Later in the eighteenth century, in the gracious version of Georgian Britain, notably in the three capitals, London, Edinburgh and Dublin, the family living-rooms were on the first floor. The dining- and sitting-rooms were often connected by folding doors, hence the term 'withdrawing' or 'drawing-room' – the room to which one withdrew after dinner. Houses were entered from the street, usually up steps which arched over the basement area and servants' entrance. Behind the basement, there was a straight strip of garden between walls.

In France the layout of the town

252 | Houses by the Amstel, Amsterdam

houses called 'hôtels' was much less uniform in regard to the number of floors and patterns of accommodation. A central gateway in the street façade, with a concierge on guard, very commonly gave access to a courtyard around which lay service wings, stables and later coach-house wings (*fig. 251*). Behind the far side of the courtyard was a formal walled garden. The later development was to set the living quarters across the back of the service courtyard, with the salon and display rooms overlooking the garden behind. More modest were some early terraced planned schemes like that of Henri IV's Place de Vosges (until 1800 called the Place Royale) of 1605–12. It consisted of quiet, practical houses of brick, with stone window surrounds and quoins (corner edges) and dormers in the mansard roofs, laid out in a scheme alongside his new Pont Neuf, which joined islands in the Seine–the first Paris bridge to have no houses on it. In Brussels, the Grand' Place surrounded by guild houses was built after the siege of 1695. It was the last example of the public square that was once standard in medieval Flemish towns, and has a typical Low Countries Renaissance collection of Gothic decorative detail mixed with porticoes supporting balustraded balconies, restrained pilasters and pedi-

mented gable-ends, some with a clutter of urns and shells added at a later date.

In the seventeenth century, Holland was the place for the mature creation of Renaissance town housing on a large scale. The houses along canals, such as the Prinsengracht in Amsterdam, are tall and narrow, built in a terrace with their gable-ends on to road or canal. But they are not uniform. The narrow frontage announces few rooms per floor. Unlike the English, the Dutch, constrained by the canals, retained into the twentieth century the steep narrow enclosed flights of stairs of the Middle Ages. The corollary was large windows, for furniture had to be hauled into upstairs rooms on ropes. The Prinsengracht was the fashionable street for noblemen, the Heerengracht

253 | **Jacob van Campen**, *Mauritzhuis*, The Hague, Netherlands, 1633–5

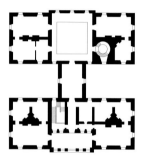

for gentlemen, but many humbler streets are equally charming, with their rising and dipping skylines of curved gables (*fig. 252*). The interiors of some of these houses, with patterned floors in black and white tiling and the distinctive contrasts of light sources with smudged shadow, have been preserved in the paintings of Vermeer and Pieter de Hooch. Similarly varied skylines were created elsewhere in Europe, for instance in the old Moravian town of Telc in the Czech Republic.

It was Holland that produced outstanding examples of another very northern translation of the Renaissance: small palaces, neat and compact which yet retain dignity and elegance. Such is the Mauritshuis in The Hague–a small-scale palace beside a lake, built in 1633–5 by Jacob van Campen (*fig. 253*). Its rooms are set symmetrically about a central stairway, and the exterior is given an appearance of natural and quiet imperiousness by the use of giant pilasters. The inspiration for these buildings was, of course, Palladio. But the Dutch discovered a scale fitting for both dignity and domestic comfort. Such Palladian buildings are so complete and contained that they fulfil Alberti's prescription that the proportions of all parts should be so integrated that nothing can be added or taken away without destroying the harmony of the whole.

The same qualities and the same influence are apparent in England in the work of Inigo Jones (1573–1652), who discovered Palladio on a journey through Europe at the age of 40, and became so enamoured that he covered the flyleaf of his copy of Palladio's *Quattro libri dell' architettura* with attempts to make his signature like that of his hero. Before becoming interested in architecture, Jones had excelled in designing costumes and theatrical effects for the mythological masques beloved of James I and his court. Perhaps by this time he had had enough of excesses; at any rate he took his new art very seriously. After he was appointed Royal Surveyor, he returned to Italy for serious study. In the Queen's House at Greenwich, the Banqueting House in Whitehall, and Wilton House in Wiltshire, he conceived both plan and façade in a Palladian unity of proportion and design. In all three he used the cube. 'The outward ornaments', he wrote, 'ought to be solid, proportionable according to the rules, masculine and unaffected.'

The Queen's House (1616–35), the first English villa in the Italian style, was originally built, by a whim of Queen Anne of Denmark, in two wings of three cubes each, connected by a bridge that straddled the main London to Dover road. After Jones's death his pupil, John Webb, added two further bridges in 1662 to make the total building a cube; later the

256 | **Inigo Jones**, *Banqueting House*, Whitehall, London, 1619–22

road was re-routed and long, flat-roofed colonnades were built where the road had been, to connect the two wing pavilions (*figs. 254, 255*). The rooms are beautifully proportioned, and the framed Tulip Staircase, whose wrought-iron balustrade is composed of swaying tulips, spirals upwards in a breathtaking curve, delicate as the whorl of a shell. The Banqueting House in Whitehall (1619–22; *fig. 256*) was built to replace the Old Banqueting Hall that was destroyed by fire. Rows of Ionic and Composite columns on the classical exterior suggest that it is two-storey, but inside there is one superb double-cube room, with a gallery at first-floor level, and a magnificent ceiling painted by Rubens. It was from the upper windows that a platform was built out into Whitehall for the execution of Charles I.

Briefly imprisoned by the Parliamentarians in the Civil War, Inigo Jones was released to work with John Webb on the reconstruction of Wilton House after a fire in 1647. Here there are two state rooms, a single and a double cube, the latter with white and gold décor to show off a collection of portraits by Van Dyck (*fig. 257*). To balance the excessive height demanded by the double-cube proportion, Inigo Jones used what is known as

a coved ceiling, where a deeply curved section joins the walls to the ceiling. Here it is richly painted and delineated with gilt swags of fruit.

The wealth and diversity of inspiration in Renaissance architecture escalated into an even more richly spectacular movement in the seventeenth century – the Baroque.

257 | **Inigo Jones**, *Wilton House*, Wiltshire, double-cube room, *c*.1647

In Italy, the Renaissance return to classicism lasted for 200 years. During the second half of this period, as we have seen, there was a growing dissatisfaction with the strict, rational ordering of the elements of building, which was the essence of the style; people had begun to find it mechanical, boring or constricting; the quest for the ideal and for perfect equilibrium no longer seemed significant.

Beginning where Michelangelo left off, a new generation of Roman architects abandoned the antique and threw themselves into an art that overspilled all established boundaries and conventions. Some people consider this effusiveness bad taste and speak of Baroque architecture as decadent Renaissance. We can see what is meant by this if we look at the extreme form that developed in Spain, in the work of a family of stuccoists called Churriguera. The sacristy of La Cartuja (Charterhouse) at Granada (1727–64; *fig. 259*), shows this incredible style at its most prolific, with an embarrassment of mouldings in white stucco, repeated three or four times like a series of little pleats or folds. Others respond to Baroque as the artists intended them to: they involve themselves in the drama and excitement that the artists sought to communicate, and are carried away by the infectious vitality of the art. For those who respond in this way, the Baroque period constitutes not a distasteful exhibition of excess, but the glorious fulfilment of the Renaissance.

Artistically, the Baroque was a very rich movement in painting, sculpture, interior decoration and music. The Renaissance proper had not concentrated especially on music; but now the Baroque countries led the field. It was from the curved walls of Italian churches that the Mass settings of Monteverdi and Vivaldi first reverberated, and from the palace salons of Germany and Austria, from gold-legged chairs between walls decorated with white and gold stucco and beneath ceilings crowded with tumbling figures trailing draperies in rich blues and reds, that the chamber music of Haydn, Mozart and Bach was played. It was probably about this time, too, that the process of composing music to fit the room was reversed and a start was made on the science of acoustics in architecture. Rooms were built that had the reverberation time that music required. Theatre made a comeback at this period, and opera, which had originated in Italy at the end of the sixteenth century, came into its own and spread throughout Europe as a popular art form.

This exuberant architecture, starting in Rome, was at first confined within a territory which included Italy and Spain, Austria, Hungary and Catholic Germany. France really came into the story only at the end of the period, in the first decades

258 | **Egid Quirin Asam**, *St John Nepomuk*, Munich, 1733–46

259 | *La Cartuja (Charterhouse)*, Granada, Spain, 1727–64

Younger (1654–1728). What the original Baroque countries had in common is that they remained Catholic after the Reformation.

The Jesuits, the spearhead of the Counter-Reformation, who planned their missionary forays with all the care of a military campaign, recruited some of the leading exponents of the Baroque movement. In *The Architecture of Humanism* Geoffrey Scott suggests that it was a piece of conscious (and brilliant) psychological insight on the part of the Jesuits to use the exciting forms of the Baroque to 'enlist in the service of religion the most theatrical instincts of mankind'.

And unquestionably Baroque was dramatic. The adjective applies to all the things by which we distinguish Baroque from Renaissance architecture. Brunelleschi, it is said, desired to please, Bramante to ennoble. But both were very concerned with whether their work was correct. Neither of the third or fourth Bs by which we can remember the founding fathers of the Renaissance's stylistic phases, Bernini and Borromini, had any such concern. The Baroque has no pedantic desire to teach, no moralistic desire to judge if the finished object is up to standard. It seeks only to carry us away with emotion.

Baroque architects deserted symmetry and equilibrium to experiment with new and vigorous massing. We can see this in the Belvedere, Vienna (*fig. 260*), built in 1720–4 for Prince Eugene of Savoy by Lucas von Hildebrandt (1668–1745). The Belvedere has a wide, expansive

of the eighteenth century, with the elegant form of interior decoration called Rococo. On the other hand, parts of the Holy Roman Empire – southern Germany, Austria and Hungary – were to produce many of the richest and most magnificent examples of Baroque, like the abbey church at Rohr near Regensburg (1717–22), the abbey church of Ottobeuren (1748–67), and the pilgrimage church at Vierzehnheiligen (1743–72), in Germany. Several German provinces and the Vorarlberg in Austria became nurseries of craftsmen-builders, sculptors and stuccoists, and there are lavishly decorated Baroque palaces in Russia and Scandinavia, like the Royal Palace in Stockholm (1690–1754) by Nicodemus Tessin the

260 | **Lucas von Hildebrandt**, *Belvedere Palace*, Vienna, 1720–4

261 | **Matthaeus Pöppelmann**, *Zwinger*, Dresden, 1711–22

window-patterned façade, low-domed turrets at the sides and a dramatic stepping roof line, all pulled together by the great centrepiece with giant triple-arched doorway and giant curving pediment. It is symmetrical, but not with any pompous regularity. We can see similar banked-up massing, with detail converging to a central point, on many other places. There is the Stupinigi at Turin (1729–33) by Filippo Juvarra (1678–1736), which, although a mere hunting-lodge, has a ballroom three storeys high; the Zwinger, Dresden (1711–22; *fig. 261*), a pavilion by Matthaeus Pöppelmann (1662–1736), whose upper floor is an open gazebo topped by an ornate crown lantern and whose crazy festivity tells all the world of the flamboyant purpose for which it was built – as orangery, play-house, art gallery and background to the great open square in which Augustus the Strong of Saxony intended to devote himself and his court to games, jousting and feasting in the medieval manner.

That was the Baroque's first bid for freedom. The second was that it deserted the static form of the square and of the circle for shapes that swirl and move: S-curves, undulating façades and plans based on ovals. The influence of the Catholic Church is apparent here, for at the Council of Trent, which in 1545

ushered in the Counter-Reformation, the square and the circle were declared to be too pagan for Christian churches. We can look at no better example than Borromini's first church, his tiny, exquisite San Carlo alle Quattro Fontane in Rome, the façade of which was finished in 1677 (*figs. 262, 263*). Although he had to squash it into a very cramped site, both the plan and the rippling front set the pattern for future Baroque church experiments.

The third breakaway feature of the Baroque was an extreme form of theatricality, which involved the creating of illusion. The Baroque is fertile with examples of *trompe-l'oeil*; there are the carved curtain swags of red painted wood above the curtains in Harewood House, Yorkshire, and a violin appears to hang from a ribbon on the back of the music-room door at Chatsworth,

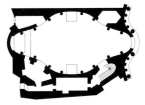

262 | *San Carlo alle Quattro Fontane*, plan

263 | **Francesco Borromini**, *San Carlo alle Quattro Fontane*, Rome, 1638–77

264 | **Gian Lorenzo Bernini**, *Ecstacy of St Theresa*, Cornaro Chapel, Santa Maria della Vittoria, Rome, 1646

Derbyshire, amazingly realistic, with the door appearing to stand slightly ajar.

The sculptor Gian Lorenzo Bernini (1598–1680) makes it quite clear in the *Ecstasy of St Theresa* (1646; *fig. 264*) in the Cornaro Chapel of Santa Maria della Vittoria in Rome, that he is staging a little play, for although St Theresa's central figure is agonizingly realistic, he has carved theatre boxes near the tableau and set members of the Cornaro family in them, watching.

Let us look at some of these Baroque effects in actual use. The two founding figures of the Baroque were Bernini and Borromini. They set the style; but their genius was too incendiary for general export, and it was the rather milder

forms of their innovations propagated by Carlo Fontana (1638–1714) that spread throughout Europe as 'late international Baroque'. Architects came to Rome to study under Fontana. He taught two of the great Austrian architects, Von Hildebrandt, designer of the Belvedere, and his fellow church and palace builder Johann Bernhardt Fischer von Erlach (1656–1723), as well as Filippo Juvarra (1678–1736), whose work is largely round Turin, and the Scotsman, James Gibbs (1682–1754). Another fascinating figure was Juvarra's predecessor, Guarino Guarini (1624–83). Like Juvarra, he was a priest – indeed a professor of philosophy and mathematics – who turned to architecture and created the highly influential churches of San Lorenzo, Turin (1668–87; *fig. 265*), and the Chapel of the Holy Shroud (Il Sindone, 1667–90) which houses the famous and disputed length of linen that is said to bear the marks of Christ's body.

Bernini opened the Baroque with a fanfare of trumpets from where Michelangelo had left off, first by building inside St Peter's an ornate canopy over the tomb of St Peter directly under the dome, secondly by creating an illusion

266 | *St Peter's*, Rome, 1506–1626, and **Bernini**'s double colonnade, 1656–71

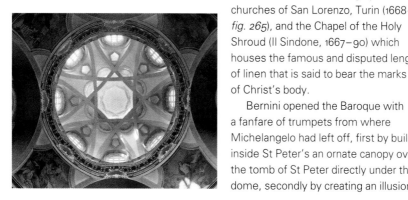

265 | **Guarino Guarini**, *San Lorenzo*, Turin, 1668–87, interior of dome

of a burst of heavenly glory round the ancient wooden throne reputed to be St Peter's, and finally by erecting the double colonnade which clasps the vast piazza before the cathedral.

Bernini had more things in common with Michelangelo than his association with St Peter's. His first medium was sculpture. He was an infant prodigy. Like Michelangelo, he lived into his eighties. Like Sir John Vanbrugh's, his versatility extended to the theatre, for he wrote plays and operas; in fact, the typical background for an architect to have at this period, other than the plastic arts, was either the theatre or military engineering. The English essayist and traveller, John Evelyn, describes how, when in Rome in 1644, he attended the opera for which Bernini had 'painted the scenes, cut the statues, invented the engines, composed the music, wrote the comedy and built the theatre'.

The bronze baldacchino (1624–33), a tall canopy standing over the tomb of St Peter, has four twisted pillars, modelled on the pillars of the old St Peter's which were reputed to have come from the Temple in Jerusalem. The illusory scalloped awnings round the top, also in bronze and reminiscent of a medieval general's tent, are regarded by experts as the most superb feats of bronze casting. It certainly took so much bronze that they ran out of the material, and by order of Pope Urban VIII removed the bronze coffering from inside the vestibule of the Pantheon. In the wall above the baldacchino, Bernini built the ancient chair, reputed to be St Peter's throne, into another illusion, known as the Cathedra Petri (1657–66).

The mixture of architecture, sculpture, painting and trickery in these two pieces is excelled and exceeded in a more purely architectural work of Bernini's, or at least a work of architecture and planning, for half the magic of the colonnade he built round the piazza at St Peter's (1656–71;

fig. 266) comes from its relationship with the environment. The colonnades, kept low to relate to Carlo Maderna's front, and providing welcome shade in the midday sun, have a profound symbolic significance. They suggest the embracing, protective arms of Mother Church, wrapped round the faithful in the piazza. Also, according to Bernini's brief, they draw the eye to the steps or to the window and balcony in the Vatican Palace from which the pope gives his blessing.

Francesco Borromini (1599–1667), sculptor and mason, was very different from Bernini. He went to Rome in 1614 to train under Maderna and Bernini. At the age of 68 he died by his own hand. The complex, tortuous forms he evolved in his churches, particularly in San Carlo alle Quattro Fontane, begun in 1638, are difficult for either layman or expert to under-

267 | **Balthasar Neumann**, *Vierzehnheiligen Pilgrimage Church*, Germany, 1743–72

268 | *Vierzehnheiligen*, plan

The Drama of Shapes and Space: *Baroque and Rococo*

stand without hard study, and probably mirror the intricate, obsessive labyrinths within his mind. For two centuries after his death he was considered deranged, and the choice by nineteenth-century art historians of the word 'Baroque', which meant misshapen, particularly of pearls, may have had something to do with the feeling in the eighteenth and nineteenth centuries that Borromini and his shifting architecture were uneasy and abnormal.

It is Borromini's juggling with shapes that is so fascinating. The fact that he had to work on tiny or awkwardly shaped sites does not seem to have curbed his swelling imagination, and this no doubt gave confidence to those who followed him, like the brothers Cosmas Damian Asam (1686–1739) and Egid Quirin Asam (1692–1750) in Munich. The latter decided to build a little church, St John Nepomuk (1733–46; *fig. 258*), on a site only 30 feet (9 metres) wide that adjoined his own house. He managed to pack the interior with swirling balconies and twisted pillars, throbbing passionately in gold, dark browns and reds. Borromini's San Ivo della Sapienza, the university church in Rome, was started in 1642 to fill in the end of an arcaded courtyard patterned with a star on its floor. But his plan for the church of wisdom looks back to the temple of wise Solomon and makes no concession to site difficulties. Its plan is formed by two triangles that interlock to form a star of David, whose points end, alternately, in semicircles and half-octagons. The front giving on to the court is concave, and over all rises a rippling dome, very steep, in the form of a six-lobed cupola which is surmounted by a spiral lantern holding up the flame of truth. This form was to influence Guarini in his Chapel of the Holy Shroud in Turin.

However, the oval is the classic shape of the Baroque. Ovals had been used before, of course. Serlio established the principle of using them in the fifth book of his treatise *L'Architettura* in 1547, and

Vignola used a longitudinal oval in Sant' Anna dei Palafrenieri, Rome (1565–76). Now ovals may lie in the long direction of the church—from east to west—or transversely; several may be used, or they may be split in half and set back to back to give concave curves on the exterior. Bernini used an oval across the width of the church of Sant' Andrea al Quirinale (1658–70), which is known as the oval Pantheon. Carlo Rainaldi (1611–91) in the church of Sant' Agnese in Piazza Navona (1652–66), on which Borromini put the façade, added two apse-like chapels at choir and entrance ends to make the plan of an octagon within a square into an east–west oval. Secular buildings were also oval, as, for example, the little Rococo Amalienburg Pavilion in the park of Schloss Nymphenburg, Munich, by François Cuvilliés (1695–1768), and François Mansart's château at Maisons-Laffitte near Paris (1642–6) has oval rooms in its side wings. The château of Vaux-le-Vicomte (1657) by Louis Le Vau (1612–70) has a central oval salon covered by a dome.

In San Carlo, Borromini twisted the four quadrants of a basically oval plan inwards to give undulating walls, and then used semicircular arches above the cornice to bring the walls back to the oval, from whence springs the coffered dome. The plan of the Abbey Church at Banz, Bavaria (1710–18; *fig. 269*), designed by Johann Dietzenhofer (1663–1726), is a spiral of interlacing ovals. Sant' Andrea and San Carlo both have oval domes, and the form even appears in oval staircases built into the fabric of a building. The magnificent staircase that Balthasar Neumann (1687–1753) built into the Episcopal Palace at Bruchsal, south Germany, in 1732, at the end of the Baroque period, gives the impression that one is spiralling through space, from one podium to another.

Vierzehnheiligen (*figs. 267, 268*), also designed by Neumann, is perhaps the

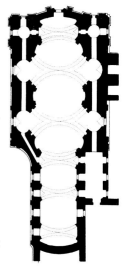

269 | **Johann Dientzenhofer**, *Banz Abbey Church*, Germany, 1710–18, plan

270 | **Balthasar Neumann,**
Lucas von Hildebrandt and
others, *staircase of Bishop's*
Palace (Residenz), Würzburg,
Germany, 1719–44

most complex of all Baroque churches.
From outside it looks regular – a Greek-cross church with extended nave and aisles, polygonal side-chapels for transepts, altar in the east and twin towers on the façade. Inside, the visitor is stunned by the light and shadows that swell and ebb around the swooping vaults, by the Baroque architectural and decorative shapes in galleries or stucco; by much gold on white, and deep colours on the painted ceiling. There are no aisles; the church is open to shifting inter-penetrating spaces. There is no dome; the altar is situated in the large longitudinal central oval which forms the nave, an anchored island floating in a sea of liquid light. When we examine the plan we see that this nave is strung between two

smaller ovals, one forming the choir, the other the entry to the church, and bulging outwards a little on the façade to give the undulating wall line. The chapels in the arms of the cross are semicircular. Pillars and concave curves in the side walls indicate the position of two further ovals placed transversely between the altar and the entry area.

Its complexity applies to the structure. Baroque structures were very advanced. If, after examining Vierzehnheiligen, we look back to the early Renaissance buildings, we are struck by their structural simplicity – almost naivety. The Palazzo Rucellai, for instance, consists of four solid walls holding up a shallow pent roof – about as primitive a structure as one could have. Rusticated stonework, pilasters, cornices, window frames are practically engraved on the side. In contrast, the Baroque architects' structural confidence seems unbounded. These men were in fact well capable of calculation. Many were engineers; Neumann and Guarini were mathematicians of note; Sir Christopher Wren (1632–1723), architect of St Paul's, London, was reckoned a scientific genius, Professor of Astronomy at both London and Oxford Universities and a founder member of the Royal Society. They were ready to exploit the structural knowledge and expertise of the past without aesthetic or moral prejudice. So, in Sant' Andrea we have Bernini carving up his solid walls into niches, as did the ancient Romans; we have Guarini weaving ribs like webbing in catenary curves to support spires and domes in San Lorenzo and Il Sindone, relying on his knowledge of Gothic vaulting, spiced with piquancy of detail from Moorish vaults in Spain. And we find James Gibbs and Nicholas Hawksmoor (1661–1736), who with Vanbrugh worked in Wren's office, setting Gothic spires on top of classical churches. Curving wings and blocks, swirling vaults: the truth is that the Baroque had gone as far as it was

271 | **Gian Lorenzo Bernini**,
Trevi fountain, Rome, 1732–7

possible with masonry structure. Further structural development had to await the discovery of new materials and the demand for new forms in the nineteenth century.

The Baroque architects matched their free-ranging experiments in structure by demolishing boundaries between one medium and another. Architecture and painting have their moment of intercommunion in the painted ceilings which opened up the roof to heaven by means of what the Italians called *'sotto in su'* (from below upwards). These were typical Baroque effects, common in both churches and palaces. Among the most famous are the ceilings of Il Gesù, and of the Zimmermann brothers' pilgrim church at Steinhausen, Swabia (1728–31), where colourful figures come and go above the false arches, painted in perspective, that frame the roof supposedly open to the heavens. In Bernini's Sant' Andrea, the theme of the saint's martyrdom, painted behind the altar, is carried upwards in a sculpture of his soul being carried to heaven, which is presumably located in the dome, where nude figures dangle

their legs over the cornice and gossiping cherubs perch all around like roosting doves. Sculpture is called in to support the fiction of a roof opening to heaven in the palace built for the Prince-Bishops of Würzburg (1719–44) by Neumann, Hildebrandt and others. Here, the staircase with its flowing patterns of balustrades (*fig. 270*) sweeps up towards a ceiling on which Tiepolo depicted the four continents–a riot of violin bows, whirling cloaks, feathered head-dresses, girls riding crocodiles, ostrichs and camels. The gilt frame cannot contain the activity, and figures overspill the stage-like theatre-in-the-round. A gallant's legs hang over the edge, and a wolfhound and a little fat soldier appear to have toppled out on to the ledge below. Just as invention and reality mix, in the same way sculpture and architecture become interchangeable. In a similar conceit, shown at the garden room of the Belvedere, pillars assume the shapes of muscular giants carrying the weight on their shoulders.

Materials are also transmuted in these illusions: wood is carved and painted to look like cloth, rays lit by yellow light from

272 | **Francesco de' Sanctis**, *Spanish Steps*, Rome, 1723–5

a concealed source are fashioned from gilt and stream down on St Theresa, and on the Cathedra Petri, while in the Trevi Fountain in Rome (1732–7; *fig. 271*) stone is carved to resemble spray and spouting water. It is a transfixing experience to chance on the Fountain after wending through narrow back streets. Bernini conceived it, and two architects and two sculptors carried out this monument – to the indomitable spirit of man – that laps at the buildings on one side of a small enclosed square. It is impossible to separate the real from the sham in this powerful combination of classical figures and seething scatter of rocks, out of which wild sea horses and real waters froth and foam. There is a similar set piece in the grounds of the palace that Luigi Vanvitelli (1700–73) built for the Spanish King of Naples, Charles III, the Palazzo Reale at Caserta (1752–72). In one of two pieces depicting the legend of Diana and Actaeon, the sculptor has placed Actaeon, caught at the moment of being turned into a stag, at the base of the Great Cascade, cornered by slavering hounds, which leap up the rocks at him from the pool's edge. Vanvitelli's son, Carlo, finished the landscaping after his father's death, using several sculptors.

This kind of effect was sought in two major planning schemes in Rome by the

popes. One was the Piazza Navona, now considered a museum of the Baroque, since it contains Rainaldi's Sant' Agnese with a front by Borromini, two fountains by Bernini and, in the Pamphili family palace, a gallery painted by Cortona. The most famous fountain, that of the four rivers (1648–51), depicts the Danube, the Plate, the Nile and the Ganges, testifying, as does the ceiling at Würzburg, to the enormous interest in the countries being opened up to east and west by explorers and colonists. The other major townplanning scheme is the Piazza del Popolo (1662–79). It is a highly self-conscious piece of town planning and contains an obelisk between two churches, which appear to have twin elevations and domes. In fact, they stand on sites of different widths, and Carlo Rainaldi had to deploy some ingenious internal planning to create the matching effect on the outside.

We have seen how, in Würzburg and Bruchsal, Baroque architects delighted in getting effects with flights of stairs. Bernini's Scala Regia (1663–6), an early example, is perhaps the most famous. As in much of the best Baroque architecture, he was presented with a challenge – to make a 'royal' staircase leading into the Vatican Palace alongside the frontage and colonnade of St Peter's without detracting one from the other. Moreover, there was not much space. His solution was to have a passageway leading from the colonnade to the exit of the Cathedral's

273 | *Bom Jesus do Monte*, near Braga, Portugal, approach steps, 1723–44

274 | **Filippo Juvarra**, *church at Superga*, Turin, 1717–31

Galilee Porch. Here, a dramatic statue of the Emperor Constantine on a white horse distracts us cleverly from an inappropriate turn before the staircase is reached. Lined with arcades the grand staircase itself then ascends steeply, narrowing into a dignified tunnel-shaft, in the Mannerist manner.

Possibilities of using staircases outdoors for scenic effect were early appreciated in a hilly city like Rome. Francesco de' Sanctis (?1693–1731) produced a masterpiece, the Spanish Steps, Rome (1723– 5; *fig. 272*). Unexpected curves, lines of steps and balustrades, where today flowers and souvenirs are sold, wind past the house where Keats died to where the sixteenth-century church with a frontage by Maderna, SS. Trinità de' Monti, stands at the head of the steps like a *grande dame* receiving visitors.

The use of steps in conjunction with a church is also to be found in Portugal. The approach to the Bom Jesus do Monte, a twin-towered church near Braga, was laid out in 1723–44 according to the Stations of the Cross, the stages of Christ's journey from Pilate's Hall to his death on the cross. Zig-zag flights with fountains and obelisks at the angles link the chapels commemorating the fourteen Stations

until the church at the top is reached (*fig. 273*).

Sometimes it is the siting that gives a building presence and drama. Juvarra assured the dominance of his basilica at Superga (1717–31; *fig. 274*) by not only giving it a dome like St Peter's, but also by setting it on a hill high above Turin. The Venetian church of Santa Maria della Salute (1630–87; *fig. 275*), by Baldassare Longhena (1598–1683), with its crested pediments lapping halfway up its walls, seems a creation of the sea because of its position, white as creamed surf among the red-tiled roofs, at the entrance to the Grand Canal.

But probably the most superlative siting is that of the Benedictine Monastery at Melk, Lower Austria (1702–14), built by Jacob Prandtauer (1660–1725) on a bluff above the Danube (*fig. 276*). Above the brown-green river and the grey-green outcrops of rock, the twin towers on the façade, the dome and the grey-green roofs of the detached church rise imperiously up from within a surround of monastic ranges with red-tiled roofs.

275 | **Baldassare Longhena**, *Santa Maria della Salute*, Venice, 1630–87

276 | **Jacob Prandtauer**, *Benedictine Monastery*, Melk, Austria, 1702–14

The British variations on this Continental style have been left to the end of this chapter, since their individuality sets them out of step with their European contemporaries, if for no other reason than that, unlike the other countries in which the Baroque flourished, England was Protestant. Anglican churches were therefore open halls and Protestant churches of the period present a harder outline in contrast to the curvaceous Baroque. A first glance at Sir Christopher Wren's greatest work, St Paul's Cathedral, London (1675–1710; *fig. 277*), with its high serene dome set around with cool, contained, closely-spaced slim columns – more like Bramante's Tempietto than like St Peter's – suggests that

he belongs to the Renaissance rather than to the Baroque, but further study does not support this. On the secular palace-type side elevations, a swirling façade replaces transepts; and the front bulges between two towers reminiscent of Borromini's work. When one ventures inside and examines the black-and-white chequered tiling, the bold structure of the Whispering Gallery encircling the dome, and then moves on to consider the piers that are hollowed out into enormous niches and placed diagonally to support a dome as wide as nave and aisles together, one recognizes the intrepid effrontery of Baroque massing. In the rebuilding of 51 churches in the City of London, after the four terrible days and nights of September 1666, during which four-fifths of the city was burned down, Wren showed an adventurously versatile eclectic response to the mammoth task before him, combining Gothic and Renaissance details and structure.

If there is a temptation to assign Wren to an earlier age, there is no question of this with Sir John Vanbrugh (1664–1726). The 'mighty forces struggling against overwhelming weights' of Baroque massing and the stirring panache of his soaring, vertical pillars, windows and turrets above the lake on Blenheim Palace, Oxfordshire (1705–24), and at Castle Howard, Yorkshire, have the unquestioned theatrical hallmark of the Baroque. After a brief association with Hawksmoor in Wren's office, Vanbrugh gained his first commission, Castle Howard, for the Earl of Carlisle in 1699. Untrained but confident, he came swaggering on to the architectural scene from more swashbuckling arenas: he had previously been an army captain, but had been arrested as a spy in France and imprisoned in the Bastille, and had later gained fame as a Restoration dramatist. Walpole considered 'sublime' that quality of powerful excitement with which he would invest classical forms. That quality is to be found

277 | **Sir Christopher Wren**, *St Paul's Cathedral*, London, 1675–1710

Bramante's Tempietto and is accounted by some critics England's most beautiful building.

The last phase of the Baroque in France was called Rococo, an elegant, light-hearted style of décor, invented to suit Parisian tastes. The style first appeared when the classicist Jules-Hardouin Mansart (1646–1708) moved from creating the Galerie des Glaces at Versailles for Louis XIV, to create designs for the Château de la Ménagerie, which was to be built for the 13-year old fiancée of Louis's eldest grandson. In response to the King's objections that the projected decoration was too sombre for a child, Claude Andran, the painter Watteau's master, evolved a light delicate decoration of arabesques and filigree depicting hunting dogs, maidens, birds, garlands, ribbons, plant fronds and tendrils. Then, in 1699, Pierre Lepautre applied arabesques to the mirrors and door-frames of the King's own apartments at Marly. The style was launched. By 1701 it had appeared at Versailles (1655–82), the great palace created for Louis XIV by Louis Le Vau and Jules-Hardouin Mansart.

It took its name from *rocaille*, meaning rocks and shells, to indicate the natural forms of its decorations: leaf- and branch-shape, sea-shapes – shells, surf, coral, seaweed, spray and spume – scrolls, C- and S-shapes. In France it remained

at Castle Howard (*fig. 278*), in the dome rising majestically above the pedimented south front, in the famed Great Hall with its shifting spaces and quivering shadowy hollows, and in the narrow vaulted Antique Passage. He boasted of his special feeling for 'the castle air', and this is probably justified at Blenheim Palace, named after the victory in the War of the Spanish Succession and presented by a grateful nation to the conquering general, the Duke of Marlborough. Its presence and enormous scale recall Versailles. But unquestionably he would have been incapable of building it had he not recruited Hawksmoor from Wren's office to be his assistant. Hawksmoor was no architectural menial, as we can see from his Mausoleum in the grounds of Castle Howard (1729), which owes much to

278 | **Sir John Vanbrugh**, *Castle Howard*, Yorkshire, 1699–

279 | **Jules-Hardouin Mansart**, *Galerie des Glaces*, Versailles, 1678–84

delicate and elegant, providing exquisite rooms for the fashionable and intimate pursuits of dancing, chamber music, etiquette, letter writing, conversation and seduction. The architecture supporting the decoration became simpler. Rooms were more likely to be rectangular, possibly with the corners rounded off, painted in ivory white or a pastel tone, lacking pillars or pilasters and all but the simplest mouldings, so as not to detract from the gold arabesques with which they were covered. It was at this period that the term 'French window' came in to describe the fashionable attenuated windows which often stretched from floor to ceiling. Mirrors had already been used for brilliance of effect in grand salons, such as Louis XIV's Galerie des Glaces at Versailles (1678–84; *fig. 279*), a barrel-vaulted room with a rich painted ceiling, whose arcade of 17 windows down one side was matched by an arcade of 17 mirrors down the other. In 1695 Fischer von Erlach added a more delicate version of the Galerie des Glaces – indeed, one that might almost be called flimsy – to the 'Viennese Versailles' – the Schönbrunn Palace, Vienna, built in rivalry of Louis XIV. Now mirrors of the flattering con-

temporary dark glass became customary over the mantelpiece; and walls were patterned with mirrors of all shapes, regular and irregular, whose frames were made of twigs or leafy shoots in gilt – slim, wispy, often trailing away in a vague open-ended S- or C-shape that knew nothing of symmetry.

By 1735, when Germain Boffrand (1667–1754) created the Salon de la Princesse for the young bride of the elderly Prince de Soubise in his hôtel, or town house, in Paris, French Rococo was at its height (*fig. 280*). It had spread even to town-planning in the Place de la Carrière, Nancy. The château built there for the French Queen's father, the dethroned Polish King Stanislas Leczinsky, was destroyed. But the Polish king's taste for the Rococo is still testified to by the curving arcades of open arches, built after 1720. They define spaces that open intriguingly out of each other, and involve an oval court, a triumphal arch and beautiful wrought-iron gates.

280 | **Germain Boffrand**, *Salon de la Princesse*, Hôtel de Soubise, Paris, 1735–9

281 | **François Cuvilliés**, *Amalienburg Pavilion*, Schloss Nymphenburg, Munich, 1734–9

Some time before that, Elector Max Emmanuel of Bavaria had discovered that the court dwarf, François Cuvilliés, had a talent for architecture and in 1720 sent him to Paris to study for four years. He worked in the Munich Residenz, and between 1734 and 1739 he created the Amalienburg, the best-known of the four Rococo pavilions erected in the extensive grounds of Schloss Nymphenburg on the outskirts of Munich. This stylish little *Pavillon de plaisance* (*fig. 281*), with a deceptively smooth and simple exterior, is embellished with charming details, such as a flight of hemispherical steps leading to the curving projecting porch under a prow-shaped pediment, the corners sculpted to make them concave, and the slim bow-shaped pediments elegantly raised. Inside, a central circular hall, about

40 feet (12 metres) in diameter, curving with the curve of the front façade, is provided on either side with the necessary services, bedrooms and gunroom. The hall, washed pale blue like the first morning of creation, is a room of oval-headed mirrors. These alternate with the windows and doors and are set at slight angles to proliferate the summer frivolity of the decorations. Silver-stuccoed ornament covers the walls in airy screens of verdure, musical instruments, cornucopias and shells; butterflies rise from the sun-spattered leaves, and grasses quiver around the roof cornice, while birds wing their way up into the blue heaven.

Baroque and Rococo came to an abrupt end in the middle of the eighteenth century. As a rule, an artistic phase that has outlived its usefulness or relevance dies out during a span of several decades. It is very odd that this one came to an end so suddenly. With more sober and ponderous empires now assuming political power, Europe returned to a more sober and ponderous classical architecture.

There were several reasons for this. One was the changed atmosphere in Europe from early in the eighteenth century, culminating in the French Revolution of 1789, which seems to have led architects and their clients to search for more permanence and authority in their buildings than the Baroque could provide. Another was that the Baroque had only been taken up in certain countries; and with the shift in the balance of power, the architecture preferred by countries like France and Protestant Germany now came into its own. But the deciding factor in the break with the Baroque was a new enthusiasm that found expression in the fashionable taste of the time.

It was in England and Scotland that the new fashionable taste was first expressed. There the architects made an early return to classicism, not at first to the ancient forms of the Greeks, or even of the Romans (that was to come later), but to the gentler interpretation by Palladio. Between 1715 and 1717, a young Scot,

Colen Campbell (1676–1729), produced a book of over 100 engravings of houses in Britain, which he called *Vitruvius Britannicus*. In it, he praised both Palladio and Inigo Jones.

Campbell put his theories into practice by building Houghton Hall, Norfolk (1722–6), for the Prime Minister Robert Walpole, an Inigo Jones-type house, with a magnificent 40-foot (12-metre) double-cube room. He also built a villa at Mereworth, Kent (1723), which closely followed Palladio's Villa Rotonda (*fig. 235*), with a round central hall, but dispensed with Palladio's symmetrical staircases on two sides. A similar variation on the Rotonda theme was created by Lord Burlington when he built for himself, with the help of William Kent, a villa near London–Chiswick House, in 1725 (*figs. 282, 283*).

Richard Boyle, third Earl of Burlington (1694–1753), one of the Whig politicians who had come to power with the accession of George I, was an amateur architect, and brought together a group of architects who took the work of Palladio as a model. With such people as Colen Campbell, the young painter William Kent (1685–1748), whom he met while studying in Rome, and the poet Alexander Pope, Burlington established himself as the virtual dictator of taste in England until his death in 1753. The Palladian style was carried as far as Pushkin in Russia, where at Tsarskoe Selo a Scot, Charles

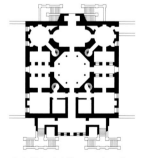

282 | *Chiswick House*, plan of ground floor

283 | **Lord Burlington** and **William Kent**, *Chiswick House*, London, 1725

284 | **Charles Cameron**, *Cameron Gallery*, Tsarskoe Selo, Pushkin, Russia, 1787

Cameron (1746–1812), added a wing to the imperial palace built by an Italian, Bartolomeo Rastrelli (1700–71) with an Ionic colonnade facing the park (*fig. 284*). Another Scot, James Gibbs (1682–1754), a Jacobite and Catholic who had at one time studied for the priesthood and had also studied the Baroque under Carlo Fontana in Rome, one would expect to be in opposition to Burlington's Whig establishment. But even Gibbs's work on the London churches, for example St Martin-in-the-Fields (1721–6; *fig. 285*), where he combined a classical portico with a spire, is never outrageously Baroque, and in the long, cool, dignified symmetry of the Senate House, Cambridge University (1722–30), he showed himself an incomparable successor to Wren. That Gibbs's style is in harmony with Palladian elegance is shown by its popularity abroad–in America, where Palladianism was much emulated, and also in the work of Australia's convict-forger architect (whom today she honours on her banknotes), Francis Greenway, in St James's Church, Sydney, of 1824 (*fig. 314*).

England at this period was going through an agricultural revolution which was to transform the appearance of the rural landscape. A foremost figure in this transformation was Thomas Coke, Earl of Leicester, for whom, in 1734, Burlington and Kent built Holkham Hall in Norfolk (*fig. 286*). The surface of the house was in yellow brick, made locally, but, at Coke's

request, fashioned after antique Roman brick. The house was planned with a central rectangular block, which presented a Palladian portico entrance to the deer park. On either side of the main block to front and back, connected by short, low, recessed links, stand four smaller rectangular blocks. As a plan, it represents a valid extension of Palladio's service wings, simply repeated so as to face the back as well as the front. Yet the entrance hall is almost Baroque in its spaces. The house had been commissioned to show off Coke's collection of antiquities, and the hall is on two levels, with an apse-like gallery round the inner end. This is reached by a staircase, gashed with a strip of red carpet, shaped like the train of a velvet cloak or an unopened peacock's tail. Brown-on-white Derbyshire alabaster pillars based on the Temple of Fortuna Virilis in Rome rise from this gallery level to support an extraordinary coved ceiling which, because it turns into the apse in a half-cup shape, reflects to some extent the curious form of the staircase.

The new elegance was not confined to country houses. John Wood the elder (1704–54) and John Wood the younger (1728–81), both architects of Palladian country houses, discovered a method of translating the simple sophistication of the Palladian way of building into the street. No later version, not even Robert Adam's planning of Charlotte Square,

285 | **James Gibbs**, *St Martin-in-the-Fields*, London, 1721–6

286 | **Lord Burlington** and
William Kent, *Holkham Hall*,
Norfolk, 1734

Edinburgh (1791–1807), as a unified palace front, is quite as dramatic as the streets the Woods created in Bath. In golden-white Bath stone, the elevations of the streets are conceived as one continuous Palladian frontage. A pediment gives emphasis to the centre of the north side of Queen Square (1729–36). Even more dramatically, an untrammelled lawn sweeps steeply down to tree fringes from the elliptical curve of Royal Crescent (1767–75; *see p.6*).

The masterly way in which the Woods evolved this new and elegant face for quality planning can be seen by juxtaposing a Palladian pilaster against the frontage of a Bath terrace and noting how the proportions and the horizontal emphases are translated from one to the other. What has happened is that the pilaster has been extended sideways in

both directions, to form the street, so that the plinth and base become the ground floor, sometimes rusticated, the shaft of the pilaster is repeated as a colonnade or in the tall narrow verticality of the first-floor windows, and the architrave and frieze are matched in the cornice mouldings, above which there may occur a pediment or attic storey.

The members of the Burlington school were important pioneers of the association of architecture and its environment which was to become part of the Romantic movement. It is to William Kent that we owe the start of the English landscape movement of the eighteenth century – the landscape of 'controlled nature'. Kent, in the phrase of the Prime Minister's son, Horace Walpole, 'leapt the fence and found all nature was a garden.'

This new awareness led to a total reversal of the Baroque relation between inside and outside that we can see in France. If we look at the famous gardens there, such as the designs by André Le Nôtre (1613–1700) for Vaux-le-Vicomte (*fig. 287*) and for Versailles, we see how carefully and geometrically they were controlled – clipped hedges defining parterres, long avenues of trees leading to geometrically organized sheets of water, diagonal paths to fountains or shrubberies. Yet the insides of Versailles and Vaux-le-Vicomte have the lavish warmth and excitement of painted vaults and carved cornices. In complete contrast, eighteenth-century English country houses have serene interiors, while outside, nature is allowed to heave into mounds or fall away; paths, streams and lakes are given licence to twist or run straight; trees to grow very much as they want. Kent was followed by Charles Bridgeman (d. 1738), who is credited with another major English innovation. That was the method whereby the entire landscape, as far as the eye could see, became part of the estate: he replaced

287 | *Château of Vaux-le-Vicomte*, France, 1657, gardens designed by **André Le Nôtre**

fences dividing gardens from the surrounding pasture land by sunken ditches called *ha-has*, which kept cattle out, but were imperceptible from the terrace or drawing-room window. The most celebrated gardener was Lancelot Brown (1716–83), nicknamed 'Capability Brown' because he always enthused about the 'capabilities' of a site. Tree-planting was an art in which he excelled. His particular art of bunching and scattering groups of trees is now taken for granted as a characteristic feature of the English landscape. So extensive was Brown's work that one landowner said he hoped to die before him since he wanted to see what heaven looked like before Capability 'improved' it.

The interaction between house and garden went one step further in what came to be known as the Picturesque movement when the garden was embellished with delightful architectural features – bridges, temples and grottoes. Bridgeman's garden for the house that the Scots architect Robert Adam

remodelled at Stowe, Buckingham (1771–), now a public school, is an architectural treasure-trove of classical temples and bridges by the most renowned practitioners – Vanbrugh, Gibbs, Kent, Capability Brown. There is even a copy of Roger Morris's Palladian bridge from Wilton House, set on a series of graceful arches. Colen Campbell made designs for

288 | **Henry** and **Richard Hoare**, gardens at Stourhead, Wiltshire, 1720s

222

289 | **Jacques Germain Soufflot**, *Panthéon*, Paris, 1755–92

a Palladian house at Stourhead, Wiltshire, for the banker Henry Hoare in the 1720s. When Hoare and his son Michael then decided to make the complementary garden (*fig. 288*), they dammed the valley to the west of the village, and, inspired by Virgil's *Aeneid*, laid it out as an allegory of man's passage through life. The idyllic route suggests, rather, a passage through Elysium to the visitor who wanders round the triangular lake by verdant copse and floating waterlily, by dank green grottoes and exquisite temples, between pink, blue and mauve hydrangeas and over bridges whose curves are reflected in the water.

This idyllic and fanciful scene was given a new – and more serious – dimension through the influence of studies both artistic and literary. The first of these studies was by an amateur in both archaeology and architecture, the Abbé Laugier (1713–69). In his search for authority, he reconsidered the basic design of the primitive hut, when architecture consisted of upright posts, cross-beams and pitched roofs, the genesis of the Greek temple. This, he contended in his *Essai sur l'architecture* of 1753, was

how architecture should be ideally, with plain walls unarticulated by pilasters, pediments, additional attic storeys, domes or decorations of any sort. The first person to translate Laugier's theories into fact was Jacques Germain Soufflot (1713–80), who built the church of Ste-Geneviève, Paris, in 1755, secularized during the Revolution and renamed the Panthéon (*fig. 289*). He did, however, use a dome, which he based on St Paul's. But he supported it entirely on pillars, joined by straight entablatures, except for the four corners, where he borrowed from Gothic structure and introduced four triangular piers, with columns standing up against them. His intention that light should pass freely through the building was foiled during the Revolution, when the windows were filled in for its use as a secular building.

Five years after the Abbe's treatise, Julien David Le Roy produced his *Ruines des plus beaux monuments de la Grèce*; but this work was outdated in 1762 by the first volume of James Stuart and Nicholas Revett's definitively comprehensive and scholarly work *The Antiquities of Athens*. It was written after the English philosopher Lord Shaftesbury persuaded the two men to visit Athens in the 1750s. In 1764 in Germany, J. J. Winckelmann brought out his history of ancient art. Winckelmann never went to Greece, but the first sentence of his *Reflections* tells us clearly where his allegiance lies: 'Good taste, which is spreading more and more throughout the world, was first formed under Greek skies.' Architects, he felt, should strive for the qualities shown by the Greeks – noble simplicity, calm grandeur and precision of contour.

It was, in other words, an architectural movement that could only be explained in literary as well as artistic terms. Probably as influential were the popular painters and engravers of the day, who liked to combine architecture, usually of an antique or ruined character, with the

290 | **Robert Adam**, *Syon House*, London, 1762–9, vestibule

'sublime' prospects of nature. Paintings by Claude Lorrain and Salvator Rosa were eagerly bought up and brought home as souvenirs from the Grand Tour which formed part of the education of young gentlemen. At the same time, a spate of books, treatises, sketches, paintings and engravings, similar to the flood that accompanied the experiments of the early Renaissance architects, poured through France, Germany, England and Italy in the 1750s and 1760s. It was partly these works, within the changing political, social and emotional atmosphere, that hastened the demise of the Baroque. The other crucial factor was the new pursuit (at this stage scarcely a science) of archaeology, and, in particular, the exploration first of Roman and then of Greek ruins, which were for the first time opened up to the gentlemen of Europe.

By the second half of the eighteenth century, in short, the fashionable classical architecture influenced by Palladio and

Inigo Jones had been superseded by a more strict and scholarly neo-classicism. The pre-eminent and dominant architect in Britain was Robert Adam (1728–92).

Adam went on the Grand tour in the 1750s. In Rome he met the celebrated etcher Giovanni Battista Piranese (1720–78), whose dramatic scenes of ancient Roman remains and prison squalor conveyed an image of Rome which did much to shape European perceptions. Piranesi's work was given an added boost through his friendship with Adam, who included rugged landscapes in his sketch designs and had made a detailed study of Diocletian's Palace at Spalato, which he published in 1764. After living for a time with Piranesi in Rome, he returned to England to design, sometimes using classical Greek and 'Etruscan' style motifs, the interiors for a series of country houses, and produced some of the finest eighteenth-century planned terraces in London and the New Town of Edinburgh. He was also a very successful supplier of fittings and furnishings.

Adam's great invention, based on Diocletian's Palace at Spalato, was his own version of Etruscan decoration. Working with his brother James, he established a vocabulary of interior decoration that became enormously influential. After the 1770s there was scarcely an Adam house that did not have an Etruscan room. The white figures, urns and garlands in low relief against a pastel background, such as Josiah Wedgwood adopted for the pottery he produced in the factory village he named Etruria in Staffordshire, are a microcosm of Adam's prolific work in furniture, wall mouldings, mantelpieces, fanlights over doorways and, most beautiful of all, ceilings in delicate relief, often with a daisy shape in the centre and fan-like webs of garlands across each corner.

His Roman rooms show deeper colour – gilt and marbles on pillars and

291 | **Sir Robert Smirke**,
British Museum, London,
1823–47

flooring in black, dark green and terracottas – as well as strongly masculine detailing, such as his trick of screening off an apse or a shallow alcove with massive pillars. The marble columns around the walls of the ante-room in Syon House, London, a Jacobean building remodelled (1762–9; *fig. 290*), were Roman originals dredged out of the River Tiber to support a decorated cornice carrying golden Greek figures.

By the end of the eighteenth century and the early years of the nineteenth, Edinburgh had become a hive of architectural industry and took to the Greek Revival style in its most exact form, earning it the sobriquet of 'the Athens of the North'. Part of the Parthenon was built on Calton Hill off the end of Princes Street, as a national monument. Thomas Hamilton (1784–1858) reinforced his reputation when he built his faultless Greek Royal High School (now scheduled as the Scottish Assembly Building, if Scotland gets devolution) in 1825–9. Later, in Glasgow, the churches of Alexander Thomson (1817–75) were so literally Greek Revival in style that he was known as Greek Thomson.

In other parts of Britain, the British Museum by Sir Robert Smirke (1780–1867), begun in 1823 (*fig. 291*), the Custom House in Dublin (1781–91) by James Gandon (1743–1823), the National Gallery in Trafalgar Square, London (1833–8),

by William Wilkins (1778–1839), the triple Ionic archway at Hyde Park Corner (1825) by Decimus Burton (1800–81), and many other formal public buildings, were part of the Greek Revival movement initiated by Robert Adam and Sir William Chambers (1723–96), who from 1760 were joint Architects of the Works to George III. Chambers was the most celebrated academician of his day. In Somerset House in the Strand, London (1776–86), with its restrained though imposing neo-Palladian façades around four sides of the courtyard, he established the neo-classical style for government buildings in England.

But such exact purity could not last. Architects needed more fun and freedom. Even Sir William Chambers was carried away by the romantic obsession with ruins and follies. When he designed a mausoleum for Frederick, Prince of Wales, in Rome, he made two meticulous drawings, one of the finished building, the other showing the building as a ruin, its beauty enhanced by the ravages of time. He published a book on Chinese architecture (1757), and his pagoda in Kew Gardens (1761) is the only survivor of a Rococo fantasy of classical temples, Roman theatres, mosques, Moorish Alhambras and Gothic cathedrals built in the gardens during the 'Picturesque' vogue of the period.

As for John Nash (1752–1835), he was prepared to direct his fertile wits and sense of humour to any style of the past.

292 | **John Nash**,
Cumberland Terrace,
Regent's Park, London,
1826–7

293 | **John Nash**, *Royal Pavilion*, Brighton, 1815–21, Banqueting Room

skyline that is a funfair of green copper domes and minarets. Inside, vulgarity of extravagance vies with exquisite craftsmanship in a series of individual rooms (*fig. 293*), all internationally eclectic, the novelty extending even to the huge kitchen with pillars in the shape of palm trees – made in the new material, cast iron.

This late period can variously be described as Picturesque, as neo-classical or by the heading chosen for this chapter – romantic classicism – which is a combination of the two. But it ends on a distinctly romantic note. The vogue for the antique and the picturesque, which we traced in Piranesi's etchings, had placed such a cachet on medodramatic ruins – the 'ivy-mantled towers' – that men with more money than sense were actually building them. A striking example of the genre was Fonthill Abbey, Wiltshire, designed for William Beckford by James Wyatt (1747–1813), a rival of the Adam brothers, in 1796. It was a country house in the disguise of a medieval monastery on an attenuated cross-plan, its long wings housing, apparently, the church and various monastic ranges, partly in ruins. Its high polygonal Gothic tower followed the fake ruins by collapsing indeed in 1807, and the rest has since joined the tower as a ruin in earnest. But even before Fonthill, Horace Walpole had promoted neo-Gothic as a country house style when he Gothicized and enlarged Strawberry Hill in Twickenham

He translated the picturesque of the country estate to the city in his neo-classical terraces round Regent's Park, London (begun in 1812; *fig. 292*), producing continuous frontages which were as impressive as those the Woods had made in Bath and as Adam, William Playfair (1790–1857) and others had made in the New Town of Edinburgh. He also anticipated garden cities with his plans for self-contained villas around the Park, each private in its own foliage but all possessing the park. He built Gothic in Devon, Italianate in Shropshire, and an Old English thatched cottage at Blaise Hamlet near Bristol. Between 1815 and 1821, he remodelled in Chinese-Hindu style a Palladian pavilion built at Brighton for the Prince Regent by Henry Holland (1745–1806) in the 1780s. He decked out the classical symmetry of the main façade in Moorish arcades, and created a

294 | **Horace Walpole**, *Strawberry Hill*, Twickenham, London, 1748–77

in Middlesex (1748–77; *fig. 294*). Clearly, he threw himself enthusiastically into what he called the 'whimsical air of novelty' in the elaborate Gothic interior detail of, for instance, his Holbein chamber.

As so often happens, one country sets the pattern for architecture development at a particular point in time. Clearly, this was Britain's moment. But we must now look at what had been happening on the Continent at the same time. Kent's contemporary in France was Ange-Jacques Gabriel (1698–1782), who succeeded his father as chief royal architect in 1742. A consistent man, he retained his classical symmetry and composure unadulterated until the end. The same cannot be said of his successor, Richard Mique (1728–94), whose structures in the gardens of Le Petit Trianon, Versailles, represent the infection of English romanticism to produce what the French call *folies*. Here he built a delightful little temple, called the Temple of Love (1778; *fig. 295*), embowered in weeping greenery, which owes something to Greece, to Rome and to England. He constructed an artificial peasant village called Le Hameau, where the capricious Marie Antoinette played at being a country girl and came to milk the goats from time to time. Mique was only one of a prolific generation of architects born between 1725 and 1750. Better-known are Claude-Nicolas Ledoux (1736–1806) and Etienne Louis Boullée (1728–99), both of whose work has an almost fantastic grandeur. In Boullée's case little ever went further than the drawing-board. He is best remembered for a design for a monument to the astronomer, Isaac Newton, an enormous sphere set into a double ring base, which demonstrates the desire to exploit the use of massive geometric figures.

Examples of Ledoux's work, on the other hand, have survived. He built a ring of 45 toll-houses around Paris, all with different plans and elevations, and basically classical in style; only four remain, of

295 | **Richard Mique**, *Temple of Love*, Le Petit Trianon, Versailles, 1778

which the best is probably La Barrière de la Villette (1785–9). As an architect to the king, he was nearly guillotined, and many of his toll-houses were destroyed in the Revolution. Before that, in the late 1770s, he built a Greek Revival theatre at Besançon. But one of his most interesting essays was an early example of industrial architecture, a city for chemical workers at a salt mine, La Saline de Chaux, at Arc-et-Senans, on the river Loue near Besançon, begun in 1775. Little is left today; the entrance is through a rough, strong row of Doric columns, stumpy and sitting on the ground without any base, while behind is a romantic grotto with round niches, in which are carved stone urns pouring out stone water.

Ledoux's columns reflect a controversy raging at the time as to what early Greek columns had really been like. The two distinguishing features of neo-classicism at this period were long colonnades and giant classical columns, whose proportions were supposed to be those of ancient Greece. It was a great shock to the classicists and antiquarians to discover that the true Doric order had been relatively short and squat, and had, most shocking of all, no base. What had always been pictured as Greek Doric – the taller, slimmer version – was in fact Roman Doric if fluted and the older Roman form, Tuscan Doric, if unfluted. It is no doubt a good thing that the purists were spared the knowledge we now possess, that the early Greek temples were decorated in vivid colours. Neo-classical buildings were very colourless.

The most eminent buildings in extreme neo-classical style, showing clearly the use of colonnades and antique columns, are to be found in Germany. Friedrich Gilly, who died in 1800 of consumption at the age of 28, left only drawings. But the dignity and quality of his designs for a memorial to Frederick the Great and the more original, less formally classical design for a national theatre in Berlin make us regret that he wasted some of his short life in studying knights' medieval castles in Prussia. His pupil Karl Friedrich Schinkel (1781–1841) had more to offer the world, for he straddled several styles and several eras. He too had his romantic side: as a painter and scenic

designer, he produced a particularly memorable neo-Egyptian palace for the Queen of the Night in a production of Mozart's opera, *The Magic Flute*, in 1815. He extended his classical debt to Gilly by learning from Ledoux and Boullée, when, in 1803, he took himself to Paris and Italy. But his eyes were not turned backwards only; he looked with keen interest towards the new productions of the Industrial Revolution – the factories and the machines they housed – and to the new materials coming into use – cast iron, papier maché, zinc. Schinkel's two best-known buildings, the Schauspielhaus (1819–21) and the Altes Museum (1823–30; *fig. 296*) in Berlin, are both in faultless Greek idiom. But there is something more than cold correctness in his work, and something almost spellbinding about the long low colonnade of the Altes Museum.

But we must recognize that, as in England, the very architects whose work exemplified the classical revival were often equally effective when working in the romantic idiom. In France, Ange-Jacques Gabriel built in the grounds of the palace of Versailles one of the first perfect (and at the same time highly romantic) neo-classical buildings, Le Petit Trianon (1762–8; *fig. 297*). A little cube house in pale limestone and rose-pink

296 | **Karl Schinkel**, *Altes Museum*, Berlin, 1823–30

297 | **Ange-Jacques Gabriel**, *Le Petit Trianon*, Versailles, 1762–8

marble with a long arcade effect across the front, it was built for Louis XV. It was later altered for Marie Antoinette. Gabriel's working life was long enough for him to complete two urban layouts, 20 years apart, the Place de la Bourse, Bordeaux, and the Place de la Concorde, Paris, both based on the Louvre colonnade. The Place de la Bourse (formerly the Place Royale) which he built between 1731 and 1755, has Ionic columns and high French roofs, while the Place de la Concorde (1753–65) shows in contrast those two most typical features of the classical revival: giant Corinthian columns and long balustrades.

It was in many ways a very literary period, in which the philosophical writers and intellectuals of the time exerted an important influence on the artistic movements as well as the great political movements which were changing the face of the world–like the French Revolution and the break-away of the American colonies.

But perhaps it is just this combination of rationalism and strict classicism with fantasy, elegance and the worship of nature and beauty which makes this period so fascinating, and which explains why the use of the label 'romantic classicism' is appropriate.

In the centuries we have just discussed, Europe had been preoccupied by what was going on within its own brilliant, vital confines. But archaeological excavations, travel, explorations and missionary work were all serving to open up territories hitherto unknown. The wider world now demands to make its contribution to our theme.

We are talking here not simply of European travellers dabbling in bits of foreign detail that they had come across in their travels, as today an artist may take a holiday in Africa, Mexico or the Andes to draw on the folk-art of an alien culture to enrich his own work with new themes and colour schemes. That kind of interaction did, of course, exist. The early association between South America and Spain and Portugal led to the importation after 1500 of American Indian details into European architecture, with notable effect on the Plateresque type of decoration and the Churrigueresque in Spain and Portugal. Again, during the eighteenth and nineteenth centuries there was a vogue among the Romantics of Europe for all things Chinese. In architecture, it was apparent in the building of follies within great gardens, pagodas and bridges — nothing very serious. And the fashion for *chinoiserie*, a delicate decoration of wall surface, and furniture and porcelain whose motifs were drawn from Chinese artefacts (of any period) was apparent inside the house. Its applications are clearly as Rococo as Adam's 'Etruscan' Greek nymphs. Any country house with a pretension to being fashionable had to have a Chinese room.

That kind of interaction was little more than petty pilfering. It was another matter where the Europeans established colonies, or where missionary activity brought areas within the sphere and responsibility of a European country. For the English in America, it was the settlements of the eastern seaboard that were their progeny; while Canada, parts of Florida and Louisiana owed their existence to France. There were Spanish settlements in Florida, too, and South America was being opened up by both Spain and Portugal. Spanish missions, originally largely Franciscan, later Dominican and Jesuit, worked their way across South America, up the western seaboard of California, and eventually across to New Mexico, leaving behind charming white-washed adobe churches with bell-towers in the gable, and mission buildings around courtyards which enclosed a garden, a graveyard for the brothers, and a fountain or well for the village water supply. The monastery of the Mercedarian order at Quito of 1630 (*fig. 299*), with its two-storey loggia around the garden courtyard, shows a more sophisticated form. But not all colonizers went west. India and Indonesia were settled,

298 | **Thomas Jefferson, William Thornton** and **Benjamin Latrobe**, *University of Virginia*, Charlottesville, Virginia, 1817–26

299 | *Mercedarian Monastery,*
Quito, Ecuador, 1630

converted and exploited by the English, the Dutch and the Portuguese; Australia had yet to enter the picture.

The architectural style adopted in the colonies was at first a primitive version of that of the parent country at the time of colonization. Bit by bit, pragmatic adaptations due to climatic conditions, to the availability of local materials and to the skills of local craftsmen, combined to produce a version that bore the hallmark of that particular country in its own right. In Brazil, where art was primitive and there was no tradition of building in stone, the architectural style tended to be a straight import from Portugal. In other areas, such as New Mexico, it was the native Indian adobe tradition that won.

In Santa Fe, New Mexico, outpost of the Spanish empire at the end of the Trail, the route south and west from Missouri before the railways were built, building heights are still strictly controlled. There is nothing today to distinguish the age and eminence of the Governor's Palace (1610–14; *fig. 300*), just off the main plaza, from the surrounding buildings. Houses, government buildings and churches all tend to be built of Indian adobe brick, with the windows and doors moulded into curves that are typical of the medium, their wooden-raftered roofs often packed with a slim local tree, the palo verde. The Palace is a long, low, one-storey building with a wooden loggia running along its length in whose

shelter Indians from nearby reservations spread out rugs, basketwork and jewellery to sell to tourists. In contrast to that, a distinctive French flavour is apparent in the grid plan of New Orleans and in the colonnaded galleries of the humid towns of Louisiana, for example Parlange, Pointe Coupee Parish, of 1750.

But it was in the churches of Mexico and Peru, some of the earliest colonial buildings still in existence, that there first appeared a combination of the traditions and talents of settlers with those of the natives. Along with their motto, 'For Christ and gold' (an echo of the 'For God and profit' that a Renaissance merchant in Florence wrote on the fly-sheet of his ledger), the conquistadores brought with them their richly decorated form of Baroque. Once churches were built with local labour, further embellishments appeared, whose origins went back to the crafts and motifs of the Aztecs and the Incas, for both these Indian peoples commanded a mastery of masonry, carving and metalwork far exceeding that of their Spanish conquerors.

The Chapel of the Three Kings (1718–37), by Jerónimo de Balbás (*c.*1680–1748), and the attached Sagrario (Sacrament Chapel) of the cathedral in Mexico City are even more exuberantly encrusted with Churrigueresque ornament than any Spanish model, and all the more astounding because so much gilt paint was used. The mouldings are

300 | *Governor's Palace,*
Santa Fe, New Mexico, 1610–14

301 | *Metropolitan Cathedral*, Mexico City, 1563–, altar and reredos

further serrated by the proliferation of a typical New World detail – the *estipite*, or broken pilaster (*fig. 301*). The cathedral, built from 1563 onwards by a series of architects, replaced a primitive structure which the conquistadores had built in order to obliterate the memory of the Aztec temple that had once stood on the same site. The neo-classical west front with its twin towers in fawn limestone was added by José Damián Ortiz in 1786, and the dome and lantern by Manuel Tolsá (1757–1816) even later, in the nineteenth century. The cathedral at Zacatecas, Mexico (1729–52), has similar Churrigueresque detail resembling lichens and plant forms swarming all over the façade and towers.

302 | *São Francisco*, Bahia (Salvador), Brazil, 1701–, main altar

The church of São Francisco at Bahia (now Salvador), on the Brazilian coast, is later than the two Mexican cathedrals since it was started in 1701, but still bears the Aztec/Baroque forms in gilt wood and plaster (*fig. 302*). The seventeenth-century cathedral in the ancient Inca city of Cuzco, in Peru, in contrast, chooses as its Spanish element the severe classicism of Philip II's Escorial, but with a different fluidity in slim pillars rising up the west front to a semicircular pediment. In similar vein, the original idea for the Jesuits' church in the same city, the Compañia (1651–), may have come from Il Gesù in Rome, but it developed twin bell-towers, topped (in a very un-European manner) with little cupolas, each with four tiny corner turrets.

The earliest church on the continent, said to have been founded by Cortez and built about 1521, is San Francisco at Tlaxcala, near Mexico City, where local cedar wood was used for beams. There is an example of late Spanish Gothic, with a Plateresque west front of 1521–41, at Santo Domingo in the Dominican Republic (*fig. 303*). At about the time the Santo Domingo cathedral was being finished another church was being built in Mexico City, San Agustin Acolman, which reveals Gothic and Moorish details grafted on to a basically Spanish Plateresque style. In the brilliant sunshine the ornament, carved by Indian craftsmen, shows up as incredibly incisive. The difficulties of responding to topographical conditions is well illustrated in the cathedral at Lima, Peru. The first vaults, built in the mid-sixteenth century, were of stone – the material they would have chosen at home. Then, after the first devastating earthquake, they tried brick. Finally, in the eighteenth century they capitulated to nature and used wooden vaults with reed and plaster in-fill – a replaceable construction for future emergencies.

By the eighteenth century, when the Baroque was already out of fashion in

303 | *Santo Domingo Cathedral*, Dominican Republic, 1521–41

233

304 | *Sagrario*, Ocotlán, Mexico, 1745

305 | **Aleijadinho**, *São Francisco de Assis*, Ouro Preto, Brazil, 1766–

São Francisco at Ouro Preto (*fig. 305*) was designed by a mulatto, Antonio Francisco Lisboa (*c*.1738–1814), better known by his nickname Aleijadinho, or Little Cripple. In 1766, in the gold-mining district of Minas Gerais, he started building this unique white church with contrasting lintels and cornices. Its proportions, the slim pillars on either side of the entrance section and the undulating cornice may suggest Borromini, but the two round towers and the extraordinary gable with spread wings are totally original. He also carved a dramatic series of life-size statues of prophets up the entrance stairway to the Conghas do Campo church, built in 1800, which has a presence reminiscent of Bom Jesus, Braga (*fig. 273*).

After that floridity – exuberant Baroque tempered with peasant innocence – it is almost a shock to find a style of severe simplicity in the dwellings of the early settlers on the eastern seaboard of North America. The Europeans who first landed in South America were conquerors; the first settlers in the New England states were pilgrims seeking freedom to worship and escape from want and fear. Their barns scattered round the United States and Canada are beautiful primitive structures in oak and thatch or aspen shingle that bespeak different European origins. They evolved a distinctive type of frame house – the balloon frame, which could easily be erected by a pioneering community, the whole village working together. The principle was to hammer together the grid frame for each side of a building flat on the ground. It was then hoisted into position with ropes, and tacked on to the corner posts which had been driven into the ground. Settlers who became established and prosperous built in the classical Georgian style that they had left behind in England – but in wood, for in the New World they found little stone or lime. Swedish settlers of the sixteenth century brought with them the log-cabin technique, and by 1649 the first

Europe, South American Baroque had found its own self-confident individuality – a combination of naivety with dazzling beauty, exemplified in two very different churches, the Sagrario at Ocotlán, Mexico, and São Francisco de Assis, at Ouro Preto, Brazil. Their common ancestor was the front added to the cathedral of Santiago de Compostella in 1738. But they created very different towers, with a change of gable and decoration, that give quite another proportion and outline to the churches.

The Sagrario at Ocotlán, a pilgrimage church of 1745 (*fig. 304*), built where an Indian had seen a vision of the Virgin, rears up against the vivid Mexican sky across a wide empty plaza, with ranges of very Moorish buildings on either side – a double-storey arcade of wide round-headed arches on very slim pillars to one side, an archway into a pishtaq-like rectangular façade on the other. A round-headed panel of carved stucco in deep relief goes all the way up the west front between the two towers. The towers are in unglazed red brick on their lower reaches, quietly patterned all over in fish-scales, but at the top they suddenly burst into two-tired, top-heavy white turrets, fretted and spiky. The interior was richly carved by a local sculptor, Francisco Miguel.

306 | *Longfellow House,* Cambridge, Massachusetts, 1759

saw-mill was working. The very earliest houses, like Parson Capen House, Topsfield, Massachusetts, of 1683 by an unknown architect, had timber frames and shingle roofs and were then clad in clapboard. The upper floor jutted out over the lower in a jetty, typical of English Elizabethan and Jacobean frame houses. The windows, on the other hand, were not recessed as in English Georgian brick or stone, but flush with the wall, as suited timber. Quite a few examples still remain in Massachusetts and Connecticut: Longfellow House, Cambridge (1759; *fig. 306*), represents the type in a later, more elegant, form. By that time the house had grown a loggia or a porch, or possibly balconies for sitting out in hot weather. The early houses with weather-boarding, small leaded window panes and a central chimney serving both downstairs rooms from fireplaces in a dividing brick wall, had coped excellently with the winter weather. Now that establishment gave more ease, consideration was given to the leisured summer hours.

Early towns like Salem, Nantucket and Charleston retain charming tree-shaded streets lined with balconied houses for which, unfortunately, we seldom know the architects. The typical low-pitched roof was often flattened at the top and edged with a wooden balustrade to form a terrace known as *captain's walk*. Handsome two-storey Palladian colonnades, with the tall slim pillars made possible by wood, and avenues of great trees were often features of the grand houses, which, like the tobacco planter's house, Shirley Plantation, on the James River in Virginia of 1723–70 (*fig. 307*), often looked out across ample parkland, in a land where there was plenty of space. George Washington's timber Georgian house at Mount Vernon, Virginia (1757–87), shows a similar shady gallery. Brick was commonly used in Virginia, and sometimes, as at Mount Pleasant

307 | *Shirley Plantation,* Virginia, 1723–70

in Philadelphia (1761), rubbled walls were stuccoed over and scored to look like stonework, while brick was used for the quoins.

In the second capital of Virginia, Williamsburg, are the earliest Renaissance buildings in North America, the College of William and Mary (1695–1702; *fig. 308*), now entirely preserved and restored. They form a U-shaped college, consisting of classrooms flanked by the

309 | **Thomas Jefferson**, *Monticello*, Charlottesville, Virginia, 1770–96

308 | *College of William and Mary*, Williamsburg, Virginia, 1695–1702

chapel and refectory wings, for which Wren may have drawn up the sketch-plans in his capacity as Royal Surveyor of England. By that time the thrifty home-spun houses of the early settlers had passed. William Byrd, for example, imported English fittings for his gracious and ample brick house, Westover, in Charles City County, Virginia (1730–4). Ballrooms and extensive gardens evoke a sophisticated society life in the Governor's Palace at Williamsburg (1706–20).

Then classicism came to America through Thomas Jefferson (1743–1826), who was to write the Declaration of Independence and become President. He had served as ambassador at Versailles,

at the time France was going through a Palladian phase, caught from the English enthusiasm. Jefferson returned to America inspired by Paris, by Palladio and by the ancient Roman remains, particularly those at Nîmes, which he saw in the 1780s. He had already built himself a Palladian villa at Monticello near Charlottesville, Virginia, in 1770, which owed much to the Villa Rotonda, and in 1796 he made use of his French experience in remodelling it (*fig. 309*). It has projecting bays and odd-shaped rooms such as he had seen in Parisian hôtels. It stands on a small hill looking towards the Blue Ridge Mountains and to the site where he later built the University of Virginia, and is full of light. It is larger than it looks at first, with extensive domestic quarters,

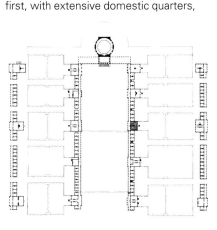

310 | **Thomas Jefferson**, **William Thornton** and **Benjamin Latrobe**, University of Virginia, Charlottesville, Virginia, 1817–26, plan

including wine cellars and stables built into a basement. It is a treasure-trove of quirky inventions – dumb waiters which swing out of sight, gadgets for opening shutters, beds that can be entered from two rooms – that testify to the genius of the man.

Jefferson, aided by William Thornton (1759–1828) and Benjamin Latrobe (1764–1820), planned his 'academical village' at Charlottesville (the University of Virginia) between 1817 and 1826 as a living museum of different sizes and types of classical buildings (*figs. 298, 310; also pp. 4–5*). Across the top is a library, modelled on the Pantheon and recently rebuilt; and then down either side of a series of leisurely sloping lawns are the buildings used as both classrooms and staff houses. This pattern became established as typical of the campus of an American university. Around the lawns are gardens of scented shrubs that separate the main quadrangle from the houses originally built to accommodate the slave servants of the early students. It is only slightly less grand than the plan created by Pierre Charles L'Enfant (1754–1825) for Washington, the gracious capital city on the banks of the Potomac river. Washington's great Mall is studded with monuments to American origins, and it is laid out in a grid crossed diagonally by avenues which bear the names of the states to which they point. The Palladian White House (1792–1829), designed by an Irishman, James Hoban (1764–1820), with porticoes added by Latrobe, stands aloof just off the Mall with a suitable air of reticence and good breeding. It does not dominate Washington; but it does reflect its elegance.

The Roman grid around the central square, where the church and the town meeting-hall stood, became typical, a planning exercise derived from France and Ireland rather than from England. The characteristic American church of the period, such as Christchurch,

Boston (1723), or St Michael's, Charleston (1752–61), was strongly in debt to Wren's city churches and to James Gibbs, particularly in the common combination of classical temple porticoes with a more Gothic spire. Then Latrobe, in the Catholic cathedral at Baltimore of 1805–18 (*fig. 311*), created a spacious, vaulted interior with America's first coffered dome by adapting the French and English classical influences of his training.

For classicism had come to America with Jefferson; at which point the new country entered the architectural lists with an originality that prefigured the major role she was to play in the next two centuries. That originality was to be seen first in the grand buildings for government, commerce and finance in which classicism had already shown its power. Latrobe's Bank of Philadelphia (1832–4) was one such example. Then William Strickland (1787–1854), the William

311 | **Benjamin Latrobe**, *Catholic Cathedral*, Baltimore, 1805–18

312 | **William Thornton**, **Benjamin Latrobe** and **Thomas Ustick Walter**, *Capitol*, Washington DC, 1793–1867

Wilkins of America, undeterred by a difficult corner site, achieved his stunning piece of Greek Revival in the Philadelphia Merchants' Exchange of 1823–4, giving his approach an elevational dignity with a colonnaded apse and, with spectacular economy, surmounting his building not with a dome but with a simple tempietto lantern based on the Choragic Monument of Lysicrates. William Thornton, an English architect and an amateur at that, started the Capitol at Washington in 1793 with a basic Parthenon shape; but the feature that gives it its world-famous silhouette, the triple-tiara dome by Thomas Ustick Walter (1804–88), places this building firmly in the nine-

teenth century: completed in 1867, it is made of cast iron (*fig. 312*).

Across the globe cast iron figured in the intricate lacework balconies and railings that were to become characteristic of suburban Melbourne and Sydney (*fig. 313*). This was a more sophisticated use of iron than the homely corrugated iron roofs that are a feature of the Australian house-type, largely because they respond so well to the summer climate. Because of the way the states sold off narrow-fronted blocks of land to settlers, the characteristic Australian development was a row of narrow one-storey boxes, often with extensions 'tacked-on' at the back, and with balconies, also roofed in corrugated iron, wrapped around as many sides of the house as the owner could afford. The less vernacular and more pretentious Georgian or classical-style buildings are generally of a lower quality than those of North America.

Not so the public buildings for New South Wales commissioned by Governor Lachlan Macquarie from his aide-de-camp, Lieutenant John Watts and the York convict-architect Francis Greenway (1777–1837), which date from 1815 onwards. They include St James's Church, Sydney (1824; *fig. 314*), with typical careful Greenway brickwork and a copper-sheathed spire. It started construction as the Law Courts and had to be redesigned by the long-suffering architect when the Commissioner from the English Home Office cancelled plans for a cathedral on another site.

Tasmania has some of the continent's oldest buildings, with some charming Georgian houses in Hobart, kin to the terraces of Brighton, Sussex, with views out to sea. Perth's Mediterranean climate encouraged a Victorian interpretation of Italian Renaissance. In the Lands Department Building (1895–6) and the Titles Office Building, Cathedral Avenue (1897), both by George Temple-Poole (1856–1934), smooth rich red brick combines with ranks of white colonnaded balconies under wide shadowy coffered eaves.

The eighteenth- and nineteenth-century upsurge of buildings of commerce and authority, erected in neo-Palladian or neo-classical style, was not limited to the Australian state capitals. Throughout the British Empire, from the West Indies to Malaysia, rose ponderously, in Palladian or Roman Doric, buildings with the 'Government look', typified in Government House, Calcutta (1799–1802; *fig. 315*), designed by Captain Charles Wyatt (1758–1819), a nephew of James Wyatt, as well as in churches built after Gibbs, such as those of Calcutta and Madras, often also designed by soldier-architects.

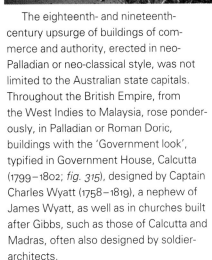

315 | **Charles Wyatt**, *Government House*, Calcutta, India, 1799–1802

313 | *Parkville*, Melbourne, Australia

314 | **Francis Greenway**, *St James's Church*, Sydney, Australia, 1824

By the opening of the nineteenth century the confidence apparent in the architecture of the age of elegance in the preceding century had evaporated. The agitation brought in by the French Revolution of 1789 had never fully subsided, and a different kind of society began to take shape; by the end of the Napoleonic wars, effectively from the 1820s, changes were becoming obvious.

It was an age of uncertainty. It was also an age that witnessed the emergence of a powerful new force in society – the bourgeoisie. The bourgeoisie were the real victors of the French Revolution and its aftermath. Work and leisure were shaped by them, no longer by the great aristocratic patrons of the eighteenth century, and not yet, if indeed ever, by the working classes in whose name the revolution was said to have been made. The fashionable architecture of the nineteenth century was designed to meet middle-class aspirations.

There was another revolution every bit as influential as the French, the Industrial Revolution. It was cradled in Britain, from roughly 1750 to 1850, although it was not seen as a revolution but only new ways of making things. It received its name in the nineteenth century.

It began with the exploitation of natural resources, especially water and coal, found its first achievements in Britain and then spread with a relentless force throughout the world. The urban population dramatically increased, towns and cities multiplied in number and size, a new urban society emerged. The demand for new buildings was greater than ever before. Many of them, as we shall see, were unprecedented, designed to satisfy the needs and demands of a changing society.

To the fashionable architects the central – and often stated – problem was to discover a style appropriate to this time of change. They had inherited from the previous century the understanding and experience of classicism, with all the clarity of its formal language. Above all, classical and neo-classical architecture expressed authority. They needed authority. The rival to the classical system was Gothic. The Romantic movement in art and literature found in the soaring attenuated forms of the Gothic style a suitable background for imagination and mystery. There were plenty of other styles, Renaissance and Baroque, Chinese, Saracenic, about which more was being discovered every year. But Classical and Gothic were the main contenders in the Battle of the Styles. Revived Gothic in particular went through the usual phases of growth and maturity – from superficial whimsy to a more basic understanding and thence to the freedom of personal expression. No one had a greater or more lasting influence than the prolific writer and critic,

316 | **Joseph Paxton**, *Crystal Palace*, London, 1851, interior

John Ruskin (1819–1900) whose *Seven Lamps of Architecture* (1849) probably had more influence on the history of taste than any other book. It was not only his massive scholarship; he provided the intellectual authority that enabled the public to feel they could distinguish the good from the bad, and recognize what was right and what was wrong.

Appropriately, the finest illustration of the stylistic predicament was the very seat of law-making in Britain, the Houses of Parliament. In 1834 a fire destroyed the Palace of Westminster, except for the Great Hall. The competition for a new palace to house Lords and Commons was won by Charles Barry (1795–1860) in 1836. Barry was a skilled exponent of the classical style. He had created the very symbol of the rise of middle-class political power in the Travellers' Club (1827) and the Reform Club (1837) in Pall Mall. Both were in his Italianate manner. Their elevations were immensely influential and, with various adaptations, spread through the country's public and commercial buildings and housing developments of the mid-century. Inside, the Reform Club had a large glazed court, a prototype of the central hall common in later

317 | **Charles Barry** and **A.W.N. Pugin**, *Houses of Parliament*, London, 1836–51

The Triumph of the Iron Masters: *The Search for a Style*

nineteenth-century monumental planning. With his usual concern for technical modernity, Barry installed a very advanced steam kitchen for the famous chef, Alexis Soyer.

Barry's problem with the Houses of Parliament (*fig. 317*) was that the government had decided that the new building should be in the style thought to represent England at its best – Elizabethan or Jacobean. That required greater knowledge of late Gothic than Barry possessed. He had produced a logical classical plan, which could easily have been given classical elevations. To make them Gothic he recruited the greatest living authority on Gothic, Augustus Welby Northmore Pugin (1812–52). Pugin designed the elevations, the details, and the interiors, using stone, brass, plaster, paper and glass with a tremendous vital intensity. The House of Commons was bombed during the Second World War and has been restored; the House of Lords remains in its full glory and testifies to the adaptability and richness of the Gothic style.

In addition to the Houses of Parliament Pugin designed several hundred churches, five cathedrals and a number of great houses, and wrote and published major works on Gothic architecture and furniture; he exhausted three wives, countless contractors, finally himself, and died insane at the age of 40. His influence was profound, for he supplied the vocabulary of Gothic. More important, he announced the two principles upon which he believed architecture should depend – that there should be no features about a building which are not necessary for convenience, construction or propriety, and that ornament should not just be applied but express the essential structure of the building. He found these characteristics in Gothic. And since Christianity, in particular Catholicism, was the way to salvation, Gothic or Pointed architecture had ultimate authority. Of his many churches

the one least changed, with its elaborate colour and furnishings, is St Giles, Cheadle, in Staffordshire, built from 1841 to 1846 (*fig. 318*).

If Pugin was the leading theorist of the Gothic Revival as well as a prolific designer, the man who created far more buildings, while recognizing Pugin as his mentor, was George Gilbert Scott (1811–78), knighted as Sir Gilbert by Queen Victoria shortly before his death. He designed a multitude of buildings of many kinds. In the context of this story, his St Pancras Station and Hotel in London (1865) are a revealing episode. For while the station front and the hotel are in Scott's Gothic style, the huge, high and wide train shed behind it, designed by the engineer W. H. Barlow (1812–92), is a dramatic contrast, a product of the new technology.

The strange thing is that although Pugin, and many architects who followed him, detested the world of industry and

318 | **A.W.N. Pugin**, *St Giles*, Cheadle, Staffordshire, 1841–6

319 | **Cuthbert Brodrick**, *Leeds Town Hall*, 1853

reacted against it strongly, which ultimately led to the Arts and Crafts movement of the end of the century, his principles, in all their seriousness and simplicity, and their emphasis on function, were those you might associate with the Industrial Revolution. It is to the effects of that revolution that we must now turn.

Leading up to it was the work of the great engineers and surveyors – Telford, who at the turn of the century and in its early decades built bridges, roads, canals and churches; the Stephensons, who built bridges and railways; Brunel, who built bridges, roads, railways and ships. The buildings and artefacts of industry provided knowledge and experience that could be adapted to architecture, which now grew at an unprecedented rate. The Albert Dock in Liverpool, for example, designed by Jesse Hartley (1780–1860) and opened by Prince Albert in 1845, was a vast warehouse scheme covering seven acres, with iron-framed buildings clad in brick and resting on massive cast-iron Doric columns, one of the masterpieces of industrial architecture. On the other side of the Pennines a young architect, Cuthbert Brodrick (1822–1905), won the competition for Leeds Town Hall in 1853, and created the very symbol of civic pride in one of the new wealthy industrial cities (*fig. 319*). It radiated confidence with its great rectangular plan and gigan-

tic Corinthian order; dominating everything was its tall French-looking Baroque tower. A few years later, Brodrick made another symbolic gesture. The Grand Hotel at Scarborough (1863–7), was, as its name implies, the grandest hotel of its time, spectacularly located on the edge of a hill above the sea. It was a middle-class dream. It used brick and terracotta and had an original roof line with bulging towers. It was brilliantly planned and used the latest service technology available.

These buildings have been selected because of their merit, but also because they represent the demand for buildings which had either not existed before or, if they had, had played only a minor role in the history of architecture. With increased wealth and increased population, the task of creating country houses for the new rich and city churches for the new urban population provided plenty of work for domestic and ecclesiastical architects. But the buildings that dominate the nineteenth century are not so much those as clubs, government buildings, town halls, hotels and a vast array of others: banks, offices, libraries, museums, galleries, exhibition buildings, shops, arcades, law courts, prisons, hospitals, schools, colleges, and the more obvious products of the industrial age – railway stations, docks, bridges, viaducts, factories and warehouses. We shall see some of these taking over the architectural scene in other countries.

That was one major change. The other major change was brought about by the Industrial Revolution itself, mainly by the

320 | **Abraham Darby**, *Iron Bridge*, Coalbrookdale, Shropshire, 1777

transformation of building technology. This came in the form of new, man-made building materials, new structural techniques and new technical services. Together they produced a universal structural system that could be applied to the new building types.

The structural possibilities of iron were first demonstrated on a dramatic scale in England in 1777 at Coalbrookdale by the iron bridge that crossed the river Severn (*fig. 320*). Within a few years iron was being extensively used for columns and frames, together with hollow clay tile floors, to provide a fireproof construction for the mills. By the beginning of the nineteenth century that system developed into a complete internal skeleton of stanchions and beams. The skeleton, which had from the beginning been one of the basic methods of building, had come into its own again.

The advantages of iron over masonry in terms of economy and strength without bulk led to its adoption for more fashionable buildings – churches, large houses with roofed courtyards, clubs, public buildings. In 1839 the roof of Chartres Cathedral was replaced with a new cast-iron roof above the stone vaults; and iron was used for the roofs of the New Palace of Westminster a few years later. After the 1850s its use declined for a time, mainly because of architects' preferences for other materials and the intellectual dominance of Ruskin. But for the bulk of ordinary buildings in what has recently come to be known as the Functional tradition – in bridges, railway stations, conservatories, market halls, shops and offices – iron was an obvious choice.

Iron – at first, cast iron and wrought iron (made more flexible and strong in tension as a result of an invention patented in 1785), and then steel, following the invention of the Bessemer process in 1856 – lent itself to the most dramatic and large-scale enterprises. Other materials familiar in preceding centuries took on a

new life or new characteristics. Advances in plate-glass manufacture in the 1840s, coupled with the lifting of duty and tax, ensured its widespread use from the 1850s onwards. Bricks, hitherto hand-made, were mechanized and there were new types and a huge variety of shapes, patterns and colours. And traditional craftsmanship began to change, sometimes to the dismay of architects and critics such as Ruskin.

Craftsmanship changed through the production of manufactured building elements and prefabrication. It followed that the operations on the site were also mechanized. That in itself required larger organizations than the old craft firms could cope with; hence the rise of the large building contractors. The needs of industry led to the development of new technical services in heating, ventilation and sanitation, which began to be applied to domestic architecture as well. Central heating, not used since the time of the Romans, reappeared in the form of steam-heating systems in the early nineteenth century; cold- and hot-water systems and sanitary plumbing developed rapidly in the second half of the century. Gas lighting came to London in 1809, and that brought a new dimension to living – urban night life. In 1801, Volta demonstrated to Napoleon the production of electricity from a pile battery; by the 1880s electric light was available to those who could afford it and were prepared to take the risk of using it. Elevators, telephones and mechanical ventilation were introduced in the last decades of the century. However much people may have regretted or been frightened by the scale and rapidity of the changes, what had been produced in a hundred years was a whole new range of possibilities, and therefore a new aesthetic and a new challenge to the designer. How was he to cope with change and express architectural qualities in such a revolutionary milieu?

321 | **Joseph Paxton**, *Crystal Palace*, London, 1851

One building more than any other in Britain brought these discoveries together and became the most influential innovation of its time, influencing, because thousands of people came to see it, the architecture of the world. That was the Crystal Palace in London, housing the Great Exhibition of 1851 (*figs. 316, 321*). Everything about it was symptomatic of the age and a portent of the future. It was the brain-child not of an architect, but of a gardener, Joseph Paxton (1801–65). He brought to the problem of a vast space the lessons he had learned in building greenhouses on the Duke of Devonshire's great country estate at Chatsworth, Derbyshire. The Crystal Palace was prefabricated, it was light and transparent, supported and enclosed by iron and glass. Its form was revolutionary in that it was indeterminate; there was no reason why it should not be made bigger or smaller, longer or

wider. It had no conventional style. Its erection depended upon railway transport and sophisticated organization on the site. It was constructed in nine months. And it could be taken down and put up again, as it was at Sydenham in 1852, where it survived until it was destroyed by fire in 1936.

Because of the vast output of construction in Britain – it must for many years have seemed like a vast building site, especially in the towns and cities – it is impossible to do more than note a few typical buildings. Of those that consciously followed some sort of style by choosing to use Romanesque or Gothic in one of its many forms or derivations are the Natural History Museum, London (1868–80; *fig. 322*), by Alfred Waterhouse (1830–1905), in yellow and blue terracotta with lively animal detail, the Law Courts, London (1874–82), by G.E. Street (1824–81), the swan-song of the Gothic revival in England and of the architect, who died of overwork, and the Royal Infirmary, Edinburgh (1872–9), by David Bryce (1803–76), a very successful Scottish architect with many dramatic buildings in Edinburgh to his credit. The most original architect within that tradition was William Butterfield (1814–1900), whose All Saints, Margaret Street, London (1847–59), was seen at the time as the complete demonstration of the principles of Pugin applied

322 | **Alfred Waterhouse**, *Natural History Museum*, London, 1868–80

323 | **Peter Ellis**, *Oriel Chambers*, Liverpool, 1864

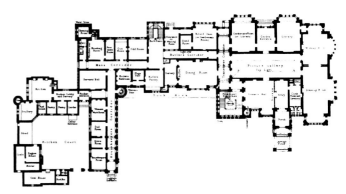

324 | **Robert Kerr**, *Bear Wood*, Berkshire, 1865–8, plan

to the High Church practice of the Church of England. The church, vicarage and hall are closely grouped around a small court; the spire is tall and the nave high. And it is full of ingenuity in, for example, the roof trusses, the highly decorated flat surfaces and the frank expression of materials with inherent colour. It is Victorian architecture at its most uncompromising. Gothic was no longer a revival; it was a vehicle for personal expression. Oriel Chambers, Liverpool (*fig. 323*), built in 1864 by Peter Ellis (1804–84), was more original in its construction as well as in its function as offices. It used a light iron frame and masonry piers, and provided a neat solution to the problem of creating an interesting rhythm with plate-glass fenestration by using shallow oriels the height of the building.

There is one other essential feature of nineteenth-century architecture which can only be appreciated by looking at a plan. Bear Wood in Berkshire (1865–8) was designed for the owner of *The Times* by Robert Kerr (1823–1904), the author of *The Gentleman's House* (1864), a standard book on nineteenth-century domestic design. In the event it was a failure as a house and in its appearance, which is not worth illustrating. But its planning illustrates Victorian architecture at its most ingenious (*fig. 324*). Advanced technology is exploited for plumbing, gas lighting, central heating and fireproof construction; the plan is a *tour de force* of planning, with intricate lines of communication between the multiplicity of rooms, the separation and definition of every function and different spaces for each, including even stairs for bachelors.

That brilliance in planning was even more dramatically demonstrated in France, with the design of the Opéra, Paris (1861–75; *figs. 325, 326*), by Charles Garnier (1825–98). Stylistically, it is a triumph of sumptuous historicism, with wonderful colour inside and out, and plastic Baroque forms and sculpture. But the plan is exquisite. Most people find it difficult to read a plan, but this one is worth studying; it shows the architect's mind working on every function and space,

325 | **Charles Garnier**, *Opéra*, Paris, 1861–75

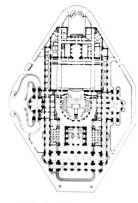

326 | *Opéra*, plan

every corner and detail. In the nineteenth century the French became the leaders of monumental planning and have remained so until today.

Apart from planning, there are two other aspects of nineteenth-century French architecture to be emphasized, which show the range of problems that architects and engineers set out to solve. The first, which affected other European countries, was, as the Opéra itself demonstrated, the theory of 'architectural polychromy'. The spokesman for the theory was a not very good architect, J.-I. Hittorff (1792–1867), who based his beliefs on discoveries made about ancient Greek buildings. In 1823 he found evidence at Selinus and Agrigentum that classical Greek buildings had been highly and even vulgarly coloured. In the 1820s and 1830s there was heated discussion; such a belief after all threatened the purity of neo-classical conventions. But Hittorff was not only interested in colour as an archaeological curiosity, he needed the authority of antiquity to back up his proposals for a new architecture. In England, Owen Jones (1806–89) took up the theory enthusiastically and brought brilliant colour into the Crystal Palace interior. In Copenhagen, Gottlieb Bindesbøll (1800–56) designed a museum in 1839 with classical shapes and rich primary colours (*fig. 327*). If the Parthenon

had been covered with vivid colour and gilt on its columns, the new architecture could afford similar splendour.

The second aspect of French nineteenth-century architecture was the exploitation of structure. The writer and architect Eugène Viollet-le-Duc (1814–79) demonstrated in his massive and influential publications on architecture (including *Entretiens sur l'architecture*, 1872) how the principles of Gothic architecture could be interpreted and developed through structural technology. The architect who made the most effective use of a structure integral with plan and appearance was Henri Labrouste (1801–75). In the Bibliothèque Sainte-Geneviève in Paris (1843–50; *fig. 329*) and in the reading-room for the Bibliothèque Nationale (1862–8), he produced light and lively interiors, however uninteresting the exteriors might be. Slender iron columns support shallow arches and delicate domes, and the spaces created inside are among the great achievements of metal architecture. By applying the new technology to his analysis of the needs of a modern library to be used by many people, he produced spaces which combines ingenuity with elegance.

If Labrouste created some of the finest rooms, it was the engineer Gustave Eiffel (1832–1923) who gave Paris its

327 | **Gottlieb Bindesbøll**, *Thorvaldsen Museum*, Copenhagen, 1839

most conspicuous and most visited monument, the Eiffel Tower (1887–9; *fig. 328*). Eiffel had designed many bridges (as well as the frame of the Statue of Liberty) and was an engineer of exceptional distinction. The Tower was the signpost of the Paris Exhibition of 1889, and for many years the world's tallest structure. Its elegance and economy, with the main structural elements strongly emphasized and knitted together with a metal web of great complexity, was a presage of the future. However much disliked and criticized at the time, it was a work of engineering that demonstrated spatial possibilities for later structures and also for the decorative arts.

In Germany and Austria, the same preoccupation with style and the same adventure with structure and space can be seen. In Austria at the height, and not long before the dissolution, of the Austro-Hungarian Empire, classical styles seemed most appropriate. There were some outstanding Gothic churches, like the Votivkirche in Vienna of 1856–79 by Heinrich von Ferstel (1828–83). More serene (and classical) is the Parliament Building (1873–83) by Theophilus Hansen (1813–91), a long symmetrical building in beautifully correct Greek style. The

328 | **Gustave Eiffel**, *Eiffel Tower*, Paris, 1887–9

Burgtheater is bolder, with its curved front facing the Ringstrasse, the road encircling the central area of Vienna and one of the first exercises in the planning of ring roads. It was a masterly feat in imaginative classicism, designed by Gottfried Semper (1803–79) and built from 1874 to 1888.

German architects, flourishing in a nation forming itself into a greater power under Bismarck, seem to have swung between a tough classicism and the most reckless fantasy. In the Alte Pinakothek in Munich (1826–36), one of the great picture galleries of the century, Leo von Klenze (1784–1864) produced a plan that

329 | **Henri Labrouste**, *Bibliothèque Sainte-Geneviève*, Paris, 1843–50

330 | **Eduard Riedel** and **Georg von Dollmann**, *Neuschwanstein*, Bavaria, Germany, 1868–86

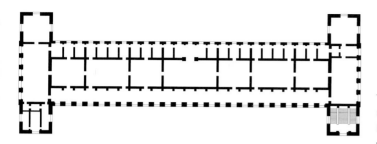

331 | **Leo von Klenze**, *Alte Pinakothek*, Munich, 1826–36, plan

was to influence the design of such buildings throughout Europe (*fig. 331*). It is High Renaissance in style, but, as in the French examples, it is the plan that makes it historically important. The immense length of 25 bays is divided into three parallel rows, the central one containing top-lit galleries, the loggia on the entrance front giving full longitudinal access to them.

The rich and mad Ludwig II of Bavaria

inspired or drove his architects into realms of fantasy, an escape from the industrial world. He built three famous palaces, whose cost eventually impoverished him. Linderhof (1874–8) is a Rococo fantasy, Herrenchiemsee (1878–86) recalls the glories of Versailles, but Neuschwanstein (1868–86) was the last word in Romanticism, a fairy castle on a mountain (*fig. 330*), complete with decorations of Wagnerian legends.

The rest of Europe reveals the same diversity, with national and regional overtones. Brussels's Palais de Justice (1866–83) by Joseph Poelaert (1817–79) was in Neo-Baroque; Amsterdam's Rijksmuseum (1877–85) was designed by Petrus Cuijpers (1827–1901) in a free Renaissance style which hid vast internal courts of iron and glass; in Milan

332 | **Giuseppe Mengoni**, *Galleria Vittorio Emanuele*, Milan, 1863–7

Giuseppe Mengoni (1829–77) produced one of the best examples of the new roofed pedestrian streets in the Galleria Vittorio Emanuele of 1863–7 (*fig. 332*). It has a vast cruciform plan, its arms meeting in a 128-foot (39-metre) diameter octagon at the centre that rises to a height of 96 feet (30 metres). It was a grand, expensive shelter for shopping and social intercourse, built with English money and technical advice. The most successful extravaganza of the whole period was in Italy in the monument to Vittorio Emanuele II, Rome, built from 1885 to 1911 by Giuseppe Sacconi (1854–1901). It towers over the Piazza Venezia and glares down the Corso, a stunning if vulgar tribute to the founder of a nation.

The main themes of nineteenth-century architecture are to be found in Europe. But by the end of the century, Europe seemed to have exhausted itself and to be waiting for disaster, and the story of architecture shifted to America, by then the centre of economic power with its vast natural resources. For most of the nineteenth century, America, Australia and New Zealand reflected the concern with style and new functions that preoccupied Europe.

Among the outstanding buildings in historical styles in the United States at this time are the Pennsylvanian Academy of the Fine Arts (1871–6) in Philadelphia by Frank Furness (1839–1912) in fanciful, colourful and original Gothic (*fig. 334*), and the Public Library (1887–95) in

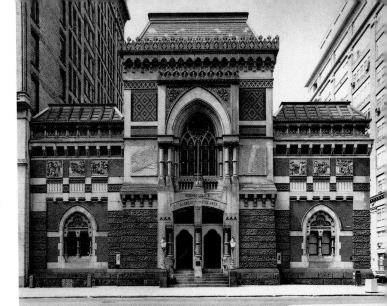

334 | Frank Furness, *Pennsylvania Academy of the Fine Arts*, Philadelphia, 1871–6

Boston, by McKim, Mead and White, a Cinquecento essay of compelling elegance and exquisite craftsmanship (*fig. 333*). As in Britain, the greatest demonstration of national pride and confidence was in government building – the Capitol in Washington. The central portion with its portico had been built at the end of the previous century and the beginning of the nineteenth. Now, from 1851 to 1867, Thomas U. Walter extended it hugely and, in effect, created a new unified complex on a dramatic scale. Its most distinguished architectural feature is the great central dome, 207 feet (63 metres) high and 94 feet (28.6 metres) in diameter, which has a cast-iron shell.

The nineteenth century had changed the whole architectural landscape with a wealth of new buildings demonstrating a massive variety of taste. The climax of nearly a century of experiment came at the turn of the century. To that climax in the United States we must now turn.

333 | McKim, Mead and White, *Public Library*, Boston, 1887–95

The period with which this chapter deals is relatively short, between 1880 and 1920. But it is a most distinctive and stimulating moment in architectural history. It saw the formulation of theories and slogans and the creation of some extraordinary masterpieces and new types of building which were to change the shape of towns and cities.

It was an exciting, almost hysterical time. In both Europe and America cities grew, and sophisticated technology developed at amazing speed. Music and the visual arts were as lively as at any time in history. In Europe it was almost as if everyone was waiting for a storm, a cataclysm, which indeed broke with the Great War of 1914–18. It was an age of apprehension. But if there was a nervous excitement in Europe, there was a growing self-confidence in America. The mounting confidence of a rich nation aware that its resources could buy almost anything was irrepressible.

In the 1880s and 1890s an architectural revolution was under way in America, in particular in Chicago. The major influence on the growth of what came to be known as the Chicago School was Henry Hobson Richardson (1838–1886), who had worked for Labrouste in Paris and returned to America at the end of the Civil War. He started his practice by winning a competition in 1866. He developed a very personal heavy style, of which the Marshall Field Warehouse in Chicago (1885–7; *fig. 335*) is a well-known example. It became the model for the new generation of Chicago architects. The building which bests gives some idea of his power as a designer is the Crane Library at Quincy, Massachusetts (1880–3; *fig. 336*). His training in Romanesque is apparent in the elevations, but the design is informal, a skilful combination of mass and line and heavy detail interpreted in a personal way.

Richardson had a national reputation. What brought the Chicago School into prominence was the disastrous fire of 1871. It swept across the river and destroyed much of the city centre, including a number of cast-iron buildings which were not fireproof. The opportunity and the challenge provided Chicago architects with a programme of building which had in its very nature to dispense with historical styles. In doing so it set the scene for the modern movement,

The crucial event in that movement was the skyscraper. It is generally accepted that the first definitive skyscraper was the Home Insurance Building, Chicago, built in 1883–5 by William le Baron Jenney (1832–1907). Of fireproof construction, it has a metal frame clad in brick and masonry. But Jenney could not quite abandon traditional detailing on the exterior and had not really mastered the challenge of giving a new shape to such a new kind of building. In the 1890s, a

335 | **Henry Hobson Richardson**, *Marshall Field Warehouse*, Chicago, 1885–7

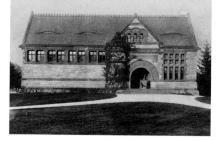

336 | **Henry Hobson Richardson**, *Crane Library*, Quincy, Massachusetts, 1880–3

few years after the fire, skyscrapers were built by the firms of Burnham and Root, Holabird and Roche, Adler and Sullivan. They effectively established the Chicago School and the essential outlines of twentieth-century commercial architecture.

What made multi-storey buildings possible was the elevator, invented in 1852 and made widely available by the invention of Siemens's electric elevator in 1880. There was now no reason why buildings should not become higher and higher. A new style of building and a new cityscape had arrived. Outstanding among the early skyscrapers in Chicago are Burnham and Root's Monadnock Building of 1884–91 (constructed of solid masonry; *fig. 337*) and Reliance Building of 1890–4 (using a metal frame; *fig. 338*). In Buffalo, in 1890, Louis Sullivan (1856–1924), one of the most cultivated of all American architects, designed the Guaranty Building. Then, in the Carson Pirie Scott Department Store, Chicago (1899–1904), he demonstrated his mastery of the new form (*fig. 339*).

Sullivan was the most intense and logical architect of his generation. A brief exploration of the Store is enough to demonstrate the essential elements that made it a prototype for countless twentieth-century offices and department stores. There are ten floors of offices, covered with white terracotta tiles hung on the steel frame, punctuated by rows of large windows. These floors sit on a two-storey base (which is what a shop needs) framed as part of the metal structure. Panels above and around the main doorways are filled with Sullivan's own luxurious decoration in cast iron. Logic and fantasy went hand in hand,

as they had in the nineteenth century; a repetitive mass building needs its own distinctive decoration. Sullivan's principle, inherited from nineteenth-century theorists, that 'form follows function' was to provide a slogan for many years to come.

The two principal materials for the new high and massive buildings were steel, which as we have seen had been pioneered in Britain and brought into general use in America, and reinforced concrete, which was developed in France. By 1892 François Hennebique (1842–1921) had perfected a system for the best location of steel reinforcement in concrete; the combination of the compressive strength of concrete with the tensile strength of steel in a homogeneous grid was one of the turning-points of architectural history. It provided a new structural material for the new forms and big spaces of modern architecture.

One of the first examples of reinforced concrete was Anatole de Baudot's church of St-Jean-de-Montmartre in Paris

337 | **Burnham and Root**, *Monadnock Building*, Chicago, 1884–91

338 | **Burnham and Root**, *Reliance Building*, Chicago, 1890–4

of 1897–1904. De Baudot (1836–1915) had been a pupil of Viollet-le-Duc and followed his master's ideal of using modern technology to develop further traditional structural principles. Starting with neo-Gothic and moving on to neo-classical, he re-examined the traditional forms and reduced them so that only the essentials remained. Elimination of unnecessary detail and expression of structure are basic to any understanding of modern architecture.

The architect who brought that approach in France to its first satisfying climax was Auguste Perret (1874–1954). In 1903 in his apartments at 25bis rue Franklin, Paris (*fig. 340*), he went further than the Chicago architects had done. He realized that the eight-storey frame made load-bearing walls unnecessary; since the walls held nothing up, the building could have open space inside. He clad the frame on the outside with tiles decorated with a flower motif. But the structural elements are freely expressed, razor-sharp and deeply modelled to give clear vertical movement to the building. Perret made the new concrete architecture respectable with that block of apartments. Twenty years later, in 1922–3, he was to reveal in a church on the outskirts of Paris, Notre-Dame-du-Raincy (*fig. 341*), how a traditional plan could lead to a spatial concept equal to the vision of the great Gothic designers. Segmental vaults of *in situ* reinforced concrete were elegantly supported on a few slender shafts, so that a new light and airy space was encircled by non-load-bearing screen walls of pre-cast concrete units filled with coloured glass.

The French delight in decorative detail led, surprisingly, to the creation of a new kind of expressive space. Hector Guimard (1867–1942), who designed the entrances to the Paris Métro in 1900, was an exponent of the fashionable Art Nouveau. Its characteristics were the whiplash line, abstracted biological and botanical decoration, asymmetry and a wide repertoire of materials, all of which allowed for personal expression and novel decorative themes.

In Brussels the initiator of Art Nouveau was Victor Horta (1861–1947), whose Hôtel Tassel (1892–3; *fig. 342*) had a novel plan and made use of many levels. But his masterpiece was the later Hôtel Solvay (1895–1900). The staircase hall has all the characteristics of Art Nouveau – flowing curves and a frankly decorative display of wrought iron. It was a theme that gave the whole interior of the house a stylistic unity. Hector Guimard gave an even fuller demonstration of Art Nouveau architecture in his Castel Béranger, Paris (1897–8). He used many different materials on the façade and made the forms flow so that they suggested living organisms. For a short time it looked as if a wildly imaginative and flexible system had been invented, which would spread

339 | **Louis Sullivan**, *Carson Pirie Scott Department Store*, Chicago, 1899–1904

340 | **Auguste Perret**, *25bis rue Franklin*, Paris, 1903

everywhere, but Art Nouveau was essentially a decorative style for special buildings; it was inappropriate for ordinary building functions.

But it did play a part in one of the most extraordinary manifestations of originality ever seen in the history of architecture. It happened in northern Spain, in the work of Antoni Gaudí. Art Nouveau in Spain was known as *Modernismo*, and Barcelona was the centre of a wave of organic design. Gaudí, born in 1852, was the most inventive and the most idiosyncratic. He died after being run over by a tram in 1926, and his funeral procession was one of the longest ever seen in the city; his death was mourned as a national calamity.

The masterpiece for which Gaudí is best known, unfinished at his death and still not completed, was the Expiatory Temple of the Sagrada Familia in Barcelona (1884–; *fig. 343*). He took over a new Gothic design by another architect and transformed it into a huge cathedral. The four tapering towers of the east transept, the Nativity facade, were one of the few parts that were completed during his lifetime. They are over 350 feet (107 metres) high, punctuated with louvres (designed to release the sound of long tubular bells) and finished at the top with fantastic finials of glass, ceramic and tile. The carvings of human figures, animals, plants and clouds are naturalistic. Every bit was supervised and some were

341 | **Auguste Perret**, *Notre-Dame-du-Raincy*, Paris, 1922–3

342 | **Victor Horta**, *Hôtel Tassel*, Brussels, stairwell, 1892–3

even put together by Gaudí himself, who gave up all other work and moved into the crypt, where he lived in monastic isolation until his death.

Gaudí's secular buildings and landscapes have an originality even more dramatic than his cathedral. The Casa Batlló in the centre of Barcelona (1904–6) is known as the House of the Bones, for its structural members at the front have warped surfaces which are bone-like in shape. In the Casa Milà (1905–10; *fig. 344*), a large block of apartment flats, also in Barcelona, the exterior seems like waves, and the interior has no right-angles. He used parabolic arches and allowed an amazing roofscape to be shaped by the differing heights caused by the differing spans. In the Güell Park (1900–14), he made a landscape of unusual diversity, with waving forms, strange stone arcades and evocative sculptures.

343 | **Antoni Gaudí**, *Sagrada Familia*, Barcelona, 1884–

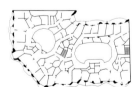

344 | **Antoni Gaudí**, *Casa Mila*, Barcelona, 1905–10, plan

He made an architecture out of his exceptional understanding of the structure of natural forms – of shells, mouths, bones, gristle, lava, vegetation, wings and petals. He created a fantasy of colour and light.

Most fascinating of all Gaudí's creations is the crypt of the church of Santa Coloma de Cervello (1898–1917; fig. *345*), where in addition to elaborating upon natural forms he worked out his own system of structural determination. He used a web of strings in tension with weights attached. The shape created thus in tension would, if you imagined it upside down, give the natural shape for a structure made of stones in compression. The strange twisted shapes of the columns and the vaults are the outcome of this experiment. No buttresses are necessary, as in Gothic buildings, he said, because the members are at the correct angle and slope to resist the forces laid upon them.

Gaudí's favourite geometric shapes were the paraboloid, the hyperboloid and the helicoid, all of them warped surfaces with differing curves, which can be found in nature. However crazy the shapes look, they are in fact carefully thought out, structurally sound and geometrically precise. He went further than anyone in creating an architecture based on the apparently irregular, but in reality functional, shapes and colours of nature.

If France, Belgium and Spain were the cradles of Art Nouveau, its sprightly forms were introduced to Britain in the illustrations of Aubrey Beardsley (1872–98). That was decorative. It was more permanent and fundamental in architecture; there it expressed itself not only in original forms, but also in the more solid and functional approach of the Arts and Crafts movement.

Pugin, as we have seen, had proclaimed the principles of a functionalist

345 | **Antoni Gaudí**, *Santa Coloma de Cervello*, Barcelona, 1898–1917, crypt

346 | **Philip Webb**,
Red House, Bexley Heath,
London, 1859–60

architecture. Ruskin had extended Pugin's ideas enormously and emphasized the importance of the craftsman in providing quality in decorative form. What was now added was the belief that architecture was an expression of society. William Morris (1834–96) was the major figure in the second half of the nineteenth century in the promotion of the Arts and Crafts movement, which he saw as not just an artistic but also a social programme. For his own house in Bexley Heath (1859–60; *fig. 346*), he commissioned Philip Webb (1831–1915) to design a dwelling which would be medieval in style, but contemporary in its frank expression of materials. It is of brick and tile, sparse in detail, substantial in construction and homely in appearance. Webb and Morris set out to create an honest architecture and succeeded; it is a landmark in architectural history, a precursor of the functional architecture of the modern movement.

Having eschewed conventional classical or Gothic detail, architects were able to point to the moral virtue of using materials honestly and at the same time enjoy the rich textures and varied forms of traditional native architecture and of craftwork made from natural materials. Hence the revival of interest in native vernacular.

The architects who dominated this period, including Webb, were Charles Annesley Voysey (1857–1941), the finest exponent of the vernacular, Richard Norman Shaw (1831–1912), the most successful architect of his generation, and Sir Edwin Lutyens (1869–1944). Lutyens designed more than a hundred houses, as well as major public buildings, of which the greatest is the Viceroy's House for the new capital of India, New Delhi (1920–31; *fig. 347*). Among his houses, the one which best exemplifies his work is the Deanery Garden at Sonning on the Thames of 1899–1902 (*fig. 348*). It is a middle-sized house set in a delightful English garden created by Gertrude Jekyll. The materials are used in a natural way and frankly expressed. But what is original about this and all of Lutyens's work is the plan.

We saw in the last chapter how the planning of buildings became a preoccupation with architects in the nineteenth century. Lutyens brought even more originality into that planning. He made access and entry to his houses an adventure full of surprises. In an apparently axial house, one might have to change direction several times before finding the main rooms. At the Deanery, the way through from the road to the garden is sometimes semi-enclosed, sometimes open, with spaces and rooms opening off it. The

347 | **Sir Edwin Lutyens**, *Viceroy's House*, New Delhi, India, 1920–31

garden elevation at the end is one of the finest asymmetrical compositions in English architecture.

Charles Rennie Mackintosh (1868–1928) is seen today as one of the most original and historically important architects of this period. He designed houses and some very original tea-rooms in Glasgow which took their character from his own version of Art Nouveau. His major work was the Glasgow School of Art, won in a competition and built in two phases, from 1896 to 1899 and 1907 to 1909. The directness of the main elevations, apart from some delightful play with curved and twisted forms in wrought iron, is the simple outcome of putting rooms and studios together in the most functional way. Inside, it is another experience. The main studios, main exhibition spaces and staircases demonstrate his mastery of the nature of different materials. The library is remarkable (*fig. 349*). Mackintosh used verticals, horizontals and gentle curves in timber to work out a richly decorative space, defined and shaped by columns, beams, cover plates and hanging frets. All the details are his – the light fittings, the door furniture, the windows, the periodicals table. He was considered a failure in his time, and he left Glasgow. He spent his later years in London and then in France, making the

most entrancing watercolours of landscapes and flowers.

The Arts and Crafts movement in England and Scotland had an influence on the Continent through a book *Das englische Haus*, by Hermann Muthesius, an attaché at the German embassy in London, and published in Berlin in 1904–5. It described and illustrated the work of most of the architects we have discussed in this chapter. From the work of the older generation, he isolated the buildings which revealed a compromise between a passion for the functional expression of structure and the sometimes fanciful exploitation of decorative detail. The exhibition hall at Darmstadt (1907), by Joseph Maria Olbrich (1867–1908) is a major example of that compromise. More expressive was the work of Otto Wagner (1841–1918) in Vienna, who set out to distil classicism to a point where all that remained was a logical statement of material, structure and function. His Majolica House of 1898 (*fig. 350*) is plain, dignified and finely proportioned; the decorative majolica spreads right across the upper four floors in coloured tiles. In the Post Office Savings Bank (1904–6) he suppressed his liking for ornament and decoration and left a beautifully constructed building that relies for its effect simply on the forthright statement of construction and function. The most extreme exponent of this kind of functionalism was Adolf Loos (1870–1933), who in 1908 wrote an article on 'Ornament and crime' which insisted that ornament should

348 | **Sir Edwin Lutyens**, *Deanery Garden*, Sonning-on-Thames, Berkshire, 1899–1902

349 | **Charles Rennie Mackintosh**, *Glasgow School of Art*, Library, 1907

be eliminated from useful objects.

In the Netherlands, the major buildings of the period were more personal and expressive. Outstanding is the Exchange, Amsterdam (1898–1903), by H.P. Berlage (1856–1934). It had a modern function that Berlage wished to express without stylistic mannerisms. But he also wanted his building to enjoy the attention and admiration of the many people who would use its halls and corridors. He therefore brought together painters, sculptors and craftsmen to work on its fine spaces. The interior has a fine massive dignity and a most attractive character.

The mood spread widely. In Silesia, Max Berg (1870–1947) was responsible in 1911–13 for the Jahrhunderthalle at Breslau, erected to mark the centenary of the nation's rise against Napoleon. It

is a stupendous structure in reinforced concrete, with the largest span of its type, great internal arches and stepped concentric rings. Even more emotional in its effect was the Town Hall at Stockholm by Ragnar Ostberg (1866–1945). It took twenty years to build, from 1904 to 1923, but has always been recognized as a triumph of what is best described as the modern traditional or romantic nationalist school (*fig. 351*). It is beautifully sited by the water, and has a romantic style that combines lightness with firmness and gives it a dignified presence as a unique national symbol.

To see the full expression of the period we must return to America. The Chicago School survived into the early years of the twentieth century, but was never again as influential as it had been in the last decade of the nineteenth. But by that time, it had produced a definitive genius, whose individuality and long career took him from that movement through at least two others and well into the middle of the twentieth century. That was Frank Lloyd Wright, who was born in 1867 (he falsified the date to 1869 to encourage a friend who financed him after his bankruptcy) and died in 1959. After working for Louis Sullivan, whom he always referred to as 'Lieber Meister'

350 | **Otto Wagner**, *Majolica House*, Vienna, 1898

351 | **Ragnar Ostberg**, *Town Hall*, Stockholm, 1904–23

('dear master'), he started his own practice in the 1890s. His work spanned seventy years of extraordinary versatility in the handling of steel, stone, redwood and reinforced concrete, extending geometrical plans and silhouettes to create a new and exhilarating relationship with the natural environment.

Wright had no doubt that he was a genius and the greatest architect of his time. His life was full of drama, including the burning of his house twice and the murder of his wife and her children. He wrote copiously and was a well-known public figure, whose autobiography is one of the most compelling accounts ever told of an architect's life. His book *Testament* (1957) brings together the theories and personal beliefs that inspired his work. He was regarded as possibly the greatest American of his generation.

In 1889 Wright built his own house in Oak Park, Chicago, and in the next few years he built many other houses in that rich suburb. They were complemented by the Unity Temple (1905–8), an influential design that took the basic elements of the scheme – church, entrance and parish hall – and composed them into simple cubic shapes. To understand his houses, it is best to look at one of his typical plans, that of the Martin House at Buffalo (1904; *fig. 352*). The basic form results from the crossing of axes. The extension of these axes into the garden forms other contained shapes which, characteristic of Wright's style, provide a single spatial experience through the interpenetration of internal and external shapes. He had an exceptional understanding of three-dimensional geometry, possibly instilled in him by his early training with Froebel's kindergarten building blocks. Especially interesting is his ability to make the internal spaces flow into one another. Corners of rooms are virtually dissolved, walls become screens, the horizontal emphasis is maintained by low sweeping ceilings and roofs and by long clerestory windows, often leaded, and the levels change so as to define rooms without barriers or doors. He created, he claimed, the open plan.

Of his many 'prairie houses', one of the best-known and most accessible is Robie House, Chicago (1908–9; *fig. 353*). In it, he combined the traditional

overleaf
353 | **Frank Lloyd Wright**, *Robie House*, Chicago, 1908–9

352 | **Frank Lloyd Wright**, *Martin House*, Buffalo, 1904, plan

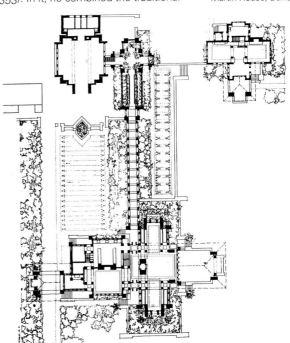

354 | **Frank Lloyd Wright**, *Fallingwater*, Bear Run, Pennsylvania, 1935–7

virtues of craftsmanship and good detail with modern technical installations. Behind the exquisitely laid brickwork, stone copings and leaded windows were electric lighting and heating systems of the most advanced type of their time. But his work demonstrated not so much the technology as the dramatic composition of roofs and the flow of the interior spaces into one another, which changed for ever the concept of a house as a collection of boxes.

Wright's career was several times given new directions by his constantly questing and inquisitive mind, and thus overlaps several of the periods defined in this book. But it is best to discuss his later buildings here because they complete a story started at the turn of the century. By the time he had finished the Imperial Hotel in Tokyo (1916–22), whose brilliantly original structure enabled it to survive the earthquake of 1926, and returned to

America he was already regarded as an old master. He then proceeded to startle the world with an even more dramatic series of houses, of which Fallingwater at Bear Run, Pennsylvania (1935–7; *fig. 354*), is probably the most frequently illustrated house of the twentieth century. Like his earlier houses, it is brilliantly organized. The stepped sections of reinforced concrete thrust outwards from a core of masonry to hover in overlapping planes above the rocks, trees and falling water. He mastered an apparently impossible site and created the most vivid example of man-made form complementing nature.

At almost the same time, he built Taliesin West at Phoenix, Arizona (1938; *fig. 355*). It was to be a winter home, which would also be a house and an atelier for his many pupils; it is still the spiritual home of the Wright admirers. Ordered by 45-degree diagonals, the structure is of

what he called desert concrete – with big boulders of local stone as aggregate, timber framing and canvas awnings – a succinct statement of his concept of organic architecture, adaptable forms and natural materials in unity with the site, in this case a response to the harmonies and rhythms of the Arizona desert.

Here there seems to be an important distinction to be made that may help to explain the nature of the modern movement. The turn of the century produced an architecture that was international in its conception, but highly personal and idiosyncratic in its national manifestations. It was the last time that architects would have the opportunity of expressing such individuality in their work. After the calamity of the First World War, Europe, the Americas and the East were entering a new phase of internationalism, which suggested not so much variation as uniformity. That was represented by the International Style.

355 | **Frank Lloyd Wright**, *Taliesin West*, Phoenix, Arizona, 1938

The term International Style was coined in 1932 by the organizers of the first International Exhibition of Modern Architecture at the Museum of Modern Art in New York. Since that time, despite many criticisms and complaints that it does not accurately reflect the actual situation, it has come to represent the mainstream of modern architecture from about the 1920s to the end of the 1950s – or possibly the 1970s. The book produced for the exhibition declared that 'there is now a single body of discipline, fixed enough to integrate contemporary style as a reality and yet elastic enough to permit individual interpretation and to encourage natural growth. … There is, first, a new conception of architecture as volume rather than mass. Secondly, regularity rather than axial symmetry serves as the chief means of ordering design.'

The need for order was in a sense true of the whole of the period. The cataclysmic events of the First World War and the Russian Revolution of 1917 changed Europe's internal order. The years that followed saw the rise of authoritarian socialist and fascist states in Europe, a succession of economic crises and finally another World War (1939–45). What emerged was a mass culture – of production, consumption and communication.

Architects and planners, as the designers of a new society, went to great trouble to identify themselves with international themes. The Congrès Internationaux d'Architecture Moderne (CIAM) was founded in 1928. Its meetings lasted in one form or another until 1959, but their earliest declarations were the most lasting in their impact. 'It is only from the present', they declared, 'that our architectural work should be derived.' They hoped to 'put architecture back on its real plane, the economic and social plane', and specifically stated that 'the most efficacious production is derived from rationalization and standardization.' The traditional street would be obsolete; instead we would have parks with separate buildings.

In order to see the movement taking shape and understand why it became an obsession with several generations, we must look at the work and ideas of some leading exponents, always recognizing that they, the mainstream architects, saw themselves as part of a social revolution; architecture was to become, not just a witness to, but a definitive agency in, the creation of a new society. It was logical and in keeping with this ideology that for the first, and possibly the only time in the history of architecture, housing for the ordinary man and woman became the vehicle for great architecture, the material out of which, like the cathedrals and palaces of an earlier epoch, great architectural statements were to be made.

The towering genius of the movement

356 | **Le Corbusier**, *Villa Savoie*, Poissy, near Paris, 1928–31

was one of the founders of CIAM, Charles-Edouard Jeanneret (1887–1966), better known as Le Corbusier. Writer, painter, architect and town-planner, he was responsible for a stream of ideas about architecture and town-planning long before he began to put up buildings. Every few years he published his designs and projects, along with his own precise aphorisms and uncompromising statements. His was the most pervasive influence on modern architecture, for good or ill. An understanding of the work of Le Corbusier is indispensable for an understanding of modern architecture.

In his seminal first book *Vers une architecture* (1923), translated into English under the title *Towards a New Architecture* (1927), Le Corbusier announced the 'five points of a new architecture' – free-standing supports (pilotis), the roof garden, the free plan, the ribbon window and the freely composed façade. We can see all of them in his Villa Savoye at Poissy (1928–31; *fig. 356*), which is an elevated white concrete box cut open horizontally and vertically. As with the paintings of the period, it is a crucial part of the concept that the observer is not standing in one fixed place, but is moving around. As he does so, the forms of the building overlap and become sometimes solid, sometimes transparent. The pilotis free the ground; at the same time the roof garden re-creates in the air the land that is lost below.

We can best understand that concept by looking at a plan. We saw how the Victorians changed the planning of buildings by analysing needs and finding a space and shape for each function. We then saw how Lutyens created new plans by making the way through a house an unusual adventure, and how Frank Lloyd Wright freed the plan altogether by opening corners, making spaces flow into each other and eventually to the outside. Le Corbusier had a quite different concept in his mind. He saw the internal

357 | **Le Corbusier**, *Dom-ino House*, 1914

space or volume as a big cube and then divided it up both horizontally and vertically, so that one part of the cube might contain taller rooms and other parts smaller and lower ones. He saw the building in the way the Cubist painter interpreted objects; he was, after all, a painter, and he saw the shapes as if *he* was in movement.

The freedom of the plan and of the façade are explained by another simple, but profoundly influential diagram. The project for the Dom-ino House was published in 1914 (*fig. 357*). It is simply a frame (the basis for low-cost housing) consisting of two concrete slabs kept apart by columns and linked only by an open stair. The plan is quite independent of the structure; the walls and windows can be put where the designer wants them, or glazed throughout. Whereas for virtually the whole of architectural history, walls were used to hold the floors and roof, now they could go anywhere and could be moved. It is a deceptively simple diagram that affected the whole future of architecture. It also explains the feature of modern architecture that is most obvious and most disliked. Flat roofs are convenient because they make possible a totally free plan. In traditional architecture, pitched roofs must rest on a wall; now you could put the walls wherever you liked.

The other crucial element in Le Corbusier's theories was the creation of the *Modulor*, a scale of architectural proportions based on the human body and the golden section (*fig. 358*). We saw that Renaissance architects, such as Alberti, worked out systems of proportion that

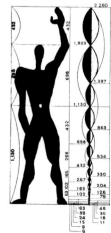

358 | **Le Corbusier**, *Modulor Man*, 1948

　　　Designing for a New Society: *The International Style*

gave their buildings authority and their followers a working set of dimensions that lasted for several centuries. Le Corbusier went further and produced a flexible system that he used in all his later buildings. It provided a range of usable dimensions all related to the human body, and related to each other so as to provide a precise formula for satisfactory proportions.

In the Pavillon Suisse at the Cité Universitaire, Paris (1930–2; *fig. 359*), he used pilotis and ribbon windows. He introduced the idea of a hierarchy of functions – the repetitive function of the 45 bedrooms for the students is expressed in a slab raised above the ground on massive supports. The communal areas at ground level flow freely, enclosed by a wall of random rubble stonework. Nearly twenty years later he applied those discoveries on a colossal scale in the revolutionary building which was the greatest single influence on mass housing in the post-war years, the Unité d'Habitation, Marseilles (1946–52; *fig. 360*).

With all its dimensions carefully taken from the Modulor, the great block of 337 split-level apartments in 23 different types rides on top of massive pilotis of concrete marked with the lines of the timber shuttering in which it was poured. The apartments have internal stairs; they are entered from wide internal corridors or streets. There are 18 floors. About a third of the way up, the internal corridor is a two-storey shopping mall. And on the top floor, there is not just a roof garden but a fantastic landscape, unlike anything Le Corbusier had done before. With concrete and planting, it incorporates a gymnasium and running track, a nursery school, tunnels and caves for children to

359 | **Le Corbusier**, *Pavillon Suisse*, Cité Universitaire, Paris, 1930–2

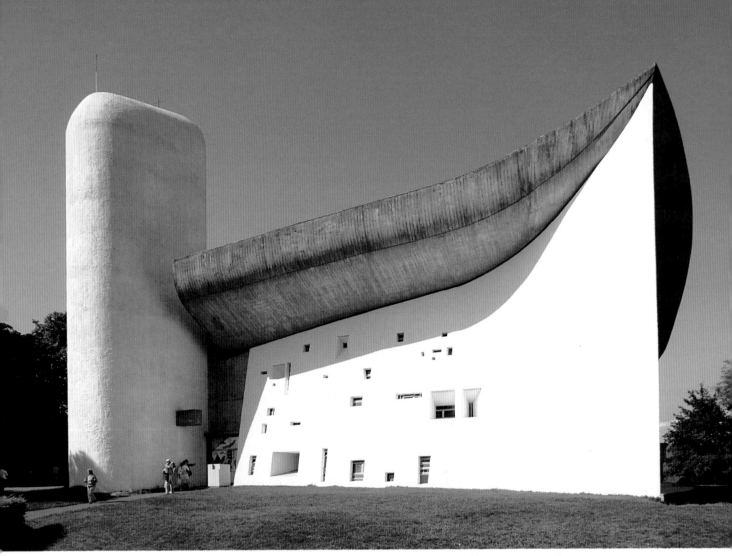

361 | **Le Corbusier**, *Notre-Dame-du-Haut*, Ronchamp, France, 1950–4

play in, a swimming pool, seats, a cantilevered balcony and a restaurant, all grouped like a huge continuous sculpture, in which the most dramatic features are the huge tapering funnels for sucking air out of the building. Far from being the cold-hearted rationalist that one of his sayings suggested, that 'the house is a machine for living in', he saw and ultimately expressed in his buildings the great ideal which he announced from the start, that 'l'architecture est le jeu savant, correct et magnifique des volumes assemblés sous la lumière' – 'architecture is the masterly, correct and magnificent play of volumes brought together in light.'

As if to confound his critics, Le

Corbusier produced in 1950–4 a small church which is considered by many to be the greatest single architectural work of the century. The Pilgrimage Chapel of Notre-Dame-du-Haut at Ronchamp (*fig. 361*) on a hilltop in the Vosges mountains contains a (reputedly) miraculous statue which attracts thousands of people on special occasions. The chapel is designed so that major services can be held outside. Inside it is small, with three smaller chapels rising up and shaped at the top to let light in. The whole chapel is a study in light. On one side the walls are immensely thick, with deep irregular windows filled with coloured glass; on other walls, tiny windows are tunnels punctured

Designing for a New Society: *The International Style*

362 | **Le Corbusier**,
Legislative Assembly Building,
Chandigarh, India, 1956

through at different angles. As the sun moves around, the whole interior changes and seems to live. The roof is a huge concrete shell sagging down in the middle and reaching up at the corners to the sky, so that the whole building is seen as pointing out as well as inviting in. For all its apparent irregularity, it is in fact planned around a series of right-angles and parallel lines, all dimensioned according to the Modulor. Le Corbusier had said 'our eyes are made to see forms in light: cubes, cones, spheres, cylinders or pyramids are the great primary forms.' They are, in short, the classical solids.

Le Corbusier's output was considerable and so was his influence. His monastery at La Tourette, near Lyons (1957), became the model for many community buildings in other countries, none more successful than St Peter's College at Cardross in Scotland by Gillespie, Kidd and Coia (1964–6). In the period of his most massive output he designed the

central government buildings in the new capital of the Punjab at Chandigarh, India with the Himalayas as a backdrop. The Legislative Assembly (1956) is a truncated cooling tower (*fig. 362*); the Courts of Justice (1951–6), in raw concrete, have a gargantuan umbrella of shallow vaults, which span the High Court, the courtrooms and the portico which lies between them. The Secretariat (1951–8) is a monolith of reinforced concrete cut open by a 'brise-soleil' ('sun-breaker') to allow the passage of breezes while giving shelter from the sun.

We have looked at some of Le Corbusier's buildings in detail because they provided much of the vocabulary of the modern architect and became effectively symbols of the time. But he was by no means alone in developing modern architecture. To see the International Style in many of its other manifestations, we must move around Europe and then cross to the Americas.

363 | **Erich Mendelsohn**, *Einstein Tower*, Potsdam, Germany, 1919–21

The sharp divisions within the movement were especially marked in Germany after the First World War. On the one hand, there was the faction represented by Erich Mendelsohn (1887–1953) in his Einstein Tower at Potsdam (1919–21; *fig. 363*). Designed as an astronomical laboratory for great scientists, it in fact enabled the architect to make an expressive statement about science in flowing sculptural forms of concrete (actually clay tiles covered with stucco). On the other hand, the dominant side of the movement was more anonymous and formal.

In 1911, Walter Gropius (1883–1969) and Adolf Meyer (1881–1929) designed the Fagus Factory at Alfeld-an-der-Leine (*fig. 364*). They interpreted its walls as a smooth glass and steel membrane barely interrupted by structural piers. Gropius went on to found a school of design, the Bauhaus, that was to have the most far-reaching effects upon architectural

education, especially in the United States. The Bauhaus was founded in 1919 at Weimar, transferred in 1925 to Dessau and closed in 1933, when its leading teachers left for the United States to escape the Nazi regime. It taught design, building and craftsmanship. Under Gropius's direction and with outstanding artists such as Paul Klee, Wassily Kandinsky and László Moholy-Nagy on the staff, it insisted, as William Morris had done, on the fundamental unity underlying all branches of design, and emphasized the necessity for a rational and systematic analysis as the start of any programme for serious building.

The buildings for the Bauhaus itself, designed by Gropius in 1925–6 (*fig. 365*), were a precise demonstration of these principles. They were composed of simple elemental shapes, articulated according to their function, arranged on a pinwheel plan with glass corners, presenting an ever-changing sequence of solid and transparent. The teaching of the Bauhaus spread world-wide. So did the form of the building. So did the influence of its teachers, above all Ludwig Mies van der Rohe (1886–1969), whose housing for an outdoor exhibition, the Weissenhofsiedlung at Stuttgart of 1927, was one of the pioneer terraces of flat-roofed housing, which, for good or ill, was to have a crucial effect on the development of domestic architecture. Mies's influence was world-wide. On the educational front

364 | **Walter Gropius** and **Adolf Meyer**, *Fagus Factory*, Alfeld-an-der-Leine, Germany, 1911

365 | **Walter Gropius**,
Bauhaus, Dessau, Germany,
1925–6

he succeeded Gropius as head of the Bauhaus school and then took its lessons with him to America. On the architectural front, in the early 1920s he designed projects for houses and skyscrapers of glass and steel, and in the German Pavilion at the Barcelona International Exhibition of 1929 (*figs. 366, 367*) he created the most pure and elemental example of the free plan under a flat roof. It influenced architects everywhere.

In the Netherlands, a group of artists and architects who called themselves De Stijl (The style) was formed in Leiden in 1917. They published an influential magazine under that name, inspired by the work of the artist Piet Mondrian, who used interlocking geometric forms, smooth bare surfaces and primary colours in his paintings and constructions. The Schröder House in Utrecht of 1923–4 by Gerrit Rietveld (1888–1964) is the outstanding example of De Stijl aesthetics (*fig. 368*). It is a cubist construction of smooth planes at right-angles, set in space and articulated by primary colours. Inside, the walls slide away to make a

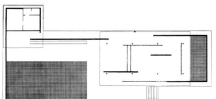

367 *Overleaf* | **Ludwig Mies van der Rohe**, *German Pavilion*, Barcelona International Exhibition, 1928–9

366 | *German Pavilion*, plan

368 | **Gerrit Rietveld**, *Schröder House*, Utrecht, The Netherlands, 1923–4

large uninterrupted space. Outside, it is an abstract sculpture, as is Rietveld's well-known chair of straight lines and primary colours for those who would sacrifice comfort rather than their deeply felt aesthetic convictions. More authoritative was Town Hall at Hilversum (1927–31) by Willem Dudok (1884–1974; *fig. 369*), which has a deceptively simple appearance, using the fine Dutch tradition of brickwork to create a dignified civic building without pomposity. Inside, the spaces and colours are finely chosen and immensely restful. With its blend of the conservative and the radical, British architects in particular found it much to their liking,

The International Style was given a sharp injection of radicalism in Britain by

a number of refugees from totalitarian regimes on the Continent. The first example of the style in Britain was the house High and Over at Amersham (1929–30) by Amyas Connell (1901–80), who had returned from a sojourn at the British School in Rome (where he had learned about the work of Le Corbusier) and designed this house for the Director of the School, to the great disgust of the local residents. Before going to America, Gropius spent some time in Britain, where he was employed on some influential school buildings and worked with the young architect Maxwell Fry (1899–1987), whose Sunhouse in Hampstead (1936) was one of the outstanding examples of International Modern before the war. But it was Berthold Lubetkin

Designing for a New Society: *The International Style*

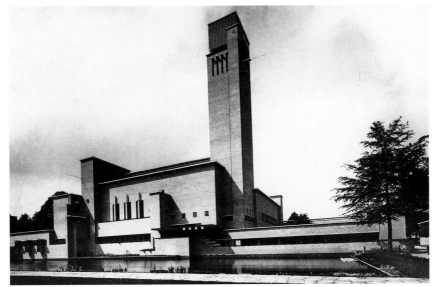

369 | **Willem Dudok**, *Hilversum Town Hall*, The Netherlands, 1927–31

(1901–90), an emigré from Russia, who made the most dramatic impact. His Penguin Pool at London Zoo (1934; *fig. 370*), its astonishingly simple spirals of concrete descending to the water, was the most sophisticated of all the animal houses in that lively zoo. With Highpoint I and II at Highgate, London (1933–8), his firm Tecton (which recruited some of the outstanding designers of the next generation) created the most accomplished examples of the International Style in Britain. Highpoint was tall, clean-lined and very expensively finished in reinforced concrete.

370 | **Berthold Lubetkin**, *Penguin Pool*, London Zoo, 1934

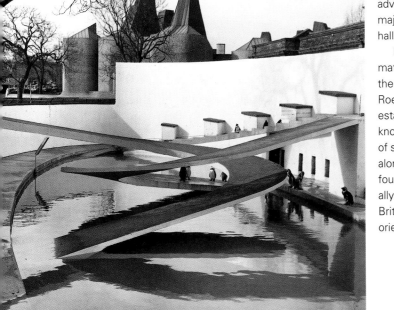

But the International Style did not really get under way in Britain until after the Second World War. Then the lead was taken by public architects' offices, notably that of the London County Council under the leadership of Robert Matthew (1906–75). The Royal Festival Hall, the centre-piece of the Festival of Britain of 1951, was a key building on three counts. First, it was the first public building to use the style; second, it had a magnificent sequence of flowing interior spaces that are wholly characteristic of the Modern Movement; and third, it was the first building comprehensively to demonstrate the application of advanced acoustics. It became the major international influence on concert-hall design.

In an undulating parkland among mature trees, the same office abandoned the street and established in 1952–5 at Roehampton, London, an outstanding estate (*fig. 371*) of what came to be known as mixed development–a mixture of slab and point blocks of eleven storeys along with single-storey, two-storey and four-storey blocks. It became internationally famous and was a characteristically British modification of Le Corbusier's theories fused with lessons learned from

371 | **London County Council**, *housing at Roehampton*, London, 1952–5

372 | **Gunnar Asplund**, *Forest Crematorium*, Stockholm, 1935–40

Scandinavia. Now that the inadequacies of high-rise living have been disclosed, the estate looks less attractive; in its day it seemed a heroic image of a post-war society housed on a massive scale.

In Scandinavia the International Style had been accepted without anxiety and struggle before the war, in domestic and in public buildings such as museums, universities, churches and hospitals. Of the best-known projects, the Forest Crematorium, Stockholm (1935–40), by Gunnar Asplund (1885–1940), gives an indelible image of dignity and repose with the simplest of geometric forms by the sensitive composition of the chapels, crematorium, columbarium and cross (*fig. 372*). The work of Alvar Aalto (1897–1976) in Finland is in a class of its own. Aalto was a public figure and a national hero – a very independent master who combined romance with technology in a number of buildings that are both practical and intensely personal. The most famous and influential was the Paimio Sanatorium (1929–33; *fig. 373*), which testifies to its architect's fame with a bust of him in the entrance hall. The most attractive is the Civic Centre at Säynätsalo of 1950–2 (*fig. 374*). It is a small collection of pitched-roof buildings in red brick, wood and copper, containing a council chamber, municipal

offices, library, shops, bank and post office, grouped around a raised green courtyard in a picturesque composition. Aalto succeeded in making a vernacular, humane architecture inspired by the landscape of his country, a free expression that totally avoids doctrinaire severity and can be described as an example of national romanticism.

But the United States, with its remarkable lack of public control and lots of available money, provided the opportunity for some of the most spectacular achievements of the modern movement. One of the first essays in the International Style was the Lovell Beach House at Newport Beach, California (1925–6), by Rudolf Schindler (1887–1953). Schindler had been born in Vienna, where he was influenced by Otto Wagner. He emigrated to the United States in 1913. But it was through commercial building that the movement was most quickly spread. The Wall Street crash of 1929 brought to an end the boom in office building which

373 | **Alvar Aalto**, *Paimio Sanatorium*, Finland, 1929–33

374 | **Alvar Aalto**, *Civic Centre*, Säynätsalo, Finland, 1950–2

had followed the First World War. By that time the Art Deco Chrysler Building, New York (1928–30; *fig. 375*) by William Van Alen (1883–1954) was already nearing completion, and the Empire State Building (1930–2) was being planned. Designed by Shreve, Lamb and Harmon, the latter was for a long time the tallest building in the world. The Rockefeller Center, New York (1930–40), by Reinhard and Hofmeister and others, applied the theme on an even more extensive scale. A group of office and leisure buildings on a 12-acre (5 hectare) site, it is a stylish composition that exploits the lines and planes of vertical movement.

The refugees from the Bauhaus had their effect. Gropius and Marcel Breuer (1902–81), the most brilliant student the Bauhaus ever had, brought its tenets to the United States in a modest little house for Gropius at Lincoln, Massachusetts (1937–8), applying American timber building techniques to the massing of European Modern. Supremely influential was Mies van der Rohe, not only in his own buildings, but also in the work of the Americans who worked with him.

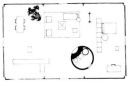

376, 377 | **Philip Johnson**, *Glass House*, New Canaan, Connecticut, 1949, plan and exterior

375 | **William Van Alen**, *Chrysler Building*, New York, 1928–30

Philip Johnson (b. 1906) took up Mies's themes of steel and glass, shown in his Bauhaus project for a glass house (1921), and created for himself at New Canaan, Connecticut, an exquisite group of buildings (1949; *figs. 376, 377*) which are a rigorous exercise in transparency, using the outside view as the walls. From Mies's projects for glass skyscrapers of 1923, the influential firm of Skidmore, Owings and Merrill found inspiration for the first actual realization of his visionary ideas. Lever House in New York (1951–2; *fig. 378*) became the model for tall buildings all over the world – the curtain wall of blue-green glass in light steel sections wrapped round the outside of the main structure, the technology of the services, which set an international standard, and the basic arrangement of a tall, thin slab above a low podium containing the entrances and larger social areas.

Mies himself went on to design, among other projects, the Lake Shore Drive Apartments, Chicago, of 1951. The 16-storey blocks have an exacting discipline, which is extended even to the tenants, who are expected to keep their standard-coloured blinds in the right position so that the elevations look properly ordered. He worked with Philip Johnson on what seems almost the final building of this school. The Seagram Building in New York of 1954–8 (*see p. 9*) was set back so as to give a full view of the 38-storey block, and to create a new civic space. The headquarters of a whiskey firm who spared no expense, it was an advance upon the Lever Building, brown in the colour of its glass and its bronze surface beams, monumental in some of

378 | **Skidmore, Owings and Merrill**, *Lever House*, New York, 1951–2

379 | **Oscar Niemeyer**,
Government Buildings,
Brasilia, 1958–60

its detail and rich in its finishing materials. After that, it was difficult to see what more could be done in the way of refinement; the next generation began to look for something more personal.

In South America a more spectacular architecture was rising. The main influence was again Le Corbusier, who had gone to Rio de Janeiro in 1936 as consultant on the design of the new Ministry of Education building (1936–45), one of his typically influential designs using a brise-soleil screen shading the glass wall. After the Second World War, Brazil exploded in a stunning architecture of its own. Lucio Costa (b. 1902) was the planner of the new capital of Brasilia, having won the competition for its design in 1957. The

architect for most of the central buildings was Oscar Niemeyer (b.1907). The President's Palace (1957), a rather pretentious version of a house on pilotis, expresses Niemeyer's flamboyant personality and probably something of Brazil's pride in its new capital. The complex at the centre (1958–60; *fig. 379*), dominating the Plaza of the Three Powers (1958–60), defines its separate functions in different elementary geometric shapes. The three smooth basic solids have almost as great a power as Boullée's visionary geometric schemes. The twin towers house the administrative offices, the dome holds the Senate Chamber and the saucer the Assembly Hall. There is something almost unreal about the pure geometry of

Designing for a New Society: *The International Style*

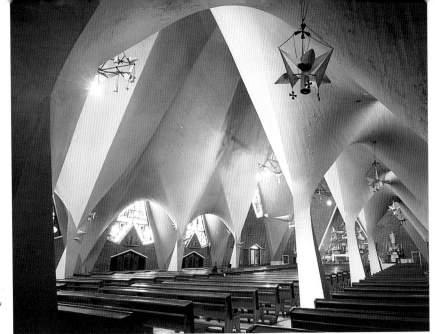

380 | **Felix Candela**, *Church of the Miraculous Virgin*, Mexico City, 1954

Brasilia, which may have something to do with its general unpopularity nowadays – an architect's dream, it is said, that paid little attention to the needs of people.

In Mexico, the new architecture was given a spectacular turning by Felix Candela (b. 1910), who came to Mexico after the Spanish Civil War and set up as an architect and builder. He is especially noted for his development of the hyperbolic paraboloid, a warped surface which is generated by straight lines and can be economical to construct. An unusual man with a rare understanding of three-dimensional geometry and of the properties of materials, he was influenced by Gaudí, as can be seen in his first major work, the Church of the Miraculous Virgin, Mexico City (1954; *fig. 380*). Its structure consists of a dramatic series of twisted columns and double-curved vaults which are in fact hyperbolic paraboloids. A conventional church plan is transformed into an original and distinctive magical interior.

Here the possibilities inherent in the International Style and the technical developments that came with it may be said to come to an end. Or it could be expressed in another way. International Modern was thought to be a total architecture, that rejected all traditional styles.

Now it was seen as just another style itself. By the end of the 1950s architects appeared to be yearning for something which would combine originality and individuality, without sacrificing the imperative of functionalism. Indeed, as the shape of the world was changing, so were the conceptions that people held about space. The search for a new style was to start again.

To the men and women responsible for the genesis of the International Style, it was the culmination of everything – an architecture for every man in every country in every way, in a brave new world that was smaller than ever before. 'It seemed', as the great architectural historian of our time (Nikolaus Pevsner) insisted, 'folly to think that anyone would wish to abandon it.' But the story of architecture has no ending. The human mind is endlessly ingenious and inventive. While some architects may have thought that they had reached a final answer, others were thinking out buildings that would upset the status quo just as the modern movement upset it early in the century.

It has been said by an informed critic of the contemporary scene that the modern movement came to an end in July 1972, when the Pruitt Igoe flats in St Louis, designed by Minoru Yamasaki (1912–86), were blown up. They had been completed in 1955; they had received an award from the American Institute of Architects. They had been vandalized, defaced, mutilated and had witnessed a higher crime rate than any other development of their type. The incident was not the last. In 1979, two multi-storey blocks of flats in Liverpool, built in 1958, were similarly demolished. Many more have been demolished since. The irony is that those buildings were major examples of social architecture. They were intended to be the architecture of every man, housing for people.

What had gone wrong during those last twenty years? What happened was that both parties – architects and observers – lost confidence in what they had seen as the modern movement. For the observers it happened mainly in the 1960s, not just in England and America, but all over the world. The buildings that dropped most in public esteem were the two kinds which made up the bulk of the later modern movement and characterized the modern cities – mass housing and office development. The arms of the movement reaching out to social democracy in housing areas and to commercial success in city centres suddenly seemed to be enfolding a monster. Critics who had previously talked of architects as the heroes of the new society now believed that actually they had been wrecking cities and treating people with contempt.

As for the designers, they were no longer so certain where they were going. As in many aspects of life, it is when people are least sure of themselves that they become most dogmatic; there is no need for dogma in a world of moral certainty. So architecture, whatever the public may have thought, started to go in many directions. Instead of recognizing one mainstream, architects started out along different paths, some of them quite irreconcilable with each other. Not only

381, 382 | **Jørn Utzon** and others, *Sydney Opera House*, 1957–73, aerial view and detail of roof shells

that. They fell for what designers have often fallen for, but not so dramatically until this century – the 'isms' of art and architecture. Apart from the revival of traditionalism, there were Brutalism, Historicism, Constructivism, Futurism, Neo-plasticism, Expressionism, Utilitarian Functionalism, the New Empiricism, Organicism, Metabolism, Neo-Metabolism, and Post-modernism. Perhaps this only means that, like most things in our society, the latest architecture is characterized by Pluralism.

383 | **Eero Saarinen**, *TWA terminal*, J. F. Kennedy International Airport, New York, 1956–62

The one style that continued and now became a fashionable style rather than an elementary way of building was the vernacular. And the one aspect of architecture that proceeded steadily on its way, sometimes despite architects, sometimes in answer to challenges presented by them, was the development of technology. Technology advanced dramatically, not so much through new discoveries as through the refinement of the innovatory ideas of the early twentieth century.

There have been significant developments in the use of most materials in structural design. Reinforced-concrete shells, used at the TWA terminal at the J.F. Kennedy International Airport, New

York, have been developed (*fig. 383*). In steel, the space frame, a three-dimensional system for evenly distributing the load in all directions, has achieved remarkable spans; if bent into a sphere, it becomes a geodesic dome. The warped surfaces introduced by Candela have spawned a large family of spatial structures, requiring different kinds of analysis from structures that could be reduced to two dimensions. Dramatic experiments have been made with cable net roofs and with pneumatic structures, in which the air inside the building, with only a little more pressure than that exerted by the air outside, holds up a plastic envelope without supports but with anchorage – a reversal of traditional structure. Such developments are only in their infancy.

Traditional structures have been much refined. In order to resist wind-loading at great heights, the traditional high-rise frame has developed hybrid structural forms such as the stiff core, the crosswall and the braced outer skin, so that the building in effect acts as a vertical cantilever. Some materials have been industrialized so that more components are prefabricated. This trend has had a very uneven history, but it may be assumed that more components are likely to be made in a factory and bought, so to speak, off the peg, as a considerable proportion of a modern building is already. If steel and concrete were the essential structural materials of the early modern movement, the ubiquitous material for today is glass. Glass has been tested and developed not only for windows but for structures and cladding and walls – and is used in electronics.

It is, however, the development of the technical services in a building, together with new ones such as air conditioning and acoustics, that has made the most fundamental alterations to the way buildings are conceived, constructed and used. High buildings in particular are differently conceived if all their services, from lifts to water and air, are controlled. On the other hand such services are intensive consumers of energy. A turning-point for some countries—and it may be for the future of architecture—was the oil crisis of 1973, as a result of which more consideration is being given to alternative sources of energy, such as sun, wind and water. There have also been many attempts to improve the efficiency of the conventional use of energy in buildings.

Ultimately the architect of today or tomorrow has to master the technology available to him on an unprecedented scale. The generation of a new building, therefore, depends greatly upon the decisions taken at the earliest moment about what portion of the cost will be spent on the technical services and what portion on the accommodation. And that will affect the whole style and appearance of the building as well as its convenience. Firmness, commodity and delight have a meaning extended by modern technology.

It became more obvious with every year that the International Style could not be the whole of architecture. Some architects looked back to classical styles; others were more positive, as in Italy, where the Velasca Tower in Milan (1956–8; fig. 384) by the firm of Belgiojoso, Peressutti and Rogers was a deliberate protest against the blandness and smoothness of International Modern. The top eight floors of the 26-storey tower are spread out on enormous chunky concrete brackets three floors deep. The windows are scattered across the façade as if someone had thrown a handful of windows at it. It was a rude comment upon the formality and smoothness of the usual modern office block.

At much the same time, Eero Saarinen (1910–61) startled America with his supple, soaring and bird-like TWA Terminal at the J.F. Kennedy International Airport, New York (1956–62). Suddenly, in place of anonymous modern, here was some-

384 | **Belgiojoso, Peressutti and Rogers**, *Velasca Tower*, Milan, 1956–8

385 | **Louis Kahn**, *Richards Medical Research Building*, University of Pennsylvania, Philadelphia, 1958–60

thing dynamic, but also symbolic of the flights which are the *raison d'être* of the building. An even more intense and dramatic designer was Louis I. Kahn (1901–74), whose Richards Medical Research Building in the University of Pennsylvania (1958–60; *fig. 385*), with its 'served' and 'servant' spaces composed so that the outside looks like huge ducts, became a model for students. His National Assembly Hall for Dacca of 1962 revived the use of the axial principles taught in the Paris Beaux-Arts school of the nineteenth century. The modern movement was taking on new and more emotional overtones.

It those buildings signalled one part of the opening campaign, the architect who expressed the mood most clearly and concisely, both in words and in actions, was Robert Venturi (b. 1925). His book *Complexity and Contradiction in Architecture* (1966) made the case for something more than the simple unitary forms of the modern movement; he wanted an architecture of meaning and popular interest

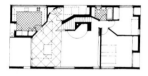

386 | **Robert Venturi**, *house at Chestnut Hill*, Philadelphia, 1962–4

387 | *House at Chestnut Hill*, ground- and first-floor plans

in place of its abstractions. The house he built for his mother at Chestnut Hill, Philadelphia, in 1962–4 (*figs. 386, 387*) is recognized as a key example of the complex, unexpected and metaphorical language of this school of design. The ambiguity is even more unexpected in buildings like Franklin Court, Philadelphia (1976), where you look at the new buildings through a steel skeleton that records the outline of the former house.

Venturi and his partners John Rauch (b. 1930) and Denise Scott-Brown (b. 1931) were expressing a mood that was to result in some unusual and exciting changes. In Spain and then in France, the Catalan architect Ricardo Bofill (b. 1939) constructed some richly colourful complex buildings. His Palais d'Abraxas on the outskirts of Paris (1978–83) is a housing mass of 10 storeys containing 400 flats, given rhythm by huge Ionic columns in concrete. The complex of Les Arcades du Lac at Marseilles (1970–5) is punctuated by five huge arches. The 386 low-cost flats have been described as monumental classicism or technological classicism; he has, not for the first time in modern history and probably disastrously, made housing into a public monument. On the other hand, the Spanish engineer Santiago Calatrava (b.1951) has produced in many parts of the world structures so elegant, dramatic and original as to be accepted as

major works of architecture. They include everything from a chair to a museum, a concert hall, several bridges, a shopping arcade, an olympic stadium, a railway station and an airport, two of the most distinctive being the Alamillo Bridge at Seville (1987–92) and the TGV station at Lyons-Satolas Airport (1988–92; *fig. 407*).

That search for a new classicism, for what has come to be known as Postmodern classicism, is nowhere more skilfully represented than by the work of Charles Moore (1925–93) in the United States, an erudite professor of architecture at the University of Los Angeles and a brilliant designer of classical pastiche. His house at Santa Barbara in California (1962) expresses the spatial concept of classical buildings. His Piazza d'Italia in New Orleans (1975–8; *fig. 388*) is a delightful public space, with fountains, coloured façades, screen walls and classical details like Ionic capitals carried out in stainless steel. At the University of Santa Cruz in California he created a stage setting called Kresge College (1973–4), an irregular walk through groups of residences and a landscape arranged in a form that would have delighted a picturesque architect of the early nineteenth century.

If the International Style was looking towards unity, anonymity and simplicity, the style that replaced it looked towards

388 | **Charles Moore**, *Piazza d'Italia*, New Orleans, 1975–8

complexity and fun. It called upon historical memories (but not historical accuracy) and the local context. It exploited the vernacular, liked buildings to be metaphorical and to have ambiguous kinds of space, used a plurality of styles, even in one building, and went in for images and symbols. No longer did the architect look for a single way to a true modern style or for utopian solutions; he looked for individuality and lots of different ways; he said goodbye to Mies van der Rohe and came back again to Gaudí and the Le Corbusier of Ronchamp.

Some of the most dramatic examples of the new pluralistic style are in America and Canada. Eamon Roche (b. 1922) and John Dinkeloo (1918–81), for example, set up the Ford Foundation Headquarters, New York, in 1967. It has a vast green-house-like foyer, soaring up 12 storeys, with offices and communal areas wrapped round two of its sides. John Portman (b. 1924) designed, and as a developer built, some astonishing Hyatt Regency Hotels, like the spectacular one in San Francisco (1974), which have vast landscaped interior volumes dripping with plants and expressing a luxury that transforms a stay in a hotel into an exotic experience. In Canada, at the Expo '67 Exhibition in Montreal, the United States employed its most brilliant as well as most verbose engineer, Buckminster Fuller (1895–1983), to make its pavilion, a huge dome 254 feet (75 metres) in diameter, a geodesic structure of triangles and hexagonal elements covered with a plastic skin (*fig. 389*). Fuller believed that whole communities could live in such a 'benign physical microcosm'. At the same exhibition the most memorable permanent exhibit was the Habitat housing by Moshe Safdie (b. 1938) and colleagues, a piling up of 158 prefabricated dwellings in a calculated appearance of disorder, an attempt to provide an informal urban life combining privacy, social contact and modern amenities (*fig. 390*).

In Germany, Hans Scharoun (1893–1972) produced in his old age the Philharmonic Concert Hall, Berlin (1956–63; *figs. 391, 392*), which may at first sight seem a wilful personal expression, but is in fact a rational solution to acoustical

389 | **Buckminster Fuller**, *United States Pavilion*, Expo '67, Montreal, 1967

390 | **Moshe Safdie**, *Habitat housing*, Montreal, 1967

problems and the desire to create a rapport between audience and orchestra. The fantastic spatial elaboration is the result of a creative acoustical arrangement of seats in 'vineyards' stepping up and around the players, a successful response to the exacting demands of the great orchestra it houses. When the Olympic Games were held in Munich in 1972, the great stadium was a vast tent roof (*fig. 393*), using the principle of tension in opposite curvatures, by the engineer Frei Otto (b. 1925) with the architects Behnisch and Partners. A web of steel cables covered by transparent plexiglass sheets was suspended from poles by steel ropes to provide an undulating translucent weather-shield that is virtually shadowless.

Britain was at first less adventurous in structure, more experimental in style and environment. After a brief interlude known as the New Brutalism, in which architects influenced by the later buildings of Le Corbusier used materials (mostly steel and concrete) 'as found', without any attempt to disguise them and make them attractive, some notable advances have been made in the environments of buildings both inside and out. The Economist Buildings, London (1962–4), by Peter (b. 1923) and Alison Smithson (b. 1928) are three towers of varying heights in an eighteenth-century setting; they were an exercise in Renaissance planning (*fig. 395*). With the Engineering Building for Leicester University (1963), James Stirling (1926–92) and James Gowan (b. 1923) created an original complex of teaching workshops, research laboratories, lecture halls, staff rooms and offices, using a ruthlessly

391 | **Hans Scharoun**, *Philharmonic Concert Hall*, Berlin, 1956–63

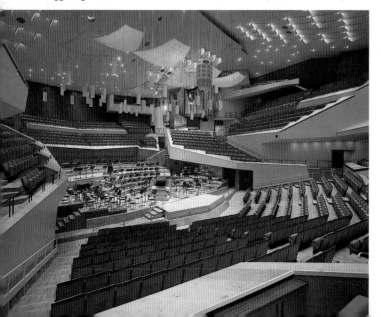

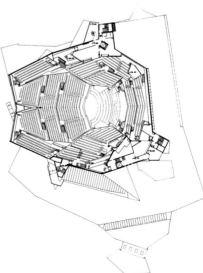

392 | *Philharmonic Concert Hall*, plan

393 | **Frei Otto, Behnisch and Partners**, *Olympic Stadium*, Munich, 1972

logical interpretation of the building's functions and economics to create distinctive imagery (*fig. 394*). In the Royal National Theatre, London, Sir Denys Lasdun (b. 1914), one of the survivors of Tecton, created a brilliantly composed but somewhat forbidding exterior in concrete, and some wonderful interior spaces surrounding and leading into the three contrasted theatres. A few years later Michael Hopkins (b. 1935) was responsible for the structurally brilliant and elegant Mound Stand at Lords cricket ground, London (1987).

But perhaps the outstanding success in Britain of the diverse movement was the offices for Willis Faber and Dumas, Ipswich, by Norman Foster (b. 1935) in 1974 (*fig. 396*). The three-storey deep-plan block covers the whole of the irregular site and is wrapped within an undulating window wall of solar-resistant glass panels, behind which highly mechanized environmental control systems provide unusually fine working conditions. The reflections in the glass wall are the dominant feature of the building, an ever-changing pattern of colour and light. Also by Foster, the Hong Kong and Shanghai Bank in Hong Kong (1979–86; *fig. 397*) enshrines, at considerable expense, the most advanced use of technology—not only in its computerized heating and ventilating systems, communications, controls, lighting and acoustics, but also in its materials, which draw upon developments in astronautics. In that, it may bring architecture full circle. For at many times in history, architecture has embodied the most advanced technology of its time. Now it promises to use the advanced technology of space. In that context and vividly expressing Sullivan's axiom that 'form follows function', Foster

394 | **James Stirling and James Gowan**, *Engineering Building*, Leicester University, 1963

has produced an even more brilliant building for Stansted Airport (1991).

And there are still more variations. With Hillingdon Civic Centre (1977), Andrew Derbyshire (b. 1926) of Robert Matthew, Johnson Marshall and Partners gave the most extensive demonstration of the 'vernacular' yet seen, with roofs cutting across at various angles and brick patterns making the most of the native tradition. But considered by many the outstanding example of the new architecture in Britain is the Byker Wall in Newcastle (1977), a long waving line of

395 | **Alison and Peter Smithson**, *Economist Buildings*, London, 1962–4

396 | **Norman Foster**, *Willis Faber and Dumas Building*, Ipswich, 1974

housing in patterned brick with dense landscape by Ralph Erskine (b. 1914), who made it an exercise in community architecture, involving the tenants at every stage of the design.

Both in Britain and in other countries some of the most successful as well as adventurous examples of recent architecture have been museums, which have the truly modern functions of housing history and attracting the public to a new social centre. They include the Neue Staatsgalerie in Stuttgart (1984; *fig. 398*), by James Stirling, the Kimbell Art Museum at Fort Worth in Texas (1972; *fig. 399*) by Louis Kahn and the Burrell Collection in Glasgow (1972), by Barry Gasson (b. 1936).

Paris received the most radical example of modern architecture reconsidered. The Centre Pompidou (1971–7; *fig. 400*), was designed by an Italian, Renzo Piano (b. 1937), and an Englishman, Richard Rogers (b. 1933). What was required was a stack of uninterrupted internal spaces and the technical infrastructure for the display of objects and for other functions, such as a library and information service. The demand was met in the most drastic modern way, by leaving the inside clear and putting all the workings on the outside–pipes, tubes, escalators and structure. The same process was followed by

Rogers in the building for Lloyds in London (1978–86). Compared with a traditional building, a modern building is upside down, inside out and back to front. In Belgium at the University of Louvain, Lucien Kroll (b. 1927) showed, in the student residences and plaza (1970–7), that it could also seem to be falling down.

In Holland, Herman Herzberger (b. 1932) created for the Central Beheer firm at Apeldoorn in 1974 a complex three-dimensional assemblage of individual work spaces, almost a workers' village with a standardized kit of parts.

In Finland, formerly dominated by the unique and thoughtful Alvar Aalto, an outstanding and even more original follower has been Reima Pietilä (b. 1923). His churches and libraries, like that at Tampere (1988), exploit organic form. He described his Official Residence for the President of Finland (1987) as expressing 'the mythological forces of the Finnish nature: receding glaciation and subsequent land upheavals'.

Japan, and other regions of the Far East, have seen some of the most dramatic examples of advanced experimental architecture. In structure, for example, Kenzo Tange (b. 1913), the brilliant disciple of Le Corbusier, created a fine exercise in imaginative structural gymnastics for the two sports halls for the Tokyo Olympics in 1964 *(fig. 401)*. They are covered with enormous tent-like roofs, whose sheets are slung from steel cables, seeming to reflect the spirit and vigour of sporting

397 | **Norman Foster**, *Hong Kong and Shanghai Bank*, Hong Kong, 1979–86

398 | **James Stirling**, *Neue Staatsgalerie*, Stuttgart, 1984

399 | **Louis Kahn**, *Kimbell Art Museum*, Fort Worth, Texas, 1972

activities. Tange had already designed some huge projects such as that for a city projecting into Tokyo Bay. The Japanese architectural scene is full of such adventures – housing reaching into or even under the sea, huge stepped housing blocks, complicated office environments, buildings capable of expansion and contraction and change – the theme of the Metabolists, who try to create architecture from an understanding of what happens in biological processes.

The most memorable is the Nakagin Capsule Tower in Tokyo by Kisho Kurokawa (b. 1934) of 1972 (fig. 402). Japan's developments in industrialized systems of prefabricated housing are among the most advanced in the world. Kurokawa provided a framework for a plug-in system of small living units comprising a bath, double bed, kitchen, storage and sitting area, all in a space measuring 8 by 12 feet (2.4 x 3.6 metres). Each unit has its own controls for heating, ventilating and air conditioning. To

the observer, it is rather like an ancient Japanese wood puzzle and the interlocking geometry of their temple timber structures. Kurokawa is said to have remarked about the capsules that: 'They're bird cages. You see in Japan we build concrete-box birds' nests with round holes and place them in the trees. I've built these birds' nests for itinerant businessmen who visit Tokyo, for bachelors who fly in with their birds.'

The most spectacular – and in some ways the most unsatisfactory – of all modern public buildings is the Opera House in Sydney (figs. 381, 382). It was started by a Danish architect Jørn Utzon (b. 1918) in 1957, after he won a competition, and

400 | **Richard Rogers and Renzo Piano**, *Centre Pompidou*, Paris, 1971–7

completed by the team of Hall, Littlemore and Todd in 1973. Utzon sketched out the most imaginative and expressive set of reinforced concrete shells on a spectacular mole jutting out into Sydney harbour. Beneath them – or within the granite-clad podium on which they sit – are a concert hall, an opera house, a theatre, a cinema and restaurants.

In fact they are not shells, which would have been impossible to construct on such a scale, but pre-cast concrete sections formed with permanent ceramic tiles on the surface. Utzon resigned before the work was finished, and the final interior bears no relation to the exterior. Yet it remains one of the most dramatic and inspiring architectural images of the twentieth century. Architecture is again capable of making a great statement and filling people with wonder.

What has happened since? Which examples best illustrate the new and lively vision which refuses to accept that the best is over and adds another family of masterpieces to the story? Among them are the brilliant glass pyramids (1989) by the American architect I. M. Pei (b. 1917), that light and give access to new acres of accommodation beneath the Napoleon Court of the Louvre in Paris (*fig. 403*), the astonishing Grande Arche de la

402 | **Kisho Kurokawa**, *Nagakin Capsule Tower*, Tokyo, 1972

Défense (1983–9) by Johann Otto von Spreckelsen (1929–87), no less than 35 storeys of offices within the carrara marble sides of a monument taller than a Gothic cathedral, the stunning mushroom-shaped water towers in Kuwait (1981) by V. B. B. Sweden, the fantastic 'water lily' concrete shells of the Baha'i Temple in Delhi (1987) by Fariburz Sabha, the 'roller coaster' football stadium in Sydney, Australia (1988), by Cox, Richardson and Taylor, and the partially underground sweeping curves of the new Parliament buildings (1988) by the firm of Mitchell/Giurgola and Thorp on a hill in Canberra that express the democratic ideology of that lively country.

More traditional in character but no less positive as architectural statements are British examples such as William Whitfield's Richmond House (1976–87) for a government ministry in Whitehall, London, or his Cathedral Library at Hereford (1996). In the former London docklands are an almost bewildering variety of new offices and houses and a memorable pumping station (1988) like a colourful modern version of a Greek temple by John Outram. These are using historic styles almost as a caricature but

401 | **Kenzo Tange**, *Olympic Stadium*, Tokyo, 1964

The Architecture of Pluralism: *The End of Certainty*

transforming them into something unmistakably of the twentieth century. Outram insists that 'we have modernized Columnar, also called "Trabeated" architecture – by finding a new identity for the column as a service duct'. He notes that most great architectures (such as the ancient Greek temples) were coloured when they were at their most perfect development. 'Colour', he says, 'is an expression of confidence and vitality.' In what has come to be known as 'romantic pragmatism', Edward Cullinan (b. 1931) has produced both original new buildings and the imaginative recasting of historic masterpieces.

In America Michael Graves (b. 1934) surprised the public with his Aztec-style Public Services Building in Portland, Oregon (1980–2; *fig. 404*), and the former disciple of Mies van der Rohe, Philip Johnson, left his mark on Manhattan, New York, with an office building for American Telephone and Telegraph (1978–83) which because of its broken pediment at the top has come to be known as the Chippendale building. In Denmark the architect of Sydney Opera House, Jørn Utzon, produced at Bagsvaerd near Copenhagen a church (1969–76) with a startlingly unpompous exterior but with an interior of wonderful curved surfaces

403 | **I. M. Pei**, *glass pyramids at the Louvre*, Paris, 1989

404 | **Michael Graves**, *Public Services Building*, Portland, Oregon, 1980–2

and finely crafted details. It is a house, a hall and a church all in one – the sort of multifunctional and expressive grouping of spaces that can increasingly be recognized in the architecture of our own time.

In the Third World countries the standard forms of modern architecture – notably in mass housing and office blocks – went up with fantastic rapidity and began to reduce the cities to copies of Western cities. It became difficult to distinguish one city from another. Where a distinctive architecture was produced it was usually a reaction against arrogant 'modern' and a recognition that what was needed was a 'sustainable' architecture – one that the country could afford.

And where that began to be seen was where architects looked back to traditional methods of construction and planning – an architecture for the poor. Regional character began to be discovered again. Vernacular architecture had a new meaning. But the change was more

profound than that. On the one hand more and more work was done in the name of 'conservation' – that is, preserving and enhancing a surviving building, often finding new uses for it; on the other, architects began to rediscover regional character and use traditional methods of construction and planning. Vernacular architecture had a new meaning. In Egypt, Hassan Fathy (1900–89) designed and advocated using traditional materials and methods and adapting vernacular styles. On a bigger scale in Jordan, Rasem Badran (b. 1945), who had trained in Germany, carried out exhaustive studies of the old buildings in every country in which he worked and so created an architecture quite unlike the International Style but seeming native to the country while modern in composition. His Grand Mosque and Justice Palace (1992) in the centre of Riyadh, the capital of Saudi Arabia, have a distinctive and apparently historical style, using natural ventilation and shelter and special techniques to avoid glare. And the buildings, including housing, are grouped in a traditional way with a view to developing a historical style suitable for modern buildings. It may be the case that in what we know as the Middle East as well as the Far East, the next chapter in the story of architecture is taking shape.

What else – amidst the enormous volume of architectural work, most of which is devoid of inspiration and notable only for scale and arrogance – has made us pause and think? It includes examples of experimentation with plans and sections, personal exercises in regional architectural character and some stupendous examples of the conservation of historic buildings and whole environments.

Perhaps the most extraordinary – and, for most observers, inexplicable – recent development is what has been defined as *Deconstructivism*. It is not one movement but an attitude that allows for colliding fragments at odd angles and irregular

405 | **Peter Eisenman**, *Wexner Center for the Visual Arts*, Ohio State University, Columbus, Ohio, 1983–9

grids. Among the more coherent designers are Peter Eisenman (b. 1932), who describes himself as a 'postfunctionalist', and said, 'My best work is without purpose – who cares about the function?' He designed the Wexner Center for the Visual Arts at Ohio State University (1983–9; *fig. 405*). Bernard Tschumi (b. 1944) designed the Parc de la Villette in Paris (1984–9; *fig. 406*), one of President Mitterand's *grands projets*, as 'a new kind of landscape for the 21st century', bright red objects scattered across the grass.

I gave the name *pluralism* to this chapter. But is there – or are there – characteristics in common? One can suggest that certain general themes seem to be characteristic of modern architecture in its later phases. They are:

Nature and growth as an inspirer of architectural form.

The Vernacular as a source of authority.

Spatial understanding as the sine qua non *of design.*

Solid geometry and mathematical proportion.

Modern technology in the control of the environment.

Continuity of form in the landscape of interior and exterior.

A psychological unity of use, movement and experience.

That suggests a new period of the Picturesque. Having witnessed a move away from the International Style and the anonymity of simple functional design, we have found that fundamental to the new architecture are spatial understanding, modern technology and continuity of form. Was it all new? In fact these characteristics could also be discovered in other periods of architectural history.

But in all periods of architectural history, what architecture has to offer – and is alone among the creative arts in offering it – is the invention and control of space; that is, unlike sculpture, *usable space*. And the technology that we now have at our command means that we can visualize and experience architectural spaces that are bigger, more original, more exciting, more memorable, than those of any earlier period. The story of architecture may be not at an end but only just beginning.

406 | **Bernard Tschumi**, *Parc de la Villete*, Paris, 1984–9

Epilogue

I set out to tell a story – The Story of Architecture – and tried to pick up the story at many times. I started with a simple account of how any kind of architecture comes to be built, and as I followed the story I recognized more and more what I had known at the beginning but never really knew in all its complexity. It is a great story – about a great subject.

The problem with calling it a 'story' is that stories traditionally have an end. But of course today's stories often end on a hollow note with many episodes unresolved. The story of architecture is like that: it has no end.

It is always tempting to tidy up the themes as the story closes – and even to find a climax and a resolution. But it would make no sense if one tried to see modern architecture – today's architecture – as a climax and satisfactory end to the unfolding history of architecture. It is nothing of the sort. The story of architecture is punctuated by climaxes and resolutions throughout. All architecture goes through periods of critical acclaim and then derision, and sometimes demolition.

Even the classifications of periods and styles that I have used throughout reflect the attitudes of the periods in which they were invented. It was a later Roman theorist, Vitruvius, who categorized the classical architecture of Greece into the orders ('order' comes from the Latin word for a rank). The term Gothic for the architecture of medieval Europe was a term of abuse invented by the Renaissance historian Vasari in 1550. And the classification of English Gothic architecture was invented by an architectural historian in the early nineteenth century. For most of history architects have not set out to design in a certain style; they set out to solve a problem and create a memorable building. Only in the last two centuries have architects felt obliged to design in a specified style, ancient or modern.

The cycle of like and dislike, the judgements of good and bad, have varied dramatically. When I was a student, the most absurd building in London was Gilbert Scott's Midland Hotel at St Pancras Station; now it is a major monument requiring preservation. In the early years of this century the building popularly regarded as the ugliest in the University of Oxford was Butterfield's Keble College (1867–83); now the university is proud of it. Similarly, the Art Deco of cinemas and factories was despised; now it is loved. Buildings that were once reviled recover their reputation and are added to the corpus of architecture and therefore to its story.

In that sense, the story of architecture can never be concluded. As every new departure changes the immediate scene, it also changes the shape of history. With every new discovery we find ourselves

407 | Santiago Calatrava, *TGV Station, Lyons-Satolas Airport*, Lyons, France, 1988–92

408 | Renzo Piano, *J. M. Tjibaou Cultural Centre*, Nouméa, New Caledonia, 1991–, model prototype of main structural system

looking back for traces of its origin – for the influences that consciously or unconsciously have played upon the designer in his search for form.

In no case is that more crucial than in the architecture of our own time. It may be possible to understand and appreciate the buildings of many historical periods by looking at their outside but it is not possible to understand a modern building without knowing its plan. For it was the plan – the grouping of the interior spaces – that the designer set out to solve. The more we study any period, the more we are filled with wonder – and pause.

But as we pause, we must ask ourselves whether there is a pattern to the story. Do certain themes emerge from this review of the whole of architecture, over something like 6,000 years, which help us to answer the question that I posed in the beginning – why is it like that? There is of course no simple answer; for the story we have been following shows that there have been many different answers and no doubt there will be many more.

It is always rash to try to forecast what those answers are likely to be in the future; several years will have to pass before we can make responsible critical judgements of the present scene. But I will take the risk. There seem to me to be two areas of architectural development that cannot fail to characterize the architecture of the new millennium.

One is that architecture as a social phenomenon will have to cater for increasing populations, unevenly distributed but usually demanding economical building often with native materials, even earth, as well as disposable man-made materials – a sustainable environment of buildings and landscape. Indeed, it is possible to chart this trend even within the work of a single architect, albeit a sophisticated one, like Renzo Piano. Piano is renowned for designing, with Richard Rogers, the Pompidou Centre in 1972 (*fig. 400*), in the days before the global energy crisis of the mid-1970s. Today he is involved in highly energy-conscious and environmentally-aware buildings such as the J M Tjibaou Cultural Centre (1991–), currently in progress on the island of Nouméa in New Caledonia (*fig. 408*). This is a building that is completely wedded to its landscape and relies on traditional building materials and techniques. In fact, it is impossible to imagine it being built anywhere else, such is its total commitment to culture and place.

The other area that cannot conceivably be ignored is the fantastic technological development that has transformed the art and science of building. Common sense as well as social need will persuade us to develop an even more sophisticated technology with a greater mastery of materials and the exercise of imagination in the fusion of technology and original form. The corollary of this, of course, is that such an architecture becomes more globally applicable, or more 'portable', relying on industrialized building systems that allow it to be landed, ready-made, in almost any location. As we have seen, such architecture is usually labelled as high-tech, but an element of 'globalism' can be detected in the work of many architects who fall outside of this camp. Santiago Calatrava, for example, has built bridges and railway stations (*fig. 407*) which seem stylistically interchangeable, and capable of being built almost anywhere in the world without needing to be modified to any real degree.

Whatever its stylistic preoccupations, though, all architecture reveals the application of human ingenuity to the satisfaction of human needs. And among those needs are not only shelter, warmth and accommodation but also the desire, felt at every moment in every part of the world in endless different ways, for something more profound, evocative and universal – for beauty, for permanence, for immortality.

Maps & Chronological Charts

1 304   **World**

2 306   **Europe, North Africa and Middle East**

1 308   **Empires and Styles:** 3000 BC - 2000 AD

2 310   **World Architecture:** 2500 BC - 1400 AD

3 312   **World Architecture:** 1400 - 1800

4 314   **World Architecture:** 1800 - 2000

NOTE. The maps include selected capital and other major cities, and principal locations of works illustrated in the book. The chronological charts include a representative selection of the principal buildings illustrated in the text, together with a summary of relevant historical names and events. Many of the dates for empires, styles and early buildings are approximate. Where a range of dates is given for a building in the text, the earlier of the two dates has been taken for the chart.

Greenland

Iceland

Alaska

Canada

Dublin
Ireland London

United
King

United States
of America

Portland

Montreal
Toronto
Chicago Buffalo Boston
Columbus Baltimore New York
Washington DC Philadelphia
Monticello
Williamsburg

Portugal Ma
Lisbon Spain

San Francisco
Santa Fe
Los Angeles
Phoenix

Cassablanca

Morocco

A

Fort Worth
New Orleans

Mexico

Ocotlan
El Tajin
Tula Mexico
Uxmal
City
Monte Alban Palenque
Tikal
Copan

Santo Domingo

Atlantic Ocean

Pacific Ocean

Quito
Ecuador

Peru

Brazil

Lima Machu Picchu
Cuzco

Salvador
(Bahia)
Brasilia

Bolivia

Ouro Preto
Rio de Janeiro
São Paulo

Paraguay

Chile

Uruguay

Argentina

0 1000 2000 3000 4000 Miles

0 1000 2000 3000 4000 5000 6000 Kilometres

Sweden
Finland
● Säynätsalo
● Helsinki
Stockholm ● St Petersburg
● Moscow

Russia

Copenhagen

Poland
Ukraine

tria
Hungary

● Istanbul
Greece   Turkey

Iraq
● Baghdad
Tehran ●
Iran
● Isfahan
● Samarkand

Shenyang ●
Beijing ●   North
Korea
Japan
Mt Wutai ●   ● Seoul   Kyoto
Mt Song   South   ● Tokyo
Korea   Osaka

Alexandria ●
● Cairo

Libya

Egypt

Saudi
Arabia
● Riyadh
● Mecca

Lahore ●   ● Chandigarh
Pakistan   ● Delhi
Karachi ●   ● Sanchi

China   Shanghai ●
● Ningbo

● Hong Kong

Khartoum ●

Sudan
● Addis Ababa
Ethiopia

Kenya
● Nairobi

India   ● Calcutta   Burma   ● Hanoi
Ellora ●   ● Ajanta
Bombay ●   ● Konarak
Karli ●   Rangoon ●

Halebid ●   ● Madras   Bangkok ●   ● Angkor Wat   ● Manila
● Mahabalipuram   ● Ho Chi Minh   Philippines
Madura ●
Colombo ●   ● Polonnaruva
Sri Lanka

Kuala Lumpur ●

Indonesia
Singapore ●

● Borobudur
Java

Pacific Ocean

Harare ●

Madagascar

Indian Ocean

New Caledonia
● Nouméa

Australia

Johannesburg ●

South Africa   Perth ●

Town   Melbourne ●   Sydney ●   ● Auckland
New Zealand

Scotland

Norway

Glasgow • • Edinburgh

Sweden

• Durham

Ireland

Denmark

Castle Howard

• Copenhagen

Dublin •

Beaumaris • • Leeds

North Sea

• Liverpool

England • Lincoln

Berlin • • Potsdam

Wales

• Birmingham

Netherlands

Germany

• Bristol

• Amsterdam

Dessau •

Dresden •

• Bath • London

• Utrecht

Atlantic Ocean

• Salisbury

• Rochester

The Hague • *Rhine*

Prague •

• Brighton

Belgium

• Cologne

Czec

Ypres • • Brussels

• Aachen

• Worms • Würzburg

• Amiens

Luxembourg

• Heidelberg • Nuremberg

Paris • • Rheims

Seine

• Augsburg • Munich

Vienn

Chartres •

St Gallen •

Loire

Bern • **Austria**

Bourges • • Autun

Switzerland

• Poitiers

Rhône

Slovenia

• Vicenza

Milan • Ljubljana •

France

• Venice

• Santiago de Compostela

Toulouse • • Orange

Po

Croatia

Portugal

• Burgos

Nîmes • Turin •

• Carcassonne

Ravenna •

• Salamanca

• Marseilles Siena

• Escorial

Pisa • • Florence

Urbino •

Lisbon • • Tomar

Spain • Madrid

Siena •

Italy

• Barcelona

• Rome

• Cordoba

Naples •

• Granada

Mediterranean Sea

• Paestum

• Gibraltar

• Cefalù

Algiers •

Rabat •

• Tunis

Morocco

• Kairouan

Malta

Tunisia

• Tripoli

Algeria

0 ⊢ 500 Miles

0 ⊢ 500 Kilometres

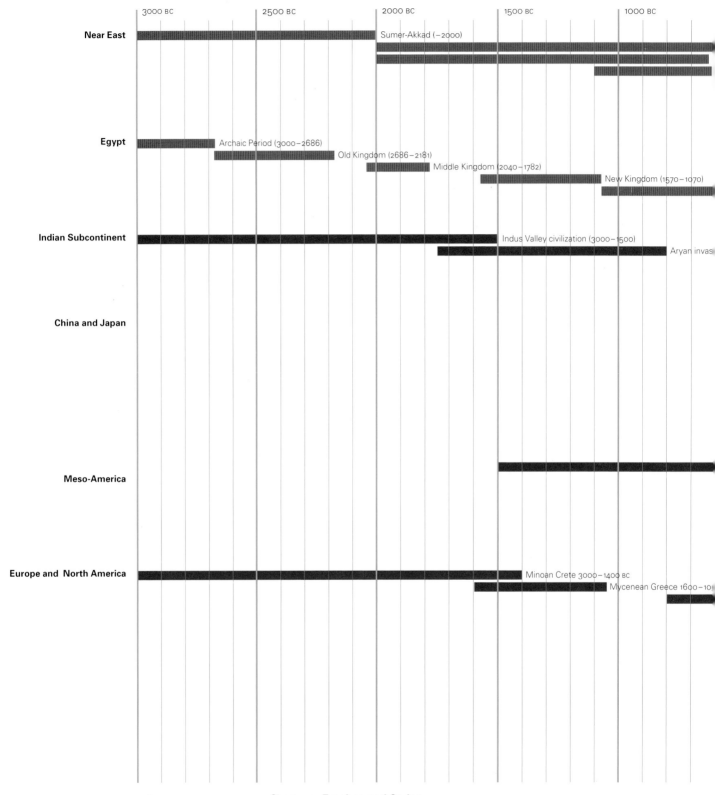

	3000 BC	2500 BC	2000 BC	1500 BC	1000 BC
Near East			Sumer-Akkad (–2000)		
Egypt	Archaic Period (3000–2686)	Old Kingdom (2686–2181)	Middle Kingdom (2040–1782)	New Kingdom (1570–1070)	
Indian Subcontinent	Indus Valley civilization (3000–1500)			Aryan invas	
China and Japan					
Meso-America					
Europe and North America	Minoan Crete 3000–1400 BC		Mycenean Greece 1600–10		

308   Chart one: **Empires and Styles**

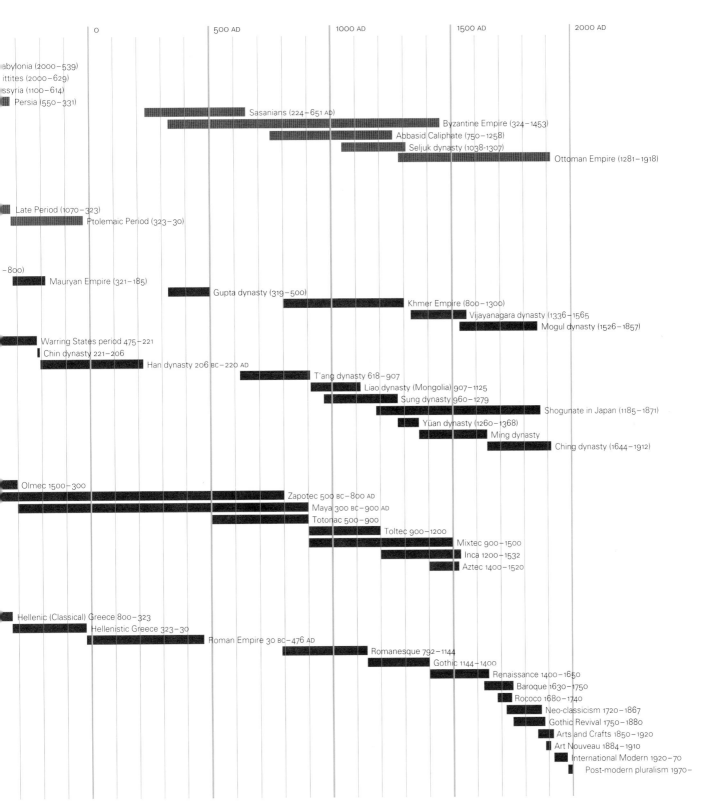

Babylonia (2000–539)
Hittites (2000–629)
Assyria (1100–614)
Persia (550–331)
Sasanians (224–651 AD)
Byzantine Empire (324–1453)
Abbasid Caliphate (750–1258)
Seljuk dynasty (1038-1307)
Ottoman Empire (1281–1918)

Late Period (1070–323)
Ptolemaic Period (323–30)

(–800)
Mauryan Empire (321–185)
Gupta dynasty (319–500)
Khmer Empire (800–1300)
Vijayanagara dynasty (1336–1565
Mogul dynasty (1526–1857)

Warring States period 475–221
Chin dynasty 221–206
Han dynasty 206 BC–220 AD
T'ang dynasty 618–907
Liao dynasty (Mongolia) 907–1125
Sung dynasty 960–1279
Shogunate in Japan (1185–1871)
Yüan dynasty (1260–1368)
Ming dynasty
Ching dynasty (1644–1912)

Olmec 1500–300
Zapotec 500 BC–800 AD
Maya 300 BC–900 AD
Totonac 500–900
Toltec 900–1200
Mixtec 900–1500
Inca 1200–1532
Aztec 1400–1520

Hellenic (Classical) Greece 800–323
Hellenistic Greece 323–30
Roman Empire 30 BC–476 AD
Romanesque 792–1144
Gothic 1144–1400
Renaissance 1400–1650
Baroque 1630–1750
Rococo 1680–1740
Neo-classicism 1720–1867
Gothic Revival 1750–1880
Arts and Crafts 1850–1920
Art Nouveau 1884–1910
International Modern 1920–70
Post-modern pluralism 1970–

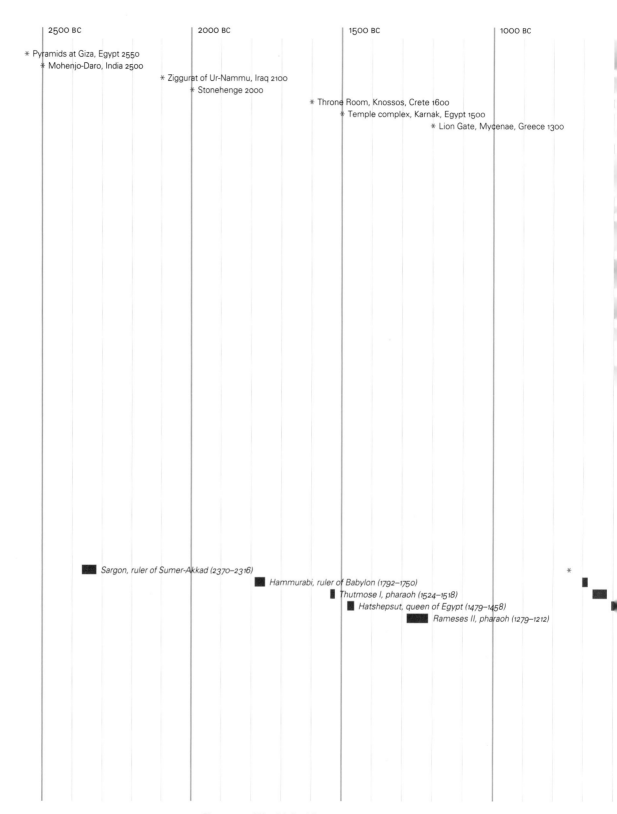

2500 BC | 2000 BC | 1500 BC | 1000 BC

* Pyramids at Giza, Egypt 2550
* Mohenjo-Daro, India 2500

* Ziggurat of Ur-Nammu, Iraq 2100
* Stonehenge 2000

* Throne Room, Knossos, Crete 1600
* Temple complex, Karnak, Egypt 1500
* Lion Gate, Mycenae, Greece 1300

Sargon, ruler of Sumer-Akkad (2370–2316)

Hammurabi, ruler of Babylon (1792–1750)

Thutmose I, pharaoh (1524–1518)

Hatshepsut, queen of Egypt (1479–1458)

Rameses II, pharaoh (1279–1212)

Chart two: **World Architecture:** 2500 BC–1400 AD

BC   O   500 AD   1000 AD   1500 AD

Ishtar Gate, Babylon, Iraq 580
Temple of Hera, Paestum, Italy 530
Persepolis, Iran 5th century
Parthenon, Athens 447
* Temple of Horus, Edfu, Egypt 237
* Great Wall of China 210
* Tikal, Guatemala 100
* Temple, Karli, India 78
* Pont du Gard, France 14 AD
* Great Stupa, Sanchi, India 1st century
* Colosseum, Rome 72
* Pantheon, Rome 120
* Teotihuacan, Mexico 150
* Basilica of Maxentius, Rome 306
* S. Maria Maggiore, Rome 432
* Songyue Pagoda, China 520
* Hagia Sophia, Istanbul, Turkey 532
* San Apollinare in classe, Ravenna, Italy 534
* Banqueting Hall, Ctesiphon, Iraq 550
* Uxmal, Mexico 600
* Shrines, Nara, Japan 7–8th century
* Great Mosque, Damascus, Syria 706
* El Aksa Mosque, Jerusalem, Israel 710
* Aachen Cathedral, Germany 792
* Borobudur Temple, Java 800
* Brahmsevara Temple, Orissa, India 9th century
* Foguang Temple, China 857
* Castillo, Chichen Itza, Mexico 1000
* Worms Cathedral, Germany 1016
* St Mark's, Venice 11th century
* St-Sernin, Toulouse, France 1050
* Durham Cathedral, England 1110
* Krak des Chevaliers, Syria 1142
* St-Denis, Paris 1144
* Chartres Cathedral, France 1194
* Cloth Hall, Ypres, Belgium 1202
* Salisbury Cathedral, England 1220
* Beaumaris Castle, Wales 1283
* Doge's Palace, Venice 1309
* Carcassonne, France 13th century
* Alhambra, Granada, Spain 1370
* Milan Cathedral, Italy 1385

Founding of Rome (753)
Sennacherib, ruler of Assyria (704–681)
Assurbanipal, ruler of Assyria (669–627)
Nebuchadnezzar II, ruler of Babylon (605–562)
Confucius (c.550–479)
Darius, ruler of Persia (521–486)
Xerxes, ruler of Persia (486–465)
Pheidias (490–430)
Greeks defeat Persians at Marathon
Greeks defeat Persians at Plataea
Peloponnesian War (431–404)
* Death of Socrates (399)
* Alexander the Great, conqueror (336–323)
Asoka, ruler in India (273–232)
* Greece conquered by Rome (146)
Augustus, first Roman Emperor (30BC–14AD)
Christ (4BC–30AD)
Vespasian, emperor (69–79)
* Eruption of Mt Vesuvius (79)
Hadrian, emperor (117–38)

Diocletian, emperor (284–305)
Constantine, emperor (306–37)
* Christianity becomes official religion of Roman Empire (313)
* Founding of Constantinople (324)
Justinian, eastern emperor (527–65)
Muhammad (570–632)
* Battle of Poitiers, Islamic invaders repulsed 732
Pepin, King of the Franks (751–87)
* Charlemagne proclaimed emperor (800)
Alfred, King of England (871–99)
* Vikings settle in France (911)
* Battle of Hastings (1066)
St Bernard (1090–1153)
* First Crusade (1096)
Frederick II, Holy Roman Emperor (1212–50)
Louis IX, King of France (1226–70)
Kublai Khan, emperor of China (1271–94)
* Black Death (1348)
Tamerlaine, Asian conqueror (1360–1404)

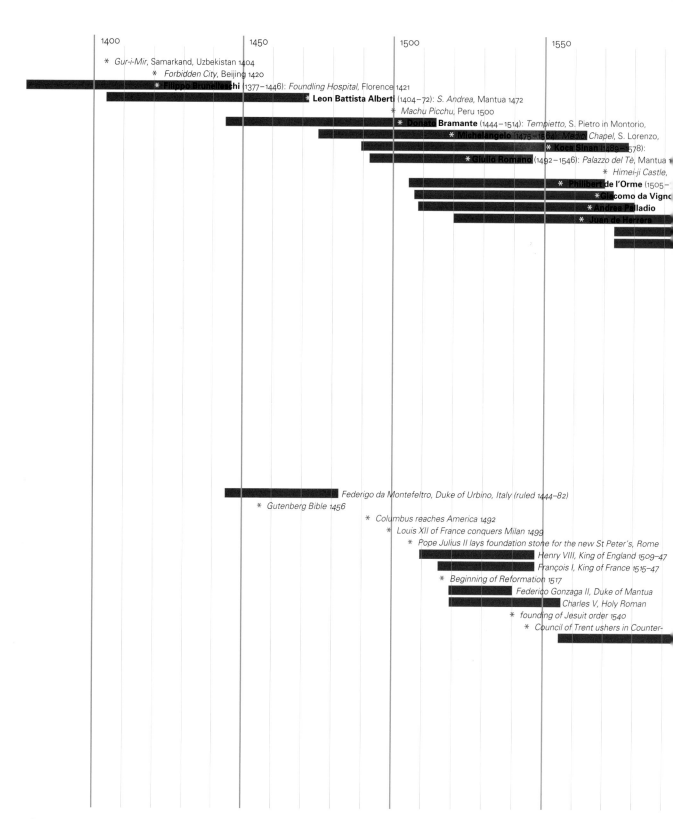

1400	1450	1500	1550

* *Gur-i-Mir*, Samarkand, Uzbekistan 1404
  * *Forbidden City*, Beijing 1420
  * **Filippo Brunelleschi** (1377–1446): *Foundling Hospital*, Florence 1421
  * **Leon Battista Alberti** (1404–72): *S. Andrea*, Mantua 1472
    * *Machu Picchu*, Peru 1500
    * **Donato Bramante** (1444–1514): *Tempietto, S. Pietro in Montorio*,
    * **Michelangelo** (1475–1564): *Medici Chapel*, S. Lorenzo,
    * **Koca Sinan** (1489–1578):
    * **Giulio Romano** (1492–1546): *Palazzo del Tè*, Mantua
      * *Himei-ji Castle*,
    * **Philibert de l'Orme** (1505–
    * **Giacomo da Vigno**
    * **Andrea Palladio**
    * **Juan de Herrera**

* Federigo da Montefeltro, Duke of Urbino, Italy (ruled 1444–82)
* Gutenberg Bible 1456
  * Columbus reaches America 1492
    * Louis XII of France conquers Milan 1499
      * Pope Julius II lays foundation stone for the new St Peter's, Rome
        Henry VIII, King of England 1509–47
        François I, King of France 1515–47
      * Beginning of Reformation 1517
        Federico Gonzaga II, Duke of Mantua
        Charles V, Holy Roman
      * founding of Jesuit order 1540
        * Council of Trent ushers in Counter-

Chart three: **World Architecture:** 1400–1800

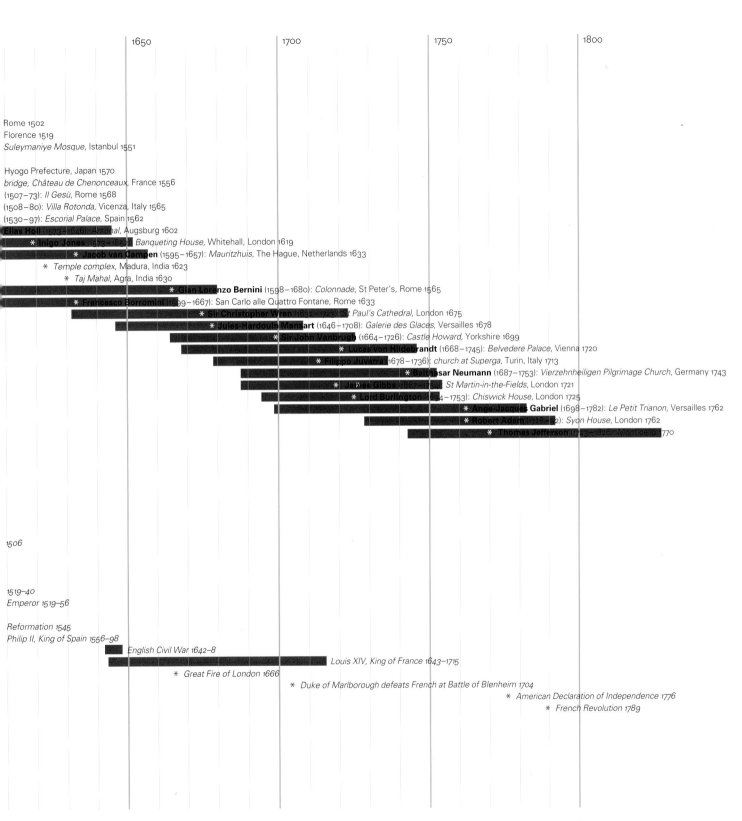

1650　　　　　　　1700　　　　　　　1750　　　　　　　1800

Rome 1502
Florence 1519
Suleymaniye Mosque, Istanbul 1551

Hyogo Prefecture, Japan 1570
bridge, *Château de Chenonceaux*, France 1556
(1507–73): *Il Gesù*, Rome 1568
(1508–80): *Villa Rotonda*, Vicenza, Italy 1565
(1530–97): *Escorial Palace*, Spain 1562
Elias Holl (1573–1646): *Arsenal*, Augsburg 1602
✳ **Inigo Jones** (1573–1652): *Banqueting House*, Whitehall, London 1619
✳ **Jacob van Campen** (1595–1657): *Mauritzhuis*, The Hague, Netherlands 1633
✳ *Temple complex*, Madura, India 1623
✳ *Taj Mahal*, Agra, India 1630
✳ **Gian Lorenzo Bernini** (1598–1680): *Colonnade*, St Peter's, Rome 1565
✳ **Francesco Borromini** (1599–1667): San Carlo alle Quattro Fontane, Rome 1633
✳ **Sir Christopher Wren** (1632–1723): *St Paul's Cathedral*, London 1675
✳ **Jules-Hardouin Mansart** (1646–1708): *Galerie des Glaces*, Versailles 1678
✳ **Sir John Vanbrugh** (1664–1726): *Castle Howard*, Yorkshire 1699
✳ **Lucas von Hildebrandt** (1668–1745): *Belvedere Palace*, Vienna 1720
✳ **Filippo Juvarra** (1678–1736): *church at Superga*, Turin, Italy 1713
✳ **Balthasar Neumann** (1687–1753): *Vierzehnheiligen Pilgrimage Church*, Germany 1743
✳ **James Gibbs** (1687–1754): *St Martin-in-the-Fields*, London 1721
✳ **Lord Burlington** (1694–1753): *Chiswick House*, London 1725
✳ **Ange-Jacques Gabriel** (1698–1782): *Le Petit Trianon*, Versailles 1762
✳ **Robert Adam** (1728–92): *Syon House*, London 1762
✳ **Thomas Jefferson** (1743–1826): *Monticello* 1770

1506

1519–40
Emperor 1519–56

Reformation 1545
Philip II, King of Spain 1556–98
English Civil War 1642–8
Louis XIV, King of France 1643–1715
✳ *Great Fire of London 1666*
✳ *Duke of Marlborough defeats French at Battle of Blenheim 1704*
✳ *American Declaration of Independence 1776*
✳ *French Revolution 1789*

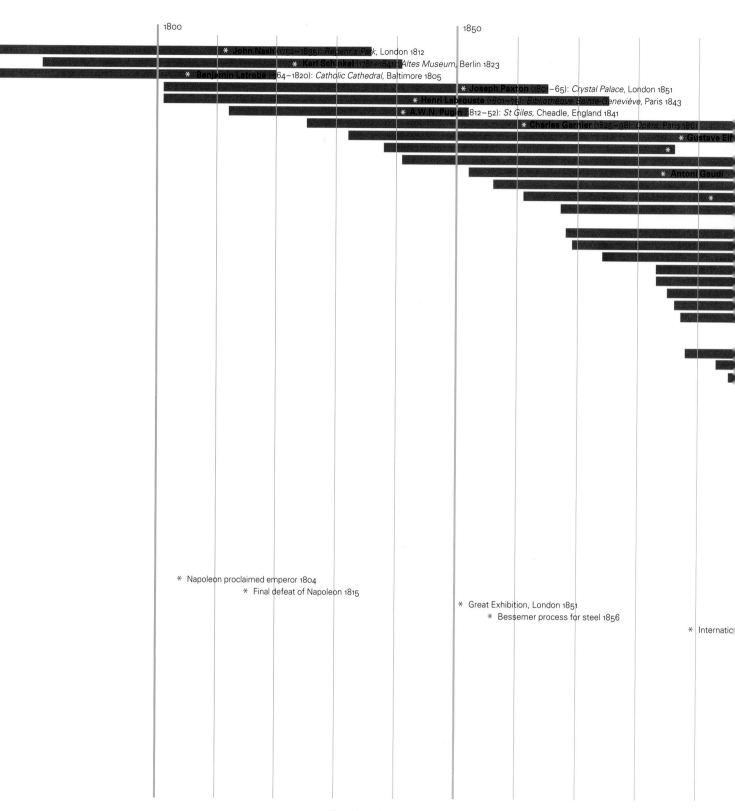

1800   1850

* **John Nash** (1752–1835): *Regent's Park*, London 1812

* **Karl Schinkel** (1781–1841): *Altes Museum*, Berlin 1823

* **Benjamin Latrobe** (1764–1820): *Catholic Cathedral*, Baltimore 1805

* **Joseph Paxton** (1801–65): *Crystal Palace*, London 1851

* **Henri Labrouste** (1801–75): *Bibliothèque Sainte-Geneviève*, Paris 1843

* **A.W.N. Pugin** (1812–52): *St Giles*, Cheadle, England 1841

* **Charles Garnier** (1825–98): *Opéra*, Paris 1861

* **Gustave Eif**

*

* **Antoni Gaudí**

*

* Napoleon proclaimed emperor 1804

     * Final defeat of Napoleon 1815

* Great Exhibition, London 1851

     * Bessemer process for steel 1856

* Internatio

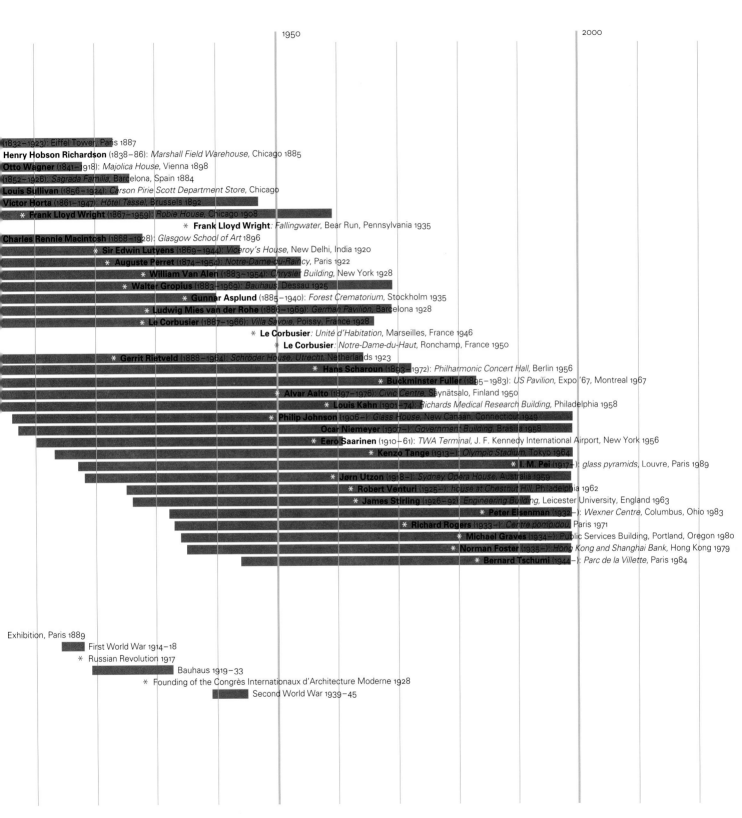

1950   2000

(1832–1923): *Eiffel Tower*, Paris 1887

Henry Hobson Richardson (1838–86): *Marshall Field Warehouse*, Chicago 1885
Otto Wagner (1841–1918): *Majolica House*, Vienna 1898
(1852–1926): *Sagrada Família*, Barcelona, Spain 1884
Louis Sullivan (1856–1924): *Carson Pirie Scott Department Store*, Chicago
Victor Horta (1861–1947): *Hôtel Tassel*, Brussels 1892
✳ **Frank Lloyd Wright** (1867–1959): *Robie House*, Chicago 1908
    ✳ **Frank Lloyd Wright**: *Fallingwater*, Bear Run, Pennsylvania 1935
Charles Rennie Macintosh (1868–1928): *Glasgow School of Art* 1896
    ✳ **Sir Edwin Lutyens** (1869–1944): *Viceroy's House*, New Delhi, India 1920
    ✳ **Auguste Perret** (1874–1954): *Notre-Dame-du-Raincy*, Paris 1922
    ✳ **William Van Alen** (1883–1954): *Chrysler Building*, New York 1928
    ✳ **Walter Gropius** (1883–1969): *Bauhaus*, Dessau 1925
        ✳ **Gunnar Asplund** (1885–1940): *Forest Crematorium*, Stockholm 1935
    ✳ **Ludwig Mies van der Rohe** (1886–1969): *German Pavilion*, Barcelona 1928
    ✳ **Le Corbusier** (1887–1966): *Villa Savoie*, Poissy, France 1928
        ✳ **Le Corbusier**: *Unité d'Habitation*, Marseilles, France 1946
        ✳ **Le Corbusier**: *Notre-Dame-du-Haut*, Ronchamp, France 1950
    ✳ **Gerrit Rietveld** (1888–1964): *Schröder House, Utrecht*, Netherlands 1923
        ✳ **Hans Scharoun** (1893–1972): *Philharmonic Concert Hall*, Berlin 1956
            ✳ **Buckminster Fuller** (1895–1983): *US Pavilion*, Expo '67, Montreal 1967
        ✳ **Alvar Aalto** (1897–1976): *Civic Centre*, Säynätsalo, Finland 1950
        ✳ **Louis Kahn** (1901–74): *Richards Medical Research Building*, Philadelphia 1958
        ✳ **Philip Johnson** (1906–): *Glass House*, New Canaan, Connecticut 1949
        Ocar Niemeyer (1907–): *Government Building*, Brasília 1958
        ✳ **Eero Saarinen** (1910–61): *TWA Terminal*, J. F. Kennedy International Airport, New York 1956
            ✳ **Kenzo Tange** (1913–): *Olympic Stadium*, Tokyo 1964
                ✳ **I. M. Pei** (1917–): *glass pyramids*, Louvre, Paris 1989
        ✳ **Jørn Utzon** (1918–): *Sydney Opera House*, Australia 1959
        ✳ **Robert Venturi** (1925–): *house at Chestnut Hill*, Philadelphia 1962
        ✳ **James Stirling** (1926–92): *Engineering Building*, Leicester University, England 1963
                ✳ **Peter Eisenman** (1932–): *Wexner Centre*, Columbus, Ohio 1983
            ✳ **Richard Rogers** (1933–): *Centre pompidou*, Paris 1971
            ✳ **Michael Graves** (1934–): *Public Services Building*, Portland, Oregon 1980
                ✳ **Norman Foster** (1935–): *Hong Kong and Shanghai Bank*, Hong Kong 1979
            ✳ **Bernard Tschumi** (1944–): *Parc de la Villette*, Paris 1984

Exhibition, Paris 1889
    First World War 1914–18
    ✳ Russian Revolution 1917
    Bauhaus 1919–33
    ✳ Founding of the Congrès Internationaux d'Architecture Moderne 1928
    Second World War 1939–45

Glossary

Abacus. The slab on top of a *capital* directly supporting the architrave.

Acanthus. A plant with sharp pointed leaves, copied in the *Corinthian* Capital.

Acropolis. The citadel of a Greek city where the temple of the patron deity was usually built.

Agora. In ancient Greece, a public space for assemblies; same as a Roman *forum*.

Aisle. In *basilican* buildings, one of the lateral divisions parallel with the *nave* but not as high. Sometimes used to include the nave as well.

Ambulatory. A continuous *aisle* forming a processional path round some larger enclosed space. In Europe the east end of a cathedral, in India the shrine of a temple.

Amphitheatre. A round or oval arena with tiers of seats all round.

Apse. Part of a building that is semicircular or U-shaped in plan; usually the east end of a chapel or *chancel*.

Arcade. A line of arches supported on piers or columns.

Arch. A structure built over an opening to hold together when supported only from the sides, the downward pressure being transformed into lateral thrust. A corbelled arch consists of blocks each overlapping the one beneath until the gap can be bridged by a single slab. A true arch is formed by radiating wedge-shaped stones known as *voussoirs*.

Architrave. The lowest point of a classical *entablature*, the stone *lintel* above the columns.

Art Nouveau. Style of decoration popular in Europe *c.*1890–1910, avoiding traditional motifs and basing itself on curving lines and vegetation-like forms.

Ashlar. Trimmed, regular masonry with flat surfaces and squared edges.

Axial planning. The placing of several buildings or rooms in a building along a single line.

Balustrade. A line of balusters, or miniature pillars, supporting a handrail.

Barbican. Fortified outwork guarding the gateway of a medieval city or castle.

Baroque. Style after *Mannerism* in Italy, *c.*1600, and later spread over Europe; characterized by dynamic lines and masses and the free use of classical motifs.

Basilica. (1) In Roman architecture, a large public hall where lawsuits were heard. (2) In early Christian and later architecture, a building consisting of *nave* and *aisles*, with windows above the level of the aisle roofs (clerestory).

Bastion. A projection from the *curtain wall* of a castle or defensive work, placed so that a zone of wall may be swept by fire from the bastions,

Bay. A compartment of a large building, consisting, e.g., in churches, of the space between one column or pier and the next, including the wall and the vault or ceiling over it. By extension, any unit of a wall surface divided by large vertical features or (on exteriors) by windows.

Bracket. Member projecting from a vertical surface to provide a horizontal support. See also *corbel* and *cantilever*.

Buttress. Masonry built against a wall to give additional support, or to resist the thrust of a vault or arch. A flying buttress is a half-arch leaning against that point in a wall where the lateral thrust of an *arch* or *vault* is being exerted, and transmitting this thrust to a body of masonry at a lower level. A characteristic of the *Gothic* style.

Byzantine. Style evolved at Constantinople about the fifth century AD and still in use in some parts of the world. The round arch, segmental dome and use of marble veneers are characteristic.

Calidarium. The hot-water room in a Roman public bath.

Canopy. Decorative covering over a small open structure such as a tomb, pulpit or niche; often supported on columns.

Cantilever. A beam or girder supported in the middle or along half its length and weighted at one end to carry a proportionate load on the other.

Capital. The upper part of a column. See *Doric*, *Ionic*, *Corinthian* and *orders*. In non-classical architecture capitals may be of any design.

Carolingian. Style originating under Charlemagne *c.*800 AD and leading to *Romanesque*.

Caryatid. Pillar in the form of a sculptured female figure.

Cenotaph. Monument to a person buried elsewhere (Greek: 'empty tomb').

Central-plan. A plan symmetrical, or nearly so, in all four directions.

Chancel. Space in a church reserved for the clergy, including the altar and the choir.

Chevet. The combination of *apse*, *ambulatory* and *radiating chapels* at the east end of a large Gothic church.

Choir. The part of a church where the choir sits. Normally the west part of the chancel. The term is often loosely applied to mean the same as chancel, although in large medieval churches the choir sat under the crossing or west of it.

Classical. Greek or Roman and their derivatives, especially the use of the *orders*.

Clerestory. The upper window-level of a large enclosed space, rising above adjacent roofs. In particular the upper window range of a *basilican* building above the *arcades* forming the *aisles*.

Cloister. A square court surrounded by an open *arcade*.

Coffering. Treatment of ceilings and domes consisting of sunk panels (coffers).

Colonnade. A row of columns.

Column. A circular pillar, a cylindrical support for part of a building. Also erected singly as a monument. See *Doric, Ionic* and *Corinthian*.

Columnar and trabeate. Using the column and beam, or *lintel*, only, i.e. not using the principle of the arch.

Composite. An *order* invented by the Romans, combining the acanthus leaves of the *Corinthian* with the volutes of the *Ionic* capital.

Concentric walls. Fortification introduced from the East by the crusaders, consisting of one complete defence system inside another.

Corbel. A *bracket,* a block of stone projecting from a wall as a horizontal support or as the *springing* of a rib. See *arch* and *vault.*

Corinthian. The last of the three classical *orders*. Characteristics: (1) high base, sometimes a pedestal; (2) slender fluted shaft with fillets; (3) ornate capital using stylized acanthus leaves.

Cornice. (1) The top, projecting section of a classical *entablature* (see *orders*). (2) In Renaissance architecture, a projecting shelf along the top of a wall supported on ornamental brackets.

Cove, coving. Concave surface connecting a wall and ceiling.

Crossing. The central space of a cruciform church where the *nave, transepts* and *chancel* meet.

Cruciform. Cross-shaped.

Crypt. Underground space below the east end of a church, originally to house the remains of saints (Greek: 'hidden').

Cupola. Sometimes means the same as *dome*. More usually in English a miniature dome or turret with a lantern-top.

Curtain wall. (1) In castles, the wall between *bastions* or towers. (2) In modern architecture, an exterior wall serving as a screen only, bearing no load. In *steel-frame* buildings all the walls are curtain walls.

Cusp. A projecting point on the inner side of an *arch*, window or roundel.

Cyclopean. Walling in very large stones without mortar.

Dagoba. A Sinhalese form of *stupa* or relic-chamber ('dhata' = relics; 'garbha' = womb).

Dais. Raised platform at the end of a hall.

Decorated. Style of architecture in England following *Early English*. Characterized by elaborate curvilinear tracery, unusual spatial effects, complicated rib vaulting, cusping, naturalistic foliage carving.

Diaphragm arch

Dome. A concave roof, roughly hemispherical, on a circular base. A section through a dome can be *semicircular, pointed,* or *segmental*. A dome with segmental section is called a saucer-dome. Most Western European domes have drums. Onion or bulb domes are external features only.

Doric. First and simplest of the classical *orders*. Characteristics: (1) no base, (2) relatively short shafts meeting in a sharp arris; (3) simple undecorated *echinus* and square *abacus*. The Roman Doric was similar but had a base.

Dormer window. Vertical window in a sloping roof.

Dromos. (1) A race-course. (2) A passage or entrance-way between high walls, e.g. to a Mycenaean tomb.

Early English. First phase of English *Gothic*, beginning c.1180. Characterized by lancet windows or (later) geometrical tracery, rib vaults, emphasis on thin linear articulation instead of mass and volume, sharp mouldings and the clear distinction of architectural members.

Eave. The lowest part of a sloping roof that projects over the wall.

Echinus. The lower element of a *Doric* capital – a circular cushion-like member under the *abacus*. Also the corresponding member of an *Ionic* capital, partly obscured by the *volutes* and carved with egg-and-dart moulding.

Engaged. Bonded into a wall; not free-standing.

Entablature. In classical architecture, everything above the columns – *architrave, frieze* and *cornice.*

Entasis. Slight bulge given to a column to correct the optical illusion that it is thinner in the middle.

Etruscan see **Tuscan**

Exedra. An apsidal recess or alcove with seat; in Renaissance architecture any niche or small apse.

Façade. The exterior of a building on one of its main sides, almost always containing an entrance.

Flamboyant. Last phase of French *Gothic* (literally 'flame-shaped'), characterized by complex curvilinear tracery and profuse ornament.

Flute, fluting. Channels or grooves, carved vertically down the shafts of classical columns.

Forum. Roman market-place or open space for assemblies, normally surrounded by public buildings.

Free-standing. Open on all sides, not attached to a wall.

Fresco. Strictly, painting applied to a wall while the plaster is still wet. Sometimes loosely used of any mural painting.

Frieze. Part of a classical *entablature*, above the *architrave* and below the *cornice*. In Doric it was divided into *triglyphs* and *metopes*. Often used for a band of figure carving; hence in Renaissance architecture it means a continuous band of relief round the top of a building or room.

Frigidarium. The cold-water swimming pool in Roman public baths.

Gable. The triangular end of a gable-roof; in classical architecture called a *pediment*. By extension, a triangular area over a doorway even when there is no roof behind, as, e.g., over French Gothic cathedral portals.

Gallery. (1) An upper floor open on one side to the main interior space of a building (e.g. galleries over the aisles of a church) or to the exterior. (2) In medieval and Renaissance houses, a long narrow room.

Giant order. Pilasters or half-columns used to articulate a façade and extending through two or more storeys.

Gothic. Name given to medieval architecture in Europe from about mid-twelfth century to the Renaissance. Characterized by the *pointed arch*, the *flying buttress* and the *rib vault*.

Groin. The ridge or arris formed by the meeting of two vaulting sections.

Hip. The line formed by two sloping roofs meeting. A hipped roof is a *truss* roof with hips instead of gables: that is, the *ridge beam* is shorter than the walls parallel with it, so that the roof slopes inwards on all four sides.

Hippodrome. In ancient Greece, a stadium for horse and chariot racing.

Hypostyle. A hall or large enclosed space in which the (usually flat) roof rests on columns throughout, not just along the sides.

Inlay. Small pieces of some rich material set into a bed or background of another.

International Style. Name given to the style of architecture evolved in Europe and America shortly before the First World War. Characterized by an emphasis on function and rejection of traditional decorative motifs.

Ionic. The second of the three classical *orders*. Characteristics: (1) elegantly moulded base; (2) tall, slender shafts with flutes separated by fillets; (3) capital using the volute, or spiral.

Joist. Horizontal beam supporting a floor or ceiling.

Kando. The main sanctuary of a Japanese Buddhist temple.

Keep. The innermost stronghold of a castle. Originally the only part built of stone, later surrounded by *concentric* walling.

King-post. Upright beam of a roof supporting the *ridge beam* and resting on the centre of the *tie beam*.

Lantern. (1) A tower open to the space underneath and with windows to admit light downwards. (2) Small turret with windows crowning a dome or cupola.

Lintel. Horizontal beam or slab spanning an opening. In classical architecture the lintel is called an *architrave*.

Loggia. A roofed space with an open *arcade* on one or more sides.

Longitudinal plan. Church plan in which the *nave*–*chancel* axis is longer than the *transepts* (as in all English cathedrals).

Mannerism. Style coming between High Renaissance and Baroque. Characterized by the idiosyncratic use of classical motifs, unnatural proportion and stylistic contradictions.

Mastaba. In Ancient Egyptian architecture, a flat-topped tomb with sloping sides, the forerunner of the pyramid.

Mausoleum. A rich and elaborate tomb, so called from the tomb of the Greek ruler Mausolus at Halicarnassus in Asia Minor.

Megaron. The principal hall of a Minoan or Homeric house (e.g. Tiryns, Mycenae).

Metope. Part of the *frieze* of a Doric entab-lature, one of the spaces between the *triglyphs*, at first left plain, later sculptured.

Mihrab. In Muslim architecture, a niche in the wall of a mosque, showing the direction of Mecca.

Minaret. Tower built near or as part of mosque, from which a muezzin calls the faithful to prayer.

Minbar. The pulpit in a mosque.

Module. A measure of proportion to which all the parts of a building are related by simple ratios. In classical architecture it is usually half the diameter of the column immediately above its base.

Mosaic. Small cubes of glass or stone (tesserae) set in a cement bedding as decoration for wall surfaces or floors.

Mosque. The Muslim place for prayer and exhortation.

Moulding. Decorative profile given to an architectural member; often a continuous band of incised or projecting patterning.

Mullion. The vertical member dividing a window of more than one light. (The horizontal members are called transoms.)

Nave. (1) The central space of a *basilica*, flanked by the *aisles* and lit by the *clerestory*. (2) All of a church west of the crossing, or if there are no transepts, west of the chancel.

Neo-classicism. A style coming after the Baroque, characterized by a more academic use of classical features.

Niche. A recess in a wall usually for a statue or ornament.

Norman. Name given to the *Romanesque* style in England.

Obelisk. A tall stone, square in section, tapering upwards and ending pyramidally.

Orders. Columns and their entablature, especially the various designs followed by Greek and Roman architects: *Doric, Ionic, Corinthian, Composite, Tuscan*. In Roman architecture, the orders came to be used as ornamental features, attached to walls and façades.

Orientation. Strictly, alignment east–west, but used loosely for any deliberate placing of a building in relation to the points of the compass.

Pagoda. A multi-storeyed Chinese or Japanese building with wide projecting roof at each storey.

Pediment. Originally the triangular *gable-*end of a Greek temple with pitched roof. Later used as a monumental feature independent of what is behind it.

Pendentive. The curved triangular surface that results when the top corner of a square space is vaulted so as to provide a circular base for a dome. If fulfils the same purpose as a *squinch*.

Peripteral. Having a single row of columns all round; a temple surrounded by a single row of columns.

Peristyle. A row of columns (1) round the outside of a building (usually a Greek temple) or (2) round the inside of a courtyard (e.g. in a Greek or Roman house) and by extension the space so enclosed.

Perpendicular. The last phase of English *Gothic*, replacing Decorated during the second half of the fourteenth century and lasting into the seventeenth. Characterized by light airy proportions, large windows, straight lattice-like tracery over both windows and wall surfaces, shallow mouldings, four-centred arches and fan vaults.

Pier. Free-standing masonry support for an arch, usually composite in section and thicker than a column, but performing the same function.

Pilaster. A flattened column, rectangular in section, attached to a wall as decoration, without structural function, but still obeying the laws governing the *orders*.

Pilotis. Posts or 'stilts' (French 'pilotis' = pile) supporting a whole building, leaving the ground storey entirely open.

Plateresque. Early Renaissance style in Spain from about 1520.

Plinth. The base of a pillar, pedestal, statue or of a whole building.

Podium. Stone platform on which a temple is built.

Portico. Colonnaded porch or vestibule. In Neoclassical houses the portico (columns and pediment) often merges into the facade.

Propylaea. (Greek: 'in front of the gate'); a monumental entrance to a sacred enclosure.

Purlin. The horizontal beam running midway along a sloping roof, resting on the principal rafters and supporting the subsidiary ones.

Pylon. Ancient Egyptian monumental gateway, usually composed of two masses of masonry with sloping sides.

Pyramid. Regular solid with a square base and sides sloping inwards to meet at a point.

Queen posts. Two upright beams in a roof, standing on the *tie-beam* and supporting a principal *rafter*.

Radiating chapels. Chapels added to an *apse* and fanning out radially.

Rafter. The sloping beams of a pitched roof, carrying the battens for the tiles.

Relief. Carving on a surface so that figures and objects are raised against a background. High relief (haut relief) is deeply cut; low relief (bas relief) is shallower.

Reticulated. Net-like. Tracery with openings like the meshes of a net, characteristic of the Decorated period in English Gothic.

Rib vault

Ridge beam. Beam running along the top of a pitched roof.

Rococo. A lighter version of the Baroque, developed in France in the late eighteenth century; characterized by flowing lines, arabesque ornament, ornate stucco-work and the obliteration of separate architectural members into a single moulded volume.

Romanesque. Style following *Carolingian* and preceding *Gothic*, characterized by massive masonry and thick proportions, the round *arch*, and the rediscovery of *vaulting* – first the barrel vault, then the groined and finally the rib vault.

Rotunda. Any round building, not necessarily domed.

Rustication. Method of leaving the outside surface of stone building blocks rough, to give an impression of strength; the edges are normally cut back, leaving deep grooves between the blocks,

Sanctuary. The most sacred part of a church or temple.

Screen. A dividing wall having no function of support, e.g. in medieval churches surrounding the *choir*.

Semidome. Half a dome leaning against part of a building (often a complete dome) and acting as an extended *flying buttress* (e.g. in Hagia Sophia, Istanbul).

Shingles. Pieces of wood used instead of tiles.

Springing. The point of an arch where the curve begins.

Squinch. A small arch built across the corner of a rectangular space to form the base for a dome.

Steel frame. A skeleton of steel girders providing all that is structurally necessary for the building to stand.

Stoa. In Greek architecture, an open colonnaded space for public business; a long *loggia*.

Stucco. Plaster or cement applied with moulds, usually to make interior decoration (e.g. Rococo), but also on exteriors and occasionally to simulate whole façades in stone (e.g. by Palladio).

Stupa. Originally a Buddhist burial mound; later a chamber for relics surrounded by an *ambulatory*.

Stylobate. The continuous base on which a *colonnade* stands.

Suspension bridge. A bridge in which the path or road is suspended from chains between towers or pylons.

Temenos. In Greek architecture, a sacred precinct enclosed by a wall and containing a temple or altar.

Tepidarium. Part of a Roman public bath containing the warm water, intermediate in temperature between the *frigidarium* and the *calidarium*.

Terracotta. Clay burnt or hard-baked in a mould; harder than brick; may be either natural brown, or painted or glazed.

Thermae. Roman public baths, containing large halls with water at various temperatures (*frigidarium, tepidarium, calidarium*) and many other amenities.

Tie beam. A beam (or rod) across the base of a pitched roof, holding the two sides together and preventing them from spreading.

Tokonoma. In Japanese houses, a niche for the exhibition of paintings or flowers.

Trabeate. Constructed with beams.

Tracery. The stone framework holding the pieces of glass which make up a large window – in practice the word means *Gothic* window tracery almost exclusively. Plate tracery, the earliest type, is basically solid wall in which holes have been cut for the glass. Bar tracery (tracery proper) uses stone ribs to form complicated patterns.

Transept. Part of a cruciform church at right angles to the *nave* and *chancel* (the north and south arms are always called 'north transept' and 'south transept'). Some cathedrals have an additional transept east of the crossing.

Triforium. The middle storey of a Romanesque or Gothic church elevation, between the *arcade* and the *clerestory*.

Triglyph. A block with three vertical strips divided by two grooves, forming (together with the *metopes*) the *frieze* of a Doric *entablature*.

Truss. A rigid triangular framework designed to span an opening and to carry tile or lead. Most wooden roofs are trussed.

Turret. A small tower, often built over a circular staircase, or as an ornamental feature.

Tuscan. A Roman addition to the classical *orders*, resembling the *Doric* but with a base and without *flutes* and *triglyphs*.

Vault. A stone ceiling. A *barrel vault* is an arched vault, either semicircular or pointed, resting on supporting walls. A *groined vault* is one where the compartments meet at a groin; a *rib vault* is the same but the joints are covered with stone ribs. A *fan vault* is a decorative type of rib vault in which the ribs fan out from the wall shafts.

Verandah. A small open gallery outside a house, with a roof supported on posts or pillars and the floor raised a few feet off the ground.

Vihara. A Buddhist monastery or hall in a monastery (originally a cave).

Volute. The spiral scroll, especially as it occurs in the *Ionic* capital.

Ziggurat. Stepped pyramid supporting an altar or temple, built in Ancient Mesopotamia and Mexico.

Bibliography

The primary sources of architecture are not books, but the buildings themselves. In writing my version of the story, I have made use of buildings, places visited, books, articles and plans too numerous to mention, and have talked to architects and critics.

The following list is not exhaustive, but is intended as a guide to the periods and places dealt with in the book. The books listed will serve as a guide to the buildings and to the available literature about them.

General

BRONOWSKI, J., *The Ascent of Man*, London, 1975

CANTACUZINO, SHERBAN, *European Domestic Architecture*, London, 1969

CLARK, KENNETH, *Civilisation*, London, 1969

CLIFTON-TAYLOR, ALEC, *The Pattern of English Building*, London, 1972

COWAN, HENRY J., *The Masterbuilders*, Sydney and London, 1977

DAVEY, NORMAN, *A History of Building Materials*, London, 1961

FLETCHER, SIR BANISTER, *A History of Architecture*, 19th edn., London, 1987

HOSKINS, W.G., *The Making of the English Landscape*, London, 1955

JELLICOE, GEOFFREY and SUSAN, *The Landscape of Man*, London, 1975

JONES, OWEN, *The Grammar of Ornament*, London, 1856; facsimile edn., London, 1986

MUMFORD, LEWIS *The City in History*, London, 1961

NUTTGENS, PATRICK (ed.), *The World's Great Architecture*, London, 1980

NUTTGENS, PATRICK, *Pocket Guide to Architecture*, London, 1980

PEVSNER, SIR NIKOLAUS, *An Outline of European Architecture*, Harmondsworth, 1943

WATKIN, DAVID, *A History of Western Architecture*, London, 1986

1 Vernacular Architecture

BRUNSKILL, R.W., *Traditional Buildings of Britain*, London, 1981

—, *Vernacular Architecture*, London, 1971

GUIDONI, ENRICO, *Primitive Architecture*, New York, 1978

RAPOPORT, AMOS, *House Form and Culture*, Englewood Cliffs, New Jersey, 1969

RUDOFSKY, BERNARD, *Architecture without Architects*, London, 1973

2 First Civilizations

BACON, EDWARD (ed.), *The Great Archeologists (from The Illustrated London News)*, New York, 1976

BORD, JANET and COLIN, *A Guide to Ancient Sites in Britain*, St Albans, 1979

BURL, AUBREY, *The Stonehenge People*, London, 1987

COTTRELL, LEONARD, *Lost Cities*, London, 1957

—, *The Bull of Minos*, London, 1955

CULICAN, WILLIAM, *The Medes and the Persians*, London, 1965

GARBINI, GIOVANNI, *The Ancient World*, London, 1967

GIEDION, SIGFRIED, *The Beginnings of Architecture*, vol. 2 of *The Eternal Present* (2 vols.), Oxford, 1964

JAMES, E.O., *From Cave to Cathedral*, London, 1965

LLOYD, S. and MULLER, H.W., *Ancient Architecture*, London, 1980

MACAULAY, ROSE, *The Pleasure of Ruins*, London, 1964

MACKENDRICK, PAUL, *The Mute Stones Speak*, London, 1960

PIGGOTT, STUART (ed.), *The Dawn of Civilization*, London, 1961

POSTGATE, NICHOLAS, *The First Empires*, Oxford, 1977

WHITEHOUSE, RUTH, *The First Cities*, Oxford, 1977

3 Ancient Egypt

DE CENIVAL, JEAN-LOUIS, *Living Architecture: Egyptian*, London, 1964

CURL, JAMES STEVENS, *A Celebration of Death*, London, 1980

EDWARDS, I.E.S., *The Pyramids of Egypt*, London, 1947

HANCOCK, GRAHAM, *Fingerprints of the Gods*, London, 1955

HUTCHINSON, WARNER, A., *Ancient Egypt*, London and New York, 1978

PEMBERTON, DELIA, *Ancient Egypt*, Harmondsworth, 1992

SMITH, W. STEVENSON, *The Art and Architecture of Ancient Egypt* (rev. edn.), Harmondsworth, 1971

4 Asian Sub-Continent

BUSSAGH, MARIO, *Oriental Architecture*, London, 1981

GRAY, BASIL (ed.), *The Arts of India*, Oxford, 1981

HARLE, J.C., *The Art and Architecture of the Indian Subcontinent*, Harmondsworth, 1986

Indian Temples and Palaces (Great Buildings of the World series), London, 1969

ROWLAND, BENJAMIN, *The Art and Architecture of India* (rev. edn.), Harmondsworth, 1971

TADGELL, CHRISTOPHER, *The History of Architecture in India*, London, 1990

VOLWAHSEN, ANDREAS, *Living Architecture: Indian*, London, 1969

5 China and Japan

AUBOYER, JEANNINE and GOEPPER, ROGER (eds.), *Oriental World*, London, 1967

COTTERELL, ARTHUR, *The First Emperor of China*, London, 1981

DEPARTMENT OF ARCHITECTURE, Qinghua University, *Historic Chinese Architecture*,

Qinghua University Press, 1985

GARDINER, STEPHEN, *The Evolution of the House*, London, 1976

KIDDER, J. EDWARD JR., *The Art of Japan*, London, 1981

LIP, EVELYN, *Chinese Geomancy*, Singapore, 1979

PAINE, ROBERT TREAT and SOPER, ALEXANDER, *The Art and Architecture of Japan* (rev. edn.), Harmondsworth, 1975

SICKMAN, LAURENCE and SOPER, ALEXANDER, *The Art and Architecture of China* (3rd edn.), Harmondsworth, 1968

TERZANI, TIZIANO, *Behind the Forbidden Door*, London, 1986

YU, ZHUOYAN, *Palaces of the Forbidden City*, Harmondsworth, 1984

6 Meso-America

HEYDEN, DORIS and GENDROP, PAUL, *Pre-Columbian Architecture of Mesoamerica*, New York, 1975, and London, 1980

—, *The Pre-Columbian Civilisations*, New York, 1979

MORRIS, CRAIG, AND VON HAGEN, ADRIANA, *The Inka Empire and its Andean Origins*, New York, 1996

ROBERTSON, DONALD, *Pre-Columbian Architecture*, Englewood Cliffs and London, 1963

7 Ancient Greece

BROWNING, ROBERT (ed.), *The Greek World*, London, 1985

GRANT, MICHAEL (ed.), *The Birth of Western Civilisation*, London, 1964

LAWRENCE, A.W., *Greek Architecture*, Harmondsworth, 1957; rev. edn., 1983

ROLAND, MARTIN, *Living Architecture: Greece*, London, 1967

ROBERTSON, D.S., *Greek and Roman Architecture*, Cambridge, 1969

SCULLY, VINCENT, *The Earth, the Temple and the Gods*, New Haven and London, 1962

SPIVEY, NIGEL, *Greek Art*, London, 1997

TAPLIN, PLIVER, *Greek Fire*, London, 1989

8 Ancient Rome

GIBBON, EDWARD, *Decline and Fall of the Roman Empire*, 1776–88; available in various modern editions and abridgements

GOODENOUGH, SIMON, *Citizens of Rome*, London, 1979

GRANT, MICHAEL, *The World of Rome*, New York, 1960

PICARD, GILBERT, *Living Architecture: Roman*, London, 1965

VITRUVIUS, *The Ten Books on Architecture*, transl. M. H. Morgan, New York, 1960

WARD-PERKINS, JOHN B., *Roman Architecture*, New York, 1977

—, *Roman Imperial Architecture*, 2nd edn., New Haven and London, 1992

9 Early christian and Byzantine

FOSTER, RICHARD, *Discovering English Churches*, London, 1980

HETHERINGTON, PAUL, *Byzantine and Medieval Greece: Churches, Castles, Art*, London, 1991

KRAUTHEIMER, RICHARD, *Early Christian and Byzantine Architecture*, Harmondsworth, 1975

LOWDEN, JOHN, *Early Christian and Byzantine Art*, London, 1997

MACDONALD, WILLIAM L., *Early Christian and Byzantine Architecture*, Englewood Cliffs and London, 1962

MAINSTONE, ROWLAND, *Hagia Sophia*, London, 1986

MANGO, CYRIL, *Byzantine Architecture*, London, 1978

STEWART, CECIL, *Early Christian, Byzantine and Romanesque Architecture*, London, 1954

TALBOT RICE, DAVID (ed.), *The Dark Ages*, London, 1965

10 Romanesque

ATROSHENKO, V.T., and COLLINS, JUDITH, *The Origins of the Romanesque*, London, 1980

CONANT, K.J., *Carolingian and Romanesque Architecture 800–1200*, London, 1959

COOK, OLIVE, *English Cathedrals*, 1989

EVANS, JOAN (ed.), *The Flowering of the Middle Ages*, London, 1985

KUBACH, HANS ERICH, *Romanesque Architecture*, New York, 1977

OURSEL, RAYMOND and ROUILLER, JACQUES, *Living Architecture: Romanesque*, London, 1967

SERVICE, ALASTAIR, *The Building of Britain: Anglo-Saxon and Norman*, London, 1982

TAYLOR, H.M. and J., *Anglo-Saxon Architecture*, Cambridge, 1965

11 Islam

BARAKAT, SULTAN (ed.), *Architecture and Development in the Islamic World*, York, 1993

BLAIR, SHEILA S., and BLOOM, JONATHAN M., *The Art and Architecture of Islam, 1250–1800*, New Haven and London, 1995

BLAIR, SHEILA S., and BLOOM, JONATHAN M., *Islamic Arts*, London, 1997

ETTINGHAUSEN, RICHARD and GRABAR, OLEG, *The Art and Architecture of Islam, 650–1250*, New Haven and London, 1992

GOODWIN, GEOFFREY, *Islamic Architecture: Ottoman Turkey*, London, 1977

—, *Sinan*, London, 1993

GRUBE, ERNST J., *The World of Islam*, London, 1966

HOAG, JOHN D., *Islamic Architecture*, New York, 1977

HUTT, ANTHONY AND HARROW, LEONARD, *Islamic Architecture: Iran*, London, 1977

HUTT, ANTHONY, *Islamic Architecture: North Africa*, London, 1977

MICHELL, GEORGE, *Architecture of the Islamic World*, London, 1978

WARREN, J. AND FETHI, I., *Traditional Houses in Baghdad*, Coach Publishing House, 1982

12 Medieval and Gothic

ACLAND, JAMES H., *Mediaeval Structure: the Gothic Vault*, Toronto and Buffalo, 1972

BRAUNFELS, WOLGANG, *Monasteries of Western Europe*, London, 1972

CHARPENTIER, LOUIS, *The Mysteries of Chartres Cathedral*, Research into Lost Knowledge Organisation, Haverhill, Suffolk, 1966

COWAN, PAINTON, *Rose Windows*, London, 1979

FRANKL, PAUL, *Gothic Architecture*, Harmondsworth, 1962

GIMPEL, JEAN, *The Cathedral Builders*, new edn., London, 1993

GRODECKI, LOUIS, *Gothic Architecture*, New York, 1977

HARVEY, JOHN, *The Medieval Architect*, London, 1972

HOFSTATTER, HANS H., *Living Architecture: Gothic*, London, 1970

JAMES, JOHN, *Chartres: the Masons Who Built a Legend*, London, 1982

MALE, EMILE, *The Gothic Image*, London, 1961

PANOFSKY, ERWIN, *Gothic Architecture and Scholasticism*, Latrobe, PA, 1951

VILLARD DE HONNECOURT, *The Sketchbooks of Villard de Honnecourt*, Bloomington, Indiana, 1959

VON SIMSON, OTTO, *The Gothic Cathedral*, London, 1962

WILSON, CHRISTOPHER, *The Gothic Cathedral*, London, 1990

13–14 The Renaissance in Italy & The Spread of the Renaissance

ACKERMANN, JAMES, *Palladio*, Harmondsworth, 1966

ALBERTI, LEON BATTISTA, *On the Art of Building*

in Ten Books, Florence, 1485; transl. J. Rykwert, N. Leach and R. Tavernor, Cambridge, Mass., 1988

ALLSOPP, BRUCE, *A History of Renaissance Architecture*, London, 1959

BENEVOLO, LEONARDO, *The Architecture of the Renaissance*, 2 vols., London, 1978

GADOL, JOAN, *Leon Battista Alberti, Universal Man of the Early Renaissance*, Chicago, 1969

HAY, DENYS (ed.), *The Age of the Renaissance*, London, 1967

HEYDENREICH, LUDWIG H., and LOTZ, WOLFGANG, *Architecture in Italy, 1400–1600*, Harmondsworth, 1974

MORRICE, RICHARD, *Buildings of Britain: Stuart and Baroque*, London, 1982

MURRAY, PETER, *Renaissance Architecture*, New York, 1971

PALLADIO, ANDREA, *The Four Books of Architecture*, Venice, 1570; Engl. transl., London, 1738, reprinted New York, 1965

PLATT, COLIN, *The Great Rebuilding of Tudor and Stuart England*, London, 1994

PORTOGHESI, PAOLO, *Rome of the Renaissance*, London, 1972

SCOTT, GEOFFREY, *The Architecture of Humanism*, London, 1914

SERLIO, SEBASTIANO, *Regolo generale di architettura*, Venice, 1537; English translation, 1611, reprinted New York, 1980

SUMMERSON, JOHN, *The Classical Language of Architecture*, London, 1963

—, *Architecture in Britain, 1530–1830*, Harmondsworth, 1953; 6th edn., 1977

WITTKOWER, RUDOLF, *Architectural Principles in the Age of Humanism*, London, 1962

VASARI, GIORGIO, *Lives of the Most Eminent Painters, Sculptors and Architects*, Florence, 1550, revised edn. 1568; transl. C. de Vere, London, 1912–15, reprinted New York, 1979

15 Baroque and Rococo

BAZIN, GERMAIN, *Baroque and Rococo*, London, 1964

BLUNT, ANTHONY (ed.), *Baroque and Rococo: Architecture and Decoration*, London, 1978

DOWNES, KERRY, *Hawksmoor*, London, 1969

DOWNES, KERRY, *Vanbrugh*, London, 1977

FISKE-KIMBALL, *The Creation of the Rococo*, New York, 1964

HARALD, BUSCH and LOHSE, BERND, *Baroque Europe*, London, 1962

HUBALA, ERICH, *Baroque & Rococo,* London, 1989

KITSON, MICHAEL, *The Age of the Baroque*, London, 1976

MILLON, HENRY A., *Baroque and Rococo Architecture*, Englewood Cliffs and London, 1961

WHINNEY, MARGARET, *Wren*, London, 1971

WITTKOWER, RUDOLPH, *Art and Architecture in Italy, 1600–1750*, Harmondsworth, 1965

16 Romantic classicism

AUNT, JOHN DIXON, and WILLIS, PETER, *The Genius of the Place: the English Landscape Garden 1620–1820*, Cambridge, Mass., 1988

BRAHAM, ALLAN, *The Architecture of the French Enlightenment*, London, 1980

CAMPBELL, COLEN (ed.), *Vitruvius Britannicus*, London, 1715–25

CROOK, J. MORDAUNT, *The Greek Revival*, London, 1972

CRUIKSHANK, DAN and WYLD, PETER, *London: The Art of Georgian Building*, London, 1975

GERMANN, GEORGE, *Gothic Revival in Europe and Britain*, London, 1972

HARRIS, JOHN, *The Palladian Revival: Lord Burlington, His Villa and Garden at Chiswick*, New Haven and London, 1996

IRWIN, DAVID, *Neoclassicism*, London, 1997

MIDDLETON, ROBIN, and WATKIN, DAVID, *Neoclassical and Nineteenth Century Architecture*, New York, 1980

STUART, JAMES and REVETT, NICOLAS, *The Antiquities of Athens*, London, 1762

SUMMERSON, JOHN, *Architecture in the Eighteenth Century*, London, 1986

TREVOR-ROPER, HUGH (ed.), *The Age of Expansion*, London, 1968

WATKIN, DAVID, *The English Vision: the Picturesque in Architecture*, London, 1982

WITTKOWER, RUDOLF, *Palladio and English Palladianism*, London, 1974

17 The Americas and Beyond

COOKE, ALASTAIR, *America*, London, 1973

DAVIES, P., *Splendours of the Raj: British Architecture in India, 1660–1947*, London, 1985

FIELDHOUSE, D.K., *The Colonial Empires*, London, 1966

HAMLIN, T.F., *Greek Revival Architecture in America*, New York, 1944 and 1964

HANDLIN, DAVID P., *American Architecture*, New York and London, 1985

HITCHCOCK, HENRY-RUSSELL, *Architecture: Nineteenth and Twentieth Centuries* (4th edn.), Harmondsworth, 1977

KUBLER, G., and SORIA, M., *Art and Architecture in Spain and Portugal and their American Dominions*, London, 1959

MORRIS, JAMES, *Heaven's Command: an Imperial Progress*, New York, 1975

O'MALLEY, DINAH, *Historic Buildings in Australia*, London, 1981

PIERSON, WILLIAM H., *American Buildings and their Architects: the Colonial and Neoclassical Styles*, New York, 1970

STACKPOLE, JOHN, *Colonial Architecture in New Zealand*, Wellington, Sydney and London, 1959

TREVOR-ROPER, HUGH (ed.), *The Age of Expansion*, London, 1968

18 The Search for a Style

ALDRICH, MEGAN, *Gothic Revival*, London, 1996

ATTERBURY, PAUL and WAINWRIGHT, CLIVE, *Pugin: A Gothic Passion*, New Haven and London, 1994

BRIGGS, ASA, *Victorian Cities*, London, 1963

CLARK, KENNETH, *The Gothic Revival*, London, 1962

COLLINS, PETER, *Changing Ideals in Modern Architecture*, London, 1966

CROOK, MORDAUNT J., *The Dilemma of Style*, London, 1989

DIXON, ROGER, and MUTHESIUS, STEFAN, *Victorian Architecture*, London, 1978

GIROUARD, MARK, *The Victorian Country House*, Oxford, 1971

GOODHART-RENDELL, H., *English Architecture since the Regency*, London, 1953

HITCHCOCK, HENRY-RUSSELL, *Architecture: Nineteenth and Twentieth Centuries* (4th edn.), Harmondsworth, 1977

IRVING, ROBERT GRANT, *Indian Summers*, New Haven and London, 1984

MAHONEY, KATHLEEN, *Gothic Style: Architecture and Interiors from the Eighteenth Century to the Present*, New York, 1995

MORRIS, IAN, with WINCHESTER, SIMON, *Stones of Empire: the Buildings of the Raj*, Oxford, 1986

MUTHESIUS, STEFAN, *The High Victorian Movement in Architecture 1850–70*, London, 1972

PEVSNER, NIKOLAUS, *A History of Building Types*, London, 1976

ROLT, L.T.C., *Isambard Kingdom Brunel*, London, 1961

STROUD, DOROTHY, *The Architecture of Sir John Soane*, London, 1962

TREVOR-ROPER, HUGH (ed.), *The Nineteenth Century*, London, 1968

WAINWRIGHT, CLIVE, *The Romantic Interior 1750–1850*, New Haven and London, 1989

19 The Turn of the Century

AMAYA, MARIO, *Art Nouveau*, London, 1985

CONDIT, CARL, W., *The Chicago School of Architecture 1875–1926*, Chicago, 1964

DAVEY, PETER, *Arts and Crafts Architecture*, London, 1980; 2nd edn., 1995

FRANKLIN, JILL., *The Gentleman's Country House, 1835–1914*, London, 1981

GAUNT, WILLIAM, *The Pre-Raphaelite Dream*, London, 1943

GUTHEIM, FRED, *Frank Lloyd Wright on Architecture*, New York, 1941

HOWARTH, THOMAS, *Charles Rennie Mackintosh*, London, 1977

HUSSEY, CHRISTOPHER, *The Life of Sir Edwin Lutyens*, Woodbridge, 1984

MACCARTHY, FIONA, *William Morris*, London, 1994

MACLEOD, ROBERT, *Charles Rennie Mackintosh*, London, 1968

MUTHESIUS, HERMANN, *Das englische Haus*, Berlin, 1904–5

NAYLOR, GILLIAN, *The Arts and Crafts Movement*, London, 1971

NUTTGENS, PATRICK (ed.), *Mackintosh and his Contemporaries*, London, 1988

PEVSNER, NIKOLAUS, *The Sources of Modern Architecture and Design*, London, 1968

RUSSELL, FRANK, *Art Nouveau Architecture*, London, 1979

SERVICE, ALASTAIR, *Edwardian Architecture*, London, 1977

SULLIVAN, LOUIS H., *Autobiography of an Idea*, New York, 1956

ZERBST, RAINER, *Antoni Gaudí*, London, 1992

20 The International Style

BANHAM, REYNER, *Theory and Design in the First Machine Age*, London, 1960

BENEVOLO, LEONARDO, *History of Modern Architecture*, 2 vols., London, 1971

DROSTE, MAGDALENA, *Bauhaus*, London, 1990

FABER, COLIN, *Candela the Shell Builder*, London and New York, 1963

GIEDION, SIGFRIED, *Space, Time and Architecture*, Cambridge, Mass., 1963

GROPIUS, WALTER, *The New Architecture and the Bauhaus*, London, 1935

HATJE, GERD (ed.), *Encyclopaedia of Modern Architecture*, London, 1963

HITCHCOCK, HENRY-RUSSELL and JOHNSON, PHILIP, *The International Style*, New York, 1932; 2nd edn., 1966

LE CORBUSIER, *Towards a New Architecture*, London, 1927; reprinted 1970

NUTTGENS, PATRICK, *Understanding Modern Architecture*, London, 1988

PEVSNER, NIKOLAUS, *The Sources of Modern Architecture and Design*, London, 1968

RICHARDS, J.M., *Guide to Finnish Architecture*, London, 1966

SCULLY, VINCENT, *Modern Architecture*, New York, 1961

WEBER, EVA, *Art Deco*, London, 1989

21 The End of Certainty

CURTIS, WILLIAM J.R., *Modern Architecture since 1900*, 3rd edn., London, 1996

GLANCEY, JONATHAN, *New British Architecture*, London, 1989

FRAMPTON, KENNETH, *Modern Architecture, a Critical History*, New York, 1980

JENCKS, CHARLES, A., *The Language of Post-Modern Architecture*, 3rd edn., London, 1981

—, *Late Modern Architecture and Other Essays*, London, 1980

ROSSI, ALDO, *The Architecture of the City*, Cambridge, Mass., 1982 (original Italian edition, Padua, 1966)

VENTURI, ROBERT, *Complexity and Contradiction in Architecture*, New York, 1966

Bibliography

Biographies of Architects

These summary biographies are of all the major architects whose works are illustrated in the book. The listing of works is selective.

Aalto, Alvar (1898–1976), the greatest Finnish architect. Brought up in the Romantic Nationalist tradition, he introduced the International Modern style to Finland, giving it a strongly personal and Finnish character. He was acutely sensitive to the landscape and made highly effective use of brick and timber.

Works: *Viipuri Library* (1927–35), *Paimio Sanatorium* (1929–33), *Villa Mairea*, Noormarkku (1938), *Baker House*, Massachusetts Institute of Technology, Cambridge (1947–8), *Civic Centre*, Säynätsalo (1950–2), *Technical University*, Otaniemi (1950–64), *Vuoksenniska Church*, Imatra (1956–9), *Public Library*, Rovaniemi (1963–8).

Adam, Robert (1728–92), greatest British architect of the second half of the eighteenth century. He devised a neo-classical style of brilliant decorative elegance that became extremely influential in America and Russia as well as Britain. Son of the famous Scottish architect William Adam (1689–1748), he and his brother James set up a highly successful business. Their *Works in Architecture* was published in 1773, 1779 and 1822. The 'Adam style' included decorative work, fittings and furniture as well as an unprecedented variety of room shapes.

Interior transformations: *Harewood House*, Yorkshire (1758–71), *Kedleston Hall*, Derbyshire (1759–), *Syon House*, London (1760–9), *Osterley Park*, Middlesex (1761–80), *Kenwood House*, London (1767–9). Architecture: *20 Portman Square*, London (1770s), *Register House*, Edinburgh

(1774–), *Culzean Castle* (1777–90), *Charlotte Square*, Edinburgh (1791–1807).

Alberti, Leon Battista (1404–72), Italian Renaissance architect and author. He moved in humanist intellectual circles, and his buildings reflect his interest in harmonic proportions and the correct use of the classical orders. His influential book *On Architecture* was written in the 1440s but not published until 1485.

Works: *Palazzo Rucellai*, Florence (1446), *façade*, S. Maria Novella, Florence (1456–70), *S. Andrea*, Mantua (1472).

Aleijadinho (António Francisco Lisboa, 1738–1814), Brazilian architect; his father a Portuguese architect, his mother a black slave. He helped create a distinctively Brazilian form of the Baroque style, with rich ornament and contorted forms, combining sculpture and architecture in a single spatial concept.

Works: *São Francisco*, Ouro Preto (1766–94), *Bom Jesus de Matozinhos*, Congonhas do Campo (1800–5).

Anathemius of Tralles, Greek geometrician turned architect who flourished in the early 6th century ad. With Isidore of Miletus he built the original church of Agia Sophia, Constantinople (532–7).

Asam, Egid Quirin (1692–1750), one of two brothers who created a distinctive Baroque style in Bavaria, Southern Germany. They mostly designed church interiors, using fresco and stucco to create fantastically rich effects.

Decoration: *Freising Cathedral* (1723–4), *St Emmeram*, Regensburg (1733) and commissions in and around Munich. Architecture: *St John Nepomuk*, Munich (1733–44),

Ursuline Church, Straubing (1736–41).

Asplund, Gunnar (1885–1940), leading Swedish architect who developed a light and graceful version of the International Modern style.

Works: *Stockholm City Library* (1920–8), *Stockholm Exhibition* (1930), *Göteborg Town Hall extension* (1934–7), *Forest Crematorium*, Stockholm (1935–40).

Barry, Sir Charles (1795–1860), versatile English architect of the early Victorian period, whose work was inspired by Renaissance models. His masterpiece is the Houses of Parliament, where the Gothic detail was supplied by Pugin.

Works: *Travellers' Club*, London (1829–31), *Houses of Parliament*, London (1836–52), *Reform Club*, London (1837), *Bridgewater House*, London (1847), *Halifax Town Hall* (1859–62).

Belgiojoso, Lodovico (b. 1909), Italian architect, founder in 1932 of the BBPR Architectural Studio in Milan, with Ernesto Rogers (1909–69) and Enrico Peressutti (1908–73) as partners. Their modernism was tempered by humour, whimsy and a willingness to make use of traditional styles.

Works: *Heliotherapy Clinic*, Legnano, Milan (1938; demolished 1956), *Post Office*, EUR quarter, Rome (1940), *Sforza Castle Museum*, Milan (1956–63), *Velasca Tower*, Milan (1956–8), *Chase Manhattan Bank*, Milan (1969).

Bernini, Gian Lorenzo (1598–1680), the greatest sculptor of his age and a dominating figure in the creation of the Baroque style. His work has a theatrical quality, blending sculpture and architecture into a unified whole.

Works (all in Rome): *Baldacchino*, St Peter's (1624–33), *Trevi Fountain* (1632–7), *Cornaro Chapel*, S. Maria della Vittoria (1646), *colonnade*, St Peter's Square (1656–71), *S. Andrea al Quirinale* (1658–70), *Palazzo Chigi-Odescalchi* (1664).

Bindesbøll, Gottlieb (1800–56), Danish architect, whose free adaptations of the Neo-classical style and bold use of colour were admired and influential. Many of his buildings use polychrome brick and also reflect the influence of vernacular traditions.

Works: *Thorvaldsen Museum*, Copenhagen (1839–48), *Habro Church* (1850–2), *Oringe Mental Hospital* (1854–7), *Veterinary School*, Copenhagen (1856).

Boffrand, Gabriel Germain (1667–1754), the greatest French Rococo architect, pupil and later partner of J.-H. Mansart. His buildings are characterized by simple exteriors and lavish interiors, of which the Hôtel de Soubise is the most famous. He became very rich, largely through building speculative private *hôtels* in Paris, but lost much of his fortune in the Mississippi Bubble of 1720.

Works: *Château de Lunéville* (1702–6), *Château de Saint Ouen* (c. 1710), *Hôtel de Montmorency*, Paris (1712), *Ducal Palace*, Nancy (1715–22; demolished 1745), *Hôtel de Soubise* (now Archives Nationales), Paris (1735–9).

Borromini, Francesco (1599–1667), brilliant Italian Baroque architect, pupil and rival of Bernini. His most famous works are small churches on awkward sites in Rome, all of which make a highly disciplined use of simple geometrical forms, resulting in outstanding clarity of structure and masterly control of space. The forms he created were bold, original and influential, yet he denied the claims of his enemies that he was breaking the rules of classical architecture. An embittered recluse in later life, he committed suicide.

Works (all in Rome): *Oratory of St Philip Neri* (1637–50), *S. Carlo alle Quattro Fontane* (1638–77), *S. Ivo della Sapienza* (1642), *façade*, S. Agnese in Piazza Navone (1652–66).

Bramante, Donato (1444–1514), Italian High Renaissance architecture whose Tempietto is often described as the perfect Renaissance building. From c.1480 he was in Milan, a contemporary of Leonardo at the court of Lodovico Sforza, and there he worked on several churches. He fled to Rome after the French invasion of 1499,

where he produced the original grandiose Greek cross plan for the new St Peter's (modified greatly in the final built structure).

Works: *S. Maria presso S. Satiro*, Milan (1482), *S. Maria delle Grazie*, Milan (1492), *cloister*, S. Maria della Pace, Rome (1500–4), *Tempietto*, S. Montorio in Monte, Rome (1502), *St Peter's*, Rome (1506–), *Palazzo Caprini*, Rome (1510).

Brodrick, Cuthbert (1822–1905), Yorkshire-based English architect of the High Victorian era, whose classical style was inspired by French Renaissance and Baroque examples.

Works: *Leeds Town Hall* (1853), *Leeds Corn Exchange* (1860–3), *Grand Hotel*, Scarborough (1863–7).

Brunelleschi, Filippo (1377–1446), Italian architect, sculptor and mathematician who pioneered the Renaissance style and is credited with the invention of perspective. Studying Antique and Romanesque models, he transformed his prototypes into a series of archetypal Renaissance buildings noted for their elegance, simplicity and perfect proportions.

Works (all in Florence): *Foundling Hospital* (1421), *Cathedral Dome* (1420–34), *S. Lorenzo* (1421–), *Pazzi Chapel*, S. Croce (1429–61), *S. Spirito* (1436–).

Bullant, Jean (c.1520–78), French Mannerist architect who combined pedantic attention to correct classical detail with the use of giant orders to create a grandiose effect. He became architect to Catherine de Medicis in 1570. He wrote *Reigle générale d'architecture* (1563).

Works: *Petit Château*, Chantilly (1560), *Hôtel de Soissons*, Paris (1572; destroyed), *bridge gallery*, Chenonceaux (1576–7).

Burlington, Lord (1694–1753), connoisseur and amateur architect who promoted Palladianism and had an enormous influence on English taste. Fastidious and puritanical, he emphasized the pure and 'absolute' classical standards of his master Palladio, and based his villa at Chiswick on the Villa Rotonda.

Works: *Dormitory*, Westminster School, London (1722–30), *Chiswick House* (1725), *Assembly Rooms*, York (1731–2).

Burnham, David H. (1846–1912), American architect and planner. In partnership with John Wellborn Root (q.v.) he played a vital role in the creation of the Chicago Style. He was Chief of Construction for the World's

Columbian Exhibition, Chicago (1893), and produced comprehensive plans for the District of Columbia (1901–2) and Chicago (1906–9).

Works: *Monadnock Building*, Chicago (1884–91), *Reliance Building*, Chicago (1890–4), *Masonic Temple*, Chicago (1891), *Flatiron Building*, New York (1902).

Calatrava, Santiago (b. 1951), Spanish-born architect and engineer based in Zurich, Switzerland. Dramatically combining architecture and advanced engineering, he has created structures that can almost be described as sculpture, with elegant and expressive three-dimensional forms that are functional and at the same time conceived in sculptural terms.

Works: *Stadelhofen Railway Station*, Zurich (1982–90), *Gallery and Heritage Square*, Toronto (1987–92), *Alamillo Bridge*, Seville (1987–92), *TGV Station*, Lyons-Satolas Airport (1988–92), *Telecommunications Tower*, Montjuic, Barcelona (1989–92), *Bilbao Airport* (1991).

Callicrates (5th century BC), leading Athenian architect, famous principally for the Parthenon, which he designed with Ictinus.

Works: *Temple of Nike Apteros*, Athens (450–424 BC), *Parthenon*, Athens (447–432 BC), part of the defensive Long Walls connecting Athens and the Piraeus (c. 440 BC).

Cameron, Charles (1746–1812), Scottish neo-classical architect, admirer and follower of Robert Adam, who went to work for Catherine the Great in Russia in 1779, and remained in Russia for the rest of his life.

Works: buildings, interiors and garden designs at *Tsarskoe Selo*, Pushkin (1780–7); *Pavlovsk Palace*, Pushkin (1781–96), *Naval Hospital and Barracks*, Kronstadt (1805).

Campen, Jacob van (1595–1657), Dutch classical architect, who introduced a version of the Palladian style into Holland that become very fashionable, and had a particular influence in England.

Works: *Mauritzhuis*, The Hague (1633–5), *Town Hall*, Amsterdam (1648–55), *New Church*, Haarlem (1654–9).

Candela, Felix (b. 1910), Spanish-born Mexican architect and engineer, whose experiments with concrete shell-vaults introduced expressive but functional paraboloid shapes into modern architecture.

Works: *Cosmic Rays Laboratory*, University Campus, Mexico City (1951), *Church of*

Biographies of Architects

the Miraculous Virgin, Mexico City (1954), *Warehouse for Ministry of Finance*, Vallejo (1954), *Textile Factory*, Coyoacan (1955), *Restaurant*, Xochimilco (1958).

Cuvilliés, François (1695–1768), Belgian-born architect who became the supreme exponent of the Rococo style in Southern Germany. Appointed court architect by the Elector of Bavaria, he was sent to Paris to study, and on returning to Munich developed a style that combined fantastic exuberance with the utmost elegance and delicacy.
    Works (in Munich): *decoration of the Residenz* (1729–37), *Amalienburg Pavilion*, Schloss Nymphenburg (1374–9), *Residenztheater* (1751–3), *façade*, St Cajetan (1767).

Dientzenhofer, Johann (1665–1726), one of a family of German Baroque architects. He visited Rome, and his early work has an Italianate character. His mature works are characterized by a dramatic and fluid conception of space.
    Works: *Cathedral*, Fulda (1701–12), *Banz Abbey Church* (1710–18), *Palace*, Pommersfelden (1711–18).

Dollmann, Georg von (1830–95), German Gothic Revival and Romantic architect. A pupil of Leo von Klenze, he succeeded Eduard Riedel (1813–85) as architect to Ludwig II of Bavaria, and became responsible for translating the king's 'fairytale' ideas into buildings incorporating clements of medieval, Baroque, Byzantine and Oriental styles.
    Works: *Parish Church*, Giesing (1865–8), *Schloss Neuschwanstein* (1872–86; begun by Riedel, 1868), *Schloss Linderhof* (1874–8), *Schloss Herrenchiemsee* (1878–86).

Dudok, Willem (1884–1974), Dutch architect based in Hilversum. Conservative in his use of brick and his respect for tradition, he absorbed the influence of De Stijl and of Frank Lloyd Wright to create a distinctive version of the International Style that was much admired, particularly in Britain.
    Works: *Dr Bavinck School*, Hilversum (1921–2), *Town Hall*, Hilversum (1927–31), *Bijenkorf Department Store*, Rotterdam (1929–30; destroyed), *Erasmus Flats*, Rotterdam (1938–9).

Eiffel, Gustave (1832–1923), French engineer who pioneered the use of latticed box girder construction, particularly for bridges. His structures combine lightness and strength with restrained elegance.
    Works: *Pont du Garabit*, Cantal, France (1870–4), *bridge over the Douro*, Porto, Portugal (1877–8), *metal frame for the Statue of Liberty*, New York (1885), *Eiffel Tower*, Paris (1887–9).

Eisenman, Peter (b. 1932), American architect, in the 1960s a member of the 'New York Five', a group who admired the classic forms of early modernism and promoted formal values at the expense of function. Describing himself as a 'post-humanist', he has become preoccupied with fragmentation, superimposed grids and arbitrary juxtapositions.
    Works: *IBA Social Housing*, Kochstrasse, Berlin (1982–7), *Wexner Center*, Columbus, Ohio (1983–9), *Max Reinhardt House* (project), Berlin (1983–9, 1994), *Greater Columbus Convention Center*, Columbus, Ohio (1989–93).

Foster, Sir Norman (b. 1935), English architect who along with Richard Rogers pioneered the 'high tech' development of modernism in Britain. His bold use of advanced technology and frank expression of structure are tempered by fluidity and formal control in his designs, and by a strong awareness of social and even spiritual needs.
    Works: *Reliance Controls Factory*, Swindon (1966), *Sainsbury Centre for the Visual Arts*, University of East Anglia (1974–8), *Willis Faber Dumas Building*, Ipswich (1974), *Hong Kong and Shanghai Bank*, Hong Kong (1979–86), *Stansted Airport* (1980–91), *Sackler Galleries*, Royal Academy (1985–93), *Carré d'Art*, Nîmes, France (1985–93), *Century Tower*, Tokyo (1987–81), *Chek Lap Kok Airport*, Hong Kong (1992–8).

Fuller, Richard Buckminster (1895–1983), American engineer and theorist. Always advocating the use of new materials and construction techniques, he invented the geodesic dome, a light construction using the principle of the space frame. Over 250,000 of these domes have been built.
    Works: *Geodesic domes* at Baton Rouge Louisiana (1959), Montreal (1967), Mt Fuji, Japan (1973), and Disneyworld, Florida (1982).

Furness, Frank (1839–1912), American architect based in Philadelphia. Richly eclectic in style, deriving mainly from French and English sources, his buildings are notable for their bold forms and colourful use of brick. Among his pupils was Louis Sullivan.
    Works (all in Philadelphia): *Pennsylvania Academy of the Fine Arts* (1871–6), *Provident Life and Trust Company Building* (1876–9), *University of Pennsylvania Library* (1887–91), *Broad Street Station* (1891–3; demolished).

Gabriel, Ange-Jacques (1698–1782), the greatest French neo-classical architect. In 1742 he succeeded his father as royal architect to Louis XV, and his principal work comprised additions and alterations to the royal palaces at Fontainebleau, Compiègne and Versailles. His finest work is characterized by dignity, simplicity and a restrained use of decoration.
    Works: *Opéra*, Versailles (1748), *Pavillon de Pompadour*, Fontainebleau (1748), *École Militaire*, Paris (1750–68), *Petit Trianon*, Versailles (1763–9), *Hunting Lodge*, La Muette (1753–4). *Place Royale*, Bordeaux (1731–55), *Place de la Concorde*, Paris (1753–65).

Garnier, Charles (1825–98), French architect. His masterpiece, the grandiose neo-Baroque Paris Opéra, is a triumph of rich colour, ornate decoration and highly disciplined control of mass and space.
    Works: *Opéra*, Paris (1861–75), *Casino*, Monte Carlo (1878), *villa*, Bordighera (1872), *Cercle de la Librairie*, Paris (1878).

Gaudí, Antoni (1852–1926), Spanish architect who created a fantastic and highly idiosyncratic version of Art Nouveau based on natural forms, characterized by curving façades and roof-lines, and by exuberant and colourful decoration.
    Works (all in Barcelona): *Church of the Sagrada Familia* (1884–), *Palacio Güell* (1885–9), *Park Güell* (1900–14), *Santa Coloma de Cervello* (1898–1917), *casa Batlló* (1904–6), *Casa Mila* (1905–10).

Gibbs, James (1682–1754), English Baroque and neo-classical architect. A pupil of Carlo Fontana in Rome, he created a restrained version of the Baroque that greatly influenced the development of the neo-classical style in Britain.
    Works: *Ditchley House*, Oxfordshire (1720–5), *St Martin-in-the-Fields*, London (1721–6), *Senate House*, Cambridge (1722–30), *Fellows' Building*, King's College, Cambridge (1724–9), *Radcliffe Camera*, Oxford (1737–49).

Giulio Romano (1492–1546), Italian architect and painter whose bold and self-conscious manipulation of the rules of classical architecture was the hallmark of the Mannerist style. He was employed by Duke Federico II Gonzaga at Mantua.

Works (all at Mantua): *Palazzo del Tè* (1525–34), *Palazzo Ducale* (1538–9), *Cathedral* (1545–7).

Gowan, James *see* **Stirling, James**

Graves, Michael (b. 1934), American architect, based in Princeton and New York. A member of the 'New York Five' (*see* Eisenman), he engaged in the formal manipulation of modern and classical prototypes, developing a style in which historical quotation is used with self-conscious irony and ambiguity.

Works: *Benacerraf House*, Princeton (1969), *Fargo-Moorhead Cultural Center*, North Dakota/Minnesota (1977–8), *Public Services Building*, Portland, Oregon (1980–3).

Gropius, Walter (1883–1969), one of the creators of the International Style in modern architecture, and founder of the Bauhaus, the most influential school of architecture and design of the twentieth century. After the Bauhaus was closed by the Nazis in 1933 he worked briefly in England (1934–7), and then emigrated to the United States where, as head of the Graduate School of Design at Harvard University, he played a major role in the dissemination of modernism.

Works: *Fagus Factory*, Alfeld-an-der-Leine (1911), *Werkbund Exhibition Pavilion*, Cologne (1914), *Bauhaus*, Dessau (1925–6), *Gropius House*, Lincoln, Mass. (1938), *Harkness Commons Dormitories*, Harvard University, Cambridge, Mass. (1948).

Guarini, Guarino (1624–83), Italian Baroque architect and mathematician. He expressed Borromini's ideas in a more monumental form, and his churches are highly complex spatially, with cone-shaped domes that were original and influential.

Works (all in Turin): *Church of the Holy Shroud* (1667–90), *San Lorenzo* (1668–87), *Collegio dei Nobili* (1678), *Palazzo Carignano* (1679).

Herrera, Juan de (c.1530–97), Spanish architect who developed a Renaissance style of great purity and simplicity, that reflected the severe taste of his patron, King Philip II. From 1572 he was in charge of completing the Escorial palace.

Works: *Aranjuez Palace* (1569), *Alcázar*, Toledo (1571–85), *El Escorial* (1572–82), begun by Juan Bautista de Toledo, 1562), *Exchange*, Seville (1582), *Valladolid Cathedral* (c.1585).

Hildebrandt, Lucas von (1668–1745), leading Baroque architect in Austria. He was a pupil of Carlo Fontana and admirer of Guarino Guarini. His façades are relatively plain, while his interiors, especially staircases, are dramatic and richly decorated. Much of his work (apart from the Belvedere) consisted of adapting existing buildings.

Works: *Schloss Pommersfelden* (1711–18), *Residenz*, Würzburg (1719–44), *Belvedere*, Vienna (1720–4), *Schloss Mirabell*, Salzburg (1721–7).

Holl, Elias (1573–1646), leading Renaissance architect in Germany, appointed city architect of Augsburg in 1602. His style was influenced by Palladio and Mannerism, but he modified the Italian style by using such typically German features as high gables.

Works (all in Augsburg): *Arsenal* (1602–7), *St Anne's Grammar School* (1613–15), *Town Hall* (1615–20), *Hospital of the Holy Ghost* (1626–30).

Horta, Victor (1861–1947), Belgian architect who in a brilliantly original series of buildings translated the sinuous lines of Art Nouveau into a 'total architecture' combining form and decoration in unified whole.

Works (all in Brussels): *Hôtel Tassel* (1892–3), *Hôtel Solvay* (1895–1900), *Maison du Peuple* (1896–9), *L'Innovation Store* (1901).

Ictinus *see* **Callicrates**

Imhotep (flourished c. 2600 BC), history's first named architect, vizier and counsellor to King Zoser of Egypt, and priest of Heliopolis. He created the huge funerary complex at Saqqara (c. 2630–2610 BC), which with its stepped pyramid, its sophisticated stonework and the use of columns set the pattern for Egyptian monuments for 2,500 years.

Isidore of Miletus *see* **Anathemius of Tralles**

James of St George (13th century), Master of the Works to King Edward I of England, responsible for overseeing a ring of 'perfected' castles on the Welsh border in the late 13th century, including Conwy, Caernarfon, Pembroke, Harlech and Beaumaris.

Jefferson, Thomas (1743–1826), American statesman, third President of the United States, who was also a gifted amateur architect. Inspired by Palladio and ancient Rome, he created a pure classical style that excercised a profound influence on public building in the United States, and he played a leading role in the planning of the new federal capital at Washington.

Works: *Monticello* (1770–96), *Virginia State Capitol*, Richmond (1796), *University of Virginia*, Charlottesville (1817–26).

Johnson, Philip (b. 1906), New York-based architect who introduced the International Style to America as co-curator of the famous exhibition of that name at New York's Museum of Modern Art in 1932. A pupil of Mies van der Rohe, he created some of the earliest and most influential steel and glass buildings in the US, notable for their purity of line. In the 1980s he pioneered the 'post-modern' quotation of historical styles in tall buildings.

Works: *Glass House*, New Canaan (1949–5), *Seagram Building*, New York (1954–8, with Mies van der Rohe), *Sheldon Memorial Art Gallery*, Lincoln, Nebraska (1963), *State Theater*, Lincoln Center, New York (1964, with Richard Foster), *John F. Kennedy Memorial*, Dallas (1970), *ATT Building*, New York (1978–83), *IBM Tower*, Atlanta (1987).

Jones, Inigo (1573–1652), brilliant architect and stage-designer who introduced the Renaissance style into England. Inspired principally by Palladio, he created England's first classical style, and he profoundly influenced the Palladian revival of the eighteenth century.

Works: *Queen's House*, Greenwich (1616–35), *Banqueting House*, Whitehall (1619–22), *Queen's Chapel*, St James's Palace, London (1623–7), *portico*, Old St Paul's Cathedral, London (1631–42), reconstruction of *Wilton House*, Wiltshire (c.1647).

Juvarra, Filippo (1678–1736), pupil of Carlo Fontana, finest Italian Baroque architect of the eighteenth century, most of whose work was in and around Turin. Showing perfect mastery of an established style rather than great originality, his buildings form imposing and finely proportioned ensembles.

Works (in or near Turin): *S. Filippo Neri* (1715), *church at Superga* (1717–31), *Palazzo*

Madama (1718–21), *Stupenigi Castle* (1729–33).

Kahn, Louis I. (1901–74), one of the greatest of the second generation of modern American architects. Restrained in his use of materials and sympathetic to tradition, he became a master of monumentality, imbuing his buildings with dignity and powerful sculptural form.

Works: *Yale University Art Gallery* (1951–3), *Richards Medical Research Laboratories*, University of Pennsylvania, Philadelphia (1957–65), *Salk Institute*, La Jolla, California (1959–65), *Indian Institute of Management*, Ahmadabad (1962–74), *National Assembly Building*, Dacca, Bangladesh (1962–75), *Kimbell Art Museum*, Fort Worth, Texas (1966–72).

Kent, William (1684–1748), English architect and landscape designer, whose revolutionary informal garden designs created a new relationship between a building and its natural setting. He was a protégé of Lord Burlington, with whom he created a pure neo-Palladian style that was hugely influential in Britain.

Works: *Chiswick House* (1725), *landscape garden*, Stowe, Buckinghamshire (1732–), *Holkham Hall*, Norfolk (1734), *landscape garden*, Rousham, Oxfordshire (1739), *44 Berkeley Square*, London (1742–4), *Horse Guards*, London (1748–59).

Klenze, Leo von (1784–1864), versatile German architect who created dignified and monumental public buildings, mainly in Southern Germany, some in the Greek style, others in the Renaissance style.

Works: *Glyptothek*, Munich (1816–31), *Leuchtenberg Palace*, Munich (1817–19), *Alte Pinakothek*, Munich (1826–36), *Walhalla*, near Regensburg (1830–42), *Hermitage*, St Petersburg (1839–52).

Kurokawa, Kisho (b. 1934), leading contemporary Japanese architect, with an international as well as Japanese practice. A member of the Metabolist group, he has developed systems based on standardized units, and has emphasized the idea of 'symbiosis' – the interactions between people and their surroundings and between different cultures. He is also a prolific writer.

Works: *Nakagin Capsule Tower*, Tokyo (1972), *Sony Tower*, Osaka (1976), *Museum of Contemporary Art*, Hiroshima (1988), *Sporting Club*, Illinois Center, Chicago (1990), *City Museum of Photography*, Nara (1992).

Labrouste, Henri (1801–75), French architect and influential exponent of rationalism, who pioneered the use of iron vaulting in buildings. Following the principle that form should follow function and materials, in his two great library commissions he exploited iron's strength to create spacious, light and elegant interiors whose influence can be seen worldwide in such structures as railway stations.

Works: *Bibliothèque Ste-Geneviève*, Paris (1843–51), *Seminary*, Rennes (1853–72), *Bibliothèque Nationale*, Paris (1854–75), *Hôtel de Vilgruy*, Paris (1865).

Latrobe, Benjamin (1764–1820), English-born architect and engineer who emigrated to the United States in 1793, was instrumental in introducing the neo-classical style into American architecture, and was one of the architects responsible for the Capitol building in Washington, DC (1803–11, 1814).

Works: *Bank of Pennsylvania*, Philadelphia (1798), *Baltimore Cathedral* (1805–18), *Markoe House*, Philadelphia (1810), *University of Virginia* (1817–26, with others), *Louisiana State Bank*, New Orleans (1819).

Laurana, Luciano (1420/5–79), Italian early Renaissance architect whose only known work is the Ducal Palace at Urbino (*c*.1454–), with commanding and spacious elevations and with refined and delicate details in the interior decoration.

Le Corbusier (Charles-Edouard Jeanneret; 1887–1965), Swiss-born architect whose archetypical forms were decisive influences on the development of modern architecture. The clean and pure lines of the Villa Savoie at Poissy are a canonical statement of modernism, and the Unité d'Habitation at Marseilles became a prototype for mass housing world-wide. Le Corbusier's later works become more rugged and poetic, reflecting a new preoccupation with landscape and natural forms.

Works: *Maison La Roche/Jeanneret*, Paris (1925), *Villa Stein/de Monzie*, Garches (1928), *Villa Savoie, Poissy* (1928–31), *Pavillon Suisse*, Cité Universitaire, Paris (1930–1), *Unité d'Habitation*, Marseilles (1946–52), *Chapel*, Ronchamp (1950–4), *Millowners' Building*, Ahmadabad (1951–4), *Chandigarh*, India (1956–), *Monastery*, La Tourette (1957), *Carpenter Center*, Harvard University (1959–63).

Le Vau, Louis (1612–70), the leading French Baroque architect, who combined grandeur and elegance in major royal projects for King Louis XIV.

Works: *Hôtel Lambert*, Paris (1639–44), *Château of Vaux-le-Vicomte* (1657), *Collège des Quatre Nations*, Paris (1662), remodelling of the *Louvre* (1664–) and of the *Palace of Versailles* (1668–).

Longhena, Baldassare (1598–1682), the greatest Venetian Baroque architect, whose work is characterized by theatricality, bold massing and richly textured surfaces. His masterpiece, S. Maria della Salute, occupied him for most of his working life.

Works (all in Venice): *S. Maria della Salute* (1630–87), *staircase*, Monastery of S. Giorgio Maggiore (1643–5), *Palazzo Belloni* (1648–65), *Palazzo Bon (Rezzonico)* (1649–82), *Palazzo Pesaro* (1652–9), *S. Maria di Nazareth* (1656–73).

L'Orme, Philibert de (1514–70), the most important French architect of the 16th century. Original and inventive, he was instrumental in creating a distinctive version of Renaissance classicism that drew on French traditions as well as Italian models. He was also influential through his books, *Nouvelles Inventions* (1561) and *Architecture* (1567). Little of his work has survived.

Works: *screen*, St-Etienne-du-Mont, Paris (1545), *Château of Anet* (1547–52; destroyed), *Bridge*, Château of Chenonceaux (1556–9), *Tuileries Palace*, Paris (1564–72; destroyed).

Lubetkin, Berthold (1901–90), Russian-born architect who emigrated to England, where he founded Tecton, a practice which created some of the earliest and most influential buildings in the International Modern style in pre-war Britain, notable for their simplicity and clean lines.

Works: *Gorilla House* and *Penguin Pool*, London Zoo (1934, 1935), *Highpoint I and II*, Highgate, London (1933–8), *Finsbury Health Centre*, London (1939).

Lutyens, Sir Edwin (1869–1944), the dominant English architect of the early 20th century, whose grand country houses and public buildings reflected the wealth and imperial grandeur of Edwardian Britain. The early works combine Arts and Craft ideas with ingenious planning and interesting façades, while he later developed an increasingly monumental classicism.

Works: *Munstead Wood*, Surrey (1896), *Tigbourne Court*, Surrey (1899–1901), *Deanery Garden*, Sonning, Berks (1899–1902), *Heathcote*, Ilkley, Yorkshire (1906),

Viceroy's House, New Delhi (1920–31), *War Memorial*, Thiepval, Belgium (1927–32), *British Embassy*, Washington DC (1927–8).

McKim, Charles (1847–1909), American architect who in partnership with William Mead (1846–1928) and Stanford White (1853–1906), ran the largest architectural practice of their time in the US. Their style was largely based on the Italian High Renaissance.

Works: *Boston Public Library* (1887–95), *Rhode Island State House*, Providence (1892–1904), *Columbia University*, New York (1892–1901), *Morgan Library*, New York (1903), *Pennsylvania Station*, New York (1902–11; demolished).

Mackintosh, Charles Rennie (1868–1928), brilliantly original architect and designer who created his own highly idiosyncratic version of Art Nouveau combining logical planning and expressive ornament. He was more influential on the Continent (notably Vienna) than in Britain.

Works: *tea-rooms for Miss Cranston*, Glasgow (1897–1911), *Glasgow School of Art* (1896–9, 1907–9), *Hill House*, Helensburgh (1902–3).

Mansart, Jules-Hardouin (1646–1708), leading French Baroque architect, appointed Royal Architect to Louis XIV in 1675. Much of his career was spent completing the palace at Versailles, where he showed himself adept at creating the required splendour and visual drama. His later work showed a lightness that foreshadowed the Rococo.

Works: *Galerie des Glaces*, Versailles (1678–84), *Chapel of the Invalides*, Paris (1680–91), *Royal Chancellery*, Place Vendôme, Paris (1698–), *Royal Chapel*, Versailles (1699–).

Mead, William *see* **McKim**

Mendelsohn, Erich (1887–1953), German architect whose early work represents an 'expressionist' tendency in modernism, with flowing forms expressed in concrete. His later works become more formal and horizontal, but always with flowing lines.

Works: *Einstein Tower*, Potsdam (1919–21), *Hat Factory*, Luckenwalde (1921–3), *Schocken Department Store*, Chemnitz (1928), *De La Warr Pavilion*, Bexhill, Sussex (1935–6, with Serge Chermayeff), *Hadassah Medical Centre*, Mount Scopus, Jerusalem (1936–8).

Mengoni, Giuseppe (1829–77), Italian architect famous for one project, the Galleria Vittorio Emanuele in Milan (1863–7). Built in a free Renaissance style, it is one of largest shopping arcades ever built.

Merrill, John *see* **Skidmore**

Michelangelo Buonarroti (1475–1564), sculptor, painter, military engineer and architect, one of the greatest geniuses of the Renaissance. By breaking rules and conceiving a building as an organically developing and sculptural form, he created a series of original and immensely influential masterpieces, none of them completely finished. His bold use of pilasters and giant orders and his dynamic conception of space opened the way for later Mannerist and Baroque developments.

Works: S. Lorenzo, Florence: *façade* (1515, not built), *Medici Chapel* (1519–) and *Laurentian Library* (1524), *Capitol*, Rome (1839–), *St Peter's*, Rome (1546–), *Capella Sforza*, S. Maria Maggiore, Rome (c.1560).

Mies van der Rohe, Ludwig (1886–1969), one of the founding fathers of modern architecture, first in Germany, and from 1938 in the US. He was director of the Bauhaus 1930–3, director of the School of Architecture at the Illinois Institute of Technology (1938–58), and one of the most influential teachers of the century. Embracing steel, glass and skeleton-frame technology, he advocated structural clarity, free floor-plans, modular designs and precision in detail. His Barcelona Pavilion and his high- and low-rise steel-frame buildings have become canonical examples of the International Style.

Works: *glass skyscraper projects* (not built) (early 1920s), *Exhibition House*, Weissenhofsiedlung, Stuttgart (1927), *German Pavilion*, Barcelona (1929), *Farnsworth House*, Plano, Illinois (1945–50), *Crown Hall*, Illinois Institute of Technology (1950–6), *Lake Shore Drive Apartments*, Chicago (1948–51), *Seagram Building*, New York (1954–8), *New National Gallery*, Berlin (1962–8).

Mique, Richard (1728–94), French neoclassical architect, designer and engineer. He became official architect to Marie-Antoinette, under whom his career progressed rapidly, but he was executed in the aftermath of the French Revolution. His finest buildings are a series of supremely elegant structures beautifully placed in landscape settings.

Works: *Porte Ste Catherine*, Nancy (1761), *Ursuline Convent*, Versailles (1766–), *Temple of Love*, Le Petit Trianon, Versailles (1778), *Cabinet Doré*, Versailles (1783), *Salon des Nobles*, Versailles (1785).

Mnesicles (5th century BC), Greek architect famed for one structure, the Propylaea on the Acropolis, Athens (c. 437 BC).

Moore, Charles (1925–93), American architect who was also notable as a university teacher and writer. A 'post-modern classicist', he advocated (and practised) the self-conscious juxtaposition and manipulation of historical styles.

Works: *houses at Sea Ranch*, California (1965–70), *Faculty Club*, University of California, Santa Barbara (1968), *Kresge College*, University of Santa Cruz (1973–4), *Piazza d'Italia*, New Orleans (1975–8).

Nash, John (1752–1835), versatile and entrepreneurial architect and town-planner whose large-scale developments have left a permanent imprint on the face of London. An energetic and a highly successful businessman, by 1812 he had built over 40 country houses in classical, Gothic and Italianate styles, as well as thatched cottages, and in all of these he was influenced by ideas of the picturesque. In 1806 he was appointed architect to the Prince of Wales, and produced his grandiose neo-classical scheme for a processional route from St James's to Regent's Park, much of which was realized, creating some of London's most famous vistas.

Works: *Cronkhill* (c.1802), *Ravensworth Castle* (1808), *Rockingham* (1810), *Blaise Hamlet* (1811), *Regent's Park and Regent Street*, London (1811–), *Brighton Pavilion* (1815), *All Souls*, Langham Place, London (1822–5), *Buckingham Palace*, London (1825–30).

Neumann, Balthasar (1687–1753), German architect whose work represents the culmination of the late Baroque style, with its swirling curves, fluid spaces and rich and colourful but delicate decoration.

Works: *Bishop's Palace (Residenz)*, Würzburg (1719–44, with others), *Holzkirchen*, near Würzburg (1726), *staircase*, Bishop's Palace, Bruchsal (1732), *Pilgrimage Church*, Vierzehnheiligen (1743–72), *Abbey Church*, Neresheim (1745–), *Marienkirche*, Limbach (1747–52).

Niemeyer, Oscar (b.1907), Brazilian architect, disciple of Le Corbusier, who developed

Biographies of Architects

a distinctive brand of modernism making sculptural use of the parabola and other simple geometric forms. In 1957 he became chief architect for the new city of Brasilia.

Works: *Ministry of Education*, Rio de Janeiro (1936–45, with Lucio Costa and Le Corbusier), *St Francis of Assisi*, Pampuhla (1942–3), *Pampuhla Casino* (1942–3), *Niemeyer House*, Rio de Janeiro (1953), *Brasilia* (1957).

Ostberg, Ragnar (1866–1945), Swedish architect and designer, known internationally for one work, the Stockholm Town Hall, in what has been called a 'romantic nationalist' style, subtly blending traditional and modern elements.

Works: *Stockholm Town Hall* (1904–23), *Östermalm Boys' School*, Stockholm (1910), *Värmland National House*, Uppsala (1930), *Marine Historical Museum*, Stockholm (1934), *Zoorn Museum*, Mora (1939).

Otto, Frei (b. 1925), German architect who pioneered advanced computing and engineering techniques to establish and develop the lightweight tent structure as a significant form in modern architecture. With their complex curvatures, his tents are highly sophisticated and at the same time sculpturally expressive and even romantic.

Works: *Riverside Dance Pavilion*, Cologne (1957), *Star Pavilions*, Hamburg (1963), *German Pavilion*, Expo '67, Montreal (1967), *retracting roof, Open-Air Theatre*, Bad Hersfeld (1968), *Olympic Stadium*, Munich (1972), *Conference Centre*, Mecca (1974).

Owings, Nathaniel *see* **Skidmore**

Palladio, Andrea (1508–80), one of the greatest and most influential Italian Renaissance architects, all of whose works were built in or near Vicenza. He drew on Vitruvius and his Renaissance predecessors to create a refined and easily imitable classical style characterized by elegance and symmetry. His influence was greatest in England and the US. He published *The Four Books of Architecture* in 1570.

Works: *Basilica*, Vicenza (1549), *Palazzo Chiericati*, Vicenza (1550), *Villa Malcontenta*, Vicenza (1560), *Palazzo Valmarana*, Vicenza (1565), *Villa Rotonda*, near Vicenza (1565–9), *S. Giorgio Maggiore*, Venice (1565–1610), *Il Redentore*, Venice (1577–92), *Teatro Olimpico*, Vicenza (1580).

Paxton, Joseph (1801–65), English garden-er, garden designer and architect. As head gardener at Chatsworth estate, he pioneered the use of glass and prefabricated iron for greenhouses, culminating in the Crystal Palace of 1851, which became a prototype for railway stations, halls and industrial buildings world-wide. As a garden designer he laid out public parks (e.g. Birkenhead, 1843–7, and as a conventional architect built Mentmore House, Buckinghamshire (1852–4).

Pei, Ieoh Ming (b. 1917), Chinese-born American architect, based in New York. A pupil of Walter Gropius, he made his name with tall commercial buildings distinguished by clean lines and sheer reflecting surfaces. His museums and public buildings also demonstrate his command of proportion and clarity of structure.

Works: *Mile High Center*, Denver, Colorado (1955), *Canadian Imperial Bank of Commerce*, Toronto (1972), *John Hancock Tower*, Boston (1973), *East Building*, National Gallery of Art, Washington DC (1978), *Bank of China*, Hong Kong (1989), *glass pyramids*, Louvre, Paris (1989).

Peressutti, Enrico *see* **Belgiojoso, Lodovico**

Perrault, Claude (1613–88), French amateur architect, a doctor by profession, known principally for the imposing east façade of the Louvre, Paris, built for Louis XIV. He was also an author, and published the first French translation of Vitruvius (1673).

Works: *east façade*, Louvre, Paris (1665), *Observatoire*, Paris (1667), *Château de Sceaux* (1673).

Perret, Auguste (1874–1954), one of the founders of modern architecture in France. A pioneer of construction in reinforced concrete, he created façades that boldly expressed structure, and free-plan interior spaces.

Works: *flats at 25bis rue Franklin*, Paris (1903), *Théâtre des Champs-Elysées*, Paris (1911–13), *Notre-Dame-du-Raincy* (1922–3), *Museum of Public Works*, Paris (1937), *Amiens Railway Station* (1945), *redevelopment of Le Havre* (1949–56).

Peruzzi, Baldassare (1481–1536), Italian High Renaissance and Mannerist architect, much indebted to Bramante, whom he assisted in the designs for St Peter's, Rome. His early work is noted for its delicacy, while his later unorthodox use of superimposed columns, original window-shapes and irregular plans heralds the Mannerist style.

Works: *Villa Farnesina*, Rome (1508–11), *S. Eligio degli Orefici*, Rome (1520), *Villa Farnese*, Caprarola (c.1530), *Palazzo Massimo alle Colonne*, Rome (1532–).

Piano, Renzo (b. 1937), Italian architect who first worked in partnership with Richard Rogers, then set up the famous Renzo Piano Workshop, based in Genoa, in 1981. Working without preconceived stylistic ideas and stressing collaboration with clients and harmony with nature, he combines advanced technology and traditional materials to create bold and colourful structures that are both functional and sensitive to their environment.

Works: *Centre Pompidou*, Paris (1972–7, with Richard Rogers), *Schlumberger Office Building*, Montrouge, Paris (1981–4), *Menil Collection Art Museum*, Houston, Texas (1981–6), *Kansai International Airport Terminal*, Osaka (1988–94), *Tjibaou Cultural Centre*, Nouméa, New Caledonia (1991–).

Pöppelmann, Matthaeus (1662–1736), German Baroque architect, from 1705 Court Architect for the Elector of Saxony in Dresden. His one masterpiece, the Zwinger, is the brilliant translation of a stage design into stone.

Works: *Taschenberg Palace*, Dresden (1705), *Zwinger*, Dresden (1711–22), *Schloss Pillnitz* (1720–32), *Augustus Bridge*, Dresden (1728).

Porta, Giacomo della (c.1537–1602), Italian Mannerist architect, who completed the façade of Vignola's Il Gesù (1568–84) and the dome of St Peter's (1588–90). He also continued Michelangelo's designs for palaces on the Capitol (1573–).

Works: *Palazzo della Sapienza*, Rome (c.1575), *S. Andrea della Valle*, Rome (1591, completed by Maderna), *Villa Aldobrandini*, Frascati (1598–1603).

Prandtauer, Jacob (1660–1726), Austrian Baroque architect. After the triumph of his dramatically sited masterwork, the monastery at Melk (1702–14), the rest of his career was devoted to building and rebuilding churches and monasteries in Austria, notably the monasteries at Garsten, Kremsmünster and St Florian, and the pilgrimage church of Sonntagberg (1706–17).

Pugin, Augustus Welby Northmore
(1812–52), English architect, designer and passionate propagandist for the Gothic style. He is best-known for his work on the architectural detail and interior decoration for the houses of Parliament (1836–51). His books set new standards in scholarship, and his analysis of the relationship between form, function and ornament greatly influenced later functionalist thinking. His writings and designs have been more influential than his buildings.

Works: *Alton Towers* (1837–52), *St Giles*, Cheadle (1841–6), *Nottingham Cathedral* (1842–4), *Ushaw College*, Durham (1848–52), *St Augustine*, Ramsgate (1846–51), *Lismore Castle*, Ireland (1849–50).

Richardson, Henry Hobson (1838–96), American architect, pupil of Labrouste in Paris, whose heavy and distinctive Romanesque-inspired buildings were a formative influence on the development of the Chicago Style of the late 19th century, the first distinctly original American style.

Works: *Trinity Church*, Boston (1872–7), *Ames Library*, North Easton, Mass. (1877), *Crane Library*, Quincy, Mass. (1880–3), *Austin Hall*, Harvard University (1881), *Court House and Jail*, Pittsburgh (1884–7), *Marshall Field Warehouse*, Chicago (1885–7), *J.J. Glessner House*, Chicago (1885–7).

Riedel, Eduard *see* **Dollmann**.

Rietveld, Gerrit (1884–1964), Dutch architect and furniture designer. Influenced by the De Stijl group, he produced the famous Red-Blue Chair (1918), and designed the Schröder House, Utrecht (1923–4), which was the first building to translate Cubist conceptions of space and fractured planes into architecture. He continued a successful architectural and design practice into the 1950s, but none of his later works has had the impact of his one masterpiece.

Rogers, Ernesto *see* **Belgiojoso, Lodovico**

Rogers, Richard (Lord Rogers of Riverside) (b. 1933), Italian-born English architect who was in partnership with Renzo Piano (1971–8), before setting up his own firm in London. Celebrating technology, he created a distinctive tubular hi-tech style with the framework and service elements boldly emphasized on the exterior.

Works: *Centre Pompidou*, Paris (1971–7, with Renzo Piano), *Lloyds Building*, London

(1978–86), *Terminal 5*, Heathrow Airport, London (1989), *Channel 4 Headquarters*, London (1990–4), *Law Courts*, Bordeaux (1993–).

Root, John Wellborn (1850–91), American architect who in partnership with Daniel Burnham (q.v.) designed pioneering tall buildings in Chicago, developing the glass and curtain wall structure typical of the Chicago School and a defining characteristic of the skyscraper. In the partnership, Root was the more original designer, while Burnham provided organization and planning.

Works (all in Chicago): *Montauk Block* (1882), *Monadnock Building* (1884–91), *The Rookery* (1886), *Masonic Temple* (1891).

Saarinen, Eero (1910–61), son of the distinguished Finnish architect Eliel Saarinen, who emigrated to the US in 1923. His style moved from cool, straight façades inspired by Mies van der Rohe to a highly personal and poetic form of expressionism based on curves and vaults.

Works: *Jefferson Memorial*, St Louis (1947–66), *General Motors Technical Centre*, Warren, Michigan (1948–56, with Eliel), *TWA Terminal*, J.F. Kennedy International Airport, New York (1956–62), *Stiles* and *Morse Colleges*, Yale University (1958–62), *Dulles Airport*, Washington DC (1958–63), *Vivian Beaumont Theater*, Lincoln Center, New York (1965).

Safdie, Moshe (b. 1938), Israeli-Canadian architect, based in Montreal since 1964. The concept of 'habitat', expressed in his projects and popularized in his writings, rejected the pure lines of modernism for assemblage, disorder and spatially complex forms that explore the relationships between architecture, the social order and the natural environment.

Works: *Habitat housing*, Montreal (1967), *Porat Joseph Rabbinical College*, Jerusalem (1971–9), *National Gallery of Canada*, Ottawa (1988), *Hebrew Union College Campus*, Jerusalem (1988), *Vancouver Library Square* (1991).

Sanctis, Francesco de' (?1693–1731), Italian Baroque architect famous for the creation of the dramatic Spanish Steps, Rome (1723–5). His only other significant work is the façade of the church of the Trinità dei Pellegrini, Rome (1722).

Scharoun, Hans (1893–1972), German architect whose early work reveals a tension

between the straight-lined severity of the International Style and a more personal style of expressive curves. He achieved international recognition in the 1950s as his expressionism became fashionable.

Works: *Exhibition House*, Weissenhofsiedlung, Stuttgart (1927), *Schminke House*, Löbau (1933), *Romeo and Juliet flats*, Stuttgart (1954–9), *Philharmonic Concert Hall*, Berlin (1956–63). *Maritime Museum*, Bremerhaven (1970), *Stadttheater*, Wolfsburg (1965–73), *National Library*, Berlin (1967–78).

Schinkel, Karl Friedrich (1781–1841), the most important and influential German architect of the early 19th century, Chief Architect of the Prussian Department of Works from 1815 and Director of Works from 1831. His perfectly composed classical façades became prototypes for public buildings world-wide, but he also built in the Gothic style, used cast iron, and designed unornamented functional buildings that influenced the developing modern movement.

Works: *New Guard*, Berlin (1817), *War Memorial*, Berlin (1818), *Schauspielhaus*, Berlin (1819–21), *Werdesche Kirche*, Berlin (1821–31), *Humboldt House*, Tegel (1822–4), *Altes Museum*, Berlin (1823–30), *Nicolai Church*, Potsdam (1829–37), *Academy of Building*, Berlin (1831–5), *Schloss Charlottenhof*, Berlin (1833–4).

Siloe, Diego de (c.1495–1563), Spanish architect and sculptor who introduced Italian Renaissance forms to Spain and played a major role in the development of the distinctive Spanish Plateresque style.

Works: *Escalera Dorada*, Burgos Cathedral (1524), *Granada Cathedral* (1549), *Salvador Church*, Ubeda (1536), *Guadix Cathedral* (1549), *S. Gabriel*, Loja (1552–68).

Sinan, Koca (1489–1578 or 1588), the greatest Turkish architect, from 1538 until his death the chief architect to the Ottoman court. Celebrated in his own lifetime and credited with no fewer than 476 mosques, schools, hospitals and other buildings, he brought to full development the classic Ottoman domed mosque.

Works: *Sehzade Mehmed Mosque*, Istanbul (1543–8), *Suleymaniye Mosque*, Istanbul (1551–8), *Suleymaniye Mosque*, Damascus (1552–9), *Mihrimah Sultan Mosque*, Edirnekapi, Istanbul (c. 1565), *Selimiye Mosque*, Edirne (1570–4).

Skidmore, Louis (1897–1967), American architect who in 1936 formed a partnership with Nathaniel Owings (1903–84) and John Merrill (1896–1975), which became one of the largest architectural practices in the US after the Second World War, specializing in large office buildings. Largely influenced by Mies van der Rohe, their work is distinguished by crispness and precision, and in their hands the steel and glass skyscraper achieved canonical form that has been imitated world-wide. Their later works use high technology, and openly express structure.

Works: *Lever House*, New York (1951–2), *Manufacturers' Trust Bank*, New York (1952–4), *Connecticut General Life Insurance Building*, Hartford (1953–7), *Chase Manhattan Bank*, New York (1962), *John Hancock Center*, Chicago (1968–70), *Hajj Airport Terminal*, Jeddah, Saudi Arabia (1980).

Smirke, Sir Robert (1781–1867), leading English Greek Revival architect responsible for many large-scale public projects and country houses, characterizedly by simplicity, dignity and grandeur.

Works: *Covent Garden Opera House*, London (1808–9; demolished), *Lowther Castle*, Cumbria (1806–11), *Eastnor Castle*, Herefordshire (1812), *St Mary's Church*, Marylebone, London (1823), *British Museum*, London (1823–47), *Royal College of Physicians and Union Club*, Trafalgar Square, London (1824–7); *Oxford and Cambridge Club*, Pall Mall, London (1835–8).

Smithson, Alison (b.1928) and **Peter** (b.1923), English husband and wife team, who in spite of having few projects realized have been influential as teachers, avant-garde propagandists and creators of imaginative schemes. They promoted 'New Brutalist' ideas.

Works: *Hunstanton School*, Norfolk (1949–54), a controversial glass-box construction inspired by Mies van der Rohe, *Economist Buildings*, London (1962–4), *Robin Hood Lane Housing*, London (1966–72).

Smythson, Robert (1536–1614), English mason and architect who developed the Elizabethan country house, in a characteristically English version of the Renaissance style with rich decoration, bold modelling and dramatic silhouettes.

Works: *Longleat* (as principal mason) (1572–5), *Wollaton Hall* (1580–8), *Hardwick Hall* (1590–7).

Soufflot, Jacques Germain (1713–80), the greatest French neo-classical architect. Trained in Italy, he built the first neo-classical buildings in France, combining the regularity and monumentality of ancient Roman models with the structural lightness that he admired in Gothic architecture.

Works: *Hôtel-Dieu*, Lyons (1741–8), *Loge au Change*, Lyons (1747–60), *Ste-Geneviève (Panthéon)*, Paris (1755–92), *École de Droit*, Paris (1771–83).

Stirling, James (1926–92), English architect whose bold and expressive forms in steel and glass anticipated 'hi-tech' imagery. To these he added the self-conscious quotation of earlier styles and deliberate juxtaposition of disparate elements in a characteristically post-modernist stance.

Works: *Ham Common Flats*, Richmond, London (1955–8), *Engineering Building*, Leicester University (1959–63), *History Faculty Library*, Cambridge University (1964–6), *Olivetti Building*, Haslemere, Surrey (1969–72), *Neue Staatsgalerie*, Stuttgart (1977–84), *Braun Headquarters*, Melsungen, Germany (1986–91).

Sullivan, Louis (1856–1924), one of the most original and influential architects of the Chicago School, who strove to develop an appropriate form and style of decoration for the new type of building, the skyscraper, basing his ideas on the dictum that 'form follows function', and seeking inspiration in natural forms. He worked in partnership with Dankmar Adler (1844–1900).

Works: *Auditorium Building*, Chicago (1886–9), *Getty Tomb*, Chicago (1890), *Wainwright Building*, St Louis (1890–1), *Schiller Theater Building*, Chicago (1892), *Guaranty Building*, Buffalo (1894–5), *Carson Pirie Scott Department Store*, Chicago (1899–1904), *National Farmers' Bank*, Owatanna, Minnesota (1906–8).

Tange, Kenzo (b.1913), leading postwar architect in Japan, much influenced by Le Corbusier, who sought to fuse the International Style with traditional Japanese monumental architecture, creating bold and sometimes heavy concrete façades, but increasingly curved and expressive rooflines.

Works: *Peace Memorial and Museum*, Hiroshima (1949–55), *Tokyo City Hall* (1955), *Kagawa Prefectural Offices*, Takamatsu (1958), *Yamanashi Press and Radio Centre*, Kofu (1961–7), *Olympic Stadium*, Tokyo (1964).

Toledo, Juan Bautista de (d.1567), Spanish architect who worked in Rome and Naples until appointed Royal Architect by Philip II of Spain in 1561. He introduced a new system of teaching architecture in Spain, and created a pure and severe classical Renaissance style that was highly influential. His only significant surviving work is his masterpiece, the Escorial Palace (1562–82), completed by his successor Juan de Herrera.

Trdat (flourished 989–1001), Armenian architect who with his followers in the Christian Byzantine period built many churches that were structurally 100 years in advance of those in the West.

Works: restoration of *Hagia Sophia*, Istanbul (989), *Ani Cathedral* (1001–15).

Tschumi, Bernard (b. 1944), Swiss-French architect based in Paris and New York, also influential as a teacher and theorist. Postmodernist and 'deconstructivist', he explores and questions assumptions about form, function and meaning, and creates an architecture based on parody, fragmentation and the manipulation of forms in space.

Works: *Parc de la Villette*, Paris (1984–9), *Glass Video Gallery*, Groningen, The Netherlands (1990), *School of Architecture*, Marne-la-Vallée, France (1991–), *Lerner Student Center*, Columbia University, New York (1991–).

Utzon, Jørn (b.1918), original and idiosyncratic Danish architect. Absorbing the influences of Aalto and Asplund, he used brick and standardized components to create housing that blended with its natural setting, and then went on to experiment with dramatic sculptural forms.

Works: *Kingo Houses*, Elsinore (1956–60), *Sydney Opera House* (1957–73), *Birkehoj Houses*, Elsinore (1963), *Bagsvaerd Church*, Copenhagen (1969–76), *National Assembly Building*, Kuwait (1972).

Van Alen, William (1883–1954), American architect who specialized in building skyscrapers in New York, only one of which is famous, the Chrysler Building (1928–30), the ultimate symbol of the Art Deco style in architecture.

Vanbrugh, Sir John (1664–1726), swashbuckling English soldier and playwright who became an architect with no formal training. Ably assisted by Nicholas Hawksmoor

(1661–1736), he designed England's largest and most flamboyant Baroque country houses, with their bold massing, giant pillars and dramatically varied skylines. His later works are more fortress-like and foreshadow the Gothic Revival.

Works: *Castle Howard*, Yorkshire (1699–1726), *Blenheim Palace*, Oxfordshire (1705–24), *King's Weston*, Bristol (1711–14), *Vanbrugh Castle*, Greenwich (1718–19), *Seaton Delaval*, Northumberland (1720–8).

Venturi, Robert (b.1925), American postmodern architect, designer and writer, who with his partners John Rauch (b.1930) and Denise Scott-Brown (b.1931) reacted against the blandness of debased modernist formulae, and proposed an architecture of complexity, irony and symbolism, embracing quotation from all styles including the vernacular and contemporary imagery.

Works: *House at Chestnut Hill*, Philadelphia (1962–4), *Guild House*, Philadelphia (1962–8), *Fire Station*, Columbus, Indiana (1966–8), *Butler College*, Princeton University (1980), *National Gallery Extension*, London (1987–91).

Vignola, Giacomo da (1507–73), Italian Mannerist architect who was the leading figure in Rome after the death of Michelangelo. Much of his work was collaborative, or completing work started by others. His design for Il Gesù, with its wide aisle-less nave focusing attention on the high altar, was immensely influential, as was his oval plan for S. Anna dei Palafrenieri.

Works: *Palazzo Farnese*, Caprarola (1547–9), *Villa Giulia*, Rome (1550–5), *Palazzo Farnese*, Piacenza (1564–), *St Peter's*, Rome (1567–73), *Il Gesù*, Rome (1568–84), *S. Anna dei Palafrenieri*, Rome (1573–).

Wagner, Otto (1841–1918), one of the founders of the modern movement in Austria, professor at the Viennese Academy from 1894 and an inspiring teacher. He rejected stylistic ecleticism and over-elaborate decoration, advocating instead simplicity, structural rationality and the use of modern materials.

Works (all in Vienna): *railway stations and bridges* (1894–1901), *Majolica House* (1898), *Post Office Savings Bank* (1904–6), *Steinhof Asylum Church* (1905–7).

Walpole, Horace (1717–97), 4th Earl of Orford, Member of Parliament, connoisseur, patron of the arts and amateur architect. He was hugely influential in promoting the

Gothic Revival through his creation of Strawberry Hill, Twickenham (1748–77). Although he employed architects (notably John Chute, Richard Bentley, Robert Adam and James Essex), the overall conception of Strawberry Hill was firmly Walpole's.

Walter, Thomas Ustick (1804–87), prominent American Greek Revival architect, a founder and 2nd president of the Institute of American architects. His numerous houses and public buildings are characterized by simplicity, regularity and restraint.

Works: *Girard College*, Philadelphia (1833–48), *Baptist Church*, Richmond (1839), *County Court House*, West Chester (1847), *Capitol*, Washington DC (1851–67).

Waterhouse, Alfred (1830–1905), leading English High Victorian proponent of the Gothic style for large public and commercial buildings. He created firm outlines and picturesque skylines, with neat and well-ordered detailing, and was bold in the use of coloured bricks and terracotta. He occasionally adopted Romanesque or Renaissance styles, but his forte was Gothic and his output prolific.

Works: *Manchester Town Hall* (1868–77), *Natural History Museum*, London (1868–80), *Blackmoor House*, Hampshire (1869), *Lyndhurst Road Chapel*, Hampstead, London (1883), *University College Hospital*, London (1896).

Webb, Philip (1831–1915), architect and designer, close friend and partner of William Morris. He built almost exclusively domestic houses, eschewing historical styles and basing his unpretentious designs on vernacular tradition, utility, local materials and sound craftsmanship. He was an important forerunner of the Arts and Crafts movement.

Works: *Red House*, Bexley Heath (1859–60), *1 Palace Green*, Kensington, London (1868), *Oast House*, Hayes Common, Middlesex (1872), *Clouds*, East Knoyle, Wiltshire (1880), *Standen*, East Grinstead, E. Sussex (1891–4).

White, Stanford *see* **McKim**

Wood, John the Younger (1728–81), English architect and town-planner who with his father, John Wood the Elder (1704–54), created much of the Georgian city of Bath (1729–75). Using giant pillars, they adapted the colonnades of the Palladian country house to the terraced street, creating

curved façades of supreme elegance, the final fulfilment of Renaissance classical ideas, and immensely influential on later town-planning.

Wren, Sir Christopher (1632–1723), England's greatest architect. A mathematician and astronomer, he came to architecture through his knowledge of structures and engineering. As Surveyor General of the King's Works (1669), he was charged with rebuilding St Paul's Cathedral and 51 City churches destroyed in the Fire of London of 1666. Rising to the opportunity, he created a series of masterpieces of restrained but varied and inventive classicism, in a modified English version of the Baroque style that emphasized lucidity and repose, and avoided the frenzy of over-exuberant decoration.

Works: *Sheldonian Theatre*, Oxford (1663–5), *St Stephen Walbrook*, London (1672), *St Paul's Cathedral*, London (1675–1710), *Trinity College Library*, Cambridge (1676–84), *Chelsea Hospital*, London (1682–92), *Hampton Court*, London (1690–1700), *Greenwich Naval Hospital*, London (1694–1716).

Wright, Frank Lloyd (1867–1959), regarded by many as the greatest American architect. As the creator of the 'prairie style' he developed the typical long roof-line, and introduced new ideas of fluid interior space, and new relations between buildings and nature. Idiosyncratic and highly original, he was little influenced by the International Modern style, following instead his own powerful imagination.

Works: *house at Oak Park*, Chicago (1889), *Martin House*, Buffalo (1904), *Unity Temple*, Oak Park, Chicago (1905–8), *Robie House*, Chicago (1908–9), *Barnsdall House*, Los Angeles (1916–21), *Imperial Hotel*, Tokyo (1916–22), *Ennis House*, Los Angeles (1923–4), *Fallingwater*, Bear Run, Pennsylvania (1935–7), *Johnson Wax Building*, Racine, Wisconsin (1936–45), *Taliesin West* (1938), *Guggenheim Museum*, New York (1943–59).

Index

Numbers in *italic* refer to the figures

Aachen Cathedral, 132; *153*
Aalto, Alvar, 278, 292
    Civic Centre, Säynätsalo, 278; *374*
    Paimio Sanatorium, 278; *373*
Abbas, Shah, 150
abbeys, 138–9; *161*
Abu Simbel, Great Temple of Rameses II, 31;
    21
Achaemenid dynasty, 26–7
Acropolis, Athens, 90, 92–6; *102–3*
Adam, James, 224
Adam, Robert, 224–5, 226, 230
    Charlotte Square, Edinburgh, 220–1
    Stowe, Buckinghamshire, 222
    Syon House, London, 225; *290*
Adler and Sullivan, 254
adobe, 232
Aegina, Temple of Aphaia, 92
Afghanistan, 51
Africa, 32
Agade, 19
Agamemnon, King, 23
Aghlabid Mosque, Kairouan, 152
Agilkia, 30
agora, 97–9
Agra, Taj Mahal, 157; *187*
Agrigentum, 248
Agrippa, 111
Aidan, St, 132
Aigues-Mortes, 172
Aihole, Hacchappayya Temple, 51
Ajanta, 50; *46*
Akkad, 19, 20
Alamillo Bridge, Seville, 288
Alaric the Goth, 118
Alberobello, 12; *6*
Albert, Prince Consort, 244
Albert Dock, Liverpool, 244
Alberti, Leon Battista, 178, 179, 180–1,

182–3, 188, 200, 268–9
    Palazzo Rucellai, Florence, 181, 210; *223*
    Palazzo Venezia, Rome, *224*
    Sant' Andrea, Mantua, 181; *222*
    Santa Maria Novella, Florence, 180–1
Alcuin, 130, 132
Aleijadinho:
    São Francisco de Assis, Ouro Preto, 234; *305*
Alexander the Great, 27, 35, 46, 86–8, 100
Alexandria, 35, 90, 126
Alfeld-an-der-Leine, Fagus Factory, 272; *363*
Alhambra, Granada, 149, 156; *178–9*
All Saints, Margaret Street, London, 246–7
Alte Pinakothek, Munich, 249–50; *331*
Altes Museum, Berlin, 228; *296*
Amalfi, 141
Amalienburg Pavilion, Munich, 209, 217; *281*
American Institute of Architects, 284
American School of Archaeology, 99
American Telephone and Telegraph Building, New York, 295
Amersham, High and Over, 276
Amiens Cathedral, 166; *202*
amphitheatres, Roman, 106–7; *116*
Amsterdam, 199–200; *252*
    Exchange, 260
    Rijksmuseum, 250
    Town Hall, 195
Anathemios of Tralles, 125
Anatolia, 13, 18, 19, 23, 26, 122, 154, 155
Ancy-le-Franc, Château d', 193
Andhra, 52
Andran, Claude, 215
Angkor Wat, 53, 54–5; *54*

Ani Cathedral, 127–8; *151*
Anne, Queen of England, 200
Antioch Kaoussie, Martyrion of St Byblas, 123
Antipater, 92
Antwerp, 196
Anuradhapura:
    Brazen Palace, 49
    Peacock Palace, 49
    Ruvanveli dagoba, 49
Apadana of Darius, Persepolis, 27, 91;
    15, 19
Apeldoorn, Central Beheer building, 292
Apulia, 12
aqueducts, 111, 136; *111*
Aquinas, St Thomas, 167
Aquitaine, 140
Arabs, 14, 137, 144, 147
Arc-et-Senans, La Saline de Chaux, 227
Les Arcades du Lac, Marseilles, 288
Arcadius, Emperor, 118
Arch of Constantine, Rome, 108; *118*
Arch of Titus, Rome, 108
arches, 12, 13; *5*
    Gothic, 160–1
    Roman, 109
    triumphal, 108; *118*
architraves, 89
Arctic, 10
Aristophanes, 99
Aristotle, 16, 88, 99
Arles, 106, 137
Armenia, 127–8
Arsenal, Augsburg, 196; *246*
Art Deco, 279, 298
Art Nouveau, 255–7, 259
Artaxerxes, King of Persia, 26
Arts and Crafts movement, 244, 257–9
Aryans, 44, 46
Asam, Cosmas Damian, 209
Asam, Egid Quirin, 209
    St John Nepomuk, Munich, 209; *258*

El-Ashair Mosque, Cairo, 154
Ashur, 19, 21
Ashurbanipal, King, 21, 24
Asia Minor, 92, 100
Gli Asinelli, Bologna, 142
Asoka, Emperor, 45, 46–7, 48
Asplund, Gunnar:
    Forest Crematorium, Stockholm,
      278; *372*
Assisi, Basilica of St Francis, 163
Assyria, 19, 21, 23–4, 26, 153
Aswan, 32, 33
Aswan Dam, 30
Athenian Treasury, Delphi, 101; *110*
Athens, 86, 88, 92–9, 100, 223
    Acropolis, 90, 92–6; *102–3*
    Choragic Monument of Lysicrates,
      92, 238; *100*
    Erechtheum, 96; *104*
    Little Metropolitan, 126
    Parthenon, 13, 86, 96–7, 248; *105–6*
    Propylaea, 90, 93, 96; *97*
    Stoa of Attalus, 99; *108*
    Temple of Hephaestus (Theseion),
      89, 90
    Temple of Nike Apteros, 93; *101*
    Temple of Olympian Zeus, 92
    Theatre of Dionysus, 99
Atlantic Ocean, 79
atrium, 102, 113
Augsburg:
    Arsenal, 196; *246*
    Town Hall, 195–6
Augustine, St, 130
Augustus, Emperor, 102, 105, 111, 113
Augustus the Strong of Saxony, 205
Australia, 238–9, 251, 293–4
Austria, 202, 204, 249
Austro-Hungarian Empire, 249
Autun Cathedral, 139–40, 141–2; *163*
Auxerre Cathedral, 166
Avignon, 138, 171, 172
Ayuwang Temple, Ningbo, *63*
Azay-le-Rideau, Château d', 194
Aztecs, 76, 78–9, 232, 233

Baalbek, 105, 112
    Temple of Bacchus, 107; *117*
Babylon, 13, 19, 20, 21–3, 26, 27, 35,
    149; *11, 15*
    Ishtar Gate, 22–3; *16*
    Temple of Etemanenki, 22
Badran, Rasem, 296
    Grand Mosque and Justice Palace,
      Riyadh, 296
Baghdad, 19, 149–50
Bagsvaerd church, 295–6
Baha'i Temple, Delhi, 294
Bahia, São Francisco, 233; *302*
Bahri Mamelukes, 154

Balbás, Jerónimo de:
    Chapel of the Three Kings, Mexico
      City, 232–3
Balkans, 122, 125–6
ball courts, Meso-America, 76, 81; *85*
Baltimore, Catholic Cathedral, 237; *311*
Bank of Philadelphia, 237
Banqueting House, Whitehall, 200,
    201; *256*
Banz Abbey Church, 209; *269*
Barcelona, 256
    Casa Batlló, 256
    Casa Mila, 256; *344*
    Cathedral, 166
    Güell Park, 256
    Sagrada Familia, 256; *343*
    Santa Coloma de Cervello, 257; *345*
Barcelona International Exhibition,
    273; *366–7*
Barlow, W.H., 243
Baroque architecture, 202–15, 218,
    224, 232, 233–4
barrel vaults, 109, 141
La Barrière de la Villette, Paris, 227
Barry, Charles:
    Houses of Parliament, London,
      242, 243; *317*
    Reform Club, London, 242–3
    Travellers' Club, London, 242
Basilica (Palazzo della Ragione),
    Vicenza, 189
Basilica of Maxentius, Rome, 115;
    128–9
Basilica Porcia, Rome, 114
Basilica of St Francis, Assisi, 163
basilicas, 114–15, 116, 118–20, 121;
    128–9, 132–5
Bath, 221, 226
Baths of Caracalla, Rome, 112; *123*
Baudot, Anatole de:
    St-Jean-de-Montmartre, Paris, 254–5
Bauhaus, 272, 273, 279, 281; *365*
Bear Wood, Berkshire, 247; *324*
Beardsley, Aubrey, 257
Beaumaris Castle, 172–3; *209*
Beauvais Cathedral, 166
Beaux-Arts school, 287
Becket, St Thomas à, 136, 171
Beckford, William, 226
Bedouin, 147, 149
Behnisch and Partners:
    Olympic Stadium, Munich, 290; *393*
Beijing, 62, 66–8; *72*
    Forbidden City, 67; *70–1*
    Summer Palace, 68–9; *73*
    Temple of Heaven, 66; *68–9*
Belgiojoso, Peressutti and Rogers:
    Velasca Tower, Milan, 287; *384*
Belgium, 292
Belvedere Palace, Vienna, 204–5,

207; *259*
Benedict, St, 138
Benedictine Monastery, Melk, 213; *276*
Benedictines, 137
Bengal, 45
Beni-Hassan, 41
Bent Pyramid of Snefaru, *24*
Berg, Max:
    Jahrhunderthalle, Breslau, 260
Berlage, H.P.:
    Exchange, Amsterdam, 260
Berlin:
    Altes Museum, 228; *296*
    Philharmonic Concert Hall, 289–90;
      391–2
    Schauspielhaus, 228
Bernard of Clairvaux, St, 138
Bernini, Gian Lorenzo, 204, 207–8, 212
    Ecstasy of St Theresa, 207; *264*
    Sant' Andrea al Quirinale, Rome,
      209, 210, 211
    St Peter's, Rome, 207–8; *266*
    Scala Regia, Rome, 212–13
    Trevi Fountain, Rome, 212; *271*
Besançon, 227
Bethlehem, Church of the Nativity,
    119–20; *134*
Bexley Heath, Red House, 258; *346*
Bhaja, 50
Bhubaneswar:
    Brahmesvara Temple, 54; *53*
    Lingaraja Temple, *50*
Bible, 18, 24, 179
Bibliothèque Nationale, Paris, 248
Bibliothèque Sainte-Geneviève, Paris, 248;
    329
Bindesbøll, Gottlieb:
    Thorvaldsen Museum,
      Copenhagen, 248; *327*
Bishop's Palace, Würzburg, 211, 212; *270*
Bismarck, Count Otto von, 249
Black Death, 171
Black Sea, 18
Blaize Hamlet, 226
Blenheim Palace, Oxfordshire, 214, 215
Blois, Château de, 194; *241*
Blue Mosque, Istanbul, 157; *186*
Bo-Hyan-Su Temple, Myohyang
    Mountains, 60–1
Boffrand, Germain:
    Hôtel de Soubise, Paris, 216; *280*
Bofill, Ricardo, 288
    Les Arcades du Lac, Marseilles, 288
    Palais d'Abraxas, Paris, 288
Bogazköy, 19
Bohemia, 167, 169
Bohier family, 194
Bolivia, 76
Bologna, 171
    Gli Asinelli, 142

La Garisenda, 142
Bom Jesus do Monte, Braga, 213, 234; *273*
Bombay, Elephanta Temple, 51
Boniface, Pope, 132
Bordeaux, 229
Borobudur Temple, Java, 54, 55, 80; *38, 55*
Borromini, Francesco, 204, 207, 208–9, 214, 234
  Sant' Agnese in Piazza Navone, Rome, 209, 212
  San Carlo alle Quattro Fontane, Rome, 205, 208, 209; *262–3*
  St Ivo della Sapienza, Rome, 209
Boston:
  Christchurch, 237
  Public Library, 251; *333*
Boullée, Etienne Louis, 227, 228, 282
Bourges, 175
  Cathedral, 163, 166, 167; *194*
  Jacques Coeur's House, 173; *212*
Bradford-on-Avon, St Lawrence, 132, 168; *157*
Braga, Bom Jesus do Monte, 213, 234; *273*
Brahmesvara Temple, Bhubaneswar, 54; *53*
Bramante, Donato, 182–3, 204
  St Peter's, Rome, 184; *226–7*
  Tempietto, Rome, 183, 215; *225*
Brasilia, Government Buildings, 282–3; *379*
Brazen Palace, Anuradhapura, 49
Brazil, 232, 233, 282
Breslau, Jahrhunderthalle, 260
Breuer, Marcel, 279
Bridgeman, Charles, 221–2
Brighton, Royal Pavilion, 226; *293*
Bristol Cathedral, 166; *203*
Britain, 13
  Art Nouveau, 257, 259
  Arts and Crafts movement, 257–9
  Baroque architecture, 214–15
  Classicism, 218–27
  Georgian architecture, 188, 198
  Gothic architecture, 164–5, 167–70, 172–3, 174
  Industrial Revolution, 240
  International Style, 276–7
  landscape gardens, 221–2
  nineteenth-century architecture, 240–7
  Norman style, 132
  Renaissance, 190, 197–8, 200–1
  twentieth-century architecture, 290–2, 294–5
British Empire, 239
British Museum, London, 225; *291*
Brodrick, Cuthbert:

Grand Hotel, Scarborough, 244
  Leeds Town Hall, 244; *319*
Bronze Age, 19
Brown, Lancelot 'Capability', 222
Bruchsal, Episcopal Palace, 209, 212
Brunel, Isambard Kingdom, 244
Brunelleschi, Filippo, 179, 204
  Florence Cathedral, 176, 185; *216*
  Foundling Hospital, Florence, 176, 178; *217*
  Pazzi Chapel, Santa Croce, Florence, 176; *218–19*
  San Lorenzo, Florence, 176
  Santo Spirito, Florence, 176; *220*
Brunswick Cathedral, 167
Brussels, 199, 255
  Hôtel Solvay, 255
  Hôtel Tassel, 255; *342*
  Palais de Justice, 250
Brutalism, 286
Bryce, David:
  Royal Infirmary, Edinburgh, 246
Buddha, 46, 104
Buddhism, 45–6, 47–9, 50, 55, 58, 62, 69
Buffalo:
  Guaranty Building, 254
  Martin House, 260; *352*
Buhen, 30
Bullant, Jean:
  Château de Chenonceaux, 194; *244*
Burgos Cathedral, 165, 170, 198; *197, 250*
Burgtheater, Vienna, 249
Burgundy, 141
Burlington, Richard Boyle, 3rd Earl of, 218
  Chiswick House, London, 218; *282–3*
  Holkham Hall, Norfolk, 220; *286*
Burma, 45, 49, 58
Burnham and Root, 254
  Monadnock Building, Chicago, 254; *337*
  Reliance Building, Chicago, 254; *338*
Burrell Collection, Glasgow, 292
Burton, Decimus:
  Hyde Park Corner, London, 225
Butterfield, William:
  All Saints, Margaret Street, London, 246–7
  Keble College, Oxford, 198
buttresses, 111, 162, 166
Byker Wall, Newcastle, 291–2
Byrd, William:
  Westover, Charles City County, 236
Byzantine Empire, 114, 115, 119–29
Byzantium *see* Constantinople

Caernarfon Castle, 172
Caesar, Julius, 90, 102
Cairo, 35, 153

El-Ashair Mosque, 154
  Ibn Tulun Mosque, 151; *181*
  Madresa of Sultan Hassan, 154
Calatrava, Santiago, 288
  Alamillo Bridge, Seville, 288
  TGV station, Lyons-Satolas Airport, 288, 301; *407*
Calcutta, Government House, 239; *315*
Callicrates:
  Parthenon, Athens, 96–7; *105–6*
  Temple of Nike Apteros, Athens, 93; *101*
Cambodia, 53, 54–5
Cambridge:
  King's College Chapel, 170
  Senate House, 220
Cambridge, Mass., Longfellow House, 235; *306*
Cameron, Charles:
  Tsarskoye Selo, 218–20; *284*
campaniles, 120
Campbell, Colen, 218
  Houghton Hall, Norfolk, 218
  Mereworth, Kent, 218
  Stourhead, Wiltshire, 222–3
Campen, Jacob van:
  Amsterdam Town Hall, 195
  Mauritzhuis, The Hague, 200; *253*
Canada, 230, 234, 289
Canberra, Parliament buildings, 294
Cancelleria, Rome, 182
Candela, Felix, 283, 286
  Church of the Miraculous Virgin, Mexico City, 283; *380*
Canterbury, 136
  Cathedral, 164, 168
Cape Sounion, Temple of Poseidon, 41, 86; *96*
capitals, 35, 88–9, 92, 125; *27, 98, 146*
Capitol, Rome, 185–6
Capitol, Washington DC, 183, 238, 251; *312*
Caprarola, Palazzo Farnese, 187, 198
Caracol Observatory, Chichen Itza, 80; *84*
Carcassonne, 172; *208*
Cardross, St Peter's College, 271
Carlisle, Earl of, 214
Carolingian architecture, 132
Carson, Pirie Scott Department Store, Chicago, 254; *339*
La Cartuja, Granada, 202; *259*
Casa Batlló, Barcelona, 256
Casa Milà, Barcelona, 256; *344*
Caserta, Palazzo Reale, 212
Caspian Sea, 18
cast iron, 238
Castel Béranger, Paris, 255
Castel del Monte, Bari, 172
El Castillo, Chichen Itza, 82; *92–3*

Castle Bolton, Yorkshire, 173
Castle Howard, Yorkshire, 183, 214, 215; *278*
castles, 72, 136, 141, 142, 143, 171, 172–3; *58, 159–60, 166, 209–10*
catacombs, 116; *131*
Çatal Hüyük, 18
cathedrals:
    Gothic, 158–70; *190–205*
    Renaissance, 176; *216*
Catholic Church, 196, 197, 204, 205
Cefalù Cathedral, 125, 133, 156
Celts, 118, 132
Central America, 27
Central Beheer building, Apeldoorn, 292
Centre Pompidou, Paris, 292; *400*
centring, 109
chaityas, 50; *44, 45*
Chaldees, 19
Chambers, Sir William, 225
    Somerset House, London, 225
Chambord, Château de, 192–3, 194; *238–40*
Chandigarh:
    Courts of Justice, 271
    Legislative Assembly Building, 271; *362*
    Secretariat, 271
Chandragupta Maurya, 45, 46
Chang'an, 68
Chapel of the Holy Shroud (Il Sindone), Turin, 207, 209, 210
Chapel of the Holy Thorn, Paris, 163; *189*
Chapel of the Three Kings, Mexico City, 232–3
Charlemagne, Emperor, 130–2, 146
Charles I, King of England, 201
Charles I, King of Spain, 76
Charles III, King of Spain, 212
Charles V, Emperor, 190, 193, 196
Charles VII, King of Bohemia, 164
Charles Martel, 133, 147
Charleston, 235
    St Michael's, 237
Chartres Cathedral, 158, 162, 163, 165–6, 245; *193, 199–201*
châteaux, 172, 192–3; *238–41, 244*
Chatsworth, Derbyshire, 205–7, 246
Chaucer, Geoffrey, 136
Cheadle, St Giles, 243; *318*
Chenonceaux, Château de, 194; *244*
Cheops, Pharaoh, 35
Chicago:
    Carson, Pirie Scott Department Store, 254; *339*
    Home Insurance Building, 252
    Lake Shore Drive Apartments, 281
    Marshall Field Warehouse, 252; *335*
    Monadnock Building, 254; *337*
    Oak Park, 260
    Reliance Building, 254; *338*

Robie House, 260–4; *353*
    Unity Temple, 260
Chicago School, 252–4, 260
Chichen Itza, 78–9, 81
    Ball Court, 81; *85*
    Caracol Observatory, 80; *84*
    El Castillo, 82; *92–3*
Chile, 76
chimneys, 15, 136, 198
Ch'in dynasty, 56, 66, 69
Ch'in Shih Huang Ti, Emperor, 56, 66
China, 13, 27, 42, 56–69
Ching dynasty, 62
chinoiserie, 230
Chipping Campden, William Grevel's House, 174; *211*
Chiswick House, London, 218; *282–3*
Choragic Monument of Lysicrates, Athens, 92, 238; *100*
Christchurch, Boston, 237
Christianity, 114, 115, 116, 118–29, 132, 243
Chrysler building, New York, 279; *375*
Church of the Convent of Christ, Tomar, 196; *197*
Church of England, 247
Church of the Holy Apostles, Constantinople, 122, 126
Church of the Miraculous Virgin, Mexico City, 283; *380*
Church of the Nativity, Bethlehem, 119–20; *134*
Church of the Transfiguration, Khizi Island, 125
churches:
    Baroque, 204–11, 213; *258–9, 262–5, 267–9, 274–7*
    basilicas, 114–15, 116, 118–20, 121; *128–9, 132–5*
    Byzantine, 121–9; *139–50*
    Carolingian, 132; *153*
    centralized, 121–2; *138*
    Gothic, 158–70; *189–206*
    Renaissance, 180–1, 183–5, 189; *216, 218–22, 225–7, 229, 232–3, 236, 242*
    Romanesque, 130–41; *154–8, 162, 164, 165*
Churrigueresque style, 202, 230, 232, 233
CIAM *see* Congrès Internationaux d'Architecture Moderne
Cistercians, 138, 167–8
cities, development of, 16–27, 28
city walls, 142
Civic Centre, Säynätsalo, 278; *374*
Clark, Kenneth, 16
Classicism, 218–29, 236–8, 240
Claude Lorrain, 224
Cloaca Maxima, Rome, 111–12
Cloth Hall, Ypres, 171; *207*
Cluny, 138, 158
Coalbrookdale, Iron Bridge, 245; *320*
Colbert, Jean Baptiste, 190

College of William and Mary, Williamsburg, 236; *308*
Cologne Cathedral, 166
Colosseum, Rome, 105–7, 181; *116*
Columbus, Christopher, 76
columns:
    Composite order, 91, 107; *98*
    Corinthian order, 88, 91, 92, 107, 181; *98*
    Doric order, 88, 91–2, 181, 228; *98*
    Egyptian, 13, 35; *26–7*
    Etruscan order, 107
    giant orders, 185
    Greek, 13, 88–90, 91–2, 227–8
    Ionic order, 88, 91, 92, 181; *98*
    Persian, 26
    Renaissance, 181, 185
    Roman, 107
Compañia, Cuzco, 233
Composite order, 91, 107; *98*
concrete, 109
    reinforced concrete, 254–5
Confucianism, 69
Confucius, 69, 104
Congrès Internationaux d'Architecture Moderne (CIAM), 266
Connell, Amyas:
    High and Over, Amersham, 276
Conques, 132, 136
Constantia, 121
Constantine I, Emperor, 35, 108, 115, 118, 119–20, 122, 144, 213
Constantinople, 35, 115, 118, 120, 144
    Church of the Holy Apostles, 122, 126
    Hagia Sophia, 124–5, 127; *143–5*
    see also Istanbul
Constructivism, 286
Conwy Castle, 172
Copenhagen, Thorvaldsen Museum, *327*
Coptic Christians, 151
corbelling, 12, 13; *5*
Cordoba, Great Mosque, 146, 155; *172*
Corinthian order, 88, 91, 92, 107, 181; *98*
Cornaro family, 207
cornices, 89–90
Cortez, Hernando, 233
Costa, Lucio, 282
Cottrell, Leonard, 18
Counter-Reformation, 196, 204, 205
Courts of Justice, Chandigarh, 271
courtyards, 15; *3*
Coutances, 163
Cox, Richardson and Taylor, 294
Crane Library, Quincy, Mass., 252; *336*
Crete, 25–6, 27, 88
cruck frames, 13
Crusades, 137–8, 144, 149, 155, 158, 164, 171
Crystal Palace, London, 246, 248; *316, 321*
Ctesiphon, 26, 149; *20*
Cubism, 268
Cuijpers, Petrus:

Rijksmuseum, Amsterdam, 250
Cullinan, Edward, 295
Cumberland Terrace, Regent's Park,
  London, 226; *292*
Curvilinear Gothic style, 164, 165
Custom House, Dublin, 225
Cuvilliés, François, 217
  Amalienburg Pavilion, Munich, 209, 217; *281*
Cuzco, 84–5, 233
  Cathedral, 233
  Compañia, 233
Cyprus, 18, 100
Czech Republic, 200

Dacca, National Assembly Hall, 287
Dal, Lake, Shalimar Garden, 148; *177*
Damascus, 153
  Great Mosque, 146; *173*
Daphni, Monastery Church, 125–6; *147*
Darby, Abraham:
  Iron Bridge, Coalbrookdale, 245; *320*
Darius I, King of Persia, 26, 27, 35, 91
Dark Ages, 116, 130
Darmstadt, 259
Deanery Garden, Sonning, 258–9; *348*
Deccan, 51
Deconstructivism, 296–7
Decorated Gothic style, 164
Deir el-Bahri, Funerary Temple of Queen
  Hatshepsut, 41; *36*
Deir el-Medina, 28
Delhi:
  Baha'i Temple, 294
  Quwwat-ul-Islam, *184*
  Tomb of Humayan, 157
Delphi, 100–1; *110*
  Athenian Treasury, 101; *110*
  Temple of Apollo, 101; *110*
  Theatre, 101; *110*
  Tholos, 101
Dendera, 41
Denmark, 295–6
Derbyshire, Andrew:
  Hillingdon Civic Centre, 291
Dessau, 272
Devonshire, Duke of, 246
Diane de Poitiers, 194
Dientzenhofer, Johann:
  Banz Abbey Church, 209; *269*
Dietterlin, Wendel, 195
Dinkeloo, John:
  Ford Foundation Headquarters, New York,
  289
Diocletian, Emperor, 114, 116–18
Diocletian's palace, Split (Spalato), 114, 121,
  224
Doge's Palace, Venice, 174–5; *213*
Dollmann, Georg von:
  Neuschwanstein, 250; *330*
Dom-ino House, 268; *357*

Dome of the Rock, Jerusalem, 144–6; *169*
Domenico da Cortona, 212
  Château de Chambord, 192–3; *238–40*
domes:
  Byzantine, 121, 123–5; *141–5*
  Indian, 157
  Islamic, 156–7; *186*
  onion domes, 128
  Renaissance, 176
  Roman, 110–11
  trulli, 12; *6*
Dominican Republic, 233
Dominicans, 230
Domitian, Emperor, 106
Doric order, 88, 91–2, 181, 228; *98*
Dougga, *113*
drainage, 111–12
Dravidians, 44, 46, 52
Dresden, Zwinger, 205; *261*
Dublin, 198
  Custom House, 225
Dudok, Willem:
  Hilversum Town Hall, 276; *369*
Durham Cathedral, 132, 168; *155*

Eastern Church, 122
Economist Buildings, London, 290; *395*
Eden, Garden of, 18
Edfu, Temple of Horus, 37, 41; *31*
Edinburgh, 198, 220–1, 224, 225, 226
  Royal High School, 225
  Royal Infirmary, 246
Edirne, Selimiye Mosque, 157
Edo, 73
Edward I, King of England, 172, 173
Eginhart, *161*
Egypt, 122, 154, 296
Egypt, Ancient, 10, 13, 16, 26, 27, 28–41, 88
Eiffel, Gustave:
  Eiffel Tower, Paris, 248–9; *328*
Einstein Tower, Potsdam, 272; *363*
Eisenman, Peter:
  Wexner Center for the Visual Arts, Ohio
  State University, 297; *405*
El Aksa Mosque, Jerusalem, 144, 146; *170*
El-Deir (Monastery) Temple, Petra, 109; *119*
El Tajin, Pyramid of the Niches, 80, 84; *94*
Elam, 25
Elephanta Temple, Bombay, 51
Elephantine, 28
elevators, 254
Elizabeth I, Queen of England, 190
Ellis, Peter:
  Oriel Chambers, Liverpool, 247; *323*
Ellora, Kailasa Temple, 50; *47*
Ely Cathedral, 169
  Lady Chapel, 164
Empire State Building, New York, 279
Enemy Observation Pagoda, Kaiyuan Temple,
  62; *65*

Engineering Building, Leicester University,
  290–1; *394*
England *see* Britain
Ensinger, Ulrich:
  Ulm Minster, 167
entablature, 90
entasis, 96
Ephesus, Temple of Artemis, 92
Epidauros, Theatre, 99–100; *107*
Episcopal Palace, Bruchsal, 209, 212
Erechtheum, Athens, 96; *104*
Eridu, 19
Erskine, Ralph:
  Byker Wall, Newcastle, 291–2
Escorial Palace, 196–7, 198, 233; *248*
Eskimos, 10
Etienne de Bonneuil, 164
Etruria, Staffordshire, 224
Etruscan order, 107
Etruscans, 104–5, 112, 224
Eudes de Montreuil, 166
Eugene, Prince of Savoy, 204
Euphrates, river, 18, 21
Europe, 10, 15
Exchange, Amsterdam, 260
Exeter Cathedral, 169
Expo '67, 289; *389*
Expressionism, 286
Ezarhaddon, King, 24

Fagus Factory, Alfeld-an-der-Leine, 272; *363*
Fallingwater, Bear Run, 264; *354*
Fathy, Hassan, 296
Feng-shui, 58–9, 64–6
Ferstel, Heinrich von:
  Votivkirche, Vienna, 249
Festival of Britain (1951), 277
feudalism, 133–6
Finland, 292
fireplaces, 15
First World War, 252, 265, 266
Firuzabad, 123
Fischer von Erlach, Johann Bernhardt, 207
  Schönbrunn Palace, Vienna, 216
Flamboyant Gothic style, 165, 167
Florence, 178, 232
  Cathedral, 176, 185; *216*
  Foundling Hospital, 176, 178; *217*
  Laurentian Library, 185; *228*
  Medici Chapel, San Lorenzo, 185; *229*
  Palazzo Pitti, 181
  Palazzo Rucellai, 181, 210; *223*
  Palazzo Vecchio, 175
  Pazzi Chapel, Santa Croce, 176; *218–19*
  San Lorenzo, 176
  San Miniato al Monte, 130, 140; *154*
  Santa Maria Novella, 180–1
  Santo Spirito, 176; *220*
  Uffizi, 185
Florida, 230

Floris, Cornelius, 195, 196
Foguang Temple, Mount Wutai, 60; *61*
Fontainebleau, 194; *237*
Fontana, Carlo, 207, 220
Fontana, Domenico, 184
  St Peter's, Rome, 184
Fonthill Abbey, Wiltshire, 226
Forbidden City, Beijing, 67; *70–1*
Ford Foundation Headquarters, New York, 289
Forde, Dorset, 174
Forest Crematorium, Stockholm, 278; *372*
Fort Worth, Kimbell Art Museum, 292; *399*
Foster, Norman:
  Hong Kong and Shanghai Bank, Hong Kong, 291; *397*
  Stansted Airport, 291
  Willis Faber and Dumas offices, Ipswich, 291; *396*
Foundling Hospital, Florence, 176, 178; *217*
Foy, Ste, 132, 136
France:
  Baroque architecture, 202–4
  Classicism, 227–9
  gardens, 221
  Gothic architecture, 158–64, 165–7, 173–4
  nineteenth-century architecture, 247–9, 254–6
  Renaissance, 190–5
  Rococo style, 215–16
  town houses, 198–9
  twentieth-century architecture, 288, 292, 294
Francesco di Giorgio, 179, 180; *221*
Francis, St, 138, 160
Franciscans, 230
François I, King of France, 190, 192, 193, 194
Franklin, Benjamin, 162
Franklin Court, Philadelphia, 288
Franks, 130–2
Frederick, Prince of Wales, 225
Frederick II, Emperor, 172
Frederick the Great, King of Prussia, 228
French Revolution, 218, 223, 229, 240
Froebel, F.W.A., 260
Fry, Maxwell:
  Sunhouse, Hampstead, 276
Fuller, Buckminster:
  United States Pavilion, Expo '67, 289; *389*
Funerary Temple of Queen Hatshepsut, Deir el-Bahri, 41; *36*
Furness, Frank:
  Pennsylvania Academy of the Fine Arts, Philadelphia, 251; *334*
Futurism, 286

Gabriel, Ange-Jacques, 227
  Le Petit Trianon, Versailles, 228–9; *297*
  Place de la Bourse, Bordeaux, 229
  Place de la Concorde, Paris, 229

Gal Vihara, Polonnaruwa, 46; *40*
Galla Placidia, 120
Galleria Vittorio Emanuele, Milan, 251; *332*
Gandon, James:
  Custom House, Dublin, 225
gardens:
  Chinese, 68–9
  Islamic, 148; *177*
  Japanese, 73–4; *80*
  landscape gardens, 221–2
La Garisenda, Bologna, 142
Garnier, Charles:
  Opéra, Paris, 247–8; *325–6*
Gasson, Barry:
  Burrell Collection, Glasgow, 292
Gaudí, Antoni, 256–7, 283, 289
  Casa Batlló, Barcelona, 256
  Casa Milà, Barcelona, 256; *344*
  Güell Park, Barcelona, 256
  Sagrada Familia, Barcelona, 256; *343*
  Santa Coloma de Cervello, Barcelona, 257; *345*
geodesic domes, 286; *389*
George, Prince Regent, 226
Georgian architecture, 188, 198, 234
German Pavilion, Barcelona International Exhibition, 273; *366–7*
Germany:
  Baroque architecture, 202, 204
  Gothic architecture, 165, 167, 170, 175
  International Style, 271–3
  nineteenth-century architecture, 249–50
  twentieth-century architecture, 289–90, 292
Il Gesù, Rome, 187, 211, 233; *232–3*
giant orders, 185
Gibbs, James, 207, 210, 220, 222, 237, 239
  Radcliffe Camera, Oxford, 183
  St Martin-in-the-Fields, London, 220; *285*
  Senate House, Cambridge University, 220
Gillespie, Kidd and Coia:
  St Peter's College, Cardross, 271
Gilly, Friedrich, 228
Gislebertus, 139–40; *163*
Giulio Romano, 179, 186
  Mantua Cathedral, 186
  Palazzo del Tè, Mantua, 194; *230*
  Palazzo Ducale, Mantua, 186
Giza, 34
  Pyramid of Cephren, 35, 36–7; *28*
  Pyramid of Cheops, 33, 35, 36–7, 38–9; *28–30*
  Pyramid of Mycerinus, 35, 36–7; *28–9*
  Pyramid of Onnos, 36
Glasgow, 225, 259
  Burrell Collection, 292
  Glasgow School of Art, 259; *349*
glass, 286
Glass House, New Canaan, 281; *376–7*
Globe Theatre, London, 171

Gloucester Cathedral, 164
Golden Pavilion, Kitayama Palace, Kyoto, 73; *78*
Gonzaga, Duke Federico, 186
Gothic architecture, 140, 158–75, 178, 190, 240
Gothic Revival, 168, 240–2, 243, 246
Goths, 116, 118
Government Buildings, Brasilia, 282–3; *379*
Government House, Calcutta, 239; *315*
Governor's Palace, Santa Fe, 232; *300*
Gowan, James:
  Engineering Building, Leicester University, 290–1; *394*
Granada, 133
  Alhambra, 149, 156; *178–9*
  La Cartuja, 202; *259*
Grand Hotel, Scarborough, 244
Grand Mosque and Justice Palace, Riyadh, 296
Grand Tour, 90, 224
Grande Arche de la Défense, Paris, 294
Graves, Michael:
  Public Services Building, Portland, 295; *404*
'Great Baths', Mohenjo-Daro, 42; *37*
Great Exhibition (1851), 246
Great Mosque, Cordoba, 146, 155; *172*
Great Mosque, Damascus, 146; *173*
Great Mosque, Kairouan, 147, 152, 153; *174*
Great Mosque, Samarkand, 150–1
Great Stupa, Sanchi, 48, 54; *41–2*
Great Temple, Madura, 52–3; *52*
Great Temple of Rameses II, Abu Simbel, 31; *21*
Great Wall of China, 56, 66; *67*
Greece, 125–6, 223
Greece, Ancient, 13, 26, 41, 86–101, 102, 105–6, 109, 224, 248, 295
Greek Revival, 225, 227, 238
Greenway, Francis:
  St James's, Sydney, 220, 239; *314*
Greenwich, Queen's House, 200–1; *254–5*
Grevel, William, 174
groin vaults, 109
Gropius, Walter, 276, 279
  Bauhaus, 272, 273; *365*
  Fagus Factory, Alfeld-an-der-Leine, 272; *363*
Guaranty Building, Buffalo, 254
Guarini, Guarino, 207, 210
  Chapel of the Holy Shroud (Il Sindone), Turin, 207, 209, 210
  San Lorenzo, Turin, 207, 210; *265*
Guatemala, 76, 82
Güell Park, Barcelona, 256
Guildhall, Lavenham, 171
Guimard, Hector, 255
  Castel Béranger, Paris, 255
Gunbad-i-Qabus, 157
Gupta dynasty, 51
Gur-i-mir, Samarkand, 157; *188*
gymnasia, 100

Habitat housing, Montreal, 289; *390*
Hacchappayya Temple, Aihole, 51
Hadrian, Emperor, 92, 110
Hadrian's Villa, Tivoli, 114; *127*
Hagia Sophia, Constantinople, 124–5, 127;
    143–5
The Hague, Mauritzhuis, 200; *253*
Halebid, Hoysalesvara Temple, 45–6; *39*
Hall, Littlemore and Todd, 294
Hamburg, 171
Hamilton, Thomas:
    Royal High School, Edinburgh, 225
Hammurabi, 21, 27
Hampstead, Sunhouse, 276
Han dynasty, 62
Hanging Gardens of Babylon, 22
Hanseatic League, 171
Hansen, Theophilus:
    Parliament Building, Vienna, 249
Harappa, 42
Hardwick Hall, Derbyshire, 197
Harewood House, Yorkshire, 205
Harlech Castle, 172
Haroun al Raschid, 149
Hartley, Jesse:
    Albert Dock, Liverpool, 244
Hatshepsut, Queen, 41; *32, 36*
Hattusash, 19, 23
    Lion Gate, *14*
Hawksmoor, Nicholas, 210, 214, 215
    Castle Howard Mausoleum, Yorkshire,
    183, 215
Heidelberg Castle, 195; *243*
Heien, 70
Hellenic period, 86
Hellenistic period, 86–8, 90, 100
Hennebique, François, 254
Henri IV, King of France, 199
Henry II, King of England, 171
Henry VIII, King of England, 190
Herculaneum, 113
Hereford Cathedral Library, 294
Herodotus, 21–2, 24–5
Herrenchiemsee, 250
Herrera, Juan de:
    Escorial Palace, 196–7, 198, 233; *248*
Herzberger, Herman:
    Central Beheer building, Apeldoorn, 292
High and Over, Amersham, 276
High Renaissance, 181–3, 250
Highpoint, London, 277
Hildebrandt, Lucas von, 207
    Belvedere Palace, Vienna, 204–5, 207; *259*
    Bishop's Palace, Würzburg, 211, 212; *270*
Hildesheim, St Michael's, 139
Hillingdon Civic Centre, 291
Hilversum Town Hall, 276; *369*
Himei-ji Castle, 72; *58*
Hinduism, 44, 45–6, 47, 50–4

Hippodamus of Miletus, 100
Historicism, 286
Hittites, 19, 23
Hittorff, J.-I., 248
Hiuen Tsang, 50
Hoare, Henry and Richard:
    Stourhead gardens, Wiltshire, 223; *288*
Hoban, James:
    White House, Washington DC, 237
Hobart, 239
Holabird and Roche, 254
Holkham Hall, Norfolk, 220; *286*
Holl, Elias:
    Arsenal, Augsburg, 196; *246*
    Augsburg Town Hall, 195–6
Holland *see* Netherlands
Holland, Henry, 226
Holy Land, 137–8, 144
Holy Roman Empire, 204
Holy Sepulchre, Jerusalem, 121
Home Insurance Building, Chicago, 252
Honduras, 76
Hong Kong and Shanghai Bank, Hong Kong,
    64, 291; *397*
Honnecourt, Villard de, 162
Honorius, Emperor, 118, 120
Hooch, Pieter de, 200
Hopkins, Michael:
    Mound Stand, Lords cricket ground, 291
Horta, Victor:
    Hôtel Solvay, Brussels, 255
    Hôtel Tassel, Brussels, 255; *342*
Horyu-ji Temple, Nara, 72; *76*
Hosios Loukas, 125–6
Hôtel de Soubise, Paris, 216; *280*
Hôtel Lambert, Paris, *251*
Hôtel Solvay, Brussels, 255
Hôtel Tassel, Brussels, 255; *342*
Houghton Hall, Norfolk, 218
House of the North, Saqqara, 35; *26*
House of the South, Saqqara, 35
House of the Vetii, Pompeii, *125–6*
Houses of Parliament, London, 242, 243; *317*
Hoysalesvara Temple, Halebid, 45–6; *39*
Hsienyang, 62
Humanists, 179, 180
Hungary, 202, 204
Huni, Pharaoh, 35
Hyatt Regency Hotel, San Francisco, 289
Hyde Park Corner, London, 225
hypocausts, 112

Ibn Tulun Mosque, Cairo, 151; *181*
Ictinus:
    Parthenon, Athens, 96–7; *105–6*
Ieyasu, 70–1
igloos, 10
Iltumish, Sultan, *184*
Imhotep, 41
    Stepped Pyramid of King Zoser, 34–5;

24–5
Imperial Forum, Rome, 102, 105; *112*
Imperial Hotel, Tokyo, 264
Incas, 84–5, 90, 232
India, 13, 27, 42–54, 58, 157, 230–2, 239, 271
Indonesia, 59, 230–2
Indus Valley, 27, 42–4
Industrial Revolution, 228, 240, 244–5
insulae, 112–13; *124*
International Exhibition of Modern Architec-
    ture, New York (1932), 266
International Style, 265, 266–83, 284, 287,
    296, 297
Ionic order, 88, 91, 92, 181; *98*
Ipswich, Willis Faber and Dumas offices,
    291; *396*
Iran, 18, 157
Iraq, 18, 22
Ireland, 13, 132
iron, 245
Iron Bridge, Coalbrookdale, 245; *320*
Ise Shrine, 56; *57*
Isfahan, 150, 164
    Masjid-i-Shah, 150; *180, 182*
Ishtar Gate, Babylon, 22–3; *16*
Isidore of Miletus, 125
Islam, 125, 132–3, 144–57
Israel, 23
Istanbul, 154
    Blue Mosque, 157; *186*
    Suleymaniye Mosque, 154; *183*
    see also Constantinople
Italy:
    Baroque architecture, 202, 205–13
    nineteenth-century architecture, 250–1
    Renaissance, 176–89, 190
    Romanesque architecture, 130, 142
Ivan the Terrible, 128
Izumo Shrine, 56

Jacques Coeur's House, Bourges, 173; *212*
Jahrhunderthalle, Breslau, 260
Jainism, 46, 47, 50
James I, King of England, 200
James of St George, 173
Jami (Friday) Mosque, Yazd, 155; *184*
Japan, 10, 13, 27, 42, 56, 59, 69–75, 292–3; *4*
Java, 54
Jefferson, Thomas, 188, 236–7
    Monticello, 189, 236–7; *309*
    University of Virginia, 237; *298, 310*
Jekyll, Gertrude, 258
Jenney, William le Baron:
    Home Insurance Building, Chicago, 252
Jericho, 18; *10*
Jerusalem, 120, 136, 144
    Dome of the Rock, 144–6; *169*
    El Aksa mosque, 144, 146; *170*
    Holy Sepulchre, 121
Jesuits, 204, 230, 233

Jews, 146
Jimmu, Emperor of Japan, 104
Johnson, Philip, 281
    American Telephone and Telegraph
        Building, New York, 295
    Glass House, New Canaan, 281; *376–7*
Jomon culture, 59, 69
Jones, Inigo, 190, 195, 200, 218, 224
    Banqueting House, Whitehall, 200, 201; *256*
    Queen's House, Greenwich, 200–1; *254–5*
    Wilton House, Wiltshire, 200, 201; *257*
Jones, Owen, 248
Jordan, 13, 18, 296
Judah, 104
Julian, Emperor, 136
Justinian, Emperor, 118, 120, 121, 124, 125
Juvarra, Filippo, 207
    church at Superga, Turin, 213; *274*
    Stupinigi, Turin, 205
Ka'aba, Mecca, 146, 153; *171*
Kabah, Palace of the Masks, 83
Kahn, Louis I.:
    Kimbell Art Museum, Fort Worth, 292; *399*
    National Assembly Hall, Dacca, 287
    Richards Medical Research Building,
        University of Pennsylvania, 287; *385*
Kailasa Temple, Ellora, 50; *47*
Kairouan:
    Aghlabid Mosque, 152
    Great Mosque, 147, 152, 153; *174*
Kaiyuan Temple, Dingxian, 62; *65*
Kalaa Sghrira, *9*
Kandinsky, Wassily, 272
Karli, Chaitya hall, 50, 51; *44–5*
Karnak, 39
    Temple of Amun-Ra, 33, 37, 39–41, 91;
        32–3
    Temple of Khons, 37, 40; *34*
Kasuga Shrine, Nara, *62*
Kathmandu Valley, Swayambhunath Stupa,
    49; *43*
Katsura Imperial Villa, Kyoto, *79*
Keble College, Oxford, 298
Kent, William, 221, 222
    Chiswick House, London, 218; *282–3*
    Holkham Hall, Norfolk, 220; *286*
Kerala, 52
Kerr, Robert:
    Bear Wood, Berkshire, 247; *324*
Kew Gardens, 225
Khirokitia, 18
Khizi Island, Church of the Transfiguration,
    125
Khmer empire, 53, 54–5
Khmer Rouge, 55
Khorsabad, 19
Kiev, Santa Sophia, 128
Kimbell Art Museum, Fort Worth, 292; *399*
King's College Chapel, Cambridge, 170
Kiosk of Trajan, Philae, 30; *22*

Kitayama Palace, Kyoto, 73; *78*
Klee, Paul, 272
Klenze, Leo von:
    Alte Pinakothek, Munich, 249–50; *331*
Knights Hospitallers, 138
Knights Templar, 138
Knossos, 25–6, 88, 91, 111
    Palace of Minos, 25; *18*
Konarak, Temple of the Sun, 50; *49*
Korea, 60
kou-tung brackets, 61–2; *60*
Krak des Chevaliers, 138; *159–60*
Kresge College, University of Santa Cruz,
    288
Kroll, Lucien:
    University of Louvain, 292
Kublai Khan, 49, 58
Kurokawa, Kisho:
    Nakagin Capsule Tower, Tokyo, 293; *402*
Kuwait, 294
Kyoto, 73
    Katsura Imperial Villa, *79*
    Kitayama Palace, 73; *78*
    Ryoan-ji Temple, *80*

La Tourette, 271
Labrouste, Henri:
    Bibliothèque Nationale, Paris, 248
    Bibliothèque Sainte-Geneviève, Paris, 248;
        329
Lagash, 19
Lake Shore Drive Apartments, Chicago, 281
Lands Department Building, Perth, 239
landscape gardens, 221–2
Lao Zi, 69
Laon Cathedral, 166
Lapland, 10
Lasdun, Sir Denys:
    National Theatre, London, 291
Latrobe, Benjamin:
    Bank of Philadelphia, 237
    Capitol, Washington DC, 238, 251; *312*
    Catholic Cathedral, Baltimore, 237; *311*
    University of Virginia, 237; *298, 310*
    White House, Washington DC, 237
Laugier, Abbé, 223
Laurana, Luciano:
    Palace of Urbino, 178
Laurentian Library, Florence, 185; *228*
Lavenham, Guildhall, 171
Law Courts, London, 246
Le Corbusier, 61, 268–71, 276, 277, 282, 290,
    292
    Courts of Justice, Chandigarh, 271
    Dom-ino House, 268; *357*
    La Tourette, 271
    Legislative Assembly Building, Chandigarh,
        271; *362*
    Ministry of Education Building, Rio de
        Janeiro, 282

Modulor Man, 268–9; *358*
Notre-Dame-du-Haut, Ronchamp, 270–1,
    289; *361*
Pavillon Suisse, Cité Universitaire, Paris,
    269; *359*
Secretariat, Chandigarh, 271
Unité d'Habitation, Marseilles, 269–70;
    360
Villa Savoie, Poissy, 268; *356*
Le Nôtre, André:
    Vaux-le-Vicomte, 221; *287*
    Versailles, 221
Le Puy, 137
Le Roy, Julien David, 223
Le Vau, Louis:
    Hôtel Lambert, Paris; *251*
    Vaux-le-Vicomte, 209
    Versailles, 215
Ledoux, Claude-Nicolas, 227, 228
    La Barrière de la Villette, Paris, 227
    La Saline de Chaux, Arc-et-Senans, 227
Leeds Town Hall, 244; *319*
Legislative Assembly Building, Chandigarh,
    271; *362*
Leicester University, Engineering Building,
    290–1; *394*
Leiden, 273
L'Enfant, Pierre Charles, 237
Leonardo da Vinci, 180, 182, 184, 193
Lepautre, Pierre, 215
Lever House, New York, 281; *378*
Li Chieh, 62
Liao dynasty, 58
Lima Cathedral, 233
Lincoln, Mass., 279
Lincoln Cathedral, 168, 170
Linderhof, 250
Lingaraja Temple, Bhubaneswar, *50*
lintels, 12–13
Lion Gate, Hattusash, *14*
Lion Gateway, Mycenae, 23; *13*
Little Metropolitan, Athens, 126
Liverpool, 284
    Albert Dock, 244
    Oriel Chambers, 247; *323*
Lloyds Building, London, 292
Loire Valley, 190, 194
Lombards, 132
Lombardy, 141
London, 224
    All Saints, Margaret Street, 246–7
    Banqueting House, Whitehall, 200, 201;
        256
    British Museum, 225; *291*
    Chiswick House, 218; *282–3*
    Crystal Palace, 246, 248; *316, 321*
    Cumberland Terrace, Regent's Park, 226;
        292
    Economist Buildings, 290; *395*
    Globe Theatre, 171

Highpoint, 277
Houses of Parliament, 242, 243; *317*
Hyde Park Corner, 225
Law Courts, 246
Lloyds Building, 292
Midland Hotel, St Pancras Station, 243, 298
National Gallery, 225
National Theatre, 291
Natural History Museum, 246; *322*
New Palace of Westminster, 245
Penguin Pool, London Zoo, 277; *370*
Reform Club, 242–3
Richmond House, 294
Royal Festival Hall, 277
St Martin-in-the-Fields, 220; *285*
St Pancras Station, 243, 298
St Paul's Cathedral, 124, 183, 214; *277*
Somerset House, 225
Syon House, 225; *290*
Tower of London, 173
Travellers' Club, 242
Westminster Abbey, 162, 168, 170; *204*
London County Council:
Roehampton housing, 277; *371*
Longfellow House, Cambridge, Mass., 235; *306*
Longhena, Baldassare:
Santa Maria della Salute, Venice, 213; *275*
Longleat, Wiltshire, 197
Loos, Adolf, 259–60
Lords cricket ground, 291
L'Orme, Philibert de, 194–5
Château de Chenonceaux, 194; *244*
St-Etienne du Mont, Paris, 195; *242*
Loti, Pierre, 55
Louis VII, King of France, 160
Louis IX (St Louis), King of France, 163, 166
Louis XII, King of France, 182, 194
Louis XIV, King of France, 190, 215, 216
Louis XV, King of France, 229
Louisiana, 230, 232
Louvain, University of, 292
Louvre Palace, Paris, 172, 190, 194, 195; *245*
Lovell Beach House, Newport Beach, 278
Low Countries, 175, 199
Lubetkin, Berthold, 276–7
Penguin Pool, London Zoo, 277; *370*
Ludwig II, King of Bavaria, 250
Lutyens, Sir Edwin, 258, 268
Deanery Garden, Sonning, 258–9; *348*
Viceroy's House, New Delhi, 258; *347*
Luxor, 39
Temple of Amun-Ra, 35, 41; *35*
Lyons-Satolas Airport, TGV Station, 288, 301; *407*

Machu Picchu, 85; *95*
McKim, Mead and White:
Boston Public Library, 251; *333*
Mackintosh, Charles Rennie, 259

Glasgow School of Art, 259; *349*
Macquarie, Lachlan, 239
Maderna, Carlo, 208
St Peter's, Rome, 184, 208
SS. Trinità de' Monti, Rome, 213
Madras, 50, 52, 239
madresa, 154
Madresa of Sultan Hassan, Cairo, 154
Madura, Great Temple, 52–3; *52*
Mahabalipuram, 50; *48*
Shore temples, 52; *51*
Maisons-Laffitte, Château, 209
Majolica House, Vienna, 259; *350*
Mali, *3*
al-Malwiya Mosque, Samarra, 153; *168*
Mamelukes, 154
Manchuria, 58
Manco II, King of the Incas, 85
Mannerism, 185, 186–7, 189, 190
mansard roofs, 193
Mansart, François, 193
Château de Blois, 194
Château Maisons-Laffitte, 209
Mansart, Jules-Hardouin:
Château de la Menagerie, 215
Versailles, 215; *279*
Mansur, Caliph, 149–50
Mantua:
Cathedral, 186
Palazzo del Tè, 186, 194; *230*
Palazzo Ducale, 186
Sant' Andrea, 181; *222*
Manueline style, 165
March, St Wendreda's, 169; *206*
Marie Antoinette, Queen of France, 227, 229
Mark, St, 126
market crosses, 171
Marlborough, Duke of, 215
Marlowe, Christopher, 27
Marly, 215
Marseilles:
Les Arcades du Lac, 288
Unité d'Habitation, 269–70; *360*
Marshall Field Warehouse, Chicago, 252; *335*
Martin House, Buffalo, 260; *352*
Martyrion of St Byblas, Antioch Kaoussie, 123
Mary, Queen of Scots, 173
Masjid-i-Shah, Isfahan, 150; *180, 182*
mastabas, 33–4
Matthew, Robert, 277
Matthew of Arras, 164
Matthew (Robert), Johnson Marshall and Partners, 291
Mauritzhuis, The Hague, 200; *253*
Mauryan dynasty, 45, 46
Mausoleum of Galla Placidia, Ravenna, 120–1; *137*
Max Emmanuel, Elector of Bavaria, 217

Maya, 76, 79, 80, 81–3, 84; *82*
Mazarin, Cardinal, 190
Mecca, 147, 148, 151, 152
Ka'aba, 146, 153; *171*
Medes, 19
Medici Chapel, San Lorenzo, Florence, 185; *229*
Medici family, 178, 185
Medina, 146, 148, 153
Prophet's House Mosque, 151–2
Mediterranean, 18, 28, 105
megaron, 15, 91; *8*
Melbourne, 238
Parkville, *313*
Melk, Benedictine Monastery, 213; *276*
Memphis, 28, 34
Menagerie, Château de la, 215
Mendelsohn, Erich:
Einstein Tower, Potsdam, 272; *363*
Menes, King, 28
Mengoni, Giuseppe:
Galleria Vittorio Emanuele, Milan, 251; *332*
Mercedarian Monastery, Quito, 230; *299*
Merchant Adventurers' Hall, York, 171
Mereworth, Kent, 218
Meso-America, 76–85
Mesopotamia, 10, 18–25, 26, 28, 151, 153, 156–7
Metabolists, 286, 293
metopes, 89
Mexico, 76–8, 232, 234, 283
Mexico City, 76, 78–9, 80
Church of the Miraculous Virgin, 283; *380*
Metropolitan Cathedral, 232–3; *301*
San Agustin Acolman, 233
Santa Cecilia Temple, 78; *83*
Meydum, 35
Meyer, Adolf:
Fagus Factory, Alfeld-an-der-Leine, 272; *363*
Michelangelo, 187, 202, 207, 208
Capitol, Rome, 185–6
Laurentian Library, Florence, 185; *228*
Medici Chapel, San Lorenzo, Florence, 185; *229*
Palazzo del Senatore, Rome, 186
Palazzo Farnese, Rome, 182
St Peter's, Rome, 184–5; *226*
Middle Ages, 23
Middle East, 10, 27, 296
Midland Hotel, St Pancras Station, London, 243, 298
Mies van der Rohe, Ludwig, 272–3, 279–81, 289, 295
German Pavilion, Barcelona International Exhibition, 273; *366–7*
Lake Shore Drive Apartments, Chicago, 281
Seagram Building, New York, 281–2; *Preface*

Weissenhofsiedlung, Stuttgart, 272
Miguel, Francisco, 234
Milan, 118
    Cathedral, 164, 176; *196*
    Galleria Vittorio Emanuele, Milan, 251; *332*
    Velasca Tower, 287; *384*
minarets, 153–4
Minas Gerais, 234
Ming dynasty, 58, 62, 66, 68
Minoan civilization, 25, 88
Mique, Richard:
    Le Petit Trianon, Versailles, 227; *295*
Mistra, 126
Mitchell/Giurgola and Thorp:
    Parliament buildings, Canberra, 294
Mitla, Palace of the Columns, 84
Mitterand, François, 297
Mixtecs, 79, 84
Mnesicles:
    Propylaea, Athens, 90, 93, 96; *97*
Modern Movement, 277
Modernismo, 256
Mogul Empire, 157
Mohenjo-Daro, 13, 42, 45
    'Great Baths', 42; *37*
Moholy-Nagy, László, 272
Monadnock Building, Chicago, 254; *337*
monasteries, 126, 138; *148*
Monastery Church, Daphni, 125–6; *147*
Monastery and pilgrim church of St Simeon
    Stylites, Qal'at Sim'an, 122; *139*
Mondrian, Piet, 273
Mongols, 56, 58, 125, 155
Monreale, 125
Monte Alban, 80
Monte Cassino, 141
Montefeltro, Federigo da, Duke of Urbino,
    178–9
Monteverdi, Claudio, 202
Montezuma II, Emperor, 76
Monticello, Charlottesville, 189, 236–7; *309*
Montreal, Habitat housing, 289; *390*
Moore, Charles, 288
    Kresge College, University of Santa Cruz,
        288
    Piazza d'Italia, New Orleans, 288; *388*
Moors, 133
Morris, Roger, 222
Morris, William, 258, 272
Morton, H.V., 38–9
mosaics, 121, 125
Moscow, St Basil's Cathedral, 128–9; *152*
mosques, 144–6, 147–8, 149, 150–4, 155,
    296; *168–74, 180–4, 186*
motte and bailey, 142
Mound Stand, Lords cricket ground, 291
Mount Athos, 126; *148*
Mount Pleasant, Philadelphia, 235–6
Mount Vernon, Virginia, 235
Mozart, Wolfgang Amadeus, 202, 228

mud bricks, 10, 19–20, 24, 32; *1*
Muhammad, Prophet, 144, 146–7, 153
Munich:
    Alte Pinakothek, 249–50; *331*
    Amalienburg Pavilion, 209, 217; *281*
    Olympic Stadium, 290; *393*
    St John Nepomuk, Munich, 209; *258*
museums, 292
Muthesius, Hermann, 259
Mycenae, 15, 23, 88, 91; *8*
    Lion Gateway, 23; *13*
Mysore, 52

Nakagin Capsule Tower, Tokyo, 293; *402*
Nancy, 216
Nantucket, 235
Naples, Castel del Monte, 172
Napoleon I, Emperor, 16, 245, 260
Nara, 72
    Horyu-ji Temple, 72; *76*
    Kasuga Shrine, *62*
    Toshodai-ji Temple, *77*
    Yakushi-ji Temple, 71–2; *75*
Nash, John, 225–6
    Blaize Hamlet, 226
    Cumberland Terrace, Regent's Park,
        London, 226; *292*
    Royal Pavilion, Brighton, 226; *293*
Nasser, Lake, 30
National Assembly Hall, Dacca, 287
National Gallery, London, 225
National Theatre, London, 291
Natural History Museum, London, 246; *322*
Nazis, 272
Nebuchadnezzar II, King of Babylon, 19, 21,
    22–3, 35
Necropolis, 32
Neo-classicism, 218–29
Neo-Metabolism, 286
Neo-plasticism, 286
Nepal, 49
Nero, Emperor, 183–4
Netherlands, 199–200, 260, 273–4, 292
Neue Staatsgalerie, Stuttgart, 292; *398*
Neumann, Balthasar, 210
    Bishop's Palace, Würzburg, 211, 212; *270*
    Episcopal Palace, Bruchsal, 209, 212
    Vierzehnheiligen Pilgrimage Church, 209–
        10; *267–8*
Neuschwanstein, 250; *330*
New Brutalism, 290
New Caledonia 301
New Canaan, Glass House, 281; *376–7*
New Delhi, Viceroy's House, 258; *347*
New Empiricism, 286
New Mexico, 230, 232
New Orleans, 232
    Piazza d'Italia, 288; *388*
New Palace of Westminster, London, 245
New South Wales, 239

New York:
    American Telephone and Telegraph
        Building, 295
    Chrysler building, 279; *375*
    Empire State Building, 279
    Ford Foundation Headquarters, 289
    Lever House, 281; *378*
    Rockefeller Center, 279
    Seagram Building, 281–2; *Preface*
    Statue of Liberty, 249
    TWA terminal, J.F. Kennedy International
        Airport, 286, 287; *383*
New Zealand, 251
Newport Beach, Lovell Beach House, 278
Nicodemia, 118
Niemeyer, Oscar:
    Government Buildings, Brasilia, 282–3;
        379
    President's Palace, Brasilia, 282
Nile, river, 28–30, 32, 33
Nîmes, 106, 236
    Pont du Gard, 111; *111*
Nimrud, 19, 24
Nineveh, 19, 21, 23
Ningbo, Ayuwang Temple, *63*
Normans, 133, 142
Norsemen, 132
North Africa, 79, 153
North American Indian tepees, 10; *2*
Norway, 164
Norwich Cathedral, 142
Notre-Dame, Paris, 166
Notre-Dame-du-Haut, Ronchamp, 270–1,
    289; *361*
Notre-Dame-du-Raincy, Paris, 255; *341*
Notre-Dame la Grande, Poitiers, 139; *162*
Nouméa, New Caledonia, Tjibaou Cultural
    Centre, 301; *408*
Novgorod, 128
Nubia, 28, 32, 39

Oak Park, Chicago, 260
Oaxaca, 84
obelisks, 37, 38; *32*
Ocotlán, Sagrario, 234; *304*
Ohio State University, Wexner Center for
    the Visual Arts, 297; *405*
Olbrich, Joseph Maria:
    exhibition hall, Darmstadt, 259
Old Basilica of St Peter, Rome, 120, 121; *135*
Olmecs, 76, 79, 81
Olympia, 100
Olympic Stadium, Munich, 290; *393*
Olympic Stadium, Tokyo, 292–3; *401*
Opéra, Paris, 247–8; *325–6*
Orange, Theatre, 106; *114–15*
orchestra, Greek theatres, 99
orders *see* columns
Organicism, 286
Oriel Chambers, Liverpool, 247; *323*

Orissa, 51, 54
Orkney, 14
Ortiz, José Damián:
   Metropolitan Cathedral, Mexico City, 233
Ostberg, Ragnar:
   Stockholm Town Hall, 260; *351*
Ostia Antica, 112; *124*
Otto, Frei:
   Olympic Stadium, Munich, 290; *393*
Ottobeuren, 204
Ottoman Empire, 154, 157
Oudenarde, Town Hall, 175; *214*
Ouro Preto, São Francisco de Assis, 234;
   305
Outram, John:
   Pumping Station, London docklands, 294
Oxford:
   Keble College, 298
   Radcliffe Camera, 183
Oxford University, 171

Paestum, Temple of Hera, 92, 96; *99*
Pagan, 49
pagodas, 62–3, 71–2; *64–6, 75*
Paimio Sanatorium, 278; *373*
Palace of the Columns, Mitla, 84
Palace of the Governor, Uxmal, 80, 81, 83;
   91
Palace of the Masks, Mayan Kabah, 83
Palace of Minos, Knossos, 25; *18*
palaces:
   Baroque, 204–5; *260*
   Islamic, 148–9; *178–9*
   Minoan, 25; *18*
   Renaissance, 178–9, 181–2, 194, 196–7,
     200; *223–4, 230–1, 245*
   Roman, 114
Palais d'Abraxas, Paris, 288
Palais de Justice, Brussels, 250
Palazzo del Senatore, Rome, 186
Palazzo del Tè, Mantua, 186, 194; *230*
Palazzo Ducale, Mantua, 186
Palazzo Farnese, Caprarola, 187, 198
Palazzo Farnese, Rome, 182
Palazzo Massimo alle Colonne, Rome, 187;
   231
Palazzo Pitti, Florence, 181
Palazzo Pubblico, Siena, 175; *215*
Palazzo Reale, Caserta, 212
Palazzo Rucellai, Florence, 181, 210; *223*
Palazzo Vecchio, Florence, 175
Palazzo Venezia, Rome, *224*
Palenque, 83
   Temple of the Inscriptions, 83
   Temple of the Sun, *89*
Palermo, 125
   Royal Palace, 156
Palestine, 144
Palladian style, 218–21, 239
Palladio, Andrea, 179, 185, 187–8, 198, 200,

218, 220, 224, 236
   Basilica (Palazzo della Ragione), Vicenza,
     189
   Il Redentore, Venice, 189; *236*
   San Giorgio Maggiore, Venice, 189
   Villa Capra (Rotonda), Vicenza, 188–9, 218,
     236; *234–5*
Pallava dynasty, 50
Pamphili family, 212
Panini, G.P., *122*
Panthéon, Paris, 223; *289*
Pantheon, Rome, 110–11, 123, 124, 125, 176,
   208, 237; *120–2*
Parc de la Villette, Paris, 297; *406*
Paris, 136, 190, 236
   La Barrière de la Villette, 227
   Bibliothèque Nationale, 248
   Bibliothèque Sainte-Geneviève, 248; *329*
   Castel Béranger, 255
   Centre Pompidou, 292; *400*
   Chapel of the Holy Thorn, 163; *189*
   Eiffel Tower, 248–9; *328*
   glass pyramids at the Louvre, 294; *403*
   Grande Arche de la Défense, 294
   Hôtel Lambert, *251*
   Hôtel de Soubise, 216; *280*
   Louvre Palace, 172, 190, 194, 195; *245*
   Métro, 255
   Notre-Dame, 166
   Notre-Dame-du-Raincy, 255; *341*
   Opéra, 247–8; *325–6*
   Palais d'Abraxas, 288
   Panthéon, 183; *289*
   Parc de la Villette, 297; *406*
   Pavillon Suisse, Cité Universitaire, 269;
     359
   Place de la Concorde, 229
   Place de Vosges, 199
   St-Etienne du Mont, Paris, 195; *242*
   St-Geneviève (Panthéon), 183; *289*
   St-Jean-de-Montmartre, 254–5
   25bis rue Franklin, 255; *340*
Paris Exhibition (1889), 249
parish churches, 168, 171
Parkville, Melbourne, *313*
Parlange, Pointe Coupee Parish, 232
Parler, Peter, 164
Parliament Building, Vienna, 249
Parson Capen House, Topsfield, Mass., 235
Parthenon, Athens, 13, 86, 96–7, 248; *105–6*
Pataliputra, 47
pattern-books, 195
Pavillon Suisse, Cité Universitaire, Paris,
   269; *359*
Paxton, Joseph:
   Crystal Palace, London, 246; *316, 321*
Pazzi Chapel, Santa Croce, Florence, 176;
   218–19
Peacock Palace, Anuradhapura, 49
Pede, Jan van:

Town Hall, Oudenarde, 175; *214*
Pei, I.M.:
   glass pyramids at the Louvre, Paris, 294;
     403
Peloponnesian Wars, 93
Pembroke Castle, 172
pendentives, 123–4; *142*
Penguin Pool, London Zoo, 277; *370*
Pennsylvania Academy of the Fine Arts,
   Philadelphia, 251; *334*
Pepin, King of the Franks, 130
Peressutti, Enrico:
   Velasca Tower, Milan, 287; *384*
Pergamum, 100
Pericles, 93, 99, 100
Perpendicular Gothic style, 164
Perrault, Claude, 195
   Louvre Palace, Paris, 190, 195; *245*
Perret, Auguste:
   Notre-Dame-du-Raincy, Paris, 255; *341*
   25bis rue Franklin, Paris, 255; *340*
Persepolis, 26–7, 35
   Apadana of Darius, 27, 91; *15, 19*
Persia, 19, 23–4, 26–7, 88, 104, 123, 141, 148,
   155, 156–7
Persian Gulf, 18, 19
Perth (Australia):
   Lands Department Building, 239
   Titles Office Building, 239
Peru, 76, 79, 84–5, 90, 232, 233
Peruzzi, Baldassare, 186
   Palazzo Massimo alle Colonne, Rome, 187;
     231
Peter, St, 183
Le Petit Trianon, Versailles, 227, 228–9; *295,
   297*
Petra, El-Deir (Monastery) Temple, 109; *119*
Pevsner, Nikolaus, 284
Phaistos, 25
Phidias, 93–6
Philadelphia:
   Chestnut Hill, 288; *386–7*
   Franklin Court, 288
   Pennsylvania Academy of the Fine Arts,
     251; *334*
   Philadelphia Merchants' Exchange, 237–8
   Richards Medical Research Building,
     University of Pennsylvania, 287; *385*
Philae, 28
   Kiosk of Trajan, 30; *22*
   Temple of Isis, 30
Philharmonic Concert Hall, Berlin, 289–90;
   391–2
Philip II, King of France, 172
Philip II, King of Spain, 190, 196, 197, 233
Phoenix, Taliesin West, 264–5; *355*
Piano, Renzo:
   Centre Pompidou, Paris, 292; *400*
   Tjibaou Cultural Centre, New Caledonia,
     301; *408*

Piazza d'Italia, New Orleans, 288; *388*
Picturesque style, 222, 225, 226, 297
Piero della Francesca, 178
Pietilä, Reima, 292
    Official Residence for the President of
        Finland, 292
pilasters, 107
Pilgrim Church of St James, Santiago de
    Compostela, 136–7; *158*
pilgrimages, 136–7, 144
Piraeus, 93, 100
Piranesi, Giovanni Battista, 224, 226
Pisa, 142; *156*
    Cathedral, 130
Pitti family, 178
Pizarro, Francisco, 84
Place de la Concorde, Paris, 229
Place de Vosges, Paris, 199
Plateresque style, 165, 196, 230, 233
Plato, 99
Playfair, William, 226
Poelaert, Joseph:
    Palais de Justice, Brussels, 250
Poggio Bracciolini, G.F., 179
Poissy, Villa Savoie, 268; *356*
Poitiers, Notre-Dame la Grande, 139; *162*
Polonnaruwa, Gal Vihara, 46; *40*
Polycrates of Pergamum, 111
Polykleitos:
    Theatre, Epidauros, 99–100; *107*
Polynesia, 79
Pompeii, 108–9, 113
    House of the Vetii, *125–6*
Pont du Gard, Nîmes, 111; *111*
Pöppelmann, Matthaeus:
    Zwinger, Dresden, 205; *261*
Porta, Giacomo della:
    Il Gesù, Rome, 187, 211, 233; *232–3*
    St Peter's, Rome, 184
Portland, Public Services Building, 295; *404*
Portman, John:
    Hyatt Regency Hotel, San Francisco, 289
Portugal, 165, 230, 232
Post-modernism, 286, 288
Post Office Savings Bank, Vienna, 259
Potsdam, Einstein Tower, 272; *363*
Poultry Cross, Salisbury, 171
Prague Cathedral, 164
Prandtauer, Jacob:
    Benedictine Monastery, Melk, 213; *276*
Prato, 172
Priene, 100; *109*
Primaticcio, Francesco, 195
    Fontainebleau, 194; *237*
Prophet's House Mosque, Medina, 151–2
Propylaea, Athens, 90, 93, 96; *97*
Protestantism, 190, 197, 214
Pruitt Igoe flats, St Louis, 284
Public Services Building, Portland, 295; *404*
pueblos, 1

Pugin, A.W.N., 243–4, 246–7, 257–8
    Houses of Parliament, London, 242, 243;
        317
    St Giles, Cheadle, 243; *318*
Punjab, 45
Puteoli, 109
Puuc, 83
pylons, 37, 38; *31*
Pyramid of Cephren, Giza, 35, 36–7; *28–9*
Pyramid of Cheops, Giza, 33, 35, 36–7,
    38–9; *28–30*
Pyramid of the Magician, Uxmal, 82–3
Pyramid of Mycerinus, Giza, 35, 36–7; *28–9*
Pyramid of the Niches, El Tajin, 80, 84; *94*
Pyramid of Onnos, Giza, 36
Pyramid of Quetzalcoatl, Xochicalco, 84
pyramids:
    Egypt, 28, 32–7, 38–9; *24–5, 28–30*
    Meso-America, 76, 78–9, 81–4; *81, 83,*
        92–3

Qal'at Sim'an, Monastery and pilgrim
    church of St Simeon Stylites, 122; *139*
Qian Long, Emperor, 67
Queen's House, Greenwich, 200–1; *254–5*
Quetzalcoatl, 76, 78; *86*
Quincy, Mass., Crane Library, 252; *336*
Quito, Mercedarian Monastery, 230; *299*
Qur'an, 147
Quwwat-ul-Islam, Delhi, *184*

Radcliffe Camera, Oxford, 183
Rainaldi, Carlo:
    Sant' Agnese in Piazza Navone, Rome,
        209, 212
Rameses II, Pharaoh, 31, 39, 109
Rangoon, Schwe Dagon Pagoda, 49
Raphael, 186
    St Peter's, Rome, 184
Rastrelli, Bartolommeo:
    Tsarskoye Selo, 220
Ravenna, 118, 119, 125
    Mausoleum of Galla Placidia, 120–1; *137*
    San Apollinare in Classe, 120; *136*
    San Vitale, 123, 132; *140, 146*
Rayonnant style, 164
Red House, Bexley Heath, 258; *346*
Red Sea, 18
Il Redentore, Venice, 189; *236*
Reform Club, London, 242–3
Reinhard and Hofmeister:
    Rockefeller Center, New York, 279
Reliance Building, Chicago, 254; *338*
Renaissance, 16, 108, 110, 112, 171, 175,
    176–89, 190–201, 202, 268–9
Revett, Nicholas, 223
Rheims:
    Cathedral, 162, 163, 165, 166–7; *192*
    St-Rémi, 120
Riario, Cardinal, 182

Richards Medical Research Building,
    University of Pennsylvania, 287; *385*
Richardson, Henry Hobson, 252
    Crane Library, Quincy, Mass., 252; *336*
    Marshall Field Warehouse, Chicago, 252;
        335
Richelieu, Cardinal, 190
Richmond House, London, 294
Riedel, Eduard:
    Neuschwanstein, 250; *330*
Rietveld, Gerrit:
    Schröder House, Utrecht, 273–6; *368*
Rijksmuseum, Amsterdam, 250
Rio de Janeiro, 282
Riyadh, Grand Mosque and Justice Palace,
    296
Robie House, Chicago, 260–4; *353*
Roche, Eamon:
    Ford Foundation Headquarters, New York,
        289
Rochester Castle, 142; *166*
Rockefeller Center, New York, 279
Rococo style, 204, 215–17, 218, 230
Roehampton, 277; *371*
Rogers, Ernesto:
    Velasca Tower, Milan, 287; *384*
Rogers, Richard:
    Centre Pompidou, Paris, 292; *400*
    Lloyds Building, London, 292
Rohr, 204
Roman Empire, 88, 92, 102–15, 116–19, 224
Romanesque architecture, 116, 130–43, 158,
    161, 252
Romantic movement, 230, 240
Rome, 116–18, 136, 181–2, 202
    Arch of Constantine, 108; *118*
    Arch of Titus, 108
    Basilica of Maxentius, 115; *128–9*
    Basilica Porcia, 114
    Baths of Caracalla, 112; *123*
    Cancelleria, 182
    Capitol, 185–6
    catacombs, 116; *131*
    Cloaca Maxima, 111–12
    Colosseum, 105–7, 181; *116*
    Il Gesù, 187, 211, 233; *232–3*
    Imperial Forum, 102, 105; *112*
    Old Basilica of St Peter, 120, 121; *135*
    Palazzo del Senatore, 186
    Palazzo Farnese, 182
    Palazzo Massimo alle Colonne, 187; *231*
    Palazzo Venezia, 224
    Pantheon, 110–11, 123, 124, 125, 176, 208,
        237; *120–2*
    Piazza del Popolo, 212
    Piazza Navone, 212
    Sant' Agnese fuori le Mura, 120
    Sant' Agnese in Piazza Navone, 209, 212
    Sant' Andrea al Quirinale, 209, 210, 211
    Sant' Anna dei Palafrenieri, 209

San Carlo alle Quattro Fontane, 205, 208, 209; *262–3*
Santa Costanza, 121, 144; *130, 138*
San Ivo della Sapienza, 209
St John Lateran, 119
Santa Maria della Vittoria, 207; *264*
Santa Maria Maggiore, 119; *132*
San Paulo fuori le Mura, 120
St Peter's, 115, 183–5, 207–8; *226–7, 266*
Santa Sabina, 118, 119, 120; *133*
SS. Trinità de' Monti, 213
Spanish Steps, 213; *272*
Tempietto, 183, 215; *225*
Temple of Minerva Medica, 121
Trevi Fountain, 212; *271*
Vittorio Emanuele II Monument, 251
Romulus Augustulus, Emperor, 118
Ronchamp, Notre-Dame-du-Haut, 270–1, 289; *361*
Rosa, Salvator, 224
Rouen, 165
Cathedral, 166
St-Maclou, 162
Royal Festival Hall, London, 277
Royal High School, Edinburgh, 225
Royal Infirmary, Edinburgh, 246
Royal Palace, Palermo, 156
Royal Palace, Stockholm, 204
Royal Pavilion, Brighton, 226; *293*
Rubens, Peter Paul, 201
Rucellai family, 178
Ruskin, John, 242, 245, 258
Russia, 125, 128, 204, 218–20
Russian Revolution, 266
Ruvanveli dagoba, Anuradhapura, 49
Ryoan-ji Temple, Kyoto, *80*

Saarinen, Eero:
TWA terminal, J.F. Kennedy International Airport, New York, 286, 287; *383*
Sabha, Fariburz:
Baha'i Temple, Delhi, 294
Sabratha, 106
Sacconi, Giuseppe:
Vittorio Emanuele II Monument, Rome, 251
Sacsahuaman, Cuzco, 84–5
Safdie, Moshe:
Habitat housing, Montreal, 289; *390*
Sagrada Familia, Barcelona, 256; *343*
Sagrario, Ocotlán, 234; *304*
Sant' Agnese fuori le Mura, Rome, 120
Sant' Agnese in Piazza Navone, Rome, 209, 212
San Agustin Acolman, Mexico City, 233
Sant' Andrea, Mantua, 181; *222*
Sant' Andrea al Quirinale, Rome, 209, 210, 211
Sant' Anna dei Palafrenieri, Rome, 209
San Apollinare in Classe, Ravenna, 120, *136*
St Basil's Cathedral, Moscow, 128–9; *152*

San Carlo alle Quattro Fontane, Rome, 205, 208, 209; *262–3*
Santa Cecilia Temple, Mexico City, 78; *83*
La Sainte-Chapelle, Paris, 163; *189*
Santa Coloma de Cervello, Barcelona, 257; *345*
Santa Costanza, Rome, 121, 144; *130, 138*
Santa Croce, Florence, 176; *218–19*
St-Denis, 137, 158–60, 163, 165; *190–1*
St-Etienne du Mont, Paris, 195; *242*
Santa Fosca, Torcello, 123; *141*
São Francisco, Bahia, 233; *302*
São Francisco de Assis, Ouro Preto, 234; *305*
San Francisco, Tlaxcala, 233
St Gall, 138, 179; *161*
St-Geneviève (Panthéon), Paris, 183; *289*
St Giles, Cheadle, 243; *318*
San Giorgio Maggiore, Venice, 189
San Ivo della Sapienza, Rome, 209
St James's, Sydney, 220, 239; *314*
St John Lateran, Rome, 119
St John Nepomuk, Munich, 209; *258*
St Lawrence, Bradford-on-Avon, 132, 168; *157*
San Lorenzo, Florence, 176, 185; *229*
San Lorenzo, Turin, 207, 210; *265*
St-Maclou, Rouen, 162
Santa Maria della Salute, Venice, 213; *275*
Santa Maria della Vittoria, Rome, 207; *264*
Santa Maria Maggiore, Rome, 119; *132*
Santa Maria Novella, Florence, 180–1
St Mark's, Venice, 126–7; *149–50*
St Martin-in-the-Fields, London, 220; *285*
St Michael's, Charleston, 237
St Michael's, Hildesheim, 139
San Miniato al Monte, Florence, 130, 140; *154*
St Pancras Station, London, 243
San Paulo fuori le Mura, Rome, 120
St Paul's Cathedral, London, 124, 183, 214; *277*
St Peter's, Rome, 115, 183–5, 207–8; *226–7, 266*
St Peter's College, Cardross, 271
St-Rémi, Rheims, 120
Santa Sabina, Rome, 118, 119, 120; *133*
St-Sernin, Toulouse, 141; *165*
Santa Sophia, Kiev, 128
Santo Spirito, Florence, 176; *220*
St Stephen's Cathedral, Vienna, 162
SS. Trinità de' Monti, Rome, 213
San Vitale, Ravenna, 123, 132; *140, 146*
St Wendreda's, March, 169; *206*
Saint Louis, Pruitt Igoe Flats, 284
Sakyamuni Pagoda, Yingxian, 62–3; *66*
Salamanca University, 196; *247*
Salamis, 100
Salem, 235
Salerno, 171
La Saline de Chaux, Arc-et-Senans, 227

Salisbury:
Cathedral, 168, *205*
Poultry Cross, 171
Samarkand, 148, 157
Gir-i-mir, 157; *188*
Great Mosque, 150–1
Samarra, al-Malwiya Mosque, 153; *168*
Samurai, *4*
San Francisco, Hyatt Regency Hotel, 289
San Gimignano, 142; *167*
Sanchi, Great Stupa, 48, 54; *41–2*
Sanctis, Francesco de':
Spanish Steps, Rome, 213; *272*
Sangallo, Antonio da, the Younger:
Palazzo Farnese, Rome, 182
Sangallo, Giuliano da:
St Peter's, Rome, 184; *226*
Sansovino, Jacopo, 186
Santa Cruz, Kresge College, 288
Santa Fe, Governor's Palace, 232; *300*
Santiago de Compostela, 141, 234
Pilgrim Church of St James, 136–7; *158*
Santo Domingo Cathedral, 233; *303*
Santorini, 26, 109
Saqqara, 34
House of the North, 35; *26*
House of the South, 35
Stepped Pyramid of King Zoser, 34–5; *24–5*
Saracens, 132–3, 137–8
Sargon I, King of Assyria, 20, 111
sash windows, 198
Sassanian dynasty, 26, 123
Saudi Arabia, 296
Säynätsalo, Civic Centre, 278; *374*
Scandinavia, 13, 132, 204, 278
Scarborough, Grand Hotel, 244
Scharoun, Hans:
Philharmonic Concert Hall, Berlin, 289–90; *391–2*
Schauspielhaus, Berlin, 228
Schindler, Rudolf:
Lovell Beach House, New Port Beach, 278
Schinkel, Karl Friedrich, 228
Altes Museum, Berlin, 228; *296*
Schauspielhaus, Berlin, 228
Schloss Nymphenburg, Munich, 209, 217; *281*
Schönbrunn Palace, Vienna, 216
Schröder House, Utrecht, 273–6; *368*
Schwe Dagon Pagoda, Rangoon, 49
Scotland, 13, 14, 218, 225, 259
Scott, Geoffrey, 204
Scott, Sir George Gilbert, 243, 298
St Pancras Station, London, 243, 298
Scott-Brown, Denise, 288
Scully, Vincent, 90
Seagram Building, New York, 281–2; *Preface*
Second World War, 266

Secretariat, Chandigarh, 271
Segovia, 111, 133
Selimiye Mosque, Edirne, 157
Selinus, 248
Seljuk dynasty, 152, 153, 154, 155
Semper, Gottfried:
    Burgtheater, Vienna, 249
Senate House, Cambridge University, 220
Sennacherib, King of Assyria, 23, 111
Sens Cathedral, 162, 165, 168
Serlio, Sebastiano, 179, 186, 209
    Château d'Ancy-le-Franc, 193
Seven Wonders of the World, 22, 92
Seville, Alamillo Bridge, 288
Shalimar Garden, Lake Dal, 148; 177
Shaw, Richard Norman, 258
Shinto, 56, 69, 72
Shirley Plantation, 235; 307
Shisanling, 59
Shokintei House, Katsura Imperial Villa,
    Kyoto, 79
Shotoku, Prince, 72
Shreve, Lamb and Harmon:
    Empire State Building, New York, 279
Shuko, 73
Sicily, 125, 133, 156
Siddhartha Gautama, 46
Siemen's, 254
Siena, Palazzo Pubblico, 175; 215
Silesia, 260
Silk Market, Valencia, 171
Siloe, Diego de:
    Escalera Dorada, Burgos Cathedral, 198;
    250
Simeon Stylites, St, 122
Sinan, Koca:
    Suleymaniye Mosque, Istanbul, 154; 183
Sind, 42
Singapore, 64
Sixtus III, Pope, 119
Skara Brae, 14
Skidmore, Owings and Merrill:
    Lever House, New York, 281; 378
skyscrapers, 252–4, 286–7
Smirke, Sir Robert:
    British Museum, London, 225; 291
Smithson, Peter and Alison:
    Economist Buildings, London, 290; 395
Smythson, Robert:
    Hardwick Hall, Derbyshire, 197
    Longleat, Wiltshire, 197
    Wollaton Hall, Nottinghamshire, 197–8;
    248
Socrates, 99
Soissons Cathedral, 166
Somerset House, London, 225
Song dynasty, 61–2
Songyue Pagoda, Mount Song, 62; 64
Sonning, Deanery Garden, 258–9; 348
Soufflot, Jacques Germain:

Panthéon, Paris, 223; 289
'soul houses', 32; 23
South America, 76, 230–2, 233–4, 282–3
South East Asia, 42, 59
Soyer, Alexis, 243
space frames, 286
Spain, 230
    Art Nouveau, 256–7
    Baroque architecture, 202
    conquistadores, 76
    Gothic architecture, 164, 165, 169, 170
    Moors, 133
    Renaissance, 196, 197
    twentieth-century architecture, 288
Spanish Steps, Rome, 213; 272
Split (Spalato), Diocletian's palace, 114, 121,
    224
Spreckelsen, Johann Otto von:
    Grande Arche de la Défense, Paris, 294
squinches, 123, 155–6
Sri Lanka, 45, 49
stadia, 100
stairways, 198
Stanislas Leczinsky, King of Poland, 216
Stansted Airport, 291
Statue of Liberty, New York, 249
steel, 245, 286
Steinhausen, 211
Stephenson, George, 244
Stephenson, Robert, 244
Stepped Pyramid of King Zoser, Saqqara,
    34–5; 24–5
De Stijl, 273
Stirling, James:
    Engineering Building, Leicester University,
    290–1; 394
    Neue Staatsgalerie, Stuttgart, 292; 398
Stoa of Attalus, Athens, 99; 108
stoas, 99; 108
Stockholm:
    Forest Crematorium, 278; 372
    Royal Palace, 204
    Town Hall, 260; 351
Stoics, 99
Stokesay Castle, 173; 210
Stone Age, 14
Stonehenge, 12, 25; 7
Stourhead, Wiltshire, 222–3; 288
Stowe, Buckinghamshire, 222
Strasbourg Cathedral, 163, 166
Strawberry Hill, Twickenham, 226–7; 294
Street, G.E.:
    Law Courts, London, 246
Strickland, William:
    Philadelphia Merchants' Exchange, 237–8
Strozzi family, 178
Stuart, James, 223
stupas, 47–9; 38, 41–3
Stupinigi, Turin, 205
Stuttgart:

Neue Staatsgalerie, 292; 398
    Weissenhofsiedlung, 272
stylobate, 92
Suger, Abbot, 138, 158, 163
Suleymaniye Mosque, Istanbul, 154; 183
Sullivan, Louis, 260
    Carson, Pirie Scott Department Store,
    Chicago, 254; 339
    Guaranty Building, Buffalo, 254
Sumer, 19–20, 22, 24, 26
Summer Palace, Beijing, 68–9; 73
Sunhouse, Hampstead, 276
Superga, 213; 274
Suryavarman III, King, 54
Swayambhunath Stupa, Kathmandu Valley,
    49; 43
Sweden, 260
Sweden, V.B.B.:
    Kuwait water towers, 294
Switzerland, 138
Sydney, 238
    St James's, 220, 239; 314
    Sydney Opera House, 293–4; 381–2
Syon House, London, 225; 290
Syria, 18, 120, 122, 148, 152

Tacitus, 112
Taj Mahal, Agra, 157; 187
Taliesin West, Phoenix, 264–5; 355
Tamerlane, 27, 155, 157
Tampere, 292
Tang dynasty, 69
Tange, Kenzo:
    Olympic Stadium, Tokyo, 292–3; 401
Taoism, 69
Tasmania, 239
tea-houses, Japanese, 73; 79
technology, 245, 286–7, 291
Tecton, 277, 291
    Highpoint, London, 277
Telc, 200
Telford, Thomas, 244
temenos, 96
Tempietto, Rome, 183, 215; 225
Temple of Amun-Ra, Karnak, 33, 37, 39–41,
    91; 32–3
Temple of Amun-Ra, Luxor, 35, 41; 35
Temple of Aphaia, Aegina, 92
Temple of Apollo, Delphi, 101; 110
Temple of Artemis, Ephesus, 92
Temple of Bacchus, Baalbek, 107; 117
Temple of Etemanenki, Babylon, 22
Temple of Heaven, Beijing, 66; 68–9
Temple of Hephaestus (Theseion), Athens,
    89, 90
Temple of Hera, Paestum, 92, 96; 99
Temple of Horus, Edfu, 37, 41; 31
Temple of the Inscriptions, Palenque, 83
Temple of Isis, Philae, 30
Temple of Khons, Karnak, 37, 40; 34

Temple of Minerva Medica, Rome, 121
Temple of Nike Apteros, Athens, 93; 101
Temple of Olympian Zeus, Athens, 92
Temple of Poseidon, Cape Sounion, 41, 86;
    96
Temple of Quetzalcoatl, Teotihuacan, 86
Temple of Quetzalcoatl, Tula, 81; 87
Temple of Rameses II, Abu Simbel, 31; 21
Temple of the Sun, Konarak, 50; 49
Temple of the Sun, Palenque, 89
Temple of Warka, Iraq, 22
Temple-Poole, George:
    Lands Department Building, Perth, 239
    Titles Office Building, Perth, 239
Temple-Pyramid I, Tikal, 81
temples:
    Buddhist, 47–9
    Chinese, 60–1; 61–3, 68–9
    Egypt, 39–41; 21, 31–6
    Greek, 41, 88–9, 90–3; 96, 99, 101–6
    Hindu, 47, 50–4, 47–53, 55
    Meso-American, 76, 78, 80–2; 81, 83,
        86–7, 89
    Mesopotamian, 20–1
    Roman, 107, 110, 116; 117, 120–2
Tenochtitlan, 76, 78–9
tents, 10, 14; 2
Teotihuacan, 80, 83–4
    Temple of Quetzalcoatl, 86
tepees, 10; 2
Tessin, Nicodemus the Younger:
    Royal Palace, Stockholm, 204
Texcoco, Lake, 78
TGV station, Lyons-Satolas Airport, 288, 301;
    407
Theatre, Delphi, 101; 110
Theatre, Epidauros, 99–100; 107
Theatre, Orange, 106; 114–15
Theatre of Dionysus, Athens, 99
theatres, Greek, 99–100, 106
Thebes, 28, 32, 39, 41, 109
Thera, 26, 109
Tholos, Delphi, 101
Thomson, Alexander, 225
Thornton, William, 237
    Capitol, Washington DC, 238, 251; 312
Thorvaldsen Museum, Copenhagen, 248;
    327
Thutmose I, Pharaoh, 37; 32
Thutmose III, Pharaoh, 41
Tiepolo, Giovanni Battista, 211
Tigris, river, 18, 21, 26, 149
Tikal, 82; 88
    Temple-Pyramid I, 81
timber-framed houses, 13
Tiryns, 23, 88
Titles Office Building, Perth, 239
Titus, Emperor, 106
Tivoli, Hadrian's Villa, 114; 127
Tjibaou Cultural Centre, Nouméa, New

Caledonia, 301; 408
Tlatelolco, 78, 79
Tlaxcala, San Francisco, 233
Tokugawa Shogunate, 70–1
Tokyo, 73
    Imperial Hotel, 264
    Nakagin Capsule Tower, 293; 402
    Olympic Stadium, 292–3; 401
Toledo, Juan Bautista de:
    Escorial Palace, 196–7, 198, 233; 248
Toledo Cathedral, 166
Tolsá, Manuel:
    Metropolitan Cathedral, Mexico City, 233
Toltecs, 79, 80–1, 83–4
Tomar, Church of the Convent of Christ,
196,
    197
Tomb of Humayan, Delhi, 157
tombs:
    Egyptian rock-cut, 37
    Islamic, 156, 157, 185
    mastabas, 33–4
Torcello, Santa Fosca, 123; 141
Toshodai-ji Temple, Nara, 77
Totonacs, 79, 80
Toulouse, 118
    St-Sernin, 141; 165
Tours, 120, 130
    Cathedral, 166
Tower of Babel, 22
Tower of London, 173
Town Hall, Oudenarde, 175; 214
town halls, 175; 214
town houses, 198–200
Travellers' Club, London, 242
Trdat:
    Ani Cathedral, 127–8; 151
Trent, Council of (1545), 205
Trevi Fountain, Rome, 212; 271
Trier, 118, 119
triforium, 166
triglyphs, 89
La Trinité, Vendôme, 162
triumphal arches, Roman, 108; 118
trompe-l'oeil, 205–7
trulli, 12, 14; 6
Tsarskoe Selo, 218–20; 284
Tschumi, Bernard:
    Parc de la Villette, Paris, 297; 406
Tula, Temple of Quetzalcoatl, 81; 87
Tunisia, 147
Turin:
    Chapel of the Holy Shroud (Il Sindone),
        207, 209, 210
    San Lorenzo, 207, 210; 265
    Stupinigi, 205
Turkey, 19, 154
Turks, 154, 155
Turtle House, Uxmal, 83; 90
Tuscany, 118

Tutankhamun, Pharaoh, 35, 37
TWA terminal, J.F. Kennedy International
Airport, New York, 286, 287; 383

Uffizi, Florence, 185
Uji, Byodoin Temple, 69; 74
Ulm Minster, 167
Unité d'Habitation, Marseilles, 269–70; 360
United States of America, 230, 232, 234–8
    Classicism, 236–8
    International Style, 278–82
    nineteenth-century architecture, 251,
        252–5, 260–5
    Palladianism, 220
    twentieth-century architecture, 289, 295
United States Pavilion, Expo '67, 289; 389
Unity Temple, Chicago, 260
universities, 171–2; 247
Uppsala, 164
Ur, 19, 20–1, 24; 12
Urban VIII, Pope, 208
Urbino, Palace, 178; Frontispiece
Uruk, 19
Utilitarian Functionalism, 286
Utrecht, Schröder House, 273–6; 368
Utzon, Jørn:
    Bagsvaerd church, 295–6
    Sydney Opera House, 293–4; 381–2
Uxmal:
    Palace of the Governor, 80, 81, 83; 91
    Pyramid of the Magician, 82–3
    Turtle House, 83; 90

Valencia, Silk Market, 171
Valley of the Kings, 37
Van, Lake, 18
Van Alen, William:
    Chrysler building, New York, 279; 375
Van Dyck, Anthony, 201
Vanbrugh, Sir John, 208, 210, 214–15, 222
    Blenheim Palace, Oxfordshire, 214, 215
    Castle Howard, Yorkshire, 214, 215; 278
Vanvitelli, Carlo, 212
Vanvitelli, Luigi:
    Palazzo Reale, Caserta, 212
Vasari, Giorgio, 160, 298
    Uffizi, Florence, 185
vaulting, 109, 141–2, 161–2, 165, 170
Vaux-le-Vicomte, 209, 221; 287
Vedas, 44
Velasca Tower, Milan, 287; 384
Vendôme, La Trinité, 162
Venice, 126, 174–5, 181, 187–8, 198
    Doge's Palace, 174–5; 213
    Il Redentore, 189; 236
    St Mark's, 126–7; 149–50
    San Giorgio Maggiore, Venice, 189
    Santa Maria della Salute, 213; 275
Venturi, Robert, 287–8

Franklin Court, Philadelphia, 288
house at Chestnut Hill, Philadelphia, 288;
386–7
Vermeer, Jan, 200
vernacular architecture, 15, 296
Versailles, 215, 216, 221, 250; *279*
Le Petit Trianon, 227, 228–9; *295, 297*
Vespasian, Emperor, 106
Vesuvius, Mount, 113
Vézelay, 137
Vicenza, 188
Basilica (Palazzo della Ragione), 189
Villa Capra (Rotonda), 188–9, 218, 236;
234–5
Viceroy's House, New Delhi, 258; *347*
Victoria, Queen of England, 243
Vienna, 259
Belvedere Palace, 204–5, 207; *259*
Burgtheater, 249
Majolica House, 259; *350*
Parliament Building, 249
Post Office Savings Bank, 259
St Stephen's Cathedral, 162
Schönbrunn Palace, 216
Votivkirche, 249
Vierzehnheiligen Pilgrimage Church, 204,
209–10; *267–8*
Vignola, Giacomo da, 179, 187
Il Gesù, Rome, 187, 211, 233; *232–3*
Palazzo Farnese, Caprarola, 187, 198
Sant' Anna dei Palafrenieri, Rome, 209
St Peter's, Rome, 184
Vijayanagara kingdom, 45
Vikings, 132
Villa Capra (Rotonda), Vicenza, 188–9, 218,
236; *234–5*
Villa Savoie, Poissy, 268; *356*
villas, Roman, 113–14; *125–7*
Viollet-le-Duc, Eugène, 248, 255
Virginia, University of, 237; *298, 310*
Visigoths, 132
Vitruvius, 8, 91, 102–4, 109, 110, 179, 180,
181, 298
Vittorio Emanuele II Monument, Rome, 251
Vladimir, Prince of Kiev, 128
Vorarlberg, 204
Votivkirche, Vienna, 249
voussoirs, 13, 109
Voysey, Charles Annesley, 258
Vries, Hans Vredeman de, 195

Wagner, Otto, 259, 278
Majolica House, Vienna, 259; *350*
Post Office Savings Bank, Vienna, 259
al Walid, Caliph, 144, 146
Walpole, Horace, 214, 221
Strawberry Hill, Twickenham, 226–7; *294*
Walpole, Robert, 218
Walter, Thomas Ustick:
Capitol, Washington DC, 238, 251; *312*

Washington, George, 235
Washington DC, 237
Capitol, 183, 238, 251; *312*
White House, 237
Waterhouse, Alfred:
Natural History Museum, London, 246;
322
Watts, Lieutenant John, 239
Webb, John:
Queen's House, Greenwich, 200–1; *254–5*
Wilton House, Wiltshire, 201
Webb, Philip:
Red House, Bexley Heath, 258; *346*
Wedgwood, Josiah, 224
Weimar, 272
Weissenhofsiedlung, Stuttgart, 272
Wells Cathedral, 162, 163; *195*
Weobley, 197
Westminster Abbey, London, 162, 168,
170; *204*
Westover, Charles City County, 236
Wexner Center for the Visual Arts, Ohio
State University, 297; *405*
White House, Washington DC, 237
Whitfield, William:
Hereford Cathedral Library, 294
Richmond House, London, 294
Wilkins, William, 237–8
National Gallery, London, 225
William of Aquitaine, 138
William the Conqueror, 132
William of Sens, 164, 168
William Grevel's House, Chipping
Campden, 174; *211*
Williamsburg:
College of William and Mary, 236; *308*
Governor's Palace, 236
Willis Faber and Dumas offices, Ipswich,
291; *396*
Wilton House, Wiltshire, 200, 201, 222; *257*
Winckelmann, J.J., 223
windows:
Gothic, 163–4, 165
Renaissance, 197–8
Wollaton Hall, Nottinghamshire, 197–8; *248*
Wood, John the elder, 220–1, 226
Wood, John the younger, 220–1, 226
Worms Cathedral, *164*
Wotton, Sir Henry, 8
Wren, Sir Christopher, 210, 236, 237
St Paul's Cathedral, London, 183, 214; *277*
Wright, Frank Lloyd, 260–5, 268
Fallingwater, Bear Run, 264; *354*
Imperial Hotel, Tokyo, 264
Martin House, Buffalo, 260; *352*
Oak Park, Chicago, 260
Robie House, Chicago, 260–4; *353*
Taliesin West, Phoenix, 264–5; *355*
Unity Temple, Chicago, 260
Würzburg, Bishop's Palace, 211, 212; *270*

Wyatt, Charles:
Government House, Calcutta, 239; *315*
Wyatt, James, 239
Fonthill Abbey, Wiltshire, 226

Xerxes I, King of Persia, 26, 27, 35
Xianyang, 66
Xochicalco, Pyramid of Quetzalcoatl, 84

Yakoi tent-houses, 13
Yakushi-ji Temple, Nara, 71–2; *75*
Yamasaki, Minoru:
Pruitt Igoe flats, St Louis, 284
Yaxchilan, *82*
Yayoi culture, 59, 69
Yazd, Jami (Friday) Mosque, 155; *184*
Yellow River, 27, 56, 59
York:
Merchant Adventurers' Hall, 171
York Minster, 162
Yoshimasa, Shogun, 73
Ypres, Cloth Hall, 171; *207*
Yuan dynasty, 58
Yucatan, 76, 80, 83

Zacatecas Cathedral, 233
Zacharias, Pope, 130
Zagros Mountains, 18
Zapotecs, 79, 80, 84
Zen Buddhism, 73
Ziggurat of Choga Zambil, 25; *17*
ziggurats, 24–5, 47, 153; *12, 17*
Zimmermann brothers:
pilgrim church at Steinhausen, 211
Zwinger, Dresden, 205; *261*

Acknowledgements

Aerofilms page 6, 209, 287; AKG, London 363; Arcaid/Richard Bryant 406; Arcaid/S. Couturier 361; Arcaid/Dennis Gilbert 400; Arcaid/Paul Rafferty 407; Dept of Archaeology and Museums, Pakistan 37; Archipress/R. Bryant 398; Archivi Alinari, Florence 99, 118, 120, 123, 136, 218, 222, 223, 224, 228, 229, 230, 231, 233, 263, 264, 266, 272, 274, 332; Artephot/Varga 280; James Austin 289; Barnaby's Picture Library 28, 303; G. Barone (Index, Florence) frontispiece, 167, 196; Basilica of the Assumption Historic Trust, Baltimore 311; Bastin & Evrard, Brussels 342; Bauhaus Archiv, Berlin 364, 365; John Bethell 68, 281, 292, 322; BIF, Mexico (Paul Czitromb) 304; Bildarchiv Foto Marburg 14, 148, 202, 207, 212, 220, 246, 261, 271, 330; Bildarchiv Preussischer Kulturbesitz 16; Boston Public Library 333; Copyright British Museum, London 2, 23; Anthony Browell 382; Caisse Nationale des Monuments Historiques et des Sites 163, 165, 193, 238, 295, 329; Martin Charles 341, 356, 372; Richard Cheek, Belmont, Mass. pages 4–5, 298; Chicago Historical Society 335, 338, 339; College of William and Mary, Williamsburg 308; Conway Library, Courtauld Institute of Art 141, 162 (Photo Julian Gardner), 198, 200, 203, 211, 214, 243, 296; Peter Cook/View 354, 360; © Corbis 107; Paul Almasy/© Corbis 21; Tony Arruza/Corbis 273; Dave Bartruff/Corbis 36; Chris Bland; Eye Ubiquitous/Corbis 194; Jan Butchofsky-Houser/Corbis 38; Macduff Everton/Corbis 127; Wolfgang Kaehler/Corbis 152; Danny Lehman/© Corbis 84, 92; Charles and Josette Lenars/Corbis 32, 55, 117; Richard T. Nowitz/Corbis 25, 112; The Purcell Team/Corbis 390; Joel Rogers/Corbis 150; Hans Georg Roth/Corbis 41; Gian Berto Vanni/Corbis 39; Ruggero Vanni/Corbis 164; Nik Wheeler/Corbis 186; Roger Wood/© Corbis 9, 15, 19, 20, 113, 174, 175, 180; Adam Woolfitt/Corbis 51, 143, 155, 213, 244, 270, 276; Alison Wright/Corbis 49; Michael S. Yamashita/Corbis 132, 393; Bernard Cox, John Bethell Photography 17, 31, 284; Bernard Cox, British Architectural Library, RIBA, London 184, 260; Roy C. Craven Jr. 90, 91, 305; Jérôme Darblay 325; Frank den Oudsten, Amsterdam 368; Deutsches Archaeologisches Institut, Athens 100; C. M. Dixon 124; Max Dupain and Associates, Sydney 314, 381; EMAP Construct 389; Ezra Stoller/© ESTO page 9, 377; Paolo Favole 168; Mark Fiennes 349; Werner Forman Archive 4, 22, 83, 94; Werner Forman Archive/National Museum of Anthropology, Mexico 82; Foster Associates (Photo Ian Lambot) 397; Fototeca Unione 128; Alison Frantz 103, 104; Gabinetto Fotografico Nazionale 133; Dennis Gilbert/View 391; Giraudon 114, 242, 297; Lauros-Giraudon 190, 237; Michael Graves, Architect (Proto Acme Photo) 404; Sonia Halliday Photographs 108, 170, (Jane Taylor) 151, (© Sonia Halliday and Laura Lushington) 189, 199; Robert Harding Picture Library, London 58, 62, 67, 116, 119, 182, 403, (Mohamed Amin) 171, (© Robert Frerck/Odyssey/Chicago) 380, (J. Pate) 3, 169, (© Roy Rainford) 288, (Adina Tovy) 78 (Adam Woolfitt) 178 and 240; Lucien Hervé 359; Hirmer Fotoarchiv 12, 26, 33, 35; © Angelo Hornak Photograph Library 156, 166, 173, 204, 215, 217, 256, 258, 275, 277, 317; Hutchison Library (Liba Taylor) 379; Ironbridge Gorge Museum Trust 320; Japan Information and Cultural Centre, London 74, 76, 79; A. F. Kersting 43, 53, 101, 111, 140, 147, 149, 159, 172, 188, 236, 241, 249, 252, 257, 265, 267, 278, 279, 285, 286, 290, 291, 294, 319, 323, 351, 370; Kimbell Art Museum, Fort Worth, Texas/Michael Bodycomb 399 (1972 photograph); Ken Kirkwood 283, 396; Balthazar Korab Ltd. 337, 353, 355, 375, 383, 385, 405; Kisho Kurokawa architect and associates 402; Library of Congress 306, 307, 312, 336; Norman McGrath 388; Ampliaciones y Reproducciones Mas 197, 247, 248, 250, 259; T. Harmon Parkhurst, Courtesy Museum of New Mexico (No. 4568) 1; Arthur Taylor, Courtesy Museum of New Mexico (No. 70211) 300; National Gallery of Art, Washington (Samuel H. Kress Collection) 122 (Photo Richard Carafelli); National Monuments Record 157, 195, 206; National Monuments Record of the Netherlands, The Hague 253; The Nelson Atkins Museum of Art, Kansas City, Missouri (Purchase: Nelson Trust) 56; Courtesy of the Pennsylvania Academy of the Fine Arts. Archives 334; Renzo Piano Building Workshop/Michel Denancé 408; Pitkin Guides Ltd. 7; Réunion des Musées Nationaux, Paris 245; Rheinisches Bildarchiv 153; British Architectural Library, RIBA, London 54 (Douglas Dickins), 57, 348, 369; Simo Rista 373, 374; Roger-Viollet 6, 192; Royal Pavilion, Art Gallery and Museums, Brighton (the Pavilion is now a tourist attraction, open daily) 293; Scala, Florence 125, 131, 137, 154, 225, 227, 234, 384; Julius Shulman 378; The Skyscan Photolibrary 210; Alison and Peter Smithson 395; South American Pictures 81, 95, (© Robert Francis) 85 and 89, (© Tony Morrison) 301, 302; The Stapleton Collection 316; Stiftsbibliothek St Gallen 161; Studio Kontos 13, 18, 96, 97, 105, 110, 144, 183; Christopher Tadgell 45, 46, 48, 177, 185, 187, 315, 347, 362; Kenzo Tange Associates 401; Edward Teitelman 309; Thorvaldsens Museum, Copenhagen 327; Rupert Truman 343, 345; School of Architecture, Tsinghua University, Beijing 59, 61, 63, 64, 65, 69, 73; University of Warwick 318; Venturi, Scott Brown and Associates 386; Courtesy of the Board of Trustees of the Victoria and Albert Museum, London 176, 321; Charlotte Wood 346.

Author's note

This book is the fruit of a collaboration. My
collaborator is my wife Bridget. At first my research
assistant, in the event she has been more than
that; she has drafted much of the book, including
some whole chapters, though I take responsibility
for all of them and for the judgements contained in
them. For this new edition we have checked every
sentence, every attribution, every date and
rewritten several chapters.

   We have been visiting buildings for some fifty
years together in many parts of the world and
talking about architecture incessantly. But this was
our first attempt at collaboration in writing and was
thus our first literary offspring.

Phaidon Press Limited
Regent's Wharf
All Saints Street
London N1 9PA

Phaidon Press Inc.
180 Varick Street
New York, NY 10014

www.phaidon.com

First published 1983
Second edition 1997
Reprinted 1998, 1999, 2001 (twice), 2003, 2004
© 1983, 1997 Phaidon Press Limited

ISBN 0 7148 3615 X (Hb)
    0 7148 3616 8 (Pb)

A CIP catalogue record for this book is
available from the British Library

Printed in China

opposite title page
Luciano Laurana, *Palace of Duke Federigo da
Montefeltro*, Urbino, Italy, *c.*1454

following title page
Thomas Jefferson, **William Thornton** and
Benjamin Latrobe, *University of Virginia*,
Charlottesville, Virginia, 1817-26

opposite contents page
John Wood the Younger, *Royal Crescent*, Bath,
England, 1767-75